Library of
Davidson College

QUESTIONS IN PARLIAMENT

QUESTIONS IN PARLIAMENT

BY

D. N. CHESTER

AND

NONA BOWRING

GREENWOOD PRESS, PUBLISHERS
WESTPORT, CONNECTICUT

Library of Congress Cataloging in Publication Data

Chester, Daniel Norman.
   Questions in Parliament.

   Reprint of the ed. published by Clarendon Press, Oxford.
   Bibliography: p.
   1. Great Britain. Parliament. House of Commons--Rules and practice. I. Bowring, Nona, joint author. II. Title.
[JN688.C47 1974]   328.42'05   74-9164
ISBN 0-8371-7614-X

© *Oxford University Press, 1962*

Originally published in 1962 by the Clarendon Press, Oxford

This reprint has been authorized by the Clarendon Press Oxford

Reprinted in 1974 by Greenwood Press,
a division of Williamhouse-Regency Inc.

Library of Congress Catalog Card Number 74-9164

ISBN 0-8371-7614-X

Printed in the United States of America

PREFACE

I STARTED work on this book as long ago as 1952. Already, however, I was very much preoccupied with the development of Nuffield College and when, in October 1954, I became Warden, this and other responsibilities caused five full years to pass very quickly and left me with very little time for research and writing. On more than one occasion I thought of abandoning the project. Fortunately, the College provided excellent research assistance. Miss Gweneth Gutch (now Mrs. R. Lloyd) was my Research Assistant until 1955 during which time she was also of great help to Lord Morrison of Lambeth in the preparation of the first edition of his *Government and Parliament*. Mrs. Nona Bowring was my Research Assistant for over four years and her enthusiasm and persistence carried the work along when others might have been tempted to give it up.

A book of this kind could not have been written without the great help of many busy people. The Clerk of the House, Sir Edward Fellowes, and his staff have been particularly helpful. There cannot be a body of public servants anywhere more interested in their craft and its history and more helpful than the staff of the House of Commons. They carry on the great tradition of Sir Thomas Erskine May in being both practitioners and scholars. Sir Charles Harris, with his unique and long experience of the working of 'the usual channels', was also of great help. Members of Parliament and civil servants have also given generously of their advice and experience. Several of my academic colleagues read and criticized the typescript in an early stage. To all these and many others we gratefully acknowledge our thanks.

My wife and I particularly wish to thank the Rockefeller Foundation for allowing us the gracious facilities of the Villa Serbelloni during the summer of 1960. Five weeks in such comfort and surroundings (with only one telephone call!) were ideal for writing and enabled me to make very substantial progress.

D.N.C.

CONTENTS

1	Introduction	*page*	1
2	Origins and Development		12
3	The Changes in 1902 and 1906		49
4	Number of Questions Since 1902		87
5	Question Time Since 1902		114
6	The Development of the Rota System		128
7	The Effect of the Rota System		145
8	Answerability, Ubiquity and Publicity		167
9	The Questions		179
10	The Questioners		192
11	Ministers and Their Answers		228
12	Conclusions		269

Appendices

    I Standing Orders of the House of Commons referring to Questions 289
    II Ministerial Responsibility and Answerability 292
    III Questions in the House of Lords 313
    IV Statistics 314
    V Sources and Select Bibliography 317

Index 327

CHAPTER 1

INTRODUCTION

THE House of Commons meets at 2.30 p.m. on Mondays, Tuesdays, Wednesdays and Thursdays,[1] and at 11.00 a.m. on Fridays during the Session. At these times the Speaker enters the Chamber and the Speaker's Chaplain then says Prayers. During Prayers only Members (apart from the Chaplain) are allowed in the Chamber, and even the several Galleries for visitors are kept closed. At the conclusion of Prayers, which take about five minutes, the Speaker takes the Chair and the House starts its business for the day.

The business for each day's sitting is mainly conveyed to Members by way of the Notice Paper of Public Business commonly known as the Order Paper. For the purpose of illustration we have chosen Thursday, 28 April 1960. On this day,[2] under the heading: 'Questions for Oral Answer' the Order Paper lists 75 numbered Questions, each with an asterisk against it. The asterisk indicates that the Member wishes the Minister to answer the Question orally, i.e. in the Chamber. These starred Questions are presented in the following form[3]:

*1. Mr. Owen: To ask the President of the Board of Trade, what recent steps have been taken by his department to call the attention of industrialists to the trade and employment prospects in the mid-Northumberland area, in view of the growing difficulty of finding employment by the disabled and able-bodied in the area.

*2. Mr. Shinwell: To ask the President of the Board of Trade, what measure he has in view for the provision of industry in the new town of Peterlee and in the adjoining area where a substantial number of former mineworkers are unemployed.

*3. Mr. Hector Hughes: To ask the President of the Board of Trade, what plans he has for restoring and increasing the traditional

---

[1] When the House adjourns for a recess on one of these days it usually meets at 11 a.m.
[2] There is no Question time on Fridays.
[3] The form of the Order Paper was changed in November 1960 and, since then, the Member's constituency is shown in brackets after his name.

trade and commerce between Aberdeen and the Scandinavian countries in order to counterbalance the loss and damage inflicted on the north-east of Scotland by the Outer Seven Agreement.

*4. Mrs. McLaughlin: To ask the President of the Board of Trade, if he has seen the report on flammability of children's nightwear in the Consumer's Guide, a copy of which has been sent to him; and what action he proposes to take to impress on the public the dangers of these garments and to prevent the manufacture of children's nightdresses from flammable materials.

The first three named are members of the Labour Party and the fourth is a Government supporter. The first 39 Questions are addressed to the President of the Board of Trade. Questions 40–43 are addressed to the Prime Minister and are followed by two more to the President of the Board of Trade. (Until July 1961 Questions to the Prime Minister appeared on the Paper not later than No. 40 on Tuesdays and Thursdays.) Then follow five Questions to the Secretary of State for the Colonies, two to the Minister of Agriculture, Fisheries and Food, eleven to the Secretary of State for the Home Department, three to the Minister of State for Commonwealth Relations, three to the Minister of Education, five to the Chancellor of the Exchequer and finally, one to the Minister of Aviation.

The Questions are very varied. Questions 19 and 21 read as follows:

*19. Mr. Marcus Lipton: To ask the President of the Board of Trade, how many firms are licensed to import Swiss watches; when they were selected; and on what basis.

*21. Mr. Bellenger: To ask the President of the Board of Trade, what was the outcome of his recent meeting with the Dutch Foreign Minister; and whether he will make a statement.

Sixteen Questions (Nos. 24–39) all ask for information about Scottish industry in relation to industry in the rest of the United Kingdom. These Questions are in the names of nine Labour Members, no Member asking more than two, which is the limit to the number of starred Questions which any Member can ask at one sitting. Two of the Questions addressed to the Prime Minister concern the release and protection of citizens of the United Kingdom and British protected persons under arrest in South Africa. Three of the Questions addressed to the Home Secretary are:

INTRODUCTION

*56. Mrs. Joyce Butler: To ask the Secretary of State for the Home Department, what progress has been made with regard to the provision of warmer clothing for the inmates of women's prisons during the winter months.

*58. Mr. George Wigg: To ask the Secretary of State for the Home Department, whether he will order the destruction of the fingerprints and photographs retained under Section 6(2) of the Prevention of Crime Act, 1871, of Mr. W. J. Darby, 17 Clee Road, Scotts Green, Dudley, which were obtained without statutory authority.

*63. Mr. Emrys Hughes: To ask the Secretary of State for the Home Department, what official expenditure he proposes to incur in connection with the royal wedding on 6th May.

Members continue to come in steadily and there is a noticeable increase shortly before the Prime Minister's Questions are due to be reached, by which time some 150 or more Members are in the House, and it looks quite full. A number of Ministers are on the Treasury Bench and the opposite front bench gradually becomes crowded with Opposition leaders.

Mr. Speaker calls out: 'Mr. Owen.' That Member stands up, says quite briefly 'Question No. 1, Sir, to the President of the Board of Trade'[1] and sits down. Then Mr. Reginald Maudling, President of the Board of Trade, rises from the Treasury Bench. He opens his file on the dispatch box in front of him and proceeds to read:

'Four firms have recently been shown locations in this area.'

He sits down. Whereupon Mr. Speaker again calls: 'Mr. Owen.' Mr. Owen says:

'It is encouraging to know that four firms have been invited, and I hope that results will follow, but is the right hon. Gentleman aware that the promoters of the Hovercraft experimental project are making inquiries for facilities apart from where they are at the moment? Will he look at the possibility of the county of Northumberland, with its wide coast-line, its reservoir of skilled workers and its training services, being considered in this respect? Further, is he aware that it is reported that Accrington R.A.F. Camp is to be closed? If that report is correct, will he carefully consider the possibility of establishing there a training centre for apprenticeship and, perhaps, a place to provide work for disabled workers?'

[1] It is usual to mention the departmental title of the Minister in the case of the first Question addressed to him, but not otherwise.

This is a supplementary Question. Immediately Mr. Owen sits down Mr. Maudling rises and replies:

'I shall certainly bear those points in mind when that firm or any other approaches us and requires permission to expand its activities.'

So, in turn, Mr. Speaker calls Mr. Shinwell, Mr. Hector Hughes, Mrs. McLaughlin. Each asks a supplementary in respect of the Minister's answer to their Question, but when Mrs. McLaughlin rises to try to ask another, Mr. Speaker exercises his control over supplementaries by refusing to call her for a second, saying: 'I hope the hon. Lady will not regard her question as a precedent for another one. It was rather on the long side.' He, however, allows two further supplementaries on the reply to Question 4, from Mr. Darling and Mrs. Slater.

Questions 6 and 7 are in the name of Mr. Randall but Mr. Speaker does not call him, for the Member cannot be present and no other Member can ask them. Mr. Speaker therefore passes to Question 8 which stands in the name of Mr. Grey.

So it goes on. No Member asks a Question unless called upon by Mr. Speaker. Most but not all replies attract a supplementary. Sometimes the Ministerial answer is received placidly, sometimes it attracts a murmur of approval or disapproval, sometimes both at the same time from different parts of the House. There are also occasional ripples, or even gusts of laughter, for the House is very ready to acknowledge a witty reply or supplementary. There is some excitement when Mr. Millan having been called and having asked Question 24, Mr. Maudling rises and says 'With permission I propose to answer Questions Nos. 24 to 39 together.' Immediately Mr. Lawson rises and says: 'On a point of order. Is it in order for a whole group of Questions dealing with quite separate matters to be taken in this way?' Thus being appealed to, Mr. Speaker rises and says: 'Being apprised of this intention, I had a look at the precedents this morning. I do not think we are in a position to stop it.' Here he is interrupted by some Members rising to catch his attention and by various shouted remarks. He goes on to explain the point of order. Various other Members then rise to raise further points of order, in particular the meaning to be attached to the Minister's opening phrase 'With permission'. When at last the Minister is allowed to rise and give his omnibus answers he says:

INTRODUCTION

'I regret that the detailed information needed to make these comparisons is not available. I am circulating in the Official Report the best information we have.

'I might add that all the statistical information available to the Government is also available already to hon. Members in the "Census of Production", the "Digest of Scottish Statistics" and the "Monthly Digest and Annual Abstracts", which are in the Library of the House of Commons."

This is followed by supplementaries and further points of order. One of these is a supplementary from Mr. Gourlay, the Labour Member for Kircaldy, who had the Questions 30 and 31 on the Paper. He says:

'Is the right hon. Gentleman aware that in the past five years, from 1954 to 1959, in the vehicle industry in Scotland there has been a reduction of 22 per cent. as against an increase of 31 per cent. in England? Does not this show that the Government are largely to blame for the present heavy unemployment in Scotland, and will the right hon. Gentleman admit that the much boosted Local Employment Act at the last General Election is completely ineffective in dealing with the unemployment position in Scotland?'

Mr. Maudling replies:

'I am not sure offhand whether those figures are accurate, but they certainly do not show that the Government are to blame.'

The very last supplementary in this exchange is asked by a Conservative Member, Sir Thomas Moore, who has sat for Ayr since 1925. He rises and says:

'Is my right hon. Friend aware that some of us are getting rather tired of this "Gimme a dime stranger" attitude, that we do not want to go cap-in-hand to the Government for everything and that we in Scotland are ready to stand on our own feet and make our own way in the world without Government assistance or help except when it is needed?'

There is no need for the Minister to reply to this supplementary, which was designed to help him. It will be noticed that the Minister was addressed by Mr. Gourlay as 'the right honourable Gentleman' whereas Sir Thomas Moore addressed him as 'my right honourable Friend', the customary usage distinguishing members of the same political party from those in opposing camps.

Mrs. Barbara Castle is now called, and she asks No. 40, the first Question addressed to the Prime Minister. He answers and then gives a single but long answer covering both Question 41 and 42. After a few supplementaries 3.30 p.m. is reached and no more Questions are called, for the Standing Orders of the House state that, with certain very limited exceptions, no Questions can be taken after 3.30 p.m. Instead Mr. Speaker calls on Mr. Harold Wilson, who is deputizing for the Leader of the Opposition, by saying: 'Mr. Harold Wilson. Business question.' Each Thursday at the end of Question time the Leader of the Opposition asks the Leader of the House to state the business for next week. Before Mr. Wilson can do so Mr. Grey raises a point of order. He wishes to know whether he can get a copy of the answer to Question No. 6, which was not called in the absence of the Member, or if he will have to wait until Hansard appears tomorrow. Mr. Speaker tells him it is not possible to obtain the answer until the Official Report is available.

A verbatim account of the proceedings of the House is available next day. It is entitled: *Parliamentary Debates (Hansard) House of Commons, Official Report*. Its popular name is Hansard. The one published on 29 April is numbered No. 102, showing that the sitting recorded was the 102nd of the current Parliamentary Session. It contains a full record of all that was said at Question time. The Questions and Replies are arranged for ease of reading and given headings such as 'Trade and Commerce', with sub-headings, 'Northumberland', 'Peterlee', 'Aberdeen' etc. Altogether the proceedings during Question time on 28 April take up 31 columns.

Questions 41 and 42, which were addressed to the Prime Minister, are recorded as follows:

UNION OF SOUTH AFRICA
(DETAINED BRITISH PERSONS)

41. Mr. Driberg asked the Prime Minister what progress has been made towards securing the release of Miss Stanton and other citizens of the United Kingdom and British-protected persons detained without trial in South Africa; and whether he will now make direct representations on behalf of those still in detention to the Prime Minister or deputy-Prime Minister of the Union of South Africa.

42. Mr. Marquand asked the Prime Minister whether he will make a statement on the result of his undertaking to do all that he can to help and protect United Kingdom citizens now under arrest in South Africa.

The Prime Minister: The United Kingdom High Commissioner has remained in close touch with South African Ministers and has been informed that Miss Stanton would be released on the undertaking that she would leave South Africa without undue delay. The question of her eventual return to the Union would be considered in the light of conditions and circumstances at the time when she applied for leave to return. Miss Stanton has, however, stated that she feels unable to give this undertaking to leave South Africa.

The only other citizen of the United Kingdom and Colonies to be detained, who is not also a South African citizen, is Dr. Letele. He has been visited by a representative of the High Commissioner, who has reported that he is in good health and has no complaints about his treatment. The High Commissioner is continuing to urge the Union Government that Dr. Letele should be released or charged as soon as possible.

As far as is known, no British-protected persons are being detained.

Four citizens of the United Kingdom and Colonies from Basutoland have been arrested on charges of public violence in connection with the disturbances on 21st March. As my hon. Friend the Minister of State for Commonwealth Relations informed the House yesterday, the High Commissioner has engaged legal advisers who are available to assist these men.

Mr. Driberg: Why should this remarkable — indeed, noble — woman be kept in prison because she refuses to be deported from the land and from the work to which she has dedicated her life? Is there any charge against her? Why is she still in prison? Does the Prime Minister remember saying a fortnight ago that this matter would not be allowed to drag on?

The Prime Minister: Yes, Sir. We made strong representations and this offer to Miss Stanton was made. She took time to consider it and arrangements were made that she should have the opportunity of discussing it with her lawyer, with her brother and with the assistant warden of the Tumelong Mission. She has now decided not to accept release on these conditions. We are, therefore, continuing our efforts to press that she should be either released unconditionally or charged.

Mr. Marquand: How long does the Prime Minister think that this process will continue? Does he realize that it is a month since these people were imprisoned without charge and that almost a fortnight has passed since he undertook to do his best? What would the Prime

Minister have done if the circumstances had arisen in a foreign country? Would he be content merely to continue to say that somebody was keeping in touch? Would he not demand immediate action, and should he not do so now?

The Prime Minister: We are, of course, demanding that action should be taken. It is only within the last few hours that I have heard that Miss Stanton had refused this offer of release on leaving the country which we had obtained.

Mr. Gresham Cooke: Will my right hon. Friend take the opportunity next week of discussing this case with Mr. Louw when he is here? Will my right hon. Friend mention to him that as the representative of this lady in my constituency, I have received fifty letters from all over the country testifying to Miss Stanton's character and mentioning, in particular, that she is of a most peaceful disposition and not likely to be mixed up in any violence? Will my right hon. Friend therefore press Mr. Louw to see whether a charge could not be brought so that she could have the opportunity of facing trial?

The Prime Minister: Yes, Sir, of course. Naturally, had the Prime Minister himself been able to come, I would have discussed it with him. As Mr. Louw is coming, I shall certainly discuss these and other questions and will have the opportunity to do so within a day or two. I or my friends concentrated on the High Commissioner's trying to get the lady released. Then, there was the condition of her leaving the country. She considered it for some days and then decided — I admire and understand her reasons — not to accept it. We are, therefore, now pressing that she should be either charged or released without conditions.

Mr. Brockway: Without in the least wishing to minimise the importance of the case of Miss Stanton, whom many of us revere, do I understand the Prime Minister to say that no citizen and no protected person under British care has been arrested? Will the right hon. Gentleman examine this matter again? Are there not thousands of protected persons from the High Commission Territories in Johannesburg? Have they not been open to arrest in the same way as other people in Johannesburg? Will the Prime Minister look into the matter so that we may be sure of the facts?

The Prime Minister: Of course, I will make further inquiries, but I have given the information which has been given to us from the High Commissioner. There is the case of Dr. Letele, with whom we have been in close touch, and we are urging that he should be either released or charged as soon as possible. We do not know of any other case of a British-protected person being detained. Four citizens from Basutoland have been arrested and charged.

Mr. Marquand: As I have pressed this matter on several occasions,

INTRODUCTION

may I say that we welcome the Prime Minister's undertaking to take up this matter with the representative of the South African Government? May we take it that when he has done that, he will make another statement to the House of Commons?

The Prime Minister: I am grateful for the forbearance of the right hon. Gentleman and his friends. He will, I think, realise that what one tries to do is to get the results. Whether one is dealing with a Commonwealth country or a foreign country, mere protestation and statements are not always enough. What we want to try to do is to get the results. I welcome the chance in the next ten days while he is here of discussing the problem with Mr. Louw and trying to point out to him personally how much it would help in the reduction of tension on other matters if he could help us over these matters.

Mr. Marquand: I asked the Prime Minister whether he would then make a statement to the House, or must I put down another Question?

The Prime Minister: Perhaps it would be simplest if the right hon. Gentleman would get in touch with me to know whether it is easier by Question or by statement. Often, a Question at Question Time is more convenient than statements after Question Time. I or one of my colleagues will keep in touch with the right hon. Gentleman and we will use the most convenient method. When the conference of Prime Ministers ends, I have to go to Paris, so it may be necessary to ask one of my hon. or right hon. Friends to make a statement on my behalf.

Mr. Callaghan: Will the Prime Minister reconsider his statement in reply to the last question that the release of this lady would reduce tension on other matters? Does he mean that to do common justice to this lady, either by charging her or by releasing her, would reduce tension on the policy of 'apartheid', which should be condemned and abhorred by every decent citizen in this country? I am sure that that is not what he means.

The Prime Minister: I hope that the hon. Member will not take away the value of some of the arguments which I might use in order to obtain what I want.

At the end of the daily record of proceedings in the House is a section headed: Written Answers to Questions.[1] Here Questions 6 and 7 and their answers are printed, for should a Member not

[1] Questions are an exception to the general rule that Hansard records only what has taken place during the proceedings of the House, for it records three categories of Questions which were neither asked nor answered in the Chamber, viz: those put on the Paper without an asterisk; those with an asterisk but not reached by the end of Question time and those with an asterisk but not answered orally, because of the absence either of the member or (rarely now) of the Minister. (Questions in the second and third categories which are deferred do not receive a written answer and, therefore, do not appear in that day's Hansard.)

be present when his name is called, his Questions are automatically given a 'written' answer unless he has asked for them to be deferred until a later date. Here also are twenty of the thirty-three starred Questions which were on the Order Paper but which were not reached, i.e. all Questions after No. 42. This Hansard deals with 44–49, 52, 60, 63 and 65–75. These are printed in the same form as the Questions answered orally. Thus Questions No. 63 and 70 are shown as follows :

63. Mr. Emrys Hughes asked the Secretary of State for the Home Department what official expenditure he proposes to incur in connection with the Royal wedding on 6th May.

Mr. R. A. Butler : None. The cost of the policing arrangements will fall on the Metropolitan Police Fund and qualify for the normal 50 per cent. Exchequer grant. The cost cannot be precisely calculated in advance.

NATIONAL FINANCE
August Bank Holiday

70. Mr. Warbey asked the Chancellor of the Exchequer what representations he has received from the Industrial Welfare Society and other bodies regarding the advantages of transferring the August Bank Holiday to a later date in the year; and what reply he has given.

Mr. Barber :[1] I have seen two memoranda by the Society. As the hon. Gentleman will be aware, my right hon. Friend the President of the Board of Trade has recently appointed an official committee to consider what action the Government can take to encourage the extension of the summer holiday season. The question of moving the August Bank Holiday to a later date in the year is one of the possibilities which this committee is considering and the views of interested organizations will be welcomed.

The other thirteen starred Questions which were not reached and yet are not dealt with among the Written Answers were deferred by the Members concerned. In other words, these Members would not be content with a written answer but hoped, on a later day[2] to have their Questions answered in the Chamber and so have the opportunity to ask a supplementary.

[1] A junior Treasury Minister.
[2] All except the remaining Question to the Prime Minister were deferred to the following Thursday, 5 May, when the Ministers concerned would each be one place higher on the rota.

INTRODUCTION

In addition to the Questions with a number against them recorded under the heading of 'Written Answers', there are nine without any number. Six of these were among the eight Questions listed at the end of the Order Paper[1] under the heading: 'Questions not for oral answer'. These are given a number on the Order Paper but without an asterisk: they are not however numbered in Hansard, and this enables one to distinguish them at a glance from Questions which, though 'starred', received only a written answer. They seem very much like many of the 75 Questions which had an asterisk against them. Two examples are:

TRANSPORT
Road Accidents (Car Drivers)

Mr. Hector Hughes asked the Minister of Transport what number and percentage of the motor car accidents, of which the police took note during the Easter weekend, were found to be due to the driver of either car being under the influence of alcoholic liquor.

Mr. Marples: Detailed reports of the accidents at Easter have not yet been received. When the detailed police reports have been received and collated I will write to the hon. and learned Member.

BRITISH ARMY
Horses

Sir L. Ropner asked the Secretary of State for War how many horses are on the establishment of the Army.

Mr. Soames: 635.

It would be necessary to sit through many Question times before experiencing all the many possible aspects and moods of this important item in the Parliamentary timetable. The purpose of this introduction is merely to enable the reader to attach a more exact meaning to the terms Question time and Question when they are used in the following pages.

[1] Notice of the other three had appeared in previous Order Papers.

CHAPTER 2

ORIGINS AND DEVELOPMENT

ORIGINS

OWING to the incomplete and haphazard character of the early records of Parliamentary proceedings, it is not possible to speak with any certainty about the origins of Parliamentary Questions.[1] It is generally agreed that the Question addressed by Earl Cowper to the Prime Minister (the Earl of Sunderland) on 9 February 1721 in the House of Lords is the first one recorded. The first Speaker's ruling in the House of Commons appears to have been in 1783. Commenting on this, Howarth says: 'After a period of uncertainty lasting more than sixty years, questions had become a fully recognized form of parliamentary procedure.'[2] This is too great a claim on the scanty evidence available. Certainly, Questions in anything like their modern usage are largely a development of the nineteenth century, particularly of the period after 1830.

The procedural significance of Questions lies in the fact that they developed as the exception to one of the basic principles of the rules of debate. The first edition of Erskine May's *Parliamentary Practice*, published in 1844, and the next eight editions, treat Questions to Ministers not as a procedure in its own right but as an exception to the general rules of debate. The basic rule was described in May's first edition thus: 'It is a rule that should always be strictly observed, that no member may speak except when there is a question[3] already before the house, or the member is about to conclude with a motion or amendment.' He then went on: 'The only exceptions which are admitted, are, 1, in putting questions to particular ministers or other members of

[1] Mr. Patrick Howarth's *Questions in the House* (1956) contains a good deal of interesting information about the developments up to 1880 but is more precise about the contents of Questions than about procedure.
[2] Howarth, op. cit., p. 43.
[3] i.e. a Motion or an amendment to a Motion, which is the normal Parliamentary usage of the word 'question'. Otherwise the term 'Questions to Ministers' is used.

ORIGINS AND DEVELOPMENT

the house; and, 2, in explaining personal matters. But in either of these cases the indulgence given to a particular member will not justify a debate.'[1]

Another basic rule of debate also had a bearing on the development of Questions. Again in the words of the first edition 'It is a rule strictly observed in both houses, that no member shall speak twice to the same question, except, 1st to explain some part of his speech, which has been misunderstood; 2dly, in certain cases, to reply at the end of a debate; and 3dly, in committee.'[1] Until well into the nineteenth century a Member had almost unlimited opportunities to speak in the House. If the issue he wished to raise was not relevant to the Motion before the House he would not have to wait long before an opportunity was provided by one of the innumerable formal Motions that were a feature of the procedure in those days. Or he could put a Motion on the paper with a fair chance of its being reached, or, if he thought the matter urgent, he could move the adjournment of the House. Nevertheless, there were two difficulties in using the ordinary processes of debate for the purpose of obtaining information. On the one hand, the Minister to be questioned had to be present in the Chamber. As there were only a handful of Ministers in the House of Commons, and as their attendance was not regular, most of the procedural opportunities might occur when the Minister concerned was not in the Chamber. On the other hand, even if he were present, the use of a Motion as a method of asking a question was subject to the limitations of the second basic rule. It would be perfectly correct for the Member to speak once and for the Minister to reply, but if that Member wished to pursue the matter further he would either have to wait for a fresh Motion, having already spoken once, or try to get away with contravening the rule against speaking twice to the same question (i.e. Motion). More important, if other Members wished to pursue the matter, each could speak but the Minister replying could speak only once, unless his further replies were allowed by the Chair as being explanations of parts of his original speech that had been misunderstood.

It being apparent that Members occasionally wished to ask a Minister for information, particularly about the course of

[1] p. 195

Business before the House or the Government's intentions,[1] and that the debate of a Motion was not the most convenient occasion for doing this, there was obviously something to be said for allowing Questions of this kind as an exception to the rules of debate. But from time to time the Speaker had to intervene to prevent the proceedings becoming disorderly.[2]

The kind of problem which arose at this early stage is well illustrated by the events of 16 March 1808. A Member asked a Question to which a Minister gave a reply. Another Member named Tierney then made some remarks to which the Minister also replied, followed, however, by another Minister. Several Members then rose, including Mr. Tierney, but were called to order by Mr. Speaker Abbot, on the ground that for some time there had been no question before the House. The Minister then rose, 'now that this conversation was finished', to move the first Order of the Day, but Mr. Tierney persisted, and when he was refused the right to speak, said he would raise the matter again. Later, a discussion took place on the propriety of the Speaker's ruling. Mr. Speaker Abbot explained that after the original questioner had received a Ministerial answer he called on a Member (Tierney), 'whose knowledge of the forms and customs of the house led me to presume that he would not pass beyond the limits which the occasion demanded'. The Member did, however, pass beyond those limits, i.e. the Member made observations which led to the Chancellor of the Exchequer feeling it necessary to retaliate. When this led to several other Members rising, Mr. Speaker said he felt it his duty 'to put an end to the conversation', and when a Minister rose and 'distinctly spoke of the conversation, no choice was left me on the subject'. Mr. Tierney wanted to prevent in future 'that species of debate which was called conversation, unless there was some motion before the House, or some understanding established as to the latitude which should be allowed in it'. The Foreign

[1] Questions to Members other than Ministers were also usually about future business e.g. on 1 June 1837 one Member asked another whether he had objection to postponing the presentation of a petition until the questioner could be present. *Mirror of Parliament* (1837), vol. iii, 1665–6.

[2] cf. the statement of Mr. Speaker Cornwall in 1783 quoted at p. 15. On 30 May 1837 Mr. P. Borthwick having received a reply from Palmerston rose and said 'The information is so far satisfactory' at which point he was interrupted by Members calling 'Spoke, spoke! Order, order!' Borthwick went on to say that he was not going to make a speech but to give notice of a Motion. *Mirror of Parliament* (1837), vol. iii, 1634.

Secretary observed that a conversation becomes irregular as soon as it is noticed. The House gave overwhelming approval to the Motion moved by the Foreign Secretary (G. Canning), highly approving of 'the upright, able and impartial conduct' of Mr. Speaker Abbot, only Mr. Tierney dissenting.[1] Thus, whilst the House was prepared to accept the occasional question and answer, it was not prepared to tolerate observations by Members on an answer, particularly those which, by introducing argument or criticism led to conversation i.e. the discussion of a topic without there being a Motion before the House.

In so far as answering Questions might be embarrassing to a Government, it may be wondered why Ministers did not take refuge either in the plea of irregularity or in their majority. There is some evidence that from time to time they tried both these defences, though not very determinedly. For one thing, Questions were at first very few in number, and judging from those recorded, were concerned with matters Ministers could hardly ignore. Many were about the Government's intentions in respect of legislation or the Business of the House. As Mr. Speaker Abbot said in 1808, 'It has ever been the usage of the House, and it has been found a most convenient usage, to permit questions to be asked, tending to facilitate the arrangement of business.'[2] There was also available to Members an already established device for obtaining information, the Motion 'to move for papers'. This Motion was used to obtain information on a variety of matters, e.g. the negotiations with another country or statistics of taxes and trade. Such Motions could be defeated, i.e. not accepted by the Government and its supporters, and according to Howarth[3] this increasingly occurred during the eighteenth century. But the tradition of the House was already established, if Sir William Pulteney's words in 1739 can be given their full weight. 'I hope we shall continue to follow the ancient maxim of this House, which has always been, to call for such papers as we thought might contribute towards giving us a full and perfect knowledge of the affair we were to enquire into.'[4] Mr. Speaker Cornwall in 1783[5] could say, that he had 'often repeated, and wished to impress it in the mind of the House, that

---

[1] Parl. Deb. (1808), 10, c. 1170–2. [2] Parl. Deb. (1808), 10, c. 1171.
[3] op. cit., pp. 16–17. [4] *Parliamentary History* (1737–9), x, c. 1008.
[5] *Parliamentary History* (1782–3), 23, c. 915 and 925.

conversations were disorderly' but that deviation from the strictness of the general rule of order 'had been at all times allowed, as a means of obtaining the House material information, which might (it had in many instances) throw a light upon the business before them, and serve to guide their judgment as to their future proceedings. The deviation from the general rule, however, ought to be adopted with great care, sobriety, and prudence, because otherwise it might put the House out of temper, and prove a source of much inconvenience.' Finally, in the words of Redlich 'the procedure of the House of Commons, was worked out, so to speak, as the *procedure of an opposition*'[1] (his italics). The famous paragraph from the *Report of the Select Committee of 1861* put the point in this fashion: 'the old rules and orders, when carefully considered and narrowly investigated, are found to be the safeguard of freedom of debate, and a sure defence against the oppression of overpowering majorities.'[2]

Thus, Questions developed as an exception to the rules of the House which controlled speaking in the Chamber. They were mainly concerned with the course of Business, or with the Government's intentions, or with obtaining information. They developed very slowly, for there were numerous other opportunities for Members to obtain information and ventilate grievances and they developed during a time when the private Member still dominated the proceedings of the House.

DEVELOPMENTS 1832–1900

By the time of the Reformed Parliament the right of Members to ask Questions of Ministers or other Members in the House was clearly recognized. During the remainder of the century two important things were to happen to Questions. On the one hand, the rules of procedure governing their form, content and place in the proceedings of the House were to be developed, refined and codified. On the other, their number was to increase so markedly that by 1900 more Questions were asked in one day than were asked during the whole of the session of 1830. There was a certain amount of interplay between these happenings. The increase in numbers led to an increasing number of rules yet, in comparison with the increasing restrictions placed on the use of

[1] *The Procedure of the House of Commons*, vol. i. 57. [2] Report, para. 57.

ORIGINS AND DEVELOPMENT

every other form of procedure, the rules developed for Questions were not so restrictive and this led to a diversion of Parliamentary activity to this procedure.

DEVELOPMENTS IN USAGE

The formal rules governing Questions developed in three main ways:
  (i) The notice to be given,
  (ii) The place in the daily timetable,
  (iii) Restrictions on scope and content.

(i) *Notice*

The practice developed of giving notice of the Question to be asked. This was done as a matter of courtesy, or to give the Minister time to secure the necessary information, or to have a better chance of the Minister being present. At first notice was given informally, e.g. by letter.

A fair sample of the way things were done is taken from Hansard for 31 May 1847. The record reads: 'Mr. Bernal Osborne wished to put to the Foreign Secretary a question of which previous notice would probably not be required' (concerning Portugal). 'Viscount Palmerston: I hold in my hand a note which I have received from a noble Lord whom I do not now see in his place — the noble Member for Lynn — giving me notice that he meant to ask that question, and to follow it by two or three other questions upon the same subject.' He answered Osborne. A little later the record reads: 'Lord G. Bentinck (who had just entered the House): I understand that my first question is answered. My second question to the noble Lord is . . . .'[1]

In 1835 the practice began of giving notice by printing the Question on the Notice Paper. Under the heading 'Notices given on Wednesday 25 February' there appears:[2]

1. Mr. Foxwell Buxton, — To put a Question relative to the measures which are in progress for the Education of the Negroes; and also relative to the appointment of Local Magistrates in Jamaica to the office of Special Magistrates (Friday 27 March).

March must have been a misprint for February, for in the next day's Papers the same wording appears under the heading

[1] Parl. Deb. (1847), 92, c. 1291–3.   [2] Notices of Motions, (1835), p. 24.

'Notices of Motions for Friday 27 February'. The Question (or rather two Questions) and the answer(s) by Mr. Gladstone (then Under Secretary for the Colonies) are recorded in Hansard for Monday 2 March 1835.

For some years Questions continued to appear under the heading 'Notices of Motions', mixed up with other items. In February 1849, however, they were grouped together and put first. The Order Paper for 27 April 1869 shows Questions for the first time under a separate heading 'Questions', followed immediately by 'Notices of Motions'.[1] The sixth edition of Erskine May states the position in 1868 as 'Notice is usually given of such questions in the Votes, unless they relate to some matter of urgency, or to the course of public business'.[2]

The custom had also developed of giving notice orally in the House. The Member would rise before the start of Public Business and say that on such and such a day he proposed to put such and such a Question. Sometimes he would follow this up by placing the Question on the Paper, sometimes he would regard the oral notice as sufficient. The practice at the time of the Select Committee of 1871 was that a Member exercised discretion whether to give public notice (i.e. orally in the House) or to hand his Question to the Clerk at the Table. In the great majority of cases the latter method was adopted.[3] The method of giving notice privately by way of a letter also continued and on occasion no notice of any kind would be given.

As the number of Questions increased, Members became irritated by the amount of time taken up by the mere reading of Questions in the House. Attention was first focussed on the reading of Questions already fully set out on the day's Paper. The normal practice was for the Member to read his Question in full when putting it to the Minister. Should he fail to do so, Members would usually shout: 'Read, Read.'[4] On 8 July

[1] Notices of Motions, (1868–9), p. 631.
[2] ibid., p. 302.
[3] Sir T. Erskine May before the Select Committee on Business of the House, 1871, qs. 287–9.
[4] 'When I first entered the House [in 1883] every Member who had a question on the notice paper read the whole of his question aloud before the Minister answered it. I remember some chaff of Mr. Gladstone, who would before replying to a question, say "The Hon. Member for so and so asks whether it is the intention of H.M. Government to, etc. . . , etc. . . ," and repeat verbatim the whole question. It was Sir Charles Dilke who first set the example of calling out the number of his question. To ears accustomed to the more lengthy process, this procedure seemed

1880,[1] however, Mr. J. Cowen asked Mr. Speaker whether in view of the fact that about an hour of the close on two hours just spent on Questions had been occupied with the reading of them, was it absolutely incumbent on Members to read them. Mr. Speaker Brand said it had been the general practice and had generally been found convenient, but there was no rule on the subject. Apparently this reply had an immediate effect, for on 5 August,[2] the Speaker said: '. . . it was formerly the practice for Members to read their Questions, and that practice has generally prevailed down to the present day. But I am bound to say that latterly the practice has prevailed of putting questions at such extraordinary length that I am inclined to think the House would do well to depart from it.' Gradually, therefore, it became the practice not to read out the Question but to refer to the number it bore on the Order Paper, though some Members continued to add a few introductory words.[3]

On 4 July 1881 Mr. Dillwyn asked whether, since they had given up the practice of reading Questions that were on the Paper, they might also dispense with the reading of Notices. Mr. Speaker Brand agreed that if the House would go still further and require that Notice should not be given at full length a further saving of time might take place.[4] Yet on 22 February 1886 Mr. Joseph Cowen could still complain that 'A quarter of an hour a night was sometimes spent in listening to Notices of Questions' on purely local subjects. 'The reading of these Questions', he said, 'was virtually a kind of Obstruction, although it might be unconcious.'[5]

somewhat bald, but the House soon adopted it and saved much time thereby. There was then no time limit for questions, as there is now; but on the other hand the number of questions was comparatively small and supplementary questions a rarity.' *A Speaker's Commentaries*, by Viscount Ullswater (Mr. Speaker Lowther), (1925), ii, 299–300.

[1] Parl. Deb. (1880), 253, c. 1920. When asked by a member of the Select Committee of 1871 whether it would be convenient to limit the putting of Questions twice over May replied: 'It has not occurred to me to consider the propriety of such a rule; the practice occupies a very short time.' (q. 289).

[2] Parl. Deb. (1880), 255, c. 311. An Irish Member had just read a Question containing nearly 500 words.

[3] On 30 May 1893 however, Mr. Weir asked the Prime Minister, 'whether with a view of saving the time of the House at Question time, a Member on being called by Mr. Speaker, may simply respond by giving the number of the question which stands in his name on the Paper instead of the usual introductory form of words.' Mr. Gladstone replied, 'My opinion is that the humblest economies of time are not to be despised. That which the Hon. Member suggests is one I should be very glad to see adopted.' Parl. Deb. (1893), 12, c. 1547.

[4] Parl. Deb. (1881), 262, c. 1966.   [5] Parl. Deb. (1886), 302, c. 930.

Apart from a saving of time, there was another reason why the Speaker wished to avoid purely oral notice. For some years now the Clerk under his authority had been 'editing' the Questions before they were printed on the Notice Paper. As the number of Speaker's rulings increased greater care was needed about the wording of Questions. Sir Erskine May told the Select Committee of 1878 that the Speaker 'does stop an infinity of questions that no one is ever aware of. Before questions appear, they are most carefully revised, and objectionable parts removed, generally with the consent of the Member, and under the direction of the Speaker.'[1] It was very difficult, indeed impossible on occasion, for the Speaker to exercise this control in respect of Questions of which the only previous notice was that given orally in the House.

On 25 February 1886 Colonel Waring, in giving notice that next Monday he would ask the Chief Secretary for Ireland a Question, proceeded to read statements from newspapers and quote other expressions of opinion. Two Members rose to ask whether Colonel Waring was in order in including opinion and argument in his Question 'contrary to the Orders and spirit of the Rules of the House'. Mr. Speaker answered by saying that he wished the House would sanction him in restraining Questions of the nature referred to, 'and also in enforcing the practice that when Questions are to be put they may be placed on the Notice Paper without previous Notice, or being required to read them'. As regards Colonel Waring's Question he said he would 'of course, before it appears on the Paper, carefully revise it'.[2]

Next day the Prime Minister (Mr. Gladstone) was asked whether he would at an early date move a Resolution embodying the Speaker's suggestions. He replied that the suggestions would be carefully considered by the Select Committee on Procedure which the House had agreed on 22 February to set up. However, on 12 March, the same day as the Hartington Committee was nominated, Sir Henry Selwin-Ibbetson (the Chief Conservative Whip) used the formal Motion preliminary to converting the House into Committee of Supply to move 'That, pending the judgment of the House on the Report of any

---

[1] Select Committee on Public Business, 1878, q. 82.
[2] Parl Deb. (1886), 302, c. 1190–1.

Committee appointed to consider the Business of the House, it shall be an order of this House:

> That Notices of Questions be given by Members in writing to the Clerk at the Table, without reading them *vivâ voce* in the House, unless the consent of the Speaker to any particular Question has been previously obtained.'

In support, he urged the need to reduce the amount of time devoted to Questions and to stop the habit that had grown up in recent years of putting long and argumentative Questions without notice. The Chancellor of the Exchequer, Sir William Harcourt, supported the proposal on behalf of the Government, suggesting that if the first clause were omitted and the last sentence agreed to it would become a Sessional Order. This was done. There was no serious opposition, though several Members wished to go much further in the control of Questions.[1] On 7 March 1888 the rule was converted word for word into the first Standing Order (No. 20) governing Questions.

Until this Resolution, it had been possible for a Member to ask a Question without giving formal previous notice of it, either on the Paper or orally in the House. But neither Ministers nor the Speaker liked this practice, and by the early 1880's formal notice was given for the vast majority of Questions. On 19 June 1882, for example, Sir Charles Dilke, then Under Secretary for Foreign Affairs, in answer to a Question about the numbers killed in the disturbances at Alexandria said: '. . . I will take this opportunity of stating that I have tried to give the House the latest possible information by answering Questions of fact without Notice; but that course of procedure has produced so large an increase in the number of Questions put, and so much inconvenience and loss of time, that I propose in future, under no circumstances to answer any Question whatever without full Notice.'[2] On the same day but in respect of another Question Mr. Speaker supported this view by saying that a Minister was not bound to answer any Question other than that on the Paper, unless he desired to do so.[3] A little earlier in the Session, Mr. Speaker had objected to the Questions that were being fired at the Under Secretary of State for Foreign Affairs about the

---
[1] Parl. Deb. (1886), 303, c. 697–702. [2] Parl. Deb. (1882), 270, c. 1582.
[3] Parl. Deb. (1882), 270, c. 1591.

political crisis in Egypt, many by the Fourth Party. He said: 'I think it is right to point out that in Questions of a grave character such as these (the Minister) is entitled to ask that Notice should be given . . . .'[1]

(ii) *Place in Daily Timetable*

The second procedural development was that a definite place came to be given to Questions in the daily timetable of the House. It is not possible to speak with any certainty about the precise order in which the House did most of its business in the eighteenth century. The great work, *Precedents of Proceedings in the House of Commons* by John Hatsell, Clerk of the House from 1768 to 1797, gives no information about the course of business or the arrangement of the daily programme. Redlich, commenting on this says: '. . . But from the facts that there are in the journals no resolutions as to principles for determining these matters, and that Hatsell does not concern himself with them, we may draw an unmistakable inference as to one characteristic of the parliamentary procedure of this period, namely, that the large and difficult problem set before the modern House of Commons in arranging its daily business and its work as a whole was entirely unknown to procedure of that day. And hence flows a further characteristic of the time — the comparative freedom of each individual member and the comparative looseness of the whole House in fixing the succession of the items of business to be taken and the debates thereon.'[2] In general, however, the practice had grown up of dealing first with Private Bills and Petitions (which were indeed the heaviest part of the work of the House until the 1830's) before proceeding to discuss the Orders of the Day and Notices of Motions.

It is not clear from the little and unreliable evidence available, just when Questions could be asked in the eighteenth or early nineteenth century. One suspects that when they were a rare event they could be asked at any convenient time.[3] In the *Mirror of Parliament*, which is a fuller record than Hansard, during the

---

[1] Parl. Deb. (1882), 270, c. 1258 and 1272. [2] Redlich, op. cit., vol. i, 65.
[3] Professor R. W. McCulloch, in an unpublished revised Doctoral Dissertation (University of Michigan), says that Questions were asked both at the beginning and at the close of the sitting, the last to be asked at the Adjournment of the House being on 21 January 1847. See Parl. Deb. (1847), 89, c. 268. We are greatly indebted to Professor McCulloch for permission to consult his work.

period 1828–33, the occasional Question is usually recorded after Petitions and Private Bills, but there does not appear to be a regular order for the variety of miscellaneous business — granting of leave of absence, motion for returns, new writs etc.[1] It is probably significant that Questions were similarly treated on the Notice Paper until 1849, when they were grouped together as the first item under the heading 'Notices of Motions.' There must indeed have been an element of opportunism in the asking of Questions, for all depended on catching the Minister. For many years after 1830 the *Mirror of Parliament* and Hansard record such phrases as 'Mr. Robinson seeing the Rt. Hon. Baronet [the Chancellor of the Exchequer] in his place, begged to embrace the opportunity of asking . . .'.[2] Or, more unkindly, 'Mr. Cochran seeing the noble Lord the Secretary of State for Foreign Affairs now in his place, which was a rare sight at the time for questions . . .'.[3] As Questions became more numerous, and formal notice of intention to ask became usual, Ministers had less excuse for not being present and their presence at a particular time in the day's proceedings set the seal on the development of a Question time. The time was fixed at the earliest that Ministers need be present. Dod's *Parliamentary Companion*, published annually since 1832, first mentions the matter in its 1865 edition. 'At half-past four public business begins, when the leading Members of the Government are expected to be in their places to answer the questions of which notice has been given.'[4] As it was customary at this time for Mr. Speaker to take the Chair at 4.0 p.m., this arrangement provided a minimum half-hour for Petitions, Private Business etc. If this preliminary business took longer than 30 minutes, Questions were delayed to that extent: if, however, it took less time, then there was a gap between the end of that business and Questions. The 1876 edition gives the earliest starting time for Questions as 15 minutes after Mr. Speaker takes the Chair, but the edition of 1895 reverts to 30 minutes though 15 minutes remained the rule for the last week or so of the Session.

No precise evidence is available as to why Question time came to be fixed in this order but a very good guess can be made. The

[1] Questions are not acts of the House and are, therefore, not recorded in the daily *Votes and Proceedings* or in the *Journals*.
[2] Parl. Deb. (1847), 26, c. 494.   [3] Parl. Deb. (1849), 105, c. 194.
[4] p. 87.

practice of taking Private Bills and Petitions as the first main business of the day was long established. Even when these items came to have less Parliamentary significance relative to other business, it was still convenient to take them early, so delaying the hour when Ministers and the mass of Members need attend. In so far as Questions involved the presence of Ministers, they were more likely to be answered if they were asked when Ministers had to attend for some other business; this was more likely to be when the Orders of the Day were reached than during the earlier proceedings. But once discussion of the Orders of the Day had started it would be inconvenient to allow Questions to be asked because of the confusion likely to arise from there not being a Motion before the House. The most convenient time procedurally for Ministers, and probably for most Members, was thus as near as possible to the discussion of the Orders of the Day.

There is no description of the order of business in the first two editions of Erskine May's *Parliamentary Practice*. But, on 26 January 1846[1] the House decided the order of business for its Wednesday sittings and this was converted word for word into a Standing Order in June 1852. The House was to meet at noon each Wednesday 'for Private Business, Petitions and Orders of the day' and to continue until 6.0 p.m. unless previously adjourned. The Standing Order of 1852 did not preclude Questions being asked on Wednesdays, and it was not the practice of Mr. Speaker or of the Clerk to refuse Questions put on the Paper for answer on that day.[2] But the general understanding was that Wednesday was a quiet interlude between the long sittings on Monday and Tuesday on the one hand and Thursday and Friday on the other. Ministers were not normally expected to be present to answer Questions put down for answer on that day.

Though from time to time the House met on Saturdays, and Ministers even occasionally answered Questions on that day, the general pattern by the middle of the century was for four long days and one short day. The House did not formally fix the order of business for any of the long days until 27 May 1867 and then only in respect of any morning sittings that might be arranged

[1] *Commons Journals* 1846–7, vol. 101, part 1, p. 14.
[2] Statement by Mr. Speaker Gully, 28 April 1902. Parl. Deb. (1902), 107, c. 121.

for Tuesdays and Fridays. In April 1869 this Rule was applied to all such sittings, the Resolution being:

'That, unless the House shall otherwise order, whenever the House shall meet at Two o'clock, the House will proceed with Private Business, Petitions .... Questions to Ministers, and such Orders of the Day as shall have been appointed for the Morning Sitting.'

In moving this Resolution Mr. Gladstone said that its purpose was to provide that when the House met at 2 p.m. it would proceed with the business usually taken at 4 p.m.[1] The Resolution had, however, already been anticipated in the first manual of the *Rules, Orders and Forms of Proceedings of the House of Commons*. Prepared by Mr. Thomas Erskine May and published in 1854, Rule 101, showed the order of the main items of business to be: Private Bills, Public Petitions, Questions, and Orders of the Day and Notices of Motions, as set down in the Order Book. The last item is now generally known as Public Business. Rule 152 stated that, 'Questions are permitted to be put to Ministers of the Crown, relating to public affairs; and to other Members, relating to any Bill, Motion or other public matter connected with the business of The House in which such a Member may be concerned'.

By the middle of the century, therefore, Questions had a recognized place in the daily timetable. More important, the place they had come to occupy in the order of business both preceded Public Business and had precedence over it. The House met at a fixed time, usually shortly before 4.0 p.m. (except on Wednesdays) and continued to deal with one item of business after another, usually without a break. When, in order to deal with arrears of urgent business, the House occasionally had a 'day' or 'morning' sitting followed by an 'evening' sitting, the business remaining from the first part of the day's proceedings flowed over to the second. Questions, by preceding Public Business, were always certain to be reached, and by having precedence over it, were always certain of being completed. Thus the way was open for an unrestricted growth in the number of Questions, leading ultimately to a clash between them and Public Business.

[1] Parl. Deb. (1869), 195, c. 1977–82. For the 1867 Resolution see *Commons Journals*, vol. 122, pp. 247–8.

(iii) *Scope and Content*

Third, a stream of rulings by Mr. Speaker defined and restricted the scope and content of Questions. The right to ask a Question, particularly one about the Business of the House, was already accepted, but the limits to the kind of Question that could be asked had still to be worked out. This was done almost entirely by a series of Speaker's rulings, usually given in the House during Question time. The purpose, form and content of Questions have never been defined in the Standing Orders.

The nineteenth century saw a great increase in the prestige of the Speaker as the impartial, non-political chairman of the House, guardian of its traditions and procedure and interpreter of its practice, rules and wishes. Rulings from the Chair came to be an increasing element in the establishment of practice and were fostered by the use made of them in the successive editions of Erskine May. The first (1844) edition gave no rulings in support of its simple statement that 'questions should be limited, as far as possible, to matters immediately connected with the business of Parliament, and should be put in a manner which does not involve argument or inference'. By the tenth edition (1893) some 80 Hansard references are quoted, and the Editor in his preface was driven to say that the practice of asking Questions had reached such a formidable dimension as to provoke an almost equally formidable crop of rulings.

The authority of Mr. Speaker to rule Questions out of order and to require changes in the wording was challenged by Dr. Kenealy on 24 May 1878. His Motion, put on going into Committee of Supply, accused Mr. Speaker Brand of a breach of privilege for refusing to accept a Question which, because it purported 'rather to impugn the accuracy of the House than to seek information of the Government', the Speaker had suggested should be brought forward on a Motion. Dr. Kenealy asserted that the Speaker possessed no right to interfere with any Question unless it trespassed against order, decency or decorum, and the only jurisdiction to which a Member so transgressing was amenable was to the House itself. In the course of a short reply Mr. Speaker Brand said: 'I am merely the mouthpiece and servant of the House, and a very honourable service it is. But I am, at the same time, the Guardian of its Rules and Orders, and there are Rules and Orders laid down by this House applying specially to Questions put before the commencement of Public Business from day to day which I am bound to see enforced, and among these Rules and Orders there is one which declares that no Question is to be offered containing argument or opinion; and the Question prepared by the hon. Member for Stoke appeared to me to be a violation of that Rule, and it was upon that ground that I objected to its being put. It appears to me that the hon. gentleman is in some confusion as to the distinction between a Question and a Motion. If a Motion is offered by a Member of this House to the House, I should not feel that I was for one moment entitled to oppose the offering of such a Motion to the House, or to alter a single word, provided that it was properly and respectfully worded. But as to Questions put before the commencement of Public Business, if these Questions involve matter of argument or opinion, or are otherwise in opposition to the Rules and Orders of the House, I consider it my duty to object to them so proposed; and I trust that in taking the course I have done I have fulfilled my duty to the House.' Dr. Kenealy received no support and his Motion was not put to a vote.[1]

The earliest purpose of the rulings was to limit the possibility of Questions leading to conversation, i.e. the discussion of a matter without there being a Motion before the House. The primary purpose was seen as the asking for information; argument and opinion were out of place in a Question and more properly the subject of a Motion. In the words of the Report of the Select Committee of 1861: 'A practice has arisen of putting questions to Ministers on notice, when no Motion is before the House.... There is some convenience in this course; but to prevent this licence degenerating into abuse, it is most important that both questions and answers should be as concise as possible, and not sustained by reasoning which might give rise to debate.'[2]

A second purpose was to apply, as far as possible, the usage and etiquette governing the speech and behaviour of Members in the House and in particular during Public Business. Thus Questions containing offensive expressions or casting aspersions on the Sovereign were out of order just as the same words would have been during debate.

[1] Parl. Deb. (1878), 240, c. 643-56.   [2] Para. 56.

The third major purpose was to confine the subject matter to the business of Parliament. The earliest recorded Questions usually concerned the future business of the House, e.g. when a particular Bill was to be expected or a debate to take place, or with major matters which obviously concerned either the Government as a whole or a particular Minister. But the very simplicity of the process later led some Members to ask Questions about almost any happening under the sun.[1] Some statement or news item in the morning newspapers would attract a Member's attention and he would ask some Minister to comment upon it. In very many cases the matter would not be the concern of the Government, no Department having any power and no Minister feeling he had any responsibility to do anything about it. If, therefore, Question time was not to be wasted it became increasingly apparent that only matters for which a Minister had some direct responsibility or for which the House in general wished him to accept some responsibility could become the subject of Questions. It must be remembered that the rules of the House have never made it compulsory for Ministers to answer Questions. Indeed in the matter of Ministerial responsibility or answerability the scope was decided by what Ministers were prepared to answer and only secondarily by Speaker's rulings, there being, however, an underlying assumption from the earliest days that Members' requests for information would not normally be refused. It was obviously easier for a Minister to refuse to answer a Question about a matter for which he had no responsibility. But where he could be shown to have some responsibility it was difficult for him to refuse to answer. After 1832 the distinction between Ministers and the rest of the House became increasingly strong due to the growth of two disciplined parties, the increasing bulk of Government business, and the growth of the statutory powers of the Departments. This distinction also led to the decline and ultimate abandonment of the practice of addressing Questions to Members other than Ministers.

Finally, some of the rulings of Mr. Speaker were for the purpose of making Members more responsible for the accuracy of the content of their Questions. It ceased to be possible for a Member to ask whether a report or statement in a newspaper

[1] See the protest by Palmerston in July 1856. Parl. Deb. (1856), 143, c. 1035.

was true. The facts on which a Question was based could be set out briefly, providing the Member asking it made himself responsible for their accuracy. Extracts from newspapers and books and quotations from speeches ceased to be admissible and if the facts in the Question were of sufficient moment the Speaker could require the Member to produce *prima facie* proof of their authenticity.

It is worth noticing that a high proportion of the Speaker's rulings date from the period after about 1880. In large part this reflects the great increase in the number of Questions, but it also follows upon changes in Members' attitudes towards the use of this developing device. This point will be expanded later in this chapter.

THE INCREASING USE OF QUESTIONS

The number of Questions grew rapidly during the last fifty years of the century. The number on the Paper had risen from some 200 in 1850 to 4,000–5,000 each year in the 1890's. This exaggerates the increase, because in the former year many Questions were asked without being put on the Paper. Even so, the increase was probably at least tenfold during the period. Moreover, in addition to the original or main Questions, Members were now asking an increasing number of supplementary or 'subsidiary' Questions. Speaking in 1886 on the Resolution requiring written notice of Questions, Sir Henry Selwin-Ibbetson claimed that 'Not only has the practice of putting Questions grown immensely, but there has arisen another practice of putting a number of supplementary Questions which spring out of the answers given, with the object of arguing against the view drawn out by the original Questions, thereby becoming a sort of speech and involving a great waste of the time of the House'.[1] In 1893 Sir William Harcourt could say, 'if we had a strict rule against subsidiary questions we might save one third of the time expended. The putting of these questions is a recent practice. . . .'[2]

The factors that led to the immense growth of 'main' and 'subsidiary' Questions can be divided into two groups: forces outside the House and changes in the practice and procedure of

[1] Parl. Deb. (1886), 303, c. 699.   [2] Parl. Deb. (1893), 12, c. 1371.

the House. The first can be dealt with quite briefly. A major factor was undoubtedly the activities of certain Irish Members. In the Debate on the procedural changes of 1882 a Member referred to the 'extravagant action of a certain section of the Irish Members during the last four or five years and the kind of monopoly which they had been allowed to establish for Irish Questions . . .'.[1] In 1885 six Irish Members asked nearly 20 per cent. of the Questions recorded in Hansard, excluding supplementaries. Most of these Questions concerned what to most Members were local and trivial happenings, e.g. the delay in postal deliveries in a particular village on a particular day.[2] They were asked partly to harass the Chief Secretary for Ireland and partly to call attention to the need for a separate Irish Parliament to deal with such matters. But they also included Questions about arrests, evictions and other elements in the 'wrongs of Ireland'.

However, even without the Irish Questions, such factors as the steady growth in the powers possessed by Government Departments, the extension of British territories and responsibilities overseas and the increasing concern of Members to give public evidence[3] of their Parliamentary activities were inducing Members to ask more Questions. Even so, it is doubtful whether the increase would have been quite so great but for certain changes that took place in other parts of the procedure of the House. Indeed the attitude of the House towards Questions was quite different from that which it adopted towards most of the other procedural devices. The 70 years after 1830 saw great restrictions placed on most of the devices available to ordinary Members. Yet the use of Questions, essentially a back-bencher device, not only flourished but was encouraged to do so. It is therefore important to ask why this comparatively new device was singled out for favourable treatment, and how changes in other forms of procedure were related to this development.

[1] Parl. Deb. (1882), 274, c. 1351.
[2] Cf. Parnell, vol. i, p. 85, by R. Barry O'Brien. Parnell entered the House in April 1875. 'How do you get materials', he asked one of the Irish Members, 'for questioning the Ministers?' 'Why', said his friend, smiling at the simplicity of the novice, 'from the newspapers, from our constituents, from many sources.' 'Ah', said Parnell, 'I must try and ask a question myself some day.'
[3] In the debate of March 1886 on Questions, the Chancellor of the Exchequer (Sir William Harcourt) said: 'in the newspapers the Questions occupy very often twice as much space as the rest of the report. So long as the newspapers thus encourage the practice it will continue.' Parl. Deb. (1886), 303, c. 701.

THE STRUGGLE FOR PARLIAMENTARY TIME

Two needs increasingly dominated thought about procedure — the need to make the 'best' use of the limited time available and the need for greater certainty in the timing and order of business. Both needs pointed to reducing the part played by individual Members in the arrangement of the business of the House. The best use of time was that which provided opportunities to debate matters which interested a large number of Members, not just one or two. The timing of business was likely to be more certain the fewer the opportunities available to every Member to divert or delay the course of business.

The extensions of the franchise greatly increased the number and the variety of matters with which Members wished the House to deal. Moreover, Members were no longer content to leave discussion to a few well-known orators and public figures. Many more wished to speak themselves and to play an active part in the proceedings of the House, partly because this is what they had come there to do and partly because they wished to bring their activities to the notice of their constituents who, with each widening of the franchise became increasingly the concern of Members. In this they were assisted and encouraged by the development of the popular press, particularly of the provincial newspapers, and the institution of Special Wires.

Writing in 1880 Henry Lucy could say:

... the creation of the Special Wire is an event which has had a very serious effect upon Parliamentary procedure. Men will not often speak in an assembly who will not hear them, nor before representatives of a Press which do not notice them. But the cheapening of telegraphic communication, leading to the institution of Special Wires, has created a system by which speeches of members are reported verbatim in the local newspapers. Thus we have members speaking, not to the House of Commons, but to their constituencies; a state of affairs which, whilst it adds to the inherent dreariness of a particular speech, makes its delivery imperative. In former days, when a man had prepared a speech, and found that the House was determined not to hear it, he, after a fair show of resistance, was accustomed to give way. Now, when a Member has prepared a speech, he takes into consideration the circumstance that the papers which his constituents read have made arrangements for fully reporting it. The local journal may, indeed, as has happened in recent Parliamentary history, already have the speech in type; whence it becomes clear that the speech must be recited, though the Heavens fall, amid the clamour of an angry House.[1]

Notwithstanding the great increase in the demands on the time of the House it proved easier, or more profitable, to try to rearrange the use rather than to increase the amount of time available. For most of the 40 years after 1830 the sittings averaged somewhat over seven hours per day each Session: for the remainder of the century they averaged over eight hours. During the debates on procedural reform in 1902 Mr. Balfour referred on several occasions to the eight-hour parliamentary day. The House generally sat for some 115–120 days each session, or about 900 hours. The average was higher in the late 1870s and early 1880s, being nearer 125 days and 1100 hours. In years of exceptional strain and argument the House sat much longer, for example in 1882 it sat 162 days for 1434 hours.[2] But few thought that the solution to the increasing pressure on time could be found by the House sitting more frequently or for longer hours, certainly not while so much time of each sitting could be wasted or misused. Moreover, as the Session usually started in January or February, it being thought necessary to reserve the Autumn for the preparation of Government business, any delays involved the House sitting well into the summer, though not usually beyond 12 August, the opening day for the traditional mass slaughter of game.

The procedure and usage of the House in 1832 was the heritage of a very different period and had been devised to meet very different circumstances. Previously the problems had been to encourage Members to take an active part in the proceedings and, by multiplying the stages to be gone through, to prevent decisions being reached too hurriedly and without sufficient notice. The new and active Members therefore found available a great variety of procedural opportunities, the use of which not only gave them access to the time of the House, but quite often enabled them to decide what business should or should not be put before the House. Changes in procedure therefore took the

[1] *A Popular Handbook of Parliamentary Procedure* (1880), p. 70.
[2] For these and other statistics of the House of Commons see A. A. Taylor, *Statistics relative to the Business and Sittings of the House* (House of Commons Library).

form of a continuous reduction in the number of opportunities and an increasing acknowledgement of the idea that the business to be discussed should not be decided by or be at the mercy of any one Member.

These two changes were accelerated by the use of these many opportunities to obstruct the wishes of the great majority of the House. The Irish Party, particularly in the period 1877–82, took full advantage of the rules of the House, but they had been anticipated by those who opposed Cardwell's Army Regulation Bill of 1871, and the activities of the Fourth Party in 1880–3 showed how a minute but determined opposition could earn Parliamentary dividends by pertinacity and the use of the existing rules. But though the overt, wilful and sustained use of procedure to achieve indirectly what could not have been achieved directly sometimes gave the final impetus to change, the main force was the difficulties created by the increasing advantage taken by all Members of the opportunities offered.

There were in effect three sets of claimants on the time of the House — the Government, the House in a corporate sense, and the Member acting purely as an individual and not as part of the first two. Competition between the claimants took two distinct forms. The first was competition for the control of Public Business, i.e. discussion of the Orders of the Day and Notices of Motions. The second was competition between Public Business and all the items which preceded it.

PUBLIC BUSINESS

Orders of the Day include all stages of legislation (except the first reading of a Bill), the Committees of Supply and Ways and Means, and any matter which the House had ordered to be discussed. Broadly speaking, the term covers the Public Business which the House has already indicated its wish to discuss, whereas Notices of Motions may or may not be matters which the House, as opposed to one or a few Members, wishes to discuss.

During the course of the century, Orders of the Day were to become much more important than Notices of Motions, and in both forms of procedure Government business and business arranged between the Government and the Opposition leaders came to dominate the scene. But this was not the case before

1830, nor for the twenty or thirty years afterwards, and indeed the general arrangement of the business of the House was still subject to a great deal of 'private enterprise', even at the end of the century. The changes in procedure and the growth of the Question must be seen, therefore, against a steadily mounting need for more time to be assured to Government business and business of general concern to the two large Parties, and a steadily mounting appreciation of that need in the House.

In 1832 numerous opportunities existed for any Member to raise, after the commencement of Public Business, a matter which interested him and him alone.[1] Among the more important were:

(i) Each Order of the Day on the Paper had to be moved, and it was possible to raise any issue by moving an amendment to this Motion, e.g. that some other subject be discussed instead. Even if the amendment were lost or subsequently withdrawn the Member moving it had nevertheless created the opportunity to make his speech and perhaps initiate a short debate.

(ii) Any Member could move the Adjournment of the House either before or during Public Business and the debate on his Motion need not be confined to the reasons for adjourning the House.

(iii) He could put a Notice of Motion on the Paper and move it when it came up for discussion in due course.

(iv) Every time the House wanted to go into Committee, for the Committee Stage of legislation, for Committee of Ways and Means or for Committee of Supply, the necessary formal Motion, 'That Mr. Speaker do now leave the Chair', provided an opportunity to raise any issue and the discussion need not be confined to whether the House should or should not go into Committee.

One by one these opportunities disappeared or were severely restricted, until, by the end of 1882, little or nothing of them remained. The first to go was the right to move an amendment to the reading of the Orders of the Day. On 24 November 1837, the

[1] There also existed numerous opportunities whereby Members, even if they could not raise and have discussed an issue of their own, could divert or delay the course of Public Business and by making a nuisance of themselves call attention to some matter that was worrying them.

House resolved that the only amendment that could be moved was that another Order be read, and after 5 April 1848, each Order of the Day was read without any Motion needing to be put, so that no amendment, even of the order of business, could be moved.

As regards the Motion for the Adjournment of the House during Public Business, the issue turned on whether such a Motion should provide an opportunity to discuss any matter that the mover wished, or be confined strictly to the reasons for wishing the House to adjourn, or even be put without debate. As early as 1848 Mr. Speaker Shaw-Lefevre had expressed himself strongly in favour of the last course, but it did not commend itself to the Select Committee of 1848. It was not until 1882, after the worst Irish obstructionism, that the House ruled that the debate of all dilatory Motions,[1] should be strictly confined to the matter of the Motion, i.e. be strictly relevant to the reason why it was desirable to adjourn. The Speaker was given the power to put such a Motion forthwith from the Chair, if in his opinion it was an abuse of the Rules of the House.

The third major opportunity lessened as Orders of the Day, and in particular business proposed by the Government or arranged between the two front benches, came to predominate over private Members' Motions. In 1846, Mondays and Thursdays were fixed as Government days by order of the House, but it became usual for a third day to be taken over by the Government later each session. By 1888, Government business had precedence, not only at 63 Monday and Thursday sittings, but also at 69 out of the 104 other sittings.[2] Many of the sittings when private Members' business had precedence were either counted out for lack of a quorum (it not being the responsibility of the Whips to 'keep a House' on these days), or were ineffective because of the small attendance. Tuesdays and Wednesdays were the usual private Members' days, but the Government took the majority of these in most years towards the end of the century. It therefore became increasingly difficult for the ordinary Member to find time to get a Motion of his own discussed. He was driven either to operate through his party leaders, if in

[1] i.e. Motions concerned with holding up or delaying the business the House was in the course of discussing and had intended to continue discussing.
[2] A. A. Taylor, op. cit., p. 110.

Opposition, or to find some opportunity other than putting a Notice of Motion on the Paper.

The fourth class of opportunity in the list has a more interesting history, and is in many ways more relevant to the development of Question time. In brief, the story of the rise and decline of this element is as follows. Arising out of the constitutional maxim that the redress of grievances should be considered before the granting of supplies, a practice had grown up permitting every description of amendment to be moved on the formal Motion, 'That Mr. Speaker do now leave the Chair', necessary to convert the House into Committee of Supply or Ways and Means. The purpose of any such amendment was to enable the Member to raise some issue or grievance. Where notice of several amendments had been given, no other amendment could be proposed once an amendment had been defeated, but amendments were usually withdrawn i.e. not pressed to a vote, thus enabling others to be moved and discussed. It also became the practice, without moving an amendment, for Members to call the attention of the House to particular subjects, the rules of relevancy in debate being wholly ignored on such occasions.[1] Increasing use of both practices was made after 1837 and some 9 or 10 such amendments were moved and probably an equal number of observations and speeches not leading to an amendment were made each year during the 1850s.[2]

A somewhat similar procedure came to be adopted in the 1850s in respect of the Friday Adjournment Motion. As the House no longer wanted to meet on Saturday and as there was still no Standing Order which fixed the days when the House was to meet it was necessary on Fridays to move that the House, at its rising, do adjourn till Monday next. It was usual to move this formal Motion early whilst there still remained a quorum present for failure to pass it would mean that the House would automatically stand adjourned until Saturday.[3]

Both these occasions, by enabling a Member to make a short speech and a Minister to reply at similar length, presented Members with greater scope than Question time, from which argument and comment were excluded. They had, however,

---

[1] T. Erskine May, *Parliamentary Practice*, Fourth edition (1859), p. 521/2.
[2] See the evidence of Mr. Erskine May to the Select Committee on Business of the House, 1871, q. 10.
[3] Fifth edition (1863), p. 215/6.

several disadvantages from the point of view of the Government and to some extent of the House as a whole. For one thing, if the Member raised the issue without moving a formal amendment both he and the Minister could speak only once i.e. to the formal Motion before the House. Therefore, if several Members raised issues affecting the same Minister, he could not reply immediately to each, but had to wait until the end and answer them all together. Again, a series of such issues and amendments could be quite time consuming and so delay and render uncertain the discussion of Supply or the Adjournment of the House on Friday.

Mr. Speaker Denison vainly tried to persuade the Select Committee of 1861 that some restriction should be placed on this use of the formal Motion to go into Committees of Supply and Ways and Means, probably by applying the so-called Rule of Progress, which since 1853 had empowered the Speaker to put the formal Motion that converted the House into a Committee for the consideration of a Bill without allowing any discussion. Instead, the Select Committee compromised by in effect amalgamating the Supply and the Friday opportunities. From 1861, a new rule provided that while the Committees of Ways and Means and of Supply were meeting the first Order of the Day on Fridays should be for one or other of these Committees. When the Committees had finished their work, which usually was late in the Session, the House was to stand adjourned until Monday 'without question put' i.e. without there being any chance to raise an issue on the formal Adjournment Motion.

The Friday Adjournment Motion thus ceased to be an opportunity, but the Motion for going into Committee of Supply or of Ways and Means remained an important opportunity, particularly on Fridays. As was to be expected, the use of this opportunity increased, and Sir Thomas E. May told the Select Committee of 1871 that for the last ten years the average number of amendments moved on going into Committee of Supply had been 33, in addition to about an equal number of Questions and discussions not ending in Amendments.[1] Mr. Speaker Denison attached great importance to certainty with regard to business. 'There cannot be anything of more con-

[1] At q. 10.

sequence to a public assembly than to know when they meet together what business is to be brought before them. But, according to the practice of late years, with from 10 to 20 Notices of Motions put down before going into Supply, that certainty has been entirely destroyed, and nobody has known how long each discussion might occupy'.[1]

As a result of the Committee's report, the House in 1872 placed certain restrictions on the use of the formal Motion necessary to convert the House into Committee of Supply, and by Standing Order No. 56, passed in November 1882 as part of the great changes in that year, the opportunity was restricted to the three occasions when each of the main branches of the estimates was first put down for consideration. The amendment moved or the issue raised had to relate to the estimates proposed to be taken on that day. Thus another opportunity available to private Members who wished to raise a grievance or issue had been virtually eliminated.

THE STRUGGLE BETWEEN PUBLIC AND OTHER BUSINESS

Before discussion of the Orders of the Day and Notices of Motions could begin, certain preliminary business had first to be completed. This was true even on days when Orders of the Day and Government business had precedence. When most of the business of the House was initiated by individual Members rather than by the Government, competition between Public Business and other items of business was less significant. But as the Governmental and the majority supported content of the former rose, the precedence accorded to the latter became increasingly irksome, for the items preceding Public Business remained the concern and under the control of individual Members rather than of the Government or of the House as a whole. Moreover, for various reasons, this preliminary business greatly increased, and therefore from time to time seriously delayed the onset of Public Business.

Three main items were taken before Public Business: Private Bills, Public Petitions and Questions. Private Bills (or Private Business in the terminology of the House), though extremely

[1] At q. 295.

numerous, seldom took up much time, because already they were dealt with by small Committees of the House and were seldom debated on the floor. There were many troubles about the proper working of these Committees, but by and large, Private Bills were not regarded as a problem in the daily time-table until the end of the century, when the desire for certainty in Public Business became overwhelming.

Public petitions, in contrast, presented an early conflict. The petition was a long-established device, whereby one or more people, either from this country or from one of the Colonies, made representations to Parliament, calling attention to a grievance or to some matter about which it was claimed that action should be taken, or expressing an opinion on some current issue. The number of petitions had increased from about 200 a year at the beginning of the century to some 8000 or more in the early 1830s. The procedure which had grown up by custom prescribed four regular Motions for each separate petition, each Motion giving the opportunity for debate. Between 1833 and 1842, however, the House agreed to drastic curtailments of these opportunities. After 1839 debate upon presentation was forbidden, save in rare instances.

Questions to Ministers took up an increasing amount of time as the century progressed, but it was a by-product of Question time rather than Question time itself which first raised a major problem. On occasion, not being satisfied with the reply, the Member would try to comment on it or to argue with the Minister. As this was conversation or irregular debate, Mr. Speaker would call the Member to order. The Member 'to put himself right' would move 'That this House do now adjourn'. He could then discuss the matter at any length. Mr. Speaker Denison in his evidence to the 1861 Committee said:[1] 'At present The House has fixed an hour at which questions may be asked, and it has very closely limited the extent which is permitted in asking these questions, but a practice has arisen which is certainly a new use of the power of moving, "That this House do now adjourn". Originally that power was reserved and used when something arose on a sudden which made it, in the opinion of the Member, desirable to make that Motion; but now Members put down questions to be asked at four o'clock, and they came into The

[1] At q. 138.

House with the deliberate purpose of raising a debate at that hour when The House says there shall be no debate ... when abuses of this kind are tolerated, every time that they are employed becomes a precedent for another occasion.' He suggested that at the time set apart for Questions it should not be competent for any Member to make a Motion. The Chairman of the Committee of Ways and Means (Mr. W. N. Massey) did not support the Speaker's suggestion. He agreed that it was regrettable that a Member should use the Motion for the Adjournment when called to order by Mr. Speaker ('almost in defiance' of him, suggested Sir James Graham), but he suggested it was a convenient if irregular mode of calling the immediate attention of the House to some matter of pressing importance. He agreed with Mr. John Bright that the 'irregularity' was most frequent when the Member was dissatisfied with the Minister's reply.[1] The Select Committee came to the conclusion that the evil had not reached a point where special interference by a new Standing Order would be expedient, and were disposed to rely on the forbearance of Members.

The Select Committee of 1871 were not worried about this aspect of current procedure, and by 1878 Sir Thomas E. May could say[2] that the practice was 'a very rare thing now, and it is much discountenanced by the Speaker'.[3] The Select Committee, therefore, made no proposals. But in the next three or four years the device was actively used, mainly, but not only, by the Irish Party. In many cases the issue discussed on the Adjournment Motion was considered by the great majority of Members to be trivial or better dealt with in another way. On 4 February 1881,[4] however, Mr. Speaker Brand announced a rule to the effect that, except by leave of the House, no Motion for the Adjournment could be made before the Orders of the Day or Notices of Motions had been entered upon. At the end of the following year a new Standing Order provided that the Adjournment could not be

[1] Select Committee, 1861, q. 418–25.   [2] Select Committee, 1878, q. 285.
[3] For examples of the Speaker trying to prevent the adjournment being moved consequent upon a Member being dissatisfied with an answer to a Question see Parl. Deb. (1877), 233, c. 978, and Parl. Deb. (1877), 234, c. 1301, both in 1877.
[4] Parl. Deb. (1881), 258, c. 162. In 1879 Mr. Speaker Brand had said '... every Member of this House has the privilege of moving the adjournment of the House at the time of Questions; but I am bound to say, that if the privilege of moving the adjournment of the House when a Member is not satisfied with an answer he receives should become a practice, that privilege will have to be restrained by the House.' H. C. Deb. 247, c. 697.

moved until after the Questions on the Paper had been disposed of, and even then, except by leave of the House, could not be moved before the commencement of Public Business unless it were moved for the purpose of discussing 'a definite matter of urgent public importance'[1] and was supported by not less than forty Members rising in their places. If fewer than forty but not less than ten Members rose in support, it was for the House to decide forthwith whether the Motion should be made. If the Motion was so supported or if the House agreed it should be made, it was taken immediately before Public Business. After this, few Motions for the Adjournment were successful, being either unsupported by 40 Members or defeated in the division or ruled out by Mr. Speaker's increasingly strict interpretation of the phrase, 'a definite matter of urgent public importance'.

Thus by the end of the century only Question time, the few Adjournment Motions under Standing Order 10 that were permitted to be moved, the occasionally disputed Private Bill, and certain miscellaneous Business that took up little or no time, were left as any real competitors to the commencement of Public Business. And by far the greatest of these was Question time.

CHANGING ATTITUDE TO QUESTIONS

The development of Questions was related to these changes in procedure in two ways. On the one hand, the existence of this device made it easier to abolish or restrict other forms of expression available to Members. The various Select Committees which considered the procedure of the House were always reluctant to restrict the rights of individual Members, particularly those hallowed by long usage. Only when it was quite clear that the House was in danger of being rendered ineffective were they ready to recommend drastic measures. Their views mirrored the general feeling of the House. Questions had the great advantage of being a private Members' device which consumed little time, or rather much less time for each issue, than any possible alternative procedures. As early as 1848 Mr. Speaker Shaw-Lefevre could express the opinion: 'I think that great public convenience

[1] Cf. remark of Mr. Speaker Denison on 3 May 1869 'the privilege of moving the Adjournment of the House upon asking a Question had been reserved by the common consent of the House for occasions of urgency'. Parl. Deb. (1869), 196, c. 19.

has arisen from the questions put to Ministers ... which frequently do away with the necessity of a debate.'¹

Sir Thomas Erskine May and others who guided the procedural changes also saw Questions as less time-consuming than some of the opportunities they wished to eliminate or restrict. May, that great reformer of procedure and certainly no friend of any rule or usage which encouraged the ordinary Member to take up the time of the House, nevertheless defended Questions before the Select Committee of 1878. He had not, he said, 'observed any very great inconvenience arising from the present rules as to questions except ... that there should be so many of them and that some of them should be so very long.' But he went on to point out that 'great advantages arise from putting questions; they often avert debate, while they serve the purpose of debate; the object of the Member in putting the question is expressed in the question itself; while the facts of the case and the grounds of any decision are also stated by the Minister in answer; and these explanations generally satisfy the House, and make it unnecessary to bring forward a motion upon the subject'.² The strictly applied rules prevented anything in the way of discussion or debate developing. Finally Questions could not interrupt the course of Public Business once it had started. One suspects, therefore, that Members who came to the Clerk or one of his Assistants for advice on how to raise a particular matter would be more likely to be encouraged to ask a Question than to indulge in some more time-consuming form of Parliamentary activity.

On the other hand, as other forms of procedure were abolished or curtailed, the pressure was diverted to some remaining form and turned this into the device currently most in use. As Sir Thomas Erskine May put it in his evidence to the Select Committee of 1871, '... though formerly Members had almost unlimited rights, they rarely availed themselves of such rights; but now every right that remains is taken advantage of so frequently

[1] Evidence to Select Committee, 1848, q. 82.
[2] At q. 79. He had seen the advantage of Questions as a time-saver much earlier than this. A member of the Select Committee of 1854 asked him whether the practice of raising an issue on going into Committee of Supply was not due to the desire of Members to make observations without concluding with a Motion, a practice not possible with the normal Notice of Motion. He replied, 'No doubt it gives them that opportunity; but in many cases, I should say, the same results might be obtained, with much greater convenience, by putting a question to a Minister and receiving an answer.' q. 365.

ORIGINS AND DEVELOPMENT

that it is necessary to revise the practice.'[1] In the more picturesque words of Mr. Joseph Cowen in 1886, 'If you attempt to dam up water in one direction it will burst forth in another; and, therefore, [because of the encroachment upon the rights of private Members] pressure has been put upon hon. Members to bring forward grievances in the shape of Questions.'[2] About this time Questions were quite often referred to as a 'safety-valve'. Thus Mr. Salt on 21 February 1887 asserted: 'Questions are a sort of safety valve; they are a safety-valve for the public and for hon. Members themselves. During the last few years the time at the disposal of private Members has been severely curtailed; therefore no one need be surprised if hon-Members run riot sometimes in Questions.'[3]

THE RISE OF THE SUPPLEMENTARY

The forms of procedure that were disappearing or being restricted allowed a Member to make a speech, start a debate and enter into argument. Questions and answers did not allow of this. To prevent the device from degenerating into irregular 'debate' had, in the words of May, led to 'the greatest pains' being taken 'to eliminate anything in the nature of argument or inference from . . . questions before they are printed'.[4] A non-argumentative Question would, or should, receive a non-argumentative reply. If the Member was only in search of factual information this limitation was no handicap. If, however, he wished to pursue the grievance of one of his constituents, or to raise a point which might lead to criticism of a Minister, the Question as originally conceived was too limited. It was not an adequate alternative to moving the Adjournment or to raising an issue on going into Committee of Supply. It was, however, made more adequate by the device of the 'supplementary'.

Supplementary Questions only became significant procedurally when notice of Questions had to be given. True, even before this, if a Member's remarks subsequent to a Minister's reply were not couched in interrogative form but were by way of comment they were out of order. Even if worded as an enquiry

[1] At q. 270. See also the Memorandum he circulated to the Cabinet late in 1881, printed in *Public Administration*, (1956), vol. 34, pp. 419–24.
[2] Parl. Deb. (1886), 303, c. 704.
[3] Parl. Deb. (1887), 311, c. 230.   [4] Select Committee, 1878, q. 80.

they were also out of order if they offended one of the growing number of rules governing form and content. For the rest, it was merely a matter of whether the Minister could answer the 'supplementary' without notice, and in most cases this would depend on how close it was to the subject matter of the main Question. The seventh edition of Erskine May (1873) says: 'Sometimes when an answer has been given, further questions are addressed to the minister upon the same subject, but no observations or comments are then permitted to be made.'[1] No concern about the practice was expressed to the Select Committee of 1871.

By the 1880s, however, the character of Question time had changed.[2] The use of main Question and supplementary had developed in such a way as to enable their combined use to be a reasonable substitute for some of the opportunities that had disappeared. Instead of being mainly a method whereby a Member extracted publicly a piece of information out of a Minister they were now being used, by a very small group it is true, to harass and cross-examine Ministers and to air Members' grievances.

The procedural development of the supplementary must have been fairly straightforward until the passing of the rule about notice. At the time when a Member was not compelled to give written notice of his Question it was difficult for the Speaker to refuse to allow him to ask a 'supplementary' arising out of the answer, providing it kept within the rules governing Questions. And in so far as the supplementary kept very close to the subject of the Question just answered, it would be difficult for a Minister to say that he could not answer it because he had not the necessary information. There is some evidence that with the growth in the number of Questions and their use to embarrass them Ministers may, not unnaturally, have tried to score off Members in their answers or at least not to give anything away.[3]

Todd, writing in 1867,[4] said that sometimes Questions are

[1] p. 321.
[2] Sir Charles Dilke said in 1901: 'it was in 1882 that the practice of asking supplementary questions in foreign affairs first began.' Parl. Deb. (1901), 89, c. 340. See also the statement of Sir Henry Selwin-Ibbetson quoted earlier at page 29.
[3] Cf. Mr. Joseph Cowen on 12 March 1886: 'Most of the abuse of questioning is not in the Questions themselves, but in the ambiguous manner in which they are answered.' Parl. Deb. (1886), 303, c. 704–5.
[4] *On Parliamentary Government in England*, (1867–9) vol. ii, p. 343.

asked which Ministers find it inconvenient to answer. Under such circumstances, he pointed out, it is not unusual for them to enter largely into detail but nevertheless to evade a direct reply, and in support of this he quoted Palmerston's remark of 1856 that this 'is a course which is often felt as becoming to adopt when questions are put to which it would be indiscreet to give a direct answer '.[1]

Sometimes it would be apparent to the Speaker that the Minister had not given a satisfactory or clear answer.[2] Having the responsibility for seeing that all Members were fairly treated, he would obviously be unwilling to prevent the Member asking another Question in the hope of obtaining a more satisfactory reply. A bigger step would be the asking of a supplementary by a Member who had not asked the original Question. But why should the Speaker have prevented any Member present from trying to clear up to his own satisfaction what the Minister had said? In any case, during the late 1870s and early 1880s, when this practice was developing, it would have been difficult for the Speaker to refuse to allow a supplementary, for formal notice was still not required for the main Question, and in any case refusal might only have increased the number of Questions put down for the next day.

There were also the wider repercussions to be taken into account in curtailing what could on occasion amount to the cross-examination of a Minister. Until 1882 there was always the threat of the Adjournment being moved. As Lord John Manners said in the Debate of November 1882, on the proposal to curtail this right, 'during recent years the number of Questions put at the commencement of Business had greatly increased . . . because the time at the disposal of private Members had been so restricted by the action of the Government that matters which formerly formed the subject of distinct Motions had been put down in the form of Questions, very much, he thought to the saving of the time of the House, and also to the convenience of the Government. But if [the right to move the adjournment of the House was so restricted] what, he asked, would be the value

[1] Parl. Deb. (1856), 143, c. 1035.
[2] 'It frequently happens, as the Committee is aware, that questions are not completely answered in the opinion of the Members putting them, and they ask for further information. I could hardly interpose in that case.' Mr. Speaker Brand in evidence (q. 353) to the Select Committee on Public Business, 1878.

of those Questions? Under the present system, an hon. Member who received an unsatisfactory reply ... was able to make himself disagreeable to the Government by moving the adjournment, and so obtaining the information that he desired; but if an essential modification was not made [to the proposed change] there would be absolutely no guarantee that a question, perhaps of the greatest interest and importance, would receive an adequate answer from the Minister of the day. The House and the country would thereby be deprived of that information which they had a right to demand, and they would be left at the mercy of a powerful Minister with a mechanical majority at his back.'[1] Sir John (then Mr.) Gorst also made the same point[2] and so did Mr. Sexton, 'the greatest exponent of the device of the Supplementary,' according to Lucy. Sexton said: '... if an Irish Member put a Question, the answer was given at present under the salutary check of the possibility of a Motion for the Adjournment of the House being moved.'[3]

The Speaker, and his adviser at this period, the influential Sir Thomas Erskine May, had to take a view of the use of the time of the House as a whole, and of course, the Government were also interested in this. If an excited Member could be satisfied by asking a few Questions without notice it might be awkward for the Minister concerned, but it was worth while if the alternative was a Motion for the immediate Adjournment of the House, or an extra amendment to delay the commencement of the Committee of Supply.

The procedural changes that took place at the end of 1882 substantially removed the need for the Speaker to have to take these alternatives into account. But it is unlikely that the Speaker or the leaders and old Members of the House were altogether happy at the drastic restrictions that had suddenly been placed on the activities of Members in order to meet Irish obstruction. The right of any Member to ask a supplementary had already been established and, in any case, it was still possible to ask a main Question without giving formal notice. This was hardly the time to attempt to curtail one of the last strongholds of the private Member. Instead, one suspects, Mr. Speaker Peel took a lenient

[1] Parl. Deb. (1882), 274, c. 1341.
[2] c. 1335. Gorst also used the same argument to object to the curtailment of amendments on Supply days.
[3] Parl. Deb. (1882), 274, c. 1476.

ORIGINS AND DEVELOPMENT

view of the development. The widening of scope and character of the supplementary must, at first at least, have seemed to be a safety valve which consumed very little time and did the least harm to the course of Public Business.

The need to give notice of Questions might have had serious consequences for the supplementary. Instead the change probably encouraged its use. The wording of the Resolution of 12 March 1886 referred to Questions in general and could, therefore, have been applied even to supplementaries. A Select Committee under Lord Hartington which reported in June of the same year put forward a proposal that was clearly intended to set out more fully the desirable practice. It proposed:

That notice of any question to Ministers or other Members shall be given, in writing only, to the Clerk at the table, and no question shall be put at the commencement of public business without notice, except questions concerning the course and arrangement of public business, or questions put for the purpose of elucidating any answer given in the House, or a question of immediate urgency upon the permission of the Speaker previously given, such question to be given to the Speaker in writing.[1]

The House was apparently content with the less specific wording of the Resolution of March 1886, for it adopted the same wording for the new Standing Order 20 in March 1888. After March 1886, the Speaker had the power to refuse to allow any Question to be asked which had not appeared on the Order Paper. He now started to use that power in the manner indicated in the proposal of the Hartington Committee, i.e. to allow three classes of question without Notice — Questions concerning the course and arrangement of Public Business; Questions which he judged to be urgent; and Questions put for the purpose of elucidating any answer given in the House — in other words, supplementaries. In all these cases his permission was needed, but formal notice was not.

The Resolution of 1886 created a new situation, in that it greatly strengthened the hand of the Speaker in controlling the use and range of supplementaries. Henceforth, he could, with the full authority of the House, require a Member to give formal notice of any supplementary. On 22 March, ten days after the

[1] Report of Select Committee on Parliamentary Procedure, 1886, p. v.

passing of the Resolution, Mr. Redmond asked the Home Secretary a Question about the conduct of the police in Leeds. The Speaker pointed out that the Question came within the new rule requiring that Notice of Questions should be given beforehand to the Clerk at the Table. Mr. Sexton then said he understood that 'according to the Rule, although a Notice of a Question could not be given orally, it would be open to Members to ask supplementary Questions in addition to those on the Paper'. Mr. Speaker Peel thereupon replied: 'I have endeavoured to put the best interpretation in my power upon the Rule. Supplementary Questions purely seeking for the elucidation of former answers are in Order; but supplementary Questions which it cannot be in the power of a Minister to answer at the moment, I regard as belonging to those of which Notice should be given.'[1]

The other side of this was that the Speaker could not very well refuse to allow a supplementary if it clearly rose out of the original Question, unless, of course, it could be refused under some ruling or usage of the House. Thus, Mr. Speaker Peel, in April 1893, though confessing that 'One would of course wish to reduce supplementary questions to the narrowest possible bounds . . .', had to say 'If supplementary questions in any way arise out of the original question of which notice has been given, it is perfectly in Order . . .'[2] Thus by the 1890s the right or privilege to ask supplementaries, though still viewed with suspicion, was well established. Use of this right prolonged Question time and sometimes embarrassed Ministers. Indeed it was these features which were creating enemies, and in 1902 supplementaries were to meet a major challenge.

[1] Parl. Deb. (1886), 303, c. 1503–4.   [2] Parl. Deb. (1893), 11, c. 1488, 1490.

CHAPTER 3

THE CHANGES IN 1902 AND 1906

AT the end of the century the House usually met at 3 p.m. on Monday, Tuesday, Thursday and Friday, and at noon on Wednesday. Opposed business normally concluded at midnight (5.30 p.m. on Wednesday), but unopposed business could continue until 1 a.m. (6 p.m. on Wednesday). Half an hour was usually taken for dinner, generally between 8 and 9 o'clock, at the discretion of the Speaker or Chairman.

The business at each Sitting was taken in a fixed order, each item being completed before starting the next. Public Business, in the form of Orders of the Day and Notices of Motions, came last on the list, being preceded by Petitions, Private Bills, Questions, the occasional Motion accepted for the Adjournment of the House on a matter of urgent public importance, and a number of other less time-consuming items.

Mondays and Thursdays were allotted to Government legislation, and Fridays were largely devoted to Supply. Tuesdays and Wednesdays were regarded as private Members' days, but many of these were taken for Government business by resolution of the House, particularly in the second half of the Session. In the five years from 1896 to 1900, private Members had twenty-four whole Tuesdays and five evening sittings, but the House was counted out for lack of a quorum on fifteen of these occasions. They also had an average of twelve Wednesdays a year during this period. Ministers normally did not attend on Wednesdays to answer Questions. Very occasionally there were sittings on Saturdays and also so-called 'morning' sittings, when the House would meet at 2 p.m. and adjourn at 7 p.m. for two hours, meeting again at 9 p.m. for the 'evening' sitting.

These arrangements had two great weaknesses. First, they left the time available for Public Business at the mercy of a variety of items of business mainly the concern of the individual Member. Second, they provided no certainty as to the time, or even the day, when particular items of business would be reached

THE CHANGES IN 1902 AND 1906

and discussed. Notwithstanding the great changes of the 1880s, procedure was still liable to be dominated by the private Member. The worst forms of obstruction had been abolished, but the procedure still gave any Member, and for that matter the Opposition, great opportunities to delay and to render uncertain the course of business desired by the majority.

So far as delays in the commencement of Public Business were concerned, there were three particular culprits: (1) opposed Private Business; (2) Questions; and (3) urgency Adjournment Motions. During the five years from 1896 to 1900 the equivalent of four whole Parliamentary days a year had been spent on the first of these, there had been nearly 5,000 Questions a year on the Paper, and the Adjournment had been accepted and moved on twenty-nine occasions.[1] It was, however, not so much the volume as the uncertain incidence of these items which caused most trouble. The big increase in the number of Questions and supplementaries meant, of course, that Public Business was usually not started upon much before 5.30 to 6 p.m. When, however, a largish number of Questions coincided with an opposed Private Bill and an Adjournment Motion, Public Business might not be reached before dinner. It should be borne in mind that quite apart from the half-hour interval (the Speaker's chop) it was not customary for the leaders on both sides of the House to speak during the hours of 7 to 10 o'clock, so many Members being at dinner during this period. In so far as these three items were used for the purpose of delaying Government business, they were likely to be most in evidence on Government days, particularly on days when the Government had important legislation or financial business to get through the House.

The bitterly-fought Session of 1901 brought matters to a head. Question time took up the equivalent of almost fifteen eight-hour days. Public Business seldom started before 6 p.m. The Government had to bring in twenty-one Motions for changing the Standing Orders for the enlargement of their share in the time of the House. The closure was applied in an unprecedented way. There was an unusually large number of divisions, 482 altogether, which, at the rate of five divisions an hour, amounted to twelve eight-hour days. Many of these divi-

[1] Sir William Walrond's Memorandum to Mr. Balfour (dated 16 October 1901), Cabinet Paper 1009.

sions were moved purposely during the period between 8 and 10 o'clock, to inconvenience those with dinner engagements. A great deal of the tension arose from the Opposition's criticisms of the policy and conduct of the South African War, but the Irish Members were also active.

There was, therefore, a good deal of talk about 'reforming' the procedure of the House. Mr. Joseph Chamberlain spoke of the need 'to give to the majority of the House of Commons a greater control over its own business and a greater control over the men who insult and outrage it'. Sir Henry Fowler, one of the Opposition leaders, spoke of the necessity of 'treating the affairs of the nation in a business-like way and applying modern resources to their despatch'.[1]

THE ORIGIN OF THE BALFOUR PROPOSALS

On 16 August 1901 Balfour, as Leader of the House and very near to being Prime Minister, circulated a Memorandum from the Government Whips[2] to the House of Commons' Members of the Cabinet with a covering note in the following terms:

I commend this paper to the earnest attention of my colleagues.

I believe it contains, in something more than germ, the elements of a very far reaching reform. I do not attach the smallest importance to the argument that the proposed system would be unfavourable to us in Opposition.[3] The Unionist Party are perfectly capable of prolonging discussion on Bills to which they object. But they are quite incapable of using with effect, or indeed of using at all, the petty methods of annoyance to which these proposals are intended to put an end. These methods are of value only to those whose object is, not solely or even principally, to criticise legislation, but to injure the House of Commons. A.J.B.

[1] Quoted by Redlich, op. cit., vol. i, p. 193.
[2] Memorandum on Hours of Business in the House of Commons, Cabinet Paper 839. Printed 16 August 1901 but dated 15 August.
[3] This was presumably a reference to the last two paragraphs in the Whips' Memorandum:
'.... we have carefully considered the effect of this proposal in case we should form the Opposition instead of the Government.

No doubt it would operate in the direction of making it easier for a Government to pass Legislation. But we do not attach much importance to preserving facilities for ourselves for petty Parliamentary obstruction. Far more important is it for the Unionist Party to make a seat in the House of Commons a highly-valued possession by the type of Representative in England, Scotland or Ireland.'

Shortly afterwards he circulated a paper of his own entitled 'The Question of Double Sittings'.[1] In October, Sir William Walrond, the Chief Government Whip, circulated two Memoranda[2] in which he set forth his own ideas for reform, differing in certain significant details from those of his colleagues. Early in November[3] Balfour circulated a further Memorandum setting forth his own ideas about the form the changes should take.

All agreed on the main objects to be achieved by the changes, and on certain main features, but there were significant differences of opinion on several important points. The two main objects were, to gain a larger and more certain share of the time of the House for Government business, and to secure greater certainty in the time and the course of the business before the House. In his second Memorandum, Balfour said:

> The present system [i.e. the arrangement of time between Government and private Members] is indefensible. By the Standing Orders private Members have certain days allowed to them which, under modern conditions, have constantly to be taken for Government business. They cannot be so taken without debate, and every time such a debate takes place three or four hours of valuable Parliamentary time are not only occupied, but absolutely wasted, in the repetition of speeches which have been made and answered hundreds of times before. It would be an immense advantage if we could devise a Standing Order dealing with this matter which would not require to be torn to pieces three or four times in the course of every Session.[4]

The Whips' Memorandum started by stating that the suggestions were made with a view to securing greater despatch of the Business of the House, 'whilst at the same time decreasing the risks of Government defeat in Divisions, diminishing the discomforts of Members and thereby inducing the best type of Parliamentary Representative to remain a Member....' It went on:

> The Session of 1901 — though not so trying to Members in the number of hours after midnight, as, for instance, the Session of 1887 — has, in our opinion, been more harassing, and has made a greater

[1] Cabinet Paper 845. Printed on 20 August, but dated 19 August.
[2] Cabinet Papers 1008–9, dated 16 October 1901. Walrond had been Patronage Secretary since June 1895 and was a Whip in 1885 and again between 1886 and 1892.
[3] Cabinet Paper 1053, 1901, dated October, but printed on 4 November 1901.
[4] Cabinet Paper 1053, p. 5.

demand upon the time and temper of the usual supporters of the Government, and has, from the large number of Divisions (the *maximum* hitherto recorded), and especially from the uncertainty of the hour at which they were expected and took place, made a larger inroad upon the private Members' avocations than any of its predecessors.

It is probable that this new Parliament contains more men engaged in commercial and professional pursuits than have hitherto been found in the ranks of the Unionist Party. Whether this be so or not, the Whips have ample evidence that there is a deep-seated and widespread feeling among the best representatives of the Party that our present method of conducting Parliamentary affairs results in an unnecessary interference with their business and other engagements produces an uncertainty in their plans, a dislocation of their arrangements which is to a large extent uncalled for, and generally leads to a strain being put upon them which is the more irksome and intolerable because they are persuaded it is avoidable by adapting our rules to modern exigencies.

We are fully persuaded that if nothing is done to meet this feeling the House of Commons, while retaining its attractions for men of political or social ambition, will rapidly cease to retain in the ranks of its Members the leading men in the professional and commercial world as well as those who are willing to give a moderate share of their leisure to public life.

These are the men to whom we look in the main to form our Committees, and already we see among such men a desire, and in several instances a determination, to shake themselves free from the Parliamentary yoke, unless something is done to relieve its pressure.

The main feature common to all the proposals was that on four days a week there should be two sittings of the House. The first would end at 7.30 p.m. and the evening sitting would commence at 9 p.m. There would thus be a certain hour and a half for dinner. There was also general agreement that the morning sittings were the most suitable for Government business and that as far as possible other business should come on from 9 p.m. onwards. The combination of double sittings, a definite and longer dinner period, and Government business coming early in the day's proceedings, had obvious advantages to the Whips, and to those Government supporters who, not having any business of their own in the Chamber, only attended in the evening if pressed by the Whips. Not only would a Government supporter be more sure when business was to be taken, but he would be no longer compelled by the Whips or his conscience to dine in the House, and therefore 'would have little or no temptation to stay away ... or, if he attended, to escape from it by any but the door of Honour'.[1]

The major differences of opinion concerned the time at which the House should meet, the time when Public Business should commence, and the time when Questions to Ministers should be taken. These three points were closely interrelated. In part they were a continuation of the argument that had gone on during the previous 20 to 30 years as to the time and significance to be attached to the three main items which preceded Public Business (Private Bills, Questions and Urgency Adjournment Motions).

All three sets of proposals assumed that the House would continue to sit on four days a week until midnight for opposed business (and until 1 a.m. for unopposed business), as was then the practice. The Whips' Memorandum, however, proposed that on these days the House should meet at 2.30 p.m. (instead of 3 p.m.), and that Public Business should commence immediately after Prayers, instead of being preceded by Private Business etc. Question time would commence at 9 p.m., and unless there was an Urgency Adjournment Motion, Private Bills would be taken immediately afterwards. Any time remaining would revert to the Government, or to private Members, if it were their day. The Whips defended this treatment of Public Business and Questions largely on the grounds of greater certainty to both Members and Ministers. They said:

The fixity of the course of business during the afternoons would give Ministers greater facilities for their administrative work, would enable them to make and keep appointments with tolerable certainty, and would substantially contribute to their private convenience.

Another advantage they claimed was that:

There would be more time to prepare the answers to Questions. Attaching, as the House of Commons does — and most wisely — enormous importance to the right to question Ministers, we do not believe that this right would be shorn of any of its advantages by putting the question hour at 9 o'clock. On the other hand, we are not without hope

---

[1] The door of Honour was the entrance watched by the Whips to 'mark-in' and keep a count of Members in the House. Apparently during 1901 there were 'leakages' by other doors which upset the calculations of the Government Whips and compelled them 'to keep far more men in the House than if all men played the door game as it should be played'. Cabinet Paper 839, p. 5.

that many frivolous Questions would cease to be put, as the House would be comparatively empty and there would not be the same inducement to waste time.

But they foresaw certain objections:

We doubt, however, whether any proposal to take Questions at a later hour than 9 p.m. would be acceptable to the House. We have not shut our eyes to the fact that Ministers would usually have to be in their places at 9 o'clock. But any Minister desirous of being absent for some special purpose could, as he does now, obtain postponement of his Questions or have them replied to by his subordinate or another Minister.

They also admitted that there was something in the objection 'hinted in some quarters, that the earlier hour will fall hardly on men in the City and on practising Barristers'. But they thought this could be met by the system of pairing, which would relieve such Members of attendance in the House until 4 or 5 p.m. Even, however, without his having paired with an Opposition Member, the Whips thought, a Member's attendance at 2.30 p.m. would hardly ever be obligatory 'until after Whitsuntide, when Committee stages of Government measures are the order of the day'.

Clearly the Memorandum was trying to anticipate Sir William Walrond's main objections. 'I do *not* think', he said, 'it would be practicable to have questions at 9 p.m., as this procedure would compel Ministers to be always in attendance at that hour, and I feel certain there would be strong and general objection to this proposal. . . .' He proposed, therefore, that the House should meet at 2.0 p.m. and that Question time should commence at 2.15 p.m. He thought that in this way 'practising Barristers and City men will be able to attend to their duties in the House, almost as soon as the real business commences'. He went on to argue that if Government Business were to commence at 2.30 p.m. as was proposed by his colleagues, i.e. immediately after Prayers, 'on many occasions the Government would be in a minority.'

In his proposals Balfour drew more from Sir William Walrond than from the Government Whips' Memorandum. Like Walrond he wanted the House to meet at 2.0 p.m. on four days a week, but apparently he was not convinced of the objections to starting Public Business so much earlier than was the current practice. He thought, however, that Private Bills could be taken immediately after Prayers as was the practice, but introduced the idea that any such business not completed by, say, 2.25 p.m. should automatically stand over until 9 p.m. He thought that by 2.25 p.m. all unopposed Bills would have been cleared. It is possible that he made this proposal so as to bring the commencement of Public Business almost to the time recommended by the Whips. But it is a very good example of Balfour's general attitude, in that, though he allowed an important item to precede Public Business, he did not allow the course of it to decide the time when Public Business was to commence. Evidently he felt very strongly about Questions, for he said:

Questions are becoming — indeed have become — something of a scandal. They take up the best hour in the day; they refer, for the most part, to very trifling subjects; they give rise to constant friction between the Chair and the Irish Members — very destructive of the dignity of Parliament; and, in the shape of supplementary questions asked without notice, they are constantly made the vehicle for calumnious attacks on individuals.

The evils, therefore, that we have to meet are due partly to the time of day at which questions come on, partly to the Rules under which they are asked. To take the latter first, I think (1) that a supplementary question should only be put by the asker of the original question, and only for the purpose of eliciting the real meaning of the answer; and (2) that no question should be put except by the Member in whose name it stands — a restriction which can lead to no hardship if it be understood that any Member 'starring' his question, or communicating privately with the Minister, can have the answer to his question sent in writing to himself and to the newspapers.

It is a more difficult matter to determine the *hour* at which questions should be put. If they are put at the morning sitting, they will take up in the future, as they have in the past, one of the most valuable hours in the Parliamentary sitting, and will very seriously curtail the length of time devoted to the principal debate of the day, which will almost always take place under the new system, before 7.15. If, on the other hand, they are asked at 9, it will not be very convenient for Ministers, and it will cut very seriously into the short three hours devoted to controversial business at the evening sitting. I propose, therefore, the following plan, which, I hope, will not be thought too drastic.

Let a brief and limited time — say 5 or 10 minutes — be devoted at the beginning of public business at the morning sitting to questions and in asking these questions, (whether they be on the paper or not) let precedence be given to ex-Ministers and Privy Councillors and to questions from private Members relating to the arrangement of Parliamentary business. Let all other questions be dealt with at 12 o'clock at night, when controversial business is concluded.[1]

I am afraid the suggestion will be thought rather startling; but, before my colleagues reject it, I hope they will consider what great advantages it is calculated to secure. It enables all questions relating to the orders of the day, or the distribution of Parliamentary time, to be asked as at present. It will allow the Front Opposition Bench to demand explanations of any important or unexpected occurrence. It will enable the Government, by way of question and answer, to make statements on subjects with regard to which anxiety is felt out of doors. But it relegates to an unimportant hour, and to a time already allocated to uncontroversial business, the piles of rubbish with which, for purposes of self-advertisement, Members now crowd the order book. Nobody but the askers of questions and the Ministers who have to answer them will be obliged to stay up; and, if it be said that this throws too great a burden on the latter, I would reply, in the first place, that it is much easier to obtain the answer to a question by midnight than by half-past 2 in the afternoon; and that, in the second place, an alteration of the Rules such as I suggest will prodigiously diminish the curiosity of Members.[2]

This is such a scathing attack on Question time, and the proposals are apparently so new, that it is worthwhile looking at Mr. Balfour's public utterances and attitude to Questions during the previous 15 or so years. As early as March 1885,[3] he had given an indication of his views. He asked Mr. Gladstone, the Prime Minister, about 'the extraordinary condition of the

[1] Cabinet Paper 1053, pp. 1–2. On 20 May 1901 Mr. Randles had asked Mr. Balfour whether he would consider the desirability of making arrangements for questions to be asked at the conclusion of Public Business or at eleven o'clock, instead of before Public Business. Mr. Balfour had replied, 'I think the suggestion of my hon. friend is an exceedingly ingenious one, and if, or perhaps I ought to say when, the subject of questions comes to be considered by the House in a practical shape this suggestion should have attention.' (Parl. Deb. (1901), 94, c. 607.)

[2] He added at the end of his Memorandum: 'I fear that the above proposals may arouse considerable opposition in Parliament, and may not even meet with the approval of my colleagues. I have a strong conviction, however, that if they were carried out, though they would not put an end to obstruction, they would put an end to much that is objectionable in our proceedings, and, among other things, to the system of petty annoyance by which the Irish hope to make themselves so eminently disagreeable to the rest of the House that we shall be glad to get rid of them, even at the price of Home Rule.' Cabinet Paper 1053, p. 7.

[3] Parl. Deb. (1885), 295, c. 890–1.

Notice Paper to-day', there being notices of 77 Questions on it, and wished 'to know whether some arrangement may not be made by which Questions of merely local or personal interest should not be put verbally in the House, but printed, with the answers to them, on the Notice Paper, Mr. Speaker having authority to decide without appeal what Questions are or are not of this character?' Mr. Gladstone thought the suggestion deserved consideration. Mr. Alexander Gordon suggested a Select Committee to consider the rules relating to Questions, but Mr. Gladstone doubted the advantage of doing that at the moment.

Two years later Mr. Balfour, by now Chief Secretary for Ireland, had to undergo a most gruelling ordeal, particularly at the hands of the Irish Members. In the session of 1887 some three months of Parliamentary time were taken up by the bitterly opposed Crimes Bill, introduced and steered through by Balfour. In addition to the tremendous strain of continuous late sittings he had to undergo a barrage of Questions every day. The great bulk of these dealt with current happenings in bloodstained Ireland. He remained Chief Secretary until October 1891. For a time during this period he practically refused to answer Questions. Colonel King-Harman was appointed Parliamentary Secretary to the Chief Secretary of Ireland, and it was he who each day read the answers prepared at Dublin Castle. In the words of Lucy: 'That was a contemptuous proceeding, bitterly resented by the men at whom it was flung. Night after night there were stormy scenes at question time. "Balfour! Balfour!" the Irish Members shouted when King-Harman appeared . . . to reply to a question addressed to the Chief Secretary. Sometimes when the storm had raged for nearly an hour Mr. Balfour strolled in, pale, defiant, contemptuous, and presently descending into the arena whence his squire had gratefully retired, he, single-handed, met the onrush of the maddened enemy. It was more or less magnificent; it certainly was not business; and when, presently, it helped to hurry poor King-Harman into his grave, Mr. Balfour abandoned an unfortunate attitude and condescended to answer questions much as other Ministers did.'[1]

When in June 1895 Mr. Balfour became Leader of the House

[1] H. W. Lucy, *A Diary of the Salisbury Parliament*, 1886–1892, pp. 437–8.

he showed an 'ominously ostentatious indifference to the question hour'.[1] By a recent custom Questions to the Leader of the House were grouped at the foot of the daily list. Mr. Balfour arrived in the House just as the first of the Questions addressed to him was reached and left as soon as he had answered the last.

A few years later Mr. Balfour, as Leader of the House, was engaged in a dispute following his announcement, on 7 February 1899, that the Under Secretary of State for Foreign Affairs (the Secretary, Lord Lansdowne, being in the Lords) would not answer supplementary Questions. One of the criticisms was that he might in time 'muzzle every Minister on the Treasury Bench'. His main defence was that 'the practice of cross-examining the Under Secretary for Foreign Affairs and expecting him to answer questions on the spur of the moment in this House is an inexpedient practice, because we see that it is impossible, if such a practice is to prevail, to carry on the difficult and delicate negotiations in which an Empire of this magnitude is constantly involved'.[2]

These episodes indicate that Mr. Balfour was not an unqualified admirer of Question time. But he was not alone in wanting to reform it. Most of the proposals for reform in the last 15 or 20 years of the century had taken the form of drawing a distinction between important and unimportant Questions and providing for only the former to receive an oral answer. This was the substance of Mr. Balfour's suggestion in March 1885 and it turned up again in his Cabinet Memorandum of October 1901. The idea was very much in the air about 1885–6. At the end of 1885, Lord Randolph Churchill (then Secretary for India) submitted a Memorandum to Lord Salisbury, the Prime Minister, in which he suggested, 'That the Speaker should appoint a Committee of three, not being Privy Councillors, who shall decide what questions can be answered in the House, and which in the votes; and that no question shall be put without notice, other than explanatory questions, except by the leave of the House on the demand of 100 members.'[3] Both Balfour and

[1] H. W. Lucy, *A Diary of the Unionist Parliament*, 1895–1900, p. 103.
[2] Parl. Deb. (1901), 89, c. 330.
[3] Winston S. Churchill, *Lord Randolph Churchill*, 1906 edition, vol. ii, p. 11. Churchill also suggested the support of 100 members, not 40 as had already been agreed, for the movement of the Adjournment during Questions.

Churchill had been members of the small group which had made such effective use of Questions during Mr. Gladstone's Administration. But their Questions and their numerous supplementaries had been concerned with foreign policy, not with local matters.

In February 1886, Mr. Joseph Cowen, a Liberal Member greatly interested in procedure, could say '... the House was not interested in the Questions, the only people who were so being the Members who read them and a section of their constituents.... All parties were agreed that the answers to the kind of Questions he had indicated might be printed and distributed with the Votes. There was no Order of the House required for doing that; and if the Speaker and Leader of the House could agree to allow purely Departmental Questions to be replied to in that way, a further saving of time would be effected.'[1] Three weeks later, in the debate on the proposed Resolution about compulsory notice of Questions, Mr. Cowen returned to the point: 'there are', he said, 'a large number of Questions which are purely of local interest... we ought to insist they and the answers should be printed and circulated.' To which Hansard adds: 'Cries of "No".'[2] In the same debate, Mr. Craig-Sellar proposed that either Mr. Speaker or a Committee should be authorized to distinguish between local and imperial Questions, and that 'local Questions which could be answered very much better by the Department should be answered... either by communication or letter from the Minister in charge of the Department whereas Imperial Questions should be answered by Ministers in the House'.[3]

The changes of 1882 had left Questions as one of the very few effective weapons remaining in the hands of individual Members, and no Government liked to appear to be restricting further these rights. In any case, as Harcourt said in August 1895: 'This subject of Questions has often been brought before the House, but no scheme has yet been devised by which useless and frivolous questions can be eliminated without at the same time eliminating useful questions to which hon. Members have a right to expect an answer. If my hon. Friend has any practical

---

[1] Parl. Deb. (1886), 302, c. 930.
[2] Parl. Deb. (1886), 303, c. 704–5.
[3] Ibid., c. 707.

THE CHANGES IN 1902 AND 1906

suggestions to make, I am sure I shall be very happy to hear them.'[1]

Mr. Balfour's proposal of October 1901 placed the choice on the Member asking the Question. It was not quite the distinction between the imperial and the local Question, but presumably it was assumed that Members with Questions of purely local interest would be satisfied with an answer in writing.

The turn of the Parliamentary Question in the long list of procedural changes made after 1832 was bound to come. Had Mr. Balfour not tackled it the high level of Parliamentary activity after 1906 would have forced the Liberals to do something. Only a major measure of devolution of detailed business to subordinate elected bodies or the granting of Irish Home Rule could have relieved the situation, and even these not for ever. Mr. Balfour's proposals were, possibly for the personal reasons already quoted, more far reaching and more designed to lower the status of Question time than had another Minister been left to reform it. In particular his proposal to move Question time to a much later hour of the sitting and to curtail so drastically the right to put supplementaries would, if accepted, have taken most of the punch and attraction out of this important procedure. This was, of course, what he intended, though it is perhaps fair to add that his primary object was to gain four or so hours before 7 p.m. for Public Business. But he misjudged the feeling of the House.

THE PROPOSALS MADE TO THE HOUSE

The Session of 1902 opened on 16 January. It was already well known that the Government intended to propose substantial changes in the procedure of the House. Sir Edgar Vincent, seconding the Address in reply to the King's Speech, said that no mention was made of procedure in the Speech, though important changes 'have been announced on high authority'. 'This omission', he said, 'was in accordance with the precedent of 1882, and [was] based on the view that a modification of our method of debate is the exclusive concern of this House.'[2] Discussion of matters arising out of the King's Speech continued until 29

[1] Parl. Deb. (1895), 36, c. 802. See also the replies of W. H. Smith in 1890 and 1891. Parl. Deb. (1890), 341, c. 443 and (1891), 350, c. 846–7.
[2] Parl. Deb. (1902), 101, c. 93.

January, and therefore the 30th was the first opportunity the House had of hearing the Government's proposals. On that day Mr. Balfour made a lengthy statement about the general character and purpose of the changes but as Members had not yet had the opportunity to study them, general discussion was deferred until 6 February.[1]

The Government's proposals involved the amendment or consolidation of sixteen of the existing Standing Orders and the creation of thirteen new ones. Most of them dealt with aspects of procedure of no consequence to Question time and need not concern us. Immediately they appeared on the Notice Paper, they attracted a substantial number of notices of amendments, and though very few of these were actually discussed in the House, it is clear from the course of the Government's attitude that some of the ideas in them bore fruit.

In his opening statement Mr. Balfour painted a vivid contrast between the Sessions of 1800 and 1901. In this speech and during the course of the debates he made it clear that whereas Mr. Gladstone and earlier reformers had been mainly concerned to curb the possibilities of waste and misuse of Parliamentary time, to plug the leaks, as it were, through which time flowed away, his main aim was to rearrange the business of the House so as to introduce a different and more certain timetable. His rearrangement was primarily concerned with settling two important conflicts in the battle for the time of the House : between Public and other business and between Government and other Members' business. The first concerned the daily and the second the weekly timetable of the House. His proposals were not put forward quite in this form. Instead, in his speech explaining the ideas behind the proposals, he said the main objects were to increase the convenience of Parliamentary life and the certainty of Public Business.

Knowing that the main attack would come from the defenders of the rights of private Members, he was anxious to show that such rights would be worth more rather than less if the House accepted his proposals. In the subsequent lengthy debates he was, however, always more clear headed as to what he wanted than his critics, with whom he dealt usually patiently, sometimes

[1] For the full text of the proposals see Notices of Motions (1902), vol. 1, p. 259 et seq.

cursorily, but always appearing to be matching his realism to their romantic ideas of how the House used to work and their fanciful picture of the importance of the ordinary Member of Parliament in modern times. He constantly stressed the advantages of his proposals to all Members, particularly the greater certainty that would result. And, to that increasing proportion of the House who had to earn a living, certainty was an advantage perhaps even more than the rearrangements which would allow an hour for dinner and the chance of a long weekend.

Certainty, to Mr. Balfour, meant certainty as to the time when any item of business would be reached, and in particular, certainty that Public Business, and therefore Government Business, would be reached. The proposals for the re-allocation of time 'were' he said, 'not devised to give the Government more time than they already get or take . . . but to allocate that time in a manner more convenient to the general body of unofficial Members of the House, and to make our proceedings secure and certain so far as concerns the hour at which Government business should come on.'[1] If there was to be any uncertainty as to the course and time of any business it should not affect Public Business. 'Public business', he said, 'should begin at a fixed hour; and if there must be uncertainty, I regret to say that private business must suffer.'[2]

Combined with his aim to secure a fixed hour for Public Business and a certain and known precedence for Government Business, went a clear view as to what was the best time for these purposes. To Mr. Balfour the afternoon was 'the kernel of the day'.[3] 'The whole scheme of the new Rules had', he said, 'been framed with the idea that the afternoon sitting from 3 to 7.30 p.m. shall be devoted to important public business.'[4]

The proposals for the weekly and daily timetable (Balfour's railway timetable, they were dubbed) followed very closely those in his Cabinet Memorandum of October 1901. He had, however, by now resolved one doubt, as to whether Fridays should in future play the role that Wednesdays then played. The Whips' Memorandum had contained a footnote saying: 'The turning of Wednesday into a full-day sitting and Friday into the

[1] 18 February 1902, Parl. Deb. (1902), 103, c. 400.
[2] Parl. Deb. (1902), 107, c. 110. By private business he meant any business preceding the commencement of Public Business.
[3] Parl. Deb. (1902), 103, c. 401.   [4] Parl. Deb. (1902), 107, c. 495.

present Wednesday sitting has been proposed in some quarters. This change may be considered on its merits, and, if desirable, could be grafted upon the present proposal.'[1] Neither Walrond nor Balfour took the point up in their Memoranda, but in his speech of 30 January 1902 Balfour said the Government preferred Wednesday to Friday as a day for Public Business, on which the Government had precedence, probably because it had for some time been difficult 'to keep a House' for an evening sitting on Friday and also because of the new habit of the 'week-end'. Balfour's declared aim, therefore, was to secure for the Government, without doubt or possible interference, the four or five hours at the beginning of the first (or morning) sitting on Monday, Tuesday, Wednesday and Thursday. This, and a little more being forthcoming, he gave the impression that the House, or rather those Members interested, could make whatever use of the remaining time they thought best.

The new daily timetable put before the House differed from that in his Cabinet Memorandum at one very significant point. Instead of Question time starting at the commencement of the second sitting (9 p.m.), as in the Whips' proposals (but not in Walrond's), or at 12 p.m., as in his own Memorandum, Balfour now proposed that it should start at the interruption of business at 7.15 p.m., and that the morning sitting should be extended until 8 p.m. for this purpose. This had the incidental effect of reducing the dinner period to one hour except on days when there were very few Questions. The proposals as thus first presented to the House amounted to treating Questions to Ministers in five different ways:

(i) Questions 'of an urgent nature relating to the order of business'[2] could be asked not earlier than 2.25 p.m. and were expected by Mr. Balfour to be over by 2.30 p.m.

(ii) Questions to which Members wanted oral answers were to be marked with an asterisk (starred),[3] and were to be

[1] Cabinet Paper (1901), 839, p. 3.
[2] Several of the amendments to this proposal placed on the Notice Paper were designed to extend the category of Questions answerable before the commencement of the Orders of the Day; e.g. one Member wished to add 'Questions upon which Ministers of the Crown desire to make a statement' and another 'Questions upon a matter of definite and urgent national importance'.
[3] It will have been noticed that in his Cabinet Memorandum Mr. Balfour used the term 'starring' to mean that that Member 'can have the answer ... sent in writing to himself and to the newspapers'.

THE CHANGES IN 1902 AND 1906

answered not earlier than 7.15 p.m., when afternoon business was interrupted, and continue to be answered until not later than 8 p.m.

(iii) Any starred Questions not answered by 8 p.m. were to be answered at midnight, except when the 12 o'clock rule was suspended, i.e. when business was not automatically interrupted at midnight.

(iv) Any starred Questions left unanswered at 1 a.m. (or at 8 p.m. when the 12 o'clock rule was suspended) were to be printed and circulated with the Votes, along with any Questions that Members had not marked with an asterisk or which they were not present to ask.

(v) Supplementary Questions could be asked in order to obtain a necessary explanation of the answers given, but only one could be asked in respect of each Question of which notice had been given, and that, only by the Member by whom the notice had been given.

In referring to the proposals concerning Questions, Balfour said in his opening statement that he thought everyone must admit two or three propositions: 'In the first place, that the number of Questions has for many years been excessive. In the second place, that a very large number of those Questions are not improper Questions to put, but they are really more of a parochial than of an Imperial character. They concern the interests of small localities rather than the general interests of the country at large. But while I lay down those two propositions, hostile to our present proposal, I would lay down a third, which is that we ought to be very careful how we curtail the liberty of putting Questions. That liberty may be abused; in my judgement it has often been abused; but I think that the liberty itself is a very important one. It may sometimes have the effect of keeping an erring Government in order; in any case, it is quite right if an important local interest is touched that the truth should be elicited by a Question put to the responsible Minister, if possible. While eliciting information is a most legitimate object, I do not regard with any great favour on general grounds, though I rather like them myself, those Questions which are intended to be merely the foundation of the cross-examination of a Minister. They are lively and agreeable, especially if you think you have a good case, but I do not think it is a proper use to which to put the time of the House.'[1] He was sanguine enough to believe that with the choice of a written instead of an oral answer and the much tighter limit on supplementaries, the time allotted between 7.15 p.m. and 8 p.m. would be 'as a rule amply sufficient to deal with the Questions which have to be orally answered'. He also made the point that the right to leave a Question without a star would be an advantage to Members over the present system. For they would have 'that authoritative answer printed and circulated with the Votes, and it will remain there on permanent record', whereas at present there was no authoritative record of answers at all.

This last argument had its attractions in the circumstances of of the time. Hansard did not become a verbatim record prepared by reporters employed by Parliament until 1909. For some years before this the right of publication was awarded to the private contractor who offered the most favourable terms. Since 1891,[2] the contract had stipulated that Questions to Ministers and their replies must be given in full, but the record was still not wholly reliable. In preparing Hansard the contractor usually sent a proof of any supplementary to the Member asking him to check it and, as a matter of courtesy, also usually sent him a proof of his main Question and the Minister's answer, even though the former could be checked from the Order Paper and only the Department could check the latter. Even then proofs were sometimes delayed for several days. Moreover there was no daily or weekly Hansard, as at present, and therefore Members had to rely on the report in *The Times* which was very full and had a high reputation for accuracy. The *Votes and Proceedings* of the House are, of course, an official record circulated to Members each day, and, therefore, if included in them, written answers would be given certain advantages over oral answers.

[1] Parl. Deb. (1902), 101, c. 1369-70.
[2] R. Donaldson Jordan, 'The Reports of Parliamentary Debates', *Economica*, vol. 11, p. 441. For some flavour of Members complaints about the inadequacy of the arrangements for recording Question time see Parl. Deb. (1898), 54, c. 842, c. 972 and c. 1249 and Parl. Deb. (1901), 94, c. 1331-3. Since February 1899 (when the Government refused to allow the Under Secretary for Foreign Affairs to answer supplementaries) a copy of every question and answer to the Foreign Office was put in the Library that same evening. But Mr. Balfour refused to extend the system to all Departments (owing to the difficulty of providing so quickly an accurate record of what he called 'subsidiary Questions', and in March 1902 Mr. Joseph Chamberlain refused to extend the system to his Department (the Colonial Office). See Parl. Debs. (1899), 66, c. 114, *et seq.* and c. 1290; (1900), 83, c. 748; and (1902), 104, c. 354.

THE DEBATES

The House had a general Debate on the twenty-four proposals on 6 February. Sir Henry Campbell-Bannerman, as Leader of the Opposition, moved that they be referred to a Select Committee. After a two-day debate, the House agreed by 250 to 160 that the proposals be considered. The Government then proceeded to put the individual proposals at a series of sittings, as opportunity offered, the last occasion being in May. The resolution dealing with Questions was the last but one to be dealt with. It was, however, never formally put to the House in its original form, for during the course of the debates on the proposed new daily timetable, the Government accepted changes which had important repercussions on their proposals for Questions.

The tenor of the two-day debate was on the whole favourable to the Government. Members no doubt enjoyed Mr. Redmond's remark, that the purposes of the proposals were to promote the domestic felicity of the idle Members;[1] to abolish private Members, and to punish the Irish Party. But most were convinced that something required to be done, though by no means all agreed that Mr. Balfour had put forward the right solution. All the main proposals received some criticism, if only from the Irish or from Mr. Gibson Bowles, that candid friend of the Government. Most criticism centred on the timetable — ranging from whether such a timetable should be attempted to the place of particular items in it — and on the proposals about Questions. On the latter point, both the time proposed and the limitation on supplementaries were criticized by a number of speakers. Campbell-Bannerman in particular, in an otherwise moderately worded speech, defended Questions very strongly (reminding Members that the House is 'the grand inquest of the nation') and attacked this part of Mr. Balfour's proposals. It is noticeable that in replying to the debate Mr. Balfour was both moderate and sweetly persuasive when dealing with the criticisms of his proposals for Questions.

On 18 February[2] the House reached the proposed new Standing Order No 1, dealing with the Sittings of the House. Immediately before embarking on a debate of the Government's

[1] The Government party were sometimes called the 'dinner-party'.
[2] Parl. Deb. (1902), 103, c. 365–460.

proposal it agreed to a Motion, moved by Mr. Balfour, that until the considerations of the proposed changes dealing with Sittings of the House, Friday Sittings, Priority of Business, Business in Supply, Questions to Members, Adjournment of the House, Private Business, Quorum of the House, and Standing Committees had been completed, none of the changes agreed should come into operation. This showed how closely related were a number of the Government's proposals. The daily timetable was the frame into which so much of the rest had to fit. The attitudes of Members towards the proposed timetable was therefore very much coloured by the view they took of the importance of a particular item of business in relation to the order accorded to it, and the debates on Standing Order No. 1 were therefore both wide ranging and of vital importance.

Amid the inevitable cross currents of ideas, two major criticisms emerged. First, a number of speakers emphasized the inconveniences of commencing the daily Sittings at 2 p.m. instead of 3 p.m. Some of the arguments used were eminently practical. It was pointed out, for example, that Private Bill Committees normally sat from 11.30 a.m. to 4 p.m. and that other Committees also sat in the morning until 2.30 p.m. It was difficult to start much earlier than 11.30 a.m. if the House was to continue to sit until midnight or later, as the Government apparently contemplated. As the Government proposed that Public Business should start promptly at 2.25 p.m. there would be a conflict of loyalties.

More far-reaching was the argument advanced by the lawyers, professional and business men, that such an early start would make it virtually impossible for them to continue to be Members and earn their living. They pointed out that under the existing arrangements the House met at 3 p.m., but the first hour and a half was normally taken up by business of a local or limited interest. Public Business seldom began before 4.15–4.30 p.m., sometimes even an hour or so later, and even if any such Member wished to ask a Question he seldom needed to attend before 4 p.m. This group of Members, and many others who disliked such an early start, were inclined to regard the proposed use of the time between 7.15 to 9 p.m. as a waste. They pointed out that though the House was to start its day one hour earlier, there was no corresponding saving at the other end of the day. The extra hour was given away in the form of a dinner hour, and in addition 7.15 until 8 p.m., and 9 until probably 10 p.m., or even later, would now be taken up with private and local matters. From the point of view of the lawyer and business man, non-attendance during the business which preceded Public Business, including most if not all of the time given to Questions, would in future be no advantage: it was more useful for their private affairs to be free in the afternoon than to have two or so hours after 7.15 p.m. free.

A second group of criticisms was directed at the time fixed for Questions. Some of these were quite specific. Thus it was pointed out that, as the House of Lords took Questions at 4.15 p.m., Ministerial replies to current rumours or criticisms might well be given in the Lords before the Commons, to the detriment of the status of the latter. Again, moving the Motion for the Adjournment of the House had come to be closely associated with unsatisfactory answers to Questions. Under the new proposals, a Member who received an unsatisfactory reply in the evening would not be able to ask leave to move the Adjournment until 2.30 p.m. the next day, and if accepted the Motion could not then be moved until 9 p.m. of that day. His only alternative would be to give notice at 2.30 p.m. of the day he was to ask the Question in anticipation of receiving an unsatisfactory answer — hardly a suitable alternative. Then there were many Members who thought that Ministers should deal with any important criticisms of queries as early as possible, and not keep the press and the public waiting. This criticism arose partly from a desire to maintain the favourable position of Questions in the present timetable from the point of view of securing press publicity, but it also reflected a fear that important Questions might remain unanswered at 8 p.m., either because the commencement of Questions had been delayed beyond 7.15 p.m., or because there were in any case more than could be answered in the 45 minutes.

The critics who wanted Public Business to start later than 2.30 p.m. and the critics who wanted Question time to start earlier than 7.15 p.m. found a large measure of common ground, but only by taking different views of the importance of Question time. For if Questions were taken early in the morning sitting, the commencement of Public Business could be delayed by that amount of time. This would satisfy those who wanted to delay their attendance until as late an hour as possible and whose attendance was not required at Question time, and also those who thought Questions so important as to warrant their being answered early in the day.

At a fairly early stage in the proceeding Sir Samuel Hoare, the Conservative Member for Norwich, suggested[1] that Public Business should not begin until 3 p.m., thus leaving half an hour for Private Business and half an hour for Questions. Public Business would then go on until 7.30 p.m. instead of until 7.15 p.m. He thought this suggestion would get over the inconvenience to members of Private Bill Committees of an early start of Public Business. Sir W. Hart Dyke, the Conservative Member for Dartford, supported this suggestion and added:[2] 'Whether the Questions remaining over should be dealt with by being printed with the answers in the Votes next day, or whether there should be a small Committee of the House to sift Questions, in the same way as there was a Committee to deal with petitions — whatever scheme was adopted — that would take them more than half way out of the dilemma, by causing the public business to commence at 3 o'clock instead of 2.30.' He appealed to Mr. Balfour to remodel his proposal on these lines, but the Leader of the House commented only on the suggestion that there should be a Committee to sift Questions, saying, 'if any scheme of that sort could be devised that would be acceptable to the House, it would be a great advantage.'[3]

Added significance was given to the suggestion by Mr. Dillon, who moved an amendment that the time for the meeting of the House should be 3 p.m. and not 2 p.m. A number of Members followed the lead of Mr. Chaplin, the Conservative Member for Sleaford, Lincs., in saying that their action on this amendment depended on how the Government proposed that Questions should be treated; in other words, were the Government prepared to take Questions earlier than 7.15 p.m.? Mr. Balfour, however, was not to be drawn completely. The most he could be got

---

[1] Parl. Deb. (1902), 103, c. 409. (Hoare was father of the late Lord Templewood.) On 29 April, Sir Samuel expressed his appreciation of Mr. Balfour's subsequent action in modifying the proposals 'to meet the feeling which he expressed and which he thought had the sympathy of a great portion of the House'. Parl. Deb. (1902), 107, c. 192.
[2] ibid., c. 418.   [3] Parl. Deb. (1902), 103, c. 419.

to say was that no one voting for a 2 p.m. commencement would be committing himself to the proposal as to the hour at which Questions should be taken.[1] It was clear, however, that something was in the wind, since in the latest printing of the Government's proposals the words 'Immediately after the interruption of business at an afternoon sitting Questions shall be taken, and no other business shall be taken after Questions' had been omitted. Mr. Balfour explained this away on the ground that these particular words were unnecessary in the Standing Order on Sittings of the House and 'if introduced there, the whole subject of Questions would be raised before we had reached the Rule about Questions'. But he went on to say that he recognized 'the great interest and anxiety felt in all parts of the House as to the way in which questions should be dealt with'. He did not in the least wish to minimize it. The Government was not unalterably attached to the plan announced on 30 January. Just before the vote was taken, Mr. Joseph Walton, the Liberal Member for Barnsley, asked whether, in the event of the House agreeing to meet at 2 p.m., Mr. Balfour would consent to Questions being taken at 2.25 p.m., with Government Business commencing at 3 p.m., the dinner being taken between 7.30 and 9 p.m. He received no reply. The House agreed by 256 to 109 to meet at 2 p.m. in future.

The House became immersed in the Estimates and discussion of the South African War and other contentious business, and did not return to the discussion of the new rule governing the Sittings of the House until 8 April. Almost the first speaker was Mr. Balfour and he announced important changes in the Government's ideas about Questions.[2] He said he was well aware 'that no portion of the proposed new Rules [had] received less favour than the proposal that there should be questions during the interval between the two sittings'. He thought, however, that any changes introduced to meet this feeling must preserve inviolate the two main objects of the Government: 'to limit the time to be taken up by Questions in any one day and to secure with certainty a solid block of time in the afternoons for the consideration of the main business.' He then set out the arguments

---

[1] Parl. Deb. (1902), 103, c. 653.
[2] For Mr. Balfour's statement and the short discussion see Parl. Deb. (1902), 105, c. 1265–77.

advanced against taking Questions so late as 7.15 p.m. He proposed to meet them by advancing the time to 2.15 p.m. At that time Questions marked with an asterisk would be answered orally and Question time would go on until 2.55 p.m. At 2.55 p.m. Questions of an urgent character of which private notice had been given and Questions relating to the business of the House could be asked. As the answers to these would take only a few minutes, he thought the Government could count on Public Business beginning at 3 o'clock. If the Questions were few in number Public Business would begin earlier than, but under no circumstances should it begin later than 3 o'clock. Words of a very stringent character should limit the class of Questions which could be asked between 2.55 and 3 p.m. 'the intention being to make this a sort of safety valve in relation to important topics or subjects upon which there is public anxiety'. After this class of Questions had been answered a Member could ask leave to bring in a Motion for the Adjournment and this, if accepted, would be made at the evening sitting.

Mr. Balfour thought that it would be admitted that 'forty minutes will afford ample time for the starred Questions. . . . It is a modest estimate to say that in that time sixty or seventy Questions can be answered . . .' and he could not believe 'that the opportunity would be insufficient to satisfy the most curious Members'. But, he went on, supposing the number exceeded sixty or seventy, Members may ask 'what security will there be that the most important Questions will not be shut out by reason of their not being reached before 2.55'. He thought there was more than one plan for avoiding this. One method was already on the Order Paper and other Members had made suggestions. His opinion was that in the arranging of Questions 'so as to secure that in the first sixty those of the most interest shall be included the order might be left to the clerks at the Table'. (There were cries of 'No' at this.) The Government however would not have 'the smallest objection to the appointment of a small Standing Committee by the Committee of Selection, upon which there would be no objection to Members of the Opposition being in the majority. It would be an extremely easy task, and would throw no undue burden of responsibility on either a Committee or the clerks.'

Mr. Balfour did not specifically state that he had dropped his original proposal, to place severe restrictions on the asking of supplementary Questions. He merely said that the restrictions were not to protect Ministers, but to limit the time taken up by Questions.[1] Presumably, now that the time available for oral answers was to be limited, the use or misuse of that time was of much less concern to Mr. Balfour. He was giving way to strong pressure within his own Party,[2] but at the same time he retained his certain 'solid block of time in the afternoons'. *The Times* leader of 9 April 1902 commented:

Mr. Balfour's revised proposals in regard to questions to Ministers are not to be discussed until they have appeared in print, but their general effect, as appears from the statement of the First Lord of the Treasury, is that much more latitude will be allowed than was at first contemplated. The right of questioning Ministers, though grossly abused in recent years, has a value as a check upon administrative blundering which ought not to be surrendered, though it may be properly limited. The Government have not deemed it advisable to ignore the protests of some 80 Unionist members against the restriction of this right which was brought before them a month ago.

It is assumed however, that whether the decision as to the working of this sort of 'safety-valve' is left to the Clerks at the Table or to a small Standing Committee, public business will begin punctually at 3 o'clock, instead of at half-past two o'clock as was originally proposed. It will be suspended at half-past seven. Though members on both sides were unwilling to commit themselves prematurely to approval of these changes, they have apparently met with a good deal of acceptance, especially among men of business and members of the Bar who objected to the opening of Parliamentary work at an hour conflicting with their engagements elsewhere....[3]

---

[1] Parl. Deb. (1902), 105, c. 1266–7.
[2] The decision to abandon the original proposals was taken in February. See letter from St. John Brodrick dated 25 February 1902 circulated to the Cabinet. 'We are now told by the Whips that our supporters having got their dinner hour, will not tolerate questions at 7 p.m., and Mr. Balfour therefore proposes to abandon this part of the scheme....'
[3] The tone is rather different from *The Times*' leader of 7 February 1902, welcoming Mr. Balfour's proposal:
'Much objection has been raised to the postponement of questions until 7.15. That some may on occasion have been answered at an earlier hour in the House of Lords is an objection which will strike the public as puerile. Questions have become a scandalous waste of time and energy. Those of importance will be just as usefully put at 7.15 as at the opening of business, while those that are worthless, and they are the majority, cannot be too severely discouraged. It may be noted, however, that much of the power of pertinacious questioners depends upon the fear that they may move the adjournment, and when that weapon is taken away questions of a frivolous kind can be much more summarily dealt with at any hour.'

When Mr. Balfour's new proposals appeared they took the form[1] of the addition of four new clauses to Standing Order No. 20 (which was still worded as it was passed in March 1888). He moved these additions on 28 April, merely remarking that he put them forward in the form of a compromise, to meet what he conceived to be the general wish, and he hoped the House would consider them in that spirit. Certainly the new proposal represented a considerable victory for the active supporters of Question time. Questions would continue to be taken before the commencement of Public Business, and, indeed, would in future be the only important work of the House to rank before such Business, for the proposed timetable implied that opposed Private Business and Motions for the Adjournment would not come on until the evening Session. The proposed restriction on supplementaries had disappeared. True, Questions would in future only have forty minutes as against their hitherto unlimited time, but having regard to the possibility of getting published Ministerial answers for unstarred Questions, forty minutes appeared not unreasonable in the light of the then experience. Anyhow, it was a certain forty minutes as against the less certain[2] forty-five minutes at 7.15 p.m., and the less desirable hour possibly available after midnight.

At the same time the compromise retained considerable gains for Mr. Balfour. It enabled him to buy off some of the opposition to the four morning Sittings starting as early as 2 p.m. Instead of a certain block of four and three quarter hours (from 2.30 to 7.15 p.m.), he would get a certain block of four and a half hours (from 3 to 7.30 p.m.) for Public Business, a considerable gain on the Government's current position. The dinner break could be made an hour and a half instead of an hour. There was one less claimant to the time after midnight. Finally, Question time would be a fixed period available to Members to use and abuse as they thought fit — any time-wasting on the part of any Member would be to the detriment of 'private' or 'unofficial' Members and would not affect the Government directly.

But the House was not yet completely satisfied. The proposals were debated for thirteen and a half hours spread over two days,

[1] Notices of Motions, 8 April 1902, p. 1200.
[2] Though, according to the original proposals, Question time was to start not earlier than 7.15 p.m. the start might be delayed because, for example, a Division was being taken at that time.

on the second of which the final vote was not taken until 2 a.m. Altogether there were eleven Divisions; the Government having a comfortable majority of around 80 in each, even in those which took place after midnight.

Three main issues emerged.[1] They concerned the time at which Questions should start and end; the increase in the amount of notice required; and the problem that the limited time available might prevent some starred Questions receiving an oral answer.

THE TIME FOR QUESTIONS

Under the new rules, Private Business would be virtually displaced from its traditional position at the commencement of the sitting. Unopposed Private Bills were to be given precedence over Opposed, but it was unlikely that much of this business could be disposed of in the 10 minutes between the end of Prayers and 2.15, when Question time was to begin, for during these few minutes such other business as any Motions for new Writs and the presentation of public petitions could also be taken. An amendment by the indefatigable Mr. Gibson Bowles, to the effect that Questions should be taken at the conclusion of Private Business, was rejected by Mr. Balfour as re-introducing the very uncertainty the new Rules were designed to avoid.[2]

This had been preceded[3] by an amendment which, if carried, would have enabled Question time to commence upon Mr. Speaker taking the Chair, i.e. immediately after Prayers. In part the support for this came from those who disliked unopposed being separated from opposed Private Business. They thought Private Bills were too important to be dealt with in this way. In part it was an objection against a rigid timetable : ten minutes of this, then forty minutes of that, then five minutes of something else. It was, however, the current practice for Question time not to commence until half an hour after the time the House met (15 minutes in the last week or so of the Session) even though Private Business and other preliminary business had been completed before this time. Now that opposed Private Bills were to

[1] The proposals were discussed on 28–29 April 1902. Parl. Deb. (1902), 107, c. 101–44 and 187–307.
[2] Parl. Deb. (1902), 107, c. 117–32.
[3] c. 106–14.

come later in the day, the preliminary business should take less than 25 minutes, and on many occasions less than 10 minutes. The Government, however, thought a fixed time for Questions had advantages, even if it meant the loss of a few minutes of Parliamentary time.

Mr. Balfour was equally opposed to an amendment that would have removed the 2.55 p.m. time limit on Question time. He pointed out that the Government had met the wishes of the House on both the main points of criticism: 'we have altered the time for Questions so as to be indeed much less convenient to Ministers, but more convenient to Members . . . and we have done away with the limitation of supplementary Questions — a limitation which I am bound to say had great justification.' He had hoped that a concession so large would have reconciled Members 'to cutting down the time for Questions to a period which will allow sixty-five to be answered in addition to the Questions with reference to the business of the House. . . . It would be an unfortunate thing . . . to allow the solid four and a half hours . . . to be intrenched upon by any overflow of irrelevant or unnecessary Questions.'[1] During the debates Mr. Balfour referred several times to the number of Questions that could be answered within the forty minutes — sixty to sixty-five verbal Questions at each sitting, plus those that could be asked in order to obtain written answers, sufficient he thought 'to bring to book even the wickedest and most flagitious Government'.[2]

Most Members appeared to agree that in the light of recent experience forty minutes would be more than sufficient. Fifteen to twenty minutes had proved sufficient on many occasions, particularly after the first fury and fervour of a new Parliament had passed away. Mr. Dillon, the Irish Nationalist, even used these figures to show that they introduced an element of uncertainty into the time for commencement of Public Business. Mr. Balfour met this by saying that Members would be able to calculate very closely the time Questions would take from the number appearing on the Paper. The fact that in the present Session there were Sittings when Questions had not occupied forty minutes 'might prove that the Rule was unnecessary, but it also proved that it was not tyrannical'.[2] The cause of an unlimited

[1] Parl. Deb. (1902), 107, c. 137–8.   [2] ibid., c. 201.

Question time was not helped by the Irish Nationalists being its main supporters.

The next amendment proposed, that 3.15 p.m. should be the time limit, not 2.55 p.m., was not open to the same kind of objection. But it would have meant on some occasions, probably an increasing number of occasions, the loss of twenty minutes out of the four and a half hours on which Mr. Balfour had set his heart. Mr. Whitley, who became Speaker in 1905, said that engineers considered it wise to set their safety valve well below the pressure at which the boiler would explode. On the same principle he suggested that the limitation on Questions should be put well above the point likely to be reached. He thought that the efficiency of the proposal depended upon its being only very occasionally brought into operation. If it were fixed at forty minutes it would come into operation at least once a week 'and there would be all the difficulties and irritation arising from deferred Questions and unsatisfactory distinctions'.[1] The amendment was defeated.

No Member moved that Questions not reached by 2.55 should automatically come up for answer at 12 midnight, or even at 9 p.m. Yet there had been provision in Mr. Balfour's original proposals for a carry-over of this kind to midnight, and the Whips and others in the internal discussions had suggested 9 p.m. or later as a suitable time for Questions. No doubt this forbearance was part of the price of compromise, for most Members thought that 40 minutes would or should suffice for starred questions. But Mr. Balfour had been right when he suggested that putting the time for Questions at 12 midnight would 'prodigiously diminish the curiosity of Members'.

THE PERIOD OF NOTICE

At this time the only requirement about notice was that the Question had to appear on the Notice Paper. Normally this was the Paper for the day the answer was required, in other words, a Member could bring his Question to the Table until the very last minute before the next day's Notice Paper went to the printer, which was usually about midnight.

When announcing his amended proposals on 8 April, Mr. Balfour had added a very important change. He hoped the House

[1] ibid., c. 223-4.

would be content to limit the answering of starred Questions 'to those which appeared on the Notice Paper the day before'. He went on: 'To require answers at two o'clock to Questions only given notice of on the previous night, and which the Department could have had no opportunity of dealing with till the same morning, would be to unduly burden the Department.' He had given some hint of this change a few minutes earlier when he said that 'the extraordinary pressure thrown upon some of those already heavily-worked Departments by the modern increase of Questions is so great that some precaution must be taken with a view to mitigating the burden which would be placed upon them if Questions were asked four hours earlier than was originally designed'.[1]

Presumably this change was a concession to St. John Brodrick (Secretary of State for War), and possibly other Ministers, who complained most strongly about the great inconvenience of departing from the original proposal to have oral Questions at 7.15. Brodrick wrote a memorandum in which he argued that Ministers were getting less consideration than Members and that Mr. Balfour was about to concede an earlier Question hour and abandon certain safeguards, the only gain to Ministers being a suggestion that notice should be given not later than 3.0 p.m. of the day before asking the Question. Balfour also circulated a memorandum to the Cabinet on 3 March 1902.[2] He defended the changed proposals and tried to show that they did not impose any additional strain on Ministers. As regards the amount of notice to be given he pointed out that it was much longer than Ministers got at the moment 'but it might, perhaps, be extended to forty-eight hours'.

Many Members wished to continue the existing usage. By this time they had also begun to appreciate the effect of moving Wednesday business to Friday. For though there was no rule against Questions being put down for answer on Wednesday, it was 'the general practice that Questions shall not be put down for that day, and consequently Ministers are not expected to attend'.[3] There was indeed an amendment moved during the Debate, the effect of which would have been to specify that

[1] Parl. Deb. (1902), 105, c. 1270 and 1267.
[2] New Rules, Mr. Brodrick's objection to the new proposal about Questions, Cabinet Paper 335.
[3] Ruling by Mr. Speaker Gully, 23 March 1901. Parl. Deb. (1901), 91, c. 994.

Questions could also be asked on Fridays in order to clarify the nature of the new proposal. Mr. Balfour replied that all the rules and customs which at present attached to Wednesdays would be transferred to Fridays. He agreed that Members had from time to time put down Questions for answer on Wednesdays, and therefore this could continue for Fridays, 'although Ministers will not, as a rule, be here to answer such Questions.'[1] If, however, the words proposed were included, it would be said that it was intended that Questions should be asked on Fridays as on other days. 'My hon. friend does not desire that, any more than I do.'[2] An Irish Member thought there was an important difference, in that in future there would be a gap of three days (Friday–Sunday), not just one (Wednesday), and Mr. Hobhouse thought that a fifteen minute limit might be imposed, as 'it would establish a new practice but would limit the right to very important Questions'. But upon the Speaker agreeing that there was nothing to prevent Questions being put down for answer on Fridays or Saturdays, 'although', he added, 'I think they have been very seldom answered' Members were satisfied and the proposed amendment was withdrawn.

When, therefore, Members came to discuss the new rule about length of notice, they were aware of the new situation on Fridays, and the two points of criticism became somewhat mixed up. If starred Questions were not normally to be answered on Fridays, and if in future Questions had to appear on the previous day's Notice Paper, the result would be delay and a large concentration of Questions for answer on Mondays. For under the new rule, a Member who missed the Wednesday Notice Paper could not get an oral answer until Monday, when his question would be competing with others added on Thursday and Friday.[3] This would greatly add to the inconvenience of the time limit of forty minutes. The bunching of Questions on Monday would mean that many starred Questions would not be reached by 2.55 p.m., while on other days there might be time to spare.

Various amendments were moved: one would have continued the existing practice; one would have fixed the time limit at 2.0 p.m. on the previous day; one suggested that Ministers should not be precluded from answering any Question at shorter notice.

[1] Parl. Deb. (1902), 107, c. 118.
[2] ibid., c. 119.   [3] A Notice Paper was sent out on **Saturdays**.

All were defeated or withdrawn. Mr. Grant Lawson, the Parliamentary Secretary to the Local Government Board, who had assisted Mr. Balfour throughout the debates, reiterated and expanded[1] the point made by Mr. Balfour when he had announced the change from 7.15 to 2.15 p.m. 'Nothing could be more futile', he said, 'than a system which allowed Questions, however intricate, ranging from China to Peru, to be put down at twelve o'clock at night, reaching the public Department at ten o'clock next morning, and an answer to be expected at half-past three that afternoon.' It was an intolerable strain to put on a public official, 'assuming Questions to be put down not for the purpose of tripping up Ministers, but with a desire to obtain accurate information.' True, a Minister could ask a Member to postpone a Question, but they did not like doing so continually — 'there was a certain *amour propre* about the matter'. Unsatisfactory answers were sometimes given 'because there was no time to go thoroughly into the facts'. The taking of Questions at 7.15 p.m. would have given an extra three and three quarter hours to prepare answers: bringing them forward to 2.15 p.m. meant even less time than at present. If Members wanted Questions to come earlier, notice would have to be given earlier. But the new rule applied only to Questions for which an oral answer was wanted. For a printed or typewritten answer, 'the Department would have all the time in office hours in which to prepare the reply,' so that notice as late as 12 o'clock the preceding night would continue to suffice. Urgent Questions could be asked at 2.55 p.m. Matters could also be raised on the nightly Motion 'That this House do now adjourn'. For the rest, if the Question was of importance only to the Member's constituents, 'an excellent way to get an immediate answer was for a Member to go to the Department and ask the Question.'

THE EFFECTS OF A LIMITED QUESTION TIME

It was generally appreciated that a limited Question time raised the problem of what should happen to the starred Questions that were not reached. The last of the four clauses in the new proposal read: 'Questions distinguished by an asterisk shall be so arranged on the Paper that those which seem of the

[1] Parl. Deb. (1902), 107, c. 236–7.

greatest general interest shall be reached before five minutes before three of the clock.'[1]

The first amendment moved to deal with this aspect of the Government's proposal was that Questions not answered on one day should have precedence on the Order Paper on the following day. This was easily disposed of: if Questions were to be arranged so that those of greatest general importance were reached before 2.55 p.m., those of least general importance would have precedence next day.[2] Mr. Charles Hobhouse, the Liberal Member for East Bristol, moved the deletion of the clause.[3] He asked how the Clerks were to judge the relative importance of Questions. 'They would naturally be influenced by the importance of the individual Member giving the notice. . . . The House ought not lightly to part with the right of priority which at present the humblest and most insignificant Member possessed over the most influential and important.' He went on to say that the point in the Question 'might be unimportant to the House or to the Member himself, but of far reaching importance to the person immediately concerned; and by the Question being put in the House the matter received that publicity through the Press which answers printed and circulated in the Votes would never get'. Mr. Dillon also thought that it would be the Questions of the obscurer Members which would be the ones to be sacrificed.

At this stage in the debate Mr. Balfour intervened to make two points. First, the Rule was 'proposed not in the interest of the Treasury Bench or the Front Opposition Bench, but in the interest of the House at large, in order that forty minutes might be devoted to Questions in which the House was interested'. Second, the task imposed on the officials of the House would not be heavy. If the number of Questions put on the Paper were less than experience showed could be answered within forty minutes,

[1] Some of the Notices given by Members to amend the original proposals reflected the interests of the House in this issue. Thus, one Member wished that 'all Questions addressed to the Leader of the House, or the Secretary or Under-Secretary for Foreign Affairs, or any other Questions which shall appear to Mr. Speaker to be of public rather than departmental interest' to be put first on the Paper. Notices of Motions (1902), vol. 1, p. 307.
[2] Parl. Deb. (1902), 107, c. 230–2. The Irish Members thought that most of their Questions would be treated as being of least general interest. If so the effect of the Amendment would have been to bring their Questions to the top every other day.
[3] Ibid. c. 261–82.

no classification would be needed. If the number exceeded sixty or so, the clerks would not have to classify all the Questions, but would take out those which raised the least general interest and put them at the end. If, however, the general view favoured a Committee, he would not shrink from such a proposal, though he thought it would be best to see how the new Standing Order worked without such a body.

The House, however, was not satisfied. Mr. Chaplin pointed out that many Questions which appeared on the paper were of a purely or largely political character. The officials at the Table[1] had no politics, and yet if the Rule were passed, they would be required to weigh the relative importance of difficult political Questions. Mr. Bryce asked the House to consider the case of an outbreak of war, or a great strike, or a matter of domestic policy affecting different parts of the country — the number of Questions might then reach 100 per day. The pressure on the Rule would then be heaviest when the Rule was unable to meet it. A Committee would not make things much better; it would have to sit daily, and it might be exceedingly difficult to get any number of Members to undertake the duty. Sir Edward Grey thought difficulties would arise if the Clerks at the Table had to exercise this discretion, some Members would be disappointed and this disappointment would concentrate itself on the officials of the House. Another Member pointed out that the new Rule might have the effect of longer notice being given. Mr. Balfour gave way to the general feeling of the House. It was not a matter, he said, in which the Government as Ministers had the smallest interest. Though he did not think the time limit would work without an arrangement of the kind he proposed, he was prepared to withdraw the clause and so allow the House to gain experience of the new Standing Order.

One other aspect of the time limit caused some discussion. Under current conditions, the arrangements at Question time were fairly informal. Questions were asked and answered in the order that they had been put on the Paper, which, apart from Questions to the Prime Minister, was in the order in which they had been handed in. If a Member was not present when his name was called, it was the practice for the Speaker to have a second or

[1] Mr. Balfour had envisaged that Mr. Speaker would 'lay down general principles, which will guide the clerks at the Table'. Parl. Deb. (1902), 105, c. 1460.

even third round, thus catching the Questions which had been missed earlier. Alternatively, the Member could depute[1] another Member to ask the Question for him. Similarly, if the Minister to whom a Question was addressed was not present when the Question was called, it would be called when he entered the Chamber, providing Public Business had not already commenced.

The amended proposals announced on 8 April paid some regard to the new situation by adding another category to the kind of Questions that could be answered at 2.55 p.m., viz. 'those not answered in consequence of the absence of the Minister to whom they are addressed'. As regards the absence of Members, the new rules proposed that in addition to Questions without an asterisk and those not reached by 2.55 p.m., a third category of Questions should receive a printed answer, viz. any not asked because the Member was not present to ask them, 'unless the Minister has consented to the postponement of the Question.'[2] Members were, however, concerned with the case of the Member who could not be present to ask his Question. It was made clear that until 2.55 p.m. was reached the old practice of a second or third round of Questions would continue. The Government, however, accepted without discussion or vote two amendments. The first specifically mentioned the absence of 'any Member deputed' by another to ask a Question and the second removed the need for Ministerial consent to the postponement and replaced that phrase by the words 'unless the Member has signified his desire to postpone'.

Finally, it is worth noticing that apart from one Irish Member (Mr. Flynn) there was no objection to the category of Questions 'which are of an urgent nature and relation ... to matters of public importance ...'. The House did not appear to doubt the ability of Mr. Speaker to decide whether a Question qualified for this favourable treatment. He had, in effect, been doing just this kind of thing since 1886 in respect of Questions which need not appear on the Paper.

Thus the great part of Mr. Balfour's original structure re-

[1] As early as 5 June 1883 Mr. Speaker had ruled that a Member must have been so requested by the Member who had put the Question on the Paper. Parl. Deb. (1883), 279, c. 1756.
[2] Mr. Balfour's explanation of this phrase (Parl. Deb. (1902), 107, c. 227) to the effect that, had it not been added, 'the Minister could have avoided answering any Question by not being present at the time it was asked,' appears to be a rare lapse of understanding on his part or is an error in reporting.

mained. Only in respect of Questions had he to make any major concessions. In future, the Government and Members would know with a high degree of certainty what business would be discussed and when it would be reached. Any major uncertainty had been shifted to the hours after dinner, the least attractive hours of the day. Public Business was to have the main and most certain place in the timetable. Question time clearly came next in importance. The Government's attack on it had been withstood with very little loss. A time limit had been imposed, but forty minutes looked ample in the circumstances of the time, and there was the device of printed answers, which opened up new possibilities. The defeat of the attempt to restrict supplementaries confirmed the importance of this recent development. The right to ask Questions was not merely a right to elicit information; it was also, within limits, a right to cross-examine Ministers and to keep them answerable to the House for all they did or might have done. But only the vigilance of the back benchers, particularly those on the Government side of the House, had prevented Question time being seriously curtailed and its importance very greatly diminished. For the time at which Questions may be asked has proved of great significance. A great deal of the popularity of Question time and of the press publicity which Questions and answers receive is due to this being the first main business of the Sitting. Had the time been transferred to midnight or even to after 7.15 p.m., much of its popularity and publicity would have been lost, as indeed Mr. Balfour knew full well. As it was, the only foreseeable cloud on the horizon was the possibility that the time limit might come into effect on many occasions, indeed on an increasing number of occasions. If so, would the limit be extended, or would the House have to work out some method of classifying oral Questions, or what would happen? This problem has dominated the developments in procedure since 1902.

THE CHANGES IN 1906

The new Rules came into operation on Monday, 5 May 1902. A Return provided at the end of the Session of 1902[1] showed that starred Questions had been completed before 2.55 p.m. on all but

[1] Parl. Deb. (1902), 117, p. xxxvii.

five occasions, and one of these was exceptional, in that Question time had been interrupted by the need for Mr. Speaker to attend the House of Lords to receive a Commission indicating the Royal Assent. On the great majority of days they had been disposed of by 2.45 p.m.

One of the first acts of Sir Henry Campbell-Bannerman's Government after its success at the election of January 1906 was to establish a Select Committee on (House of Commons) Procedure. The Committee first met on 8 March and its First Report was available on the 22nd. On 2 April the Prime Minister moved important amendments to the Standing Orders of the House. The changes proposed had their starting point in the desire to abolish the double sittings. Campbell-Bannerman 'thought it would be the general opinion of the House that the effect of the fixed dinner-hour . . . had not been satisfactory' and he gave various reasons to support that view. The present hours at which the House met and ended 'were inconveniently early and inconveniently late'.[1] This was also the unanimous view of the Select Committee. He proposed, therefore, to abolish the dinner break and use half of the time saved to enable the sitting to start at 2.45 p.m. instead of 2 p.m., and the other half so that it could end at 11.15 p.m. instead of midnight. After argument and division the House agreed to a continuous sitting on four days a week from 2.45 p.m. to 11 p.m.[2]

The changes in the hours of Sittings[3] need not, of course, have had any effect on the time available for Questions. Certainly, changes which reduced the length of the Sittings by 15 minutes each day were not propitious for an increase in Question time. The Select Committee had, however, proposed, first, that Questions should commence not later than 3 p.m. and end not later than 3.45 p.m., and second, that their commencement should not have to wait until a fixed period (15 minutes as it then was) had elapsed after the Speaker had taken the Chair, but

[1] 2 April 1906. Parl. Deb. (1906), 155, c. 217–20.
[2] Sir Henry Campbell-Bannerman accepted 11 p.m. instead of 11.15 p.m. as a compromise with Mr. Redmond, who wanted the sitting to commence at 3 p.m., as was recommended by the Select Committee. Parl. Deb. (1906), 155, c. 234.
[3] A proposal by Campbell-Bannerman that the House should revert to the pre-1902 position of Wednesday (instead of Friday) being the short day was heavily defeated on a free vote, some of the Prime Minister's Cabinet colleagues voting against it. The hours of the Friday sitting were changed from 12 p.m.–6 p.m. to 12 p.m.–5.30 p.m.

should commence immediately the previous Business was completed. The Government supported both these changes and the House accepted them without a division.

The first change gave a certain extra five minutes for Question time and the second could add nearly another fifteen minutes. The Speaker, in his evidence to the Select Committee, had suggested that the then 40 minutes should be extended to 50 minutes. Mr. Redmond and Mr. Swift MacNeill and one or two others urged the need for a certain hour being made available, but the Government carried the Division by 291 to 147, the voting following Party lines. The new arrangement, that Questions should start as soon as unopposed Private Business, Returns and other minor miscellaneous items were out of the way, had been rejected by Balfour in 1902, as offending his aim of certainty. It was, however, an obvious way of gaining extra time for Questions. It remains the rule today.

Since 24 April 1906, therefore, Question time, instead of lasting only the 40 minutes fixed by Mr. Balfour, has been more nearly the 'hour' in the popular term 'Question hour'. It is, however, not an hour, for there has to be deducted the time taken by Prayers (about 5 minutes) and by certain other Business. It can be as little as 45 minutes and never more than about 55 minutes.

The duration of Question time has thus been fixed for over half a century. Since that time major changes have taken place in the powers of the central government and in the political life and working of the House of Commons. The next two chapters will therefore be devoted to a study of the trend in the number of Questions during this period and of the changing capacity of Question time.

CHAPTER 4

NUMBER OF QUESTIONS SINCE 1902

THE total number of Questions on the Paper each Session does not provide a fair indication of the trend over the past sixty years, because of the variations in the length of Sessions. Over 27,000 Questions were asked in 1945–6 as against some 12,000 in 1923, but the House sat on almost twice as many days in the former as in the latter Session. It is preferable, therefore, to convert the sessional totals into daily averages and this is done in the following Table.[1]

Number of Questions to Ministers appearing on the Order Paper 1901–1960

Session	Starred Questions			Unstarred Questions			All Questions
	Sessional total	Question times	Daily average	Sessional total	Order papers	Daily average	Sessional total
1901	6,448	94	69	—	—	—	6,448
1902 (to May 5)	2,917	55	53	—	—	—	2,917
1902 (after May 5)	2,415	88	27	1,836	110	17	4,251
1903	2,544	91	28	1,992	113	18	4,536
1904	3,719	99	38	2,214	123	18	5,933
1905	4,120	88	47	2,124	109	19	6,244
1906	8,614	123	70	3,251	151	22	11,865
1907	7,439	104	72	2,708	129	21	10,147
1908	10,181	135	75	3,630	169	21	13,811
1909	8,799	142	62	3,452	178	19	12,251
1910	6,002	74	81	2,199	91	24	8,201
1911	11,984	138	87	3,455	166	21	15,439
1912	16,127	167	97	3,786	203	19	19,913
1913	7,162	81	88	1,774	100	18	8,936
1914	5,701	104	55	2,004	127	16	7,705
1914–16	10,535	147	72	2,441	152	16	12,976
1916	13,246	123	108	2,497	123	20	15,743
1917	16,344	177	92	2,802	177	16	19,146
1918	10,223	115	89	1,802	117	15	12,025
1919	16,378	130	126	4,145	154	27	20,523
1920–21	15,033	137	110	3,619	166	22	18,652

[1] For the number of Questions in certain years before 1901 see p. 316.

NUMBER OF QUESTIONS SINCE 1902

Session	Starred Questions — Sessional total	Question times	Daily average	Unstarred Questions — Sessional total	Order papers	Daily average	All Questions — Sessional total
1921*	11,476	114	101	2,657	141	19	14,133
1922*	10,500	102	103	2,360	129	18	12,860
1923	9,954	93	107	2,416	113	21	12,370
1924	9,987	99	101	3,105	124	25	13,092
1924–5	10,682	118	91	3,353	144	23	14,035
1926	8,264	116	71	2,449	146	17	10,713
1927	8,549	116	74	1,987	143	14	10,536
1928	6,053	91	67	1,506	113	13	7,559
1928–9	5,407	79	68	1,667	99	17	7,074
1929–30	13,907	150	93	4,420	184	24	18,327
1930–31	11,606	149	78	2,767	184	15	14,373
1931–2	8,259	120	69	1,408	148	10	9,667
1932–3	6,542	112	58	1,017	135	8	7,559
1933–4	7,340	127	58	1,428	152	9	8,768
1934–5	7,079	120	59	1,370	146	9	8,449
1935–6	8,613	105	82	1,602	128	13	10,215
1936–7	10,041	127	79	1,728	155	11	11,769
1937–8	11,419	134	85	2,368	165	14	13,787
1938–9	15,191	165	92	3,269	193	17	18,460
1939–40	10,220	122	84	3,316	125	27	13,536
1940–41	8,354	109	77	2,471	108	23	10,825
1941–2	9,029	113	80	2,563	113	23	11,592
1942–3	9,363	113	83	2,548	118	22	11,911
1943–4	8,938	116	77	2,560	150	17	11,498
1944–5	6,252	69	91	1,604	91	18	7,856
1945–6	21,135	165	128	6,178	206	30	27,313
1946–7	13,785	128	108	3,525	159	22	17,310
1947–8	12,844	133	97	3,459	168	21	16,303
1948	528	4	[132]	325	8	[41]	853
1948–9	13,690	160	86	3,644	203	18	17,334
1950	7,971	76	105	1,890	99	19	9,861
1950–51	12,995	120	108	2,725	151	18	15,720
1951–2	11,672	118	99	2,520	149	17	14,192
1952–3	11,399	125	91	2,479	159	16	13,878
1953–4	13,153	148	89	2,837	185	15	15,990
1954–5	5,852	65	90	1,410	82	17	7,262
1955–6	14,775	171	86	3,510	214	16	18,285
1956–7	11,132	124	90	3,127	157	20	14,259
1957–8	9,991	119	84	2,743	151	18	12,734
1958–9	11,149	125	89	3,369	158	21	14,518
1959–60	10,161	125	81	3,310	156	21	13,471

Source: House of Commons Records. Between May 1902 and the outbreak of war in 1939 it was possible for Members to put down Questions for oral answer on Fridays. Ministers were not, as a rule, expected to answer orally on that day but occasionally did so. On some occasions only one Minister would attend showing that this was not regarded as a Question time in the normal usage. But sometimes, usually on the Friday the House adjourned for the Whitsuntide, Summer or Christmas recess many starred Questions would be on the Paper and most would be answered. These latter occasions have been included in the number of Question times, but the decision whether or not to include has had to be somewhat arbitrary. The most convenient measure for the daily average of Questions put down for written answer (unstarred) is the number of Order Papers on which such Questions appeared in each Session.

* Two sessions in 1921 and 1922.

The total number of starred Questions in each Session has been divided by the number of Question times. As there is nothing equivalent for unstarred Questions the sessional totals for these have been divided by the number of days such Questions appeared on the Order Paper.

Four general conclusions emerge from a study of this Table:

1. There are noticeable fluctuations in the numbers asked at different periods.
2. More Questions are asked now than in the early years of the century.
3. The increase is not, however, anything like as great as might have been expected, considering the vastly increased functions and powers of Ministers and the great extensions of the franchise.
4. Questions put down for written answer have shown no increase in popularity.

1. FLUCTUATIONS IN NUMBERS

The number of Questions asked at different times has varied considerably. The Sessions of 1919 and 1945–6 show the highest daily average since the beginning of Questions, the abnormally short Session of 1948 excepted. Both were new Parliaments with an unusually high proportion of new Members. Both took place immediately after a major war, when the powers of Government still remained extremely great, even though the coming of peace had made people less ready to accept Government 'interference' without complaint. In both cases the strong desire to question Ministers spilled over into the following Sessions.

An interesting contrast is between the Sessions of 1911, 1912 and 1913, on the one hand, and the early 1930s on the other. The very high figures for the former period reflect the strong Parliamentary campaign against Mr. Lloyd George's Health Insurance measure and the generally high level of Parliamentary activity. Between 1931 and 1935 fewer Questions were asked than in any year since 1905 except 1914. These were the years when the National Government had a majority of 425; there was a strong plea for national unity as a result of the economic crisis; and the Opposition (the Labour Party) not merely had only 52 Members but, after the split in the Party, had very little fighting spirit.

Fluctuations of this character are to be expected in most forms of Parliamentary activity. In part they reflect the political problems attracting the attention of Members at different times, in part the size of the Government's majority. A vigorously led Opposition facing a Government with a small majority will try to harass Ministers in all possible ways. But a great many Questions are also asked by the Government's supporters and therefore changes in the attitude of these Members will also affect the numbers.

2. INCREASE IN NUMBERS

The number of Questions of both kinds on the Paper in these days averages about 100, twice the number asked per day during the first five years of the century. If, however, we turn to a Parliamentary period more akin to the contemporary Commons in spirit and activity — the years of the Liberal Administration — there is much less difference. Questions averaged 90–100 per day during the period 1906–13, with a peak daily average of 116 in 1912. On quite a number of days during this period there were more than 150 starred Questions on the Paper, a figure which would cause comment even in the present House.

Moreover the statistics of starred Questions for recent years exaggerate the number actually asked. Being based on the daily Order Paper they include some double and even treble counting, because they fail to allow for deferred Questions. A Member can defer to a later day a starred Question standing in his name on the day's Order Paper. He has always been able to do this but it is only in recent years, with the development of the rota system, that the practice has become popular. The usual reason for deferment is to try to make certain of an oral answer and, therefore, the number deferred is greater the larger the number of starred Questions on the Paper. Notwithstanding, however, the high daily average in certain Sessions before 1945–6 the Notice Papers do not reveal much use of deferment.[1] Nowadays, however, seldom a day goes by without some Questions being deferred. An analysis of the first 75 Question times of the Session of 1959–60 showed 6,380 starred Questions on the Order Paper,

---

[1] An exception was Thursday, 4 July 1912, when 148 starred Questions were on the Paper but only 58 received an oral answer and 21 were deferred until Monday, 8 July.

of which 756 or 12 per cent were deferred and therefore double counted. A rough check indicates that the statistics of starred Questions since about 1952 should be reduced by about 10 per cent to allow for this duplication. This would reduce the number of starred Questions in most of the 1950s to below that for several of the Sessions before 1914.

The numbers in the first fourteen or so years of the century were, however, swollen by the large number of Questions asked by a few Irish Members. During the period 1918 to 1922 the majority of the Irish Members refused to take their seats and after that the creation of the Irish Free State or Eire, and of the Government of Northern Ireland led to exclusion of the hitherto considerable number of local Questions about these areas. The proportion of Irish Questions varied. In the Session of 1905 the Ministers primarily responsible for Irish affairs answered a quarter of the written and nearly a third of the oral Questions. In addition, a substantial number of Irish Questions were addressed to the Postmaster-General. The proportion would be lower for the years immediately following. It is, however, probably safe to allow 20 per cent for Irish Questions during the period 1906–14.

If most of these Irish Questions are excluded, as being an abnormal element in the early figures, it will be seen that more starred Questions are asked nowadays than were asked before 1914, even allowing for some duplication in the recent figures. Just how many more depends on the years chosen for comparison. If the years 1902–5 are taken as the datum line there has been a very big increase — from say 20 to 30 a day to, say, 75 to 80 a day. If, however, the years 1910–13 are chosen, the increase is very small indeed — by not more than say 5 or 10 a day. Coming nearer to the present day there are more starred Questions now than there were during some of the inter-war years, but not many more, and no more than were asked during the three or four immediate pre-war years.

3. REASONS FOR THE SMALL INCREASE

The really significant feature, therefore, is not that there has been an increase but that the increase, however measured, is so small. The world of 1906, or even of 1912, notwithstanding the social programme of the Liberal Government, was, so far as the powers and activities of the central Government are concerned, an entirely different world from that of the 1950s. One was still a world of Victorian laissez-faire, the other is the era of the Welfare State. The Civil Service is now nearly three times larger than it was in 1914, there are now nine more departmental Ministers, the Statute Book is very many times fatter and the number of electors has increased fivefold. In so far as Questions are a method of securing the answerability of Ministers and of bringing their faults and the complaints of individuals to light, one would have expected that the great increase in the powers and responsibilities of Ministers would have been matched by a corresponding increase in the number of Questions. It would have been no surprise to find that the daily number of Questions, starred and unstarred, had increased four or five or even ten times since 1906. Instead, only by excluding the Irish Questions can any noticeable increase be measured. There are four reasons for this:

(*a*) The use of devices for limiting the answerability of Ministers for personal cases and for day to day administration.

(*b*) The great growth of Members' correspondence with Ministers.

(*c*) Restrictions on the number of starred Questions that may be asked by a Member on any one day.

(*d*) The congestion of Question time.

(*a*) *Question Avoiding Devices*

First, there has been a development of constitutional and administrative devices the purpose of which is to avoid a Minister having to be answerable for decisions in personal cases or for the details of day to day administration. Examples of this development can be found in most branches of state activity but they are particularly noteworthy in the field of social security and public ownership.

Social security payments are of two types: those for which the amount is fixed by Statute, and which can be claimed as of right by applicants who satisfy the statutory conditions, and discretionary payments. Both types present serious problems of departmental administration and Ministerial answerability. In the case of payments as of right, e.g. unemployment benefit and contributory old age pensions, the application of the Statutory conditions to individual cases may lead to differences of opinion between the civil servant and the applicant. For example, the applicant for Unemployment Benefit must fulfil the condition of being 'capable of and available for work'. If an unemployed man is offered a job and refuses it on the grounds that it is too heavy for his physique or is too far from his home, someone has to decide whether the refusal is reasonable, or if not, whether the man can be treated as not being available for work and therefore can be refused benefit. Decisions of this kind must in the first instance be made by the civil servant handling the case. In the absence of any alternative machinery, any complaint against a decision might be brought before the Courts if a point of law was involved but would be much more likely to be taken up with the Department by way of the aggrieved person's Member of Parliament. This problem was clearly seen when the first Insurance Act was passed in 1910, and therefore special machinery was established for dealing with differences of opinion between the Department and individual applicants. The machinery, which now applies to all forms of social insurance benefit, consists of a series of administrative tribunals. At the local level there is an official called the Statutory Officer from whom an appeal can go to a Local Tribunal and, from that, to a National Insurance Commissioner at the national level. The Minister is bound to use the machinery and cannot interfere once it has been brought into operation. When a disputed case is brought to the notice of a Member of Parliament he refers the complainant to the appeal machinery or, if he passes the complaint to the Minister, he will be told that this is the proper course. Thus, a very large number of cases of this kind are kept away from the Parliamentary process even though the service is administered by a Minister. Matters of general policy can, of course, be raised in Parliament; for example, whether a particular Statutory requirement should be modified.

Discretionary payments, now made by the National Assistance Board, are dealt with rather differently. At one time these were made by the local authorities responsible for administering the Poor Law, and individual cases were not the responsibility of any Minister. The Unemployment Assistance Act, 1934, saw the beginning of the transfer of this kind of payment to the central government. The majority of the Royal Commission of 1932 on Unemployment Insurance had reported in favour of Local Authorities continuing to administer the payment of unemployment relief on a discretionary basis according to the needs of the individual applicants. They dismissed the possibility of entrusting this service to the Ministry of Labour, because discretionary payments were foreign to the experience of the Ministry's staff, and because the vesting of such discretion in the local officers of a Government Department was incompatible with central control of decisions and Ministerial responsibility to Parliament.[1] The Government, however, decided to establish an Unemployment Assistance Board to administer this service. The device of a Board was defended as a means of freeing the Minister of Labour 'from responsibility for individual decisions while maintaining the right of Parliament to approve the general policy to be followed'.[2]

Officers of the Board were given the responsibility to determine all claims, but this did not prevent Members raising individual cases with the Minister. A series of appeals tribunals were, however, established at the same time, and the first redress of an aggrieved applicant was to appeal to his local tribunal. As the scope of 'National' Assistance expanded, so the local appeals tribunal machinery was developed. There are now 152 tribunals to whom applicants for assistance may appeal against such decisions by the Board's officers as the refusal of assistance, the amount allotted, or the conditions to which the applicant has been made subject.

The appellate machinery in the field of social security handles many thousands of cases each year. In the absence of such arrangements, a great many more constituents' letters would reach Members and more Questions would be put to the Ministers.[3]

The considerable expansion of national ownership by the Labour Governments of 1945–51 could have opened the way for a very great increase in the day to day matters and individual cases for which a Minister could be held answerable. The complaints and grievances of millions of consumers of coal, gas and

[1] J. D. Millett, *The Unemployment Assistance Board* (1940), p. 25.
[2] H.C. Deb. (1933–4), 283, c. 1093.
[3] Even as it is the National Assistance Board handles some 1500 Members' letters each year.

electricity and the users of the railways, as well as those of some two million workers employed in the nationalized industries, would have yielded a vast number of cases. But, instead, of the normal Ministerial form of management being adopted, as in the telephone service, these newly nationalized industries were vested in Statutory Boards. One of the strong arguments used in favour of this form of public management is that it enables a distinction to be drawn between matters of day to day administration and general issues of public policy, the former being kept out of the hands of the Minister. In strict theory the only Questions arising out of the activities of any nationalized industry vested in a Statutory Board which a Minister should answer are those which flow from any specific powers which he may have been given by Statute, e.g. to appoint the Members of a Board or to issue directions of a general character, or those which flow from what may be regarded as the general responsibility of the Minister for the general efficiency and well-being of the industry. In addition, a system of consumers' councils has been set up for each industry to deal with the complaints, grievances and wishes of consumers.

Thus a substantial part of the powers which have accrued to the central government during the present century have accrued not to Ministers but to bodies which are variously described as 'independent', 'semi' or 'quasi' independent or extra-governmental. There has also been a concious attempt to use these and other devices for the day-to-day handling of the mass of individual decisions and the resulting individual complaints, leaving Ministers, in theory at least, responsible and therefore answerable only for broad issues of policy. The growth in the powers of the State[1] has gone along with a retreat from the full rigours of the doctrine, brought to its fullest fruition during the nineteenth century, of Ministerial accountability. The doctrine has not changed. Ministers still remain fully answerable to the House for the use of the powers vested in them; the retreat has been achieved by devices which leave them answerable only for certain matters considered to be of general importance, there being no Ministerial answerability in the full Parliamentary

[1] The traditional method of vesting powers in locally elected Councils continues to have the advantage, among others, of relieving Ministers and the House of a great deal of detail.

sense for most of the actions of these new public bodies or for the decisions in millions of individual cases.

(b) Correspondence with Ministers

The use of Boards and similar devices has not, however, avoided a marked increase in the governmental powers for which Ministers are answerable to the House. Moreover, some of the long-established functions of government have given rise to many more individual grievances now than earlier in the century. For example, conscription and the comparatively large size of the Armed Forces during peacetime led to a large number of Service cases being brought to the attention of Members. Much more important is the very big increase in the number of voters. At the election of 1906, there were $7\frac{1}{4}$ million names on the electoral register. This jumped to over 21 million at the 1918 election and to nearly 29 million at the 1929 election, following the legislation of 1918 and 1928 extending the franchise. The number at the 1959 election was nearly 36 million. In so far, therefore, as Members draw their Questions from the complaints or suggestions of the voters in their constituency that source has considerably expanded. Finally, there is one new general factor. Nowadays, if the man in the street is not pleased about some happening he is quite likely to assume that 'they' have had something to do with it or that 'they' should do something about it — who 'they' are in any particular case may not be clear, but that deters few from interpreting it to mean a Government Department or Parliament or someone in public authority. All this has resulted in a large increase in the number of individual complaints, appeals for help and advice and similar approaches made to Members. The reason why this increase has not been reflected in the number of Questions is that Members deal with most of them by way of correspondence with Ministers.

It has been estimated that an M.P. receives 12 to 20 letters a day.[1] These fall into four main groups: expressions of opinion on topical issues; circulars from national organizations seeking support for a wide range of causes; general constituency problems; and requests for assistance and advice on personal problems. Some Members may attract a larger mail because press, radio, or television publicity has shown them to be interested in

[1] Peter G. Richards, *Honourable Members* (1959), p. 167.

a particular subject, e.g. purchase tax or African problems. Members also receive requests for help and advice in personal cases or hear of the problems or difficulties of their constituents during visits to their constituency. Many Members hold regular 'surgeries' for this purpose, by making it known that they will be available to hear the views, complaints and problems of individual constituents at an advertised time and place in their constituency.

A great variety of matters will be raised in these ways. A constituent may complain that he has been waiting for a telephone to be installed in his house for four years, whereas Mr. X., a neighbour, had one installed immediately he applied. Another constituent may ask whether it is true that his land is going to be acquired compulsorily by a Department or the local Council or complain about the inadequacy of the compensation if it has already been so acquired. The local Chamber of Trade or the Trades Council may be concerned about the amount of unemployment in the area and want certain road works to be carried out as a palliative. A complaint may reach a Member alleging unfair treatment of an African in one of the Colonies. A young soldier's parents may write about conditions in his camp or complain that he has been refused compassionate leave to see his sick mother.

In some cases the Member will be able to answer the query or deal with the matter from his own knowledge and experience. But in a high proportion of cases he can only provide an adequate and correct answer by taking the matter up with the appropriate Government Department, Local Authority, or other public body. It might be thought that it would be sufficient for the Member to pass the letter to the body concerned and ask them to reply. While this method would save a Member a good deal of time and trouble, it would have two disadvantages from his point of view. First, it would make him merely a letter-box and give him much less direct contact with his constituents. He may also hope to get some credit from dealing effectively with the problems put to him. In any case he represents them, and whether he gets any credit or not, he usually likes to feel that he is able to be of some help to them. Second, and more significantly in some cases than others, he wants to see whether the Department's reply is satisfactory. If it is not he may wish to pursue the matter further.

Constituent's letters, and the individual cases he learns about when he visits his constituency, are the main source of the Member's knowledge of what is troubling the voters in his area. He regards it as an important part of his function to take up and have remedied the genuine grievances of constituents, though whether these are genuine can be decided only in the light of the Department's reply and possibly of further enquiries of his own, following that reply.

Members deal with almost all these constituency cases by correspondence with the appropriate Ministry.[1] There are several reasons why they prefer to deal with them in this way. For one thing, the rules would prevent many of the complaints and enquiries being raised by way of Questions. The constituent may be asking for advice which is readily available if he knew where to look for it or was prepared to pay for it. Thus he may write to his Member enquiring what his rights or obligations are under a new piece of legislation. He is using his Member as a kind of Citizen's Advice Bureau. The Member could tell him to look it up for himself or could do the work for him, but in most cases the enquiry will be passed to the Department for a reply. An enquiry of this kind, unless there are unusual circumstances, would offend against the rule that Questions should not ask for information which is readily available. Again matters can be dealt with in greater detail in a letter than in an oral answer, and some of the details may be of a kind that neither the constituent nor the Member would wish to be made publicly known. There is also a general understanding among Members that Questions should not be used for individual cases, at least not until an effort has been made to settle them by correspondence. It must also be borne in mind that Questions are only answered whilst the House is sitting. During the recess Questions may be sent into the Table Office for placing on the Paper, but will not receive an answer until the House sits again. During these periods, therefore, correspondence is the only method of securing a Ministerial answer.

Finally, and perhaps this is a decisive factor in the lives of busy Members with inadequate secretarial assistance, the letter

[1] Members do not normally deal directly with civil servants, either by correspondence or by personal interview. It is not unusual, however, for a Member with a 'social security' problem to discuss it with the regional, or even with the local, manager of the National Assistance Board or of the Ministry of Pensions and National Insurance and both Departments encourage this direct contact.

to the Minister is much simpler, more convenient and less time consuming in the great majority of instances than is the Question. Constituents' queries and complaints are seldom couched in the clear, precise form required by the Table Office for a Question, nor are the facts always what they are said to be. To turn a letter from an unknown and possibly not very literate constituent into a Question would thus require the Member not only to undertake some drastic and possibly delicate rewording but also to make reasonably sure that the facts on which the complaint or query is based are accurate. The constituent who complained about the long delay in getting a telephone installed may be exaggerating when he says he applied four years ago; it may only have been two years ago, or he may have forgotten to mention that the application was for his previous house. A Member who turns letters of this kind into a Question without further investigation is obviously asking for trouble. The Minister will have all the facts checked, and his answer given in the House and published in Hansard may make the Member look rather foolish in the eyes of his fellow Members. A Member will not endear himself either to Ministers or to other Members by wasting the time of the House on Questions based on flimsy or inaccurate information.

In contrast, it is made easy for him to handle such matters by correspondence with the Minister. There are no rules of procedure to be observed. The Member's conscience and his view of what he may decently trouble Departments about are the only limitations, with the possible exception of the implications of the Strauss case.[1] Specially printed notepaper and cards for handling such correspondence are now provided free by the House. The Member, or his secretary, has only to complete the printed letter

[1] The Committee of Privileges in October 1957 expressed the opinion that, in writing a letter to a Minister, a Member was engaged in 'a proceeding in Parliament' within the meaning of the Bill of Rights of 1688 and that, therefore, a threat to sue him for libel by the body referred to in the letter was a threat to question the freedom of a Member in a Court or Place outside Parliament and accordingly the body and the solicitors acted in breach of a Privilege of Parliament. The House, however, rejected this recommendation by a majority of five on a free vote. The asking and the giving notice of a Question are, however, 'proceedings in Parliament' and, therefore, if a Member is in doubt whether a letter he is considering sending to a Minister may, if the contents are made known to the persons or body criticized, involve him in a libel action, he may refer to the letter in a Question put on the Paper purely to give him the necessary Parliamentary cover. For the Strauss case see Fifth Report from the Committee of Privileges, H. of C. Paper 305 of 1956–7 and H.C. Deb. (1957–8), 591, c. 208–346.

and send it with the constituent's letter to the appropriate Minister, and send the printed acknowledgement card to his correspondent and the job is done. The printed letter form reads:

> I shall be grateful if you will give the enclosed communication from .... your attention and send me a reply which I can forward to my constituent.
>
> Please acknowledge.

If he is a Government supporter, he is likely to start the letter: 'Dear John', 'Dear Henry' etc., it being increasingly assumed that all Members of the same Party are on Christian name terms. Opposition Members are more likely to use: 'Dear Minister', 'Dear Colonial Secretary' etc., but many of these will also address the Minister by his Christian name.

In very many cases, however, the Member will not use the printed formal letter. If he wishes to raise a matter which is causing considerable concern in his constituency, or an individual case which he has investigated personally, or an issue raised by some important group or interest in his constituency, or with which he is connected in any way, he will reveal his greater interest by sending a fuller and perhaps less neutrally worded letter of his own. He may even suggest that he should have a word with the Minister about the matter. Even in these more important cases, however, he is likely to find it simpler to deal direct with the Minister than to put down a Question.

The private office of the Minister deals with these letters, formal or informal, in very much the same way as it deals with Questions.[1] One of the Minister's Private Secretaries usually reads each letter and acknowledges it. He is thus able to sort out those in need of an urgent reply; those which should have been addressed to another Department; those which the Minister will wish to handle personally and those which can be handled in the routine manner. Usually Members' letters are put in a special folder, sometimes coloured for quick identification, or flagged with some such notice as 'Minister's or Parliamentary Correspon-

---

[1] See pp. 232–6 for the handling of Questions within the Departments.

dence'. Each goes to the appropriate branch of the Department for a draft reply to be prepared, the Assistant Secretary in charge of the branch or division usually taking responsibility for this. Letters which raise new or difficult points of Departmental policy, or present some unusual feature, may well be seen by the Permanent Head of the Department, and be carefully considered by the Minister. But the great bulk of letters will not reach such a high level in the Departmental hierarchy, and are likely to be seen and the reply agreed and signed by the Parliamentary Secretary.

When the Member receives the Minister's reply, he can, unless he wishes to send a more personal letter, merely clip on and sign the appropriate printed covering reply, also provided free by the House, worded as follows:

'I took up with the authorities the matter about which you wrote to me. I have now received a reply, which I enclose.'

Space is left for some additional wording: the Member may possibly wish to make the reply more friendly, or to add some views or advice of his own. The Departmental reply is drafted on the assumption that the Minister's letter will be forwarded to the constituent merely with a formal covering letter. It is also assumed that, unless the Minister's reply is marked 'Confidential', the Member is free to show the correspondence to the Press. Occasionally, the Minister may send the Member two replies, one which he can send to his constituent and another giving fuller information which he thinks it advisable for the Member to have, but which he wishes to be kept private. It should be remembered that the term 'constituent' is used in a very wide sense, it may be an individual or a local association or even the Town Clerk on behalf of a Local Council in the area. Similarly an enquiry or complaint may range from some small personal worry of a constituent to a local outcry about the proposed siting of a nuclear-powered electricity generating plant in the area.

In some cases, either as an addition or as an alternative to correspondence, the Member will discuss the matter with the Minister or the Parliamentary Secretary. He may even arrange for the person or body concerned to meet the Minister, and, if so, is likely to be present at the meeting. The Crichel Down case showed all these possibilities in use. It started with a friendly letter from the Member (Mr. Robert Crouch) to the Parliamentary Secretary to the Minister of Agriculture and Fisheries (Mr. Nugent) as a covering note to a longish letter from a Commander Marten, a farmer in the constituency of Mr. Crouch. The Member's letter ran:

Dear Dick,

... This is some good honest chalk land and the Crichel Estate is exceedingly well run. I would have thought it better to hand this land back to the former owners and allow them to let it to such tenants as they consider fit. The two men mentioned are really first-class farmers. I do hope that you will see your way to hand this land back. For your private information, I would say the Estate is owned by Mrs. Marten, a niece of Antony Head's, and the sole survivor of the Alington family. The Alington Estate has been well-run for generations.

Yours sincerely, Bob.[1]

Between the date that letter was received (14 June 1952) and 20 July 1954, when the Minister announced his resignation in the House of Commons, there took place interviews between the Minister, or one of his Parliamentary Secretaries, and the Member and his constituent, either together or singly, (on one occasion, two other Conservative Members from the area took part in the interview); there were letters from the Minister or Mr. Nugent on one side, and Mr. Crouch or Commander Marten on the other; there was a public meeting in the constituency; resolutions had been passed in support of Commander Marten by local Conservative Associations; the National Farmers' Union, and the County Landowners' Association had added their support; a meeting of Conservative Members concerned with agriculture had been attended by the Minister in the House; the site had been visited by both Parliamentary Secretaries to the Minister, and a fat file had accumulated in the Ministry. But it was not until 23 October 1953 (16 months after the first letter) that the first Question appeared on the Order Paper. It was unstarred, and it was arranged between the Minister and the Member for the constituency, so as to enable the former to

---

[1] Quoted by R. Douglas Brown, *The Battle of Crichel Down* (1955), p. 43. The full story is told in this book and in the report of the Enquiry. Cmnd. 9176 (1954).

announce his intention of holding a public enquiry into the procedure adopted for the disposal of Crichel Down. This was an unusual individual case, its public prominence to a large extent reflecting the growing unhappiness of Conservative backbenchers with their Government's policy in respect of compulsorily acquired land. It was, therefore, a focal point for argument within the Party, both in the House and the country at large. In the end, the agitation brought about major changes in Governmental policy. Had it been a case supported by the Opposition, it would probably have been the subject of an oral Question at an early stage: the Conservative Members concerned dealt with the matter more discreetly, but none the less effectively.

There has been no detailed study of this aspect of a Member's daily activities and functions and it is usually given little or no space in the standard exposition of the working of Parliament. All the evidence, however, points to a very big increase in the volume of correspondence between Members and Ministers about constituency matters. In 1938, for example, the Financial Secretary to the Treasury sent 610 letters to Members on matters falling within his responsibility as a Treasury Minister. In 1954 the number had increased to 3,349, a fivefold increase. Some part of this increase was undoubtedly due to the expansion of the statutory responsibilities of the Treasury: nearly one-third of the letters sent out in 1954 related to topics for which he had no responsibility in 1938. But a civil servant with several years' experience as Private Secretary to this Minister has expressed a view that the increase suggests 'that the British citizen is now more ready to write to his Member of Parliament about his grievances than he was before the war.... Clearly one reason for it is the greater consciousness which the citizen has of the part played by the State in his daily life. Perhaps he is also more conscious of the means open to him to influence the State. The Press, the radio and television have made the Member of Parliament an altogether more familiar figure to the average citizen than he was before the war.'[1]

In the case of the Post Office the number of matters raised by Members which were dealt with by a Ministerial letter increased

[1] K. E. Couzens, 'A Minister's Correspondence', *Public Administration*, Autumn 1956, vol. 34, pp. 241-2.

from, 2,000 in 1936 to 5,000 in 1948 and is now running at about 3,000 per annum. Large though these numbers are they are dwarfed by the experience of the War Office immediately after the end of the 1939-45 war. In September 1945 the War Office received 36,565 letters about release on compassionate grounds from military service, of which 3,382 were from Members of Parliament.[1] During the first three months of 1946 the Private Offices of the three Ministers in the War Office despatched to Members about 1,300 letters a week, and over 1,700 in the busiest week. The number had fallen to about 700 a week in 1947 and has progressively declined since then with the decline in the size of the Army, the transition from conscription to regular forces, and a return to more normal conditions. Even so, in 1958 the number was still running at some 6,000 a year.

The amount of such correspondence varies from Ministry to Ministry depending very largely on the extent to which the Ministry is concerned with individual cases. Thus the Ministry of Housing and Local Government have in recent years handled about 5,000 Members' letters a year, the Scottish Office about 2,000, the Home Office about 5,000, and the Ministry of Education about 2,500, whereas the Colonial Office dealt with only about 700. The recent experience of the Ministry of Power further illustrates this point. In 1954 and in 1955 about 600 Members' letters were received: in 1957, however, the number rose to 2,500, largely because of the petrol rationing scheme introduced during the Suez emergency.

Information about other Departments indicates that upwards of 50,000 letters a year now pass between Members and Ministers. Even at the beginning of the century Members received letters and complaints from their constituents and dealt with them privately with the Minister, not by putting a Question on the paper. Speaking in February 1902 Mr. Vicary Gibbs could say: 'I have now been in this House for ten years, and I do not believe that I have put more than ten Questions. But I have over and over again gone to the Minister with a private letter from one of my constituents and have said to him: "Would you kindly look at this letter and tell me what answer I have got to make to

[1] H.C. Deb. (1945-6), 414, c. 964-5. The Air Ministry were handling about 4,000 Members' letters a month, the Admiralty about 600-700 and the Ministry of Labour about 1,600. The vast majority of these concerned personal cases. H.C. Deb. (1945-6), 420, c. 1492.

it. That will save me putting a question in the House." [1] Earlier in the same debate Mr. Joseph Chamberlain had said that the great majority of Questions asked had 'absolutely no public interest whatever. Every reasonable demand would be satisfied if a Member would put his Questions in a private letter to the Minister and get a private answer . . .'.[2] It is probably true to say that throughout the past sixty years the majority of Members have handled the individual complaints and problems of their constituents privately with Ministers. The Irish home rulers did not, but then they were determined to emphasize the inconvenience to Westminster of not allowing the Irish to manage their domestic affairs. There have also been a few other Members particularly partial to the use of Questions in preference to dealing with the Minister by correspondence.

The great difference between now and 40 or 50 years ago is not that Members use correspondence with the Minister whereas they formerly asked a Question; it is that the vast increase in the number of individual cases raised by constituents has been handled by correspondence and not by Questions. Quantitatively the point can be put this way. The Sessions of 1908 and 1947–8 were of almost exactly the same length. During the former 13,800 Questions appeared on the Order Paper. No figures are available of the number of Members' letters to Ministers in that year but all the indications are that it would hardly be more than a few thousand items at the most. In the Session of 1947–8, 16,300 Questions were on the Paper but well over 100,000 Members' letters were handled by Ministers. Thus within the past 50 or so years the relative importance of the two devices has been reversed. If Questions and correspondence are seen as alternative ways in which Members raise points about the activities and omissions of Government Departments, the former are now like the upper part of the iceberg, prominent, but much the smaller part of the whole.

In passing, it is worth glancing at one important aspect of this relationship between correspondence and Questions — the speed of reply. Departmental replies to Members' queries are produced at four levels of speed. The quickest is the Private Notice Question. If Mr. Speaker accepts such a Question, the Member may ask for a reply on the afternoon of the day on which he gives

[1] Parl. Deb. (1902), 102, c. 646.   [2] Parl. Deb. (1902) 102, c. 579.

notice of it.[1] This form of Question is very strictly reserved for urgent and important matters, and usually only about forty are allowed each year.

The next quickest and the most usual is the answer to the starred Question. The general rule is that a starred Question must appear on the Notice Paper circulated two days (excluding Sunday) before that on which the answer is required. A Member may, however, claim that a starred Question submitted to the Table Office on Monday or Tuesday before 2.30 p.m. shall be answered on Wednesday or Thursday respectively and if submitted before 11 a.m. on Friday, then on the following Monday.[2] Thus he can receive a complaint one morning and get a reply two or three days later by this method. Whether he receives an oral or a written answer on that day will depend on whether his Question is reached during Question time, but in any event he will receive an answer.

The third quickest route is by way of the unstarred Question. On 8 February 1960 Mr. R. A. Butler, as Leader of the House, announced[3] that the Government proposed to issue instructions to Departments that they should exert every effort to provide an answer to unstarred Questions not less than three working days after notice had been given. Where that clearly could not be done the Department should notify the Member as soon as possible. Thus it is now possible to get a reply to an unstarred Question almost as quickly as one to a starred Question. Indeed as there is no minimum period of notice required for an unstarred Question it is possible on occasion to get an even quicker answer; for example, unstarred Questions, usually inspired by the Government, may be submitted on Thursday and answered on Friday, when oral answers are not given. But there is no Standing Order or rule of the House which requires a Department to answer an unstarred Question by a stated date.

Ministerial correspondence normally produces the slowest replies. The Select Committee of 1945–6 recommended that 'It would also help to reduce the number of Questions, oral and written, if Departments made it a rule to answer letters from Members within a fortnight'.[4] This recommendation was made

---

[1] Notice must be given to Mr. Speaker not later than 12 noon of that day.
[2] See Standing Order No. 8 in Appendix I, p. 291, for the full rules, and for the special provisions to deal with periods when the House is adjourned.
[3] H.C. Deb. (1959–60), 617, c. 43.   [4] Second Report, para. 12.

at a time when owing to the large and sudden increase in constituency letters some of the Departments were overwhelmed and there were many complaints of delays.[1] About this time many Questions were asked about personal cases because Ministerial replies by letter were so slow. Thus on 18 February 1946 Mr. Kirby put down a starred Question in the following form: 'to ask the Secretary of State for War when the hon. Member for Everton may expect a reply to his letter dated 30th October 1945 regarding 865225 Gunner P. Savage R.A. of Liverpool.' The Minister's reply was: 'I very much regret the delay in answering my hon. Friend's letter, but a reply was sent to him yesterday.'[2] Mr. Kirby had a second starred Question on the Paper that day in similar terms about another soldier and received a similar reply.[3] He and all other Members and Ministers in a similar position with their correspondence could hardly dismiss as a coincidence the answering of his letters the day before the need to answer two Questions about them. The present Clerk of the House, Mr. (now Sir) Edward Fellowes, stated in November 1945 that when Members complained of not having received a reply to an unstarred Question his reply was: 'Ring up the Department and tell them that if you do not get an answer by such-and-such a time, you will put it down starred and then they will have to answer it.'[4] This advice applies with even greater force to letters.

Nowadays most Members' letters to Ministers are answered fairly quickly, though several weeks may still elapse in some cases. Certainly the difference in time in getting a reply is not

[1] In March 1946 a Member said that for his correspondence with Departments during the last three months of 1945 the average time taken to get an answer had been: Colonial Office and Foreign Office, eight days; Ministry of Works, twelve days; Treasury, thirteen days; Ministry of Fuel and Power and Ministry of Agriculture, eighteen days; Home Office, twenty-one days; Ministry of Health and Admiralty, twenty-four days; Ministry of Labour, twenty-six days; Board of Trade, thirty days; Ministry of War Transport, thirty-three days; War Office, forty days; Ministry of Pensions, forty-one days, and the Air Ministry fifty days. H.C. Deb. (1945–6), 420, c. 1482.
[2] H.C. Deb. (1945–6), 419, c. 168.
[3] cf. the personal case raised on 19 February 1946 which caused one Member to ask whether it would be in order for all Members to put down individual cases. Mr. Speaker: 'It would be in Order, but I would deprecate unnecessary Questions of this kind without due cause.' Whereupon the Member raising the case said: 'may I point out that the facts of this case have been presented ... to the ... Department on three or four occasions since last August, and that is the reason why the Question has been put down again?' H.C. Deb., (1945–6), 419, c. 934–5.
[4] Second Report of Select Committee on Procedure, 1946, q. 1166.

sufficient to cause a Member to convert the letter into a Question. He has, however, in reserve, always the right to put down a Question should the Minister's reply be long delayed. And if he needs an answer within three or four days or does not wish to risk the uncertainty of a Ministerial letter he may very well decide to put the matter in the form of a Question. But so long as Departments maintain the present speed of replying to Members' letters this form of obtaining Ministerial answers will in the great majority of personal cases continue to have advantages over putting a Question on the Paper.

(c) *Limiting the Number of Starred Questions*

At the beginning of the century the number of Questions that a Member could put down for answer on any one day was unlimited though occasionally Mr. Speaker took upon himself the responsibility of preventing a Member putting an excessive number of Questions on the day's Order Paper.[1] When the time available for oral answers became limited a kind of gentleman's agreement limited the daily number of starred Questions to eight per Member. A breach of this agreement elicited a Speaker's ruling to this effect on 1 March 1909.[2] A certain flexibility was still allowed and if by chance the number of starred Questions standing in a Member's name on any day exceeded eight, the surplus stood over to the next day. The daily maximum was reduced to four on 24 February 1919[3] and to three in February 1920.[4] About this time the rules about carrying over any surplus to the next day were considerably tightened. The surplus ceased to be carried forward automatically; the Member had to ask specifically for this to be done otherwise any surplus over three was converted into unstarred Questions. The maximum was reduced to two on 15 February 1960.[5]

The limit is quantitatively significant only in the case of Members wishing to ask more than that number on a largish number of occasions. Even after the major reduction in 1919 the Member who found himself prevented on the odd occasion from having

[1] In March 1890 Mr. Speaker ordered notices of 28 Questions standing in the name of one Member to be removed from the Paper. *Parliamentary Practice.* Eleventh edition (1906), p. 247.
[2] H.C. Deb. (1909), 1, c. 1108.   [3] H.C. Deb. (1919), 112, c. 1382–3.
[4] H.C. Deb. (1920), 125, c. 1050–1 and 1225–7.
[5] Unstarred and Private Notice Questions have never counted for the purpose of the maximum.

more than three starred Questions down for answer on a single day could achieve his purpose by spreading the number over several days. When the reduction of the limit was discussed by the Select Committee in 1946 Mr. Speaker produced figures for 17 days in the Session of 1945–6.[1] On one of these days 28 Members had their maximum number of starred Questions on the Paper and on average during the period 17 Members exercised their full rights. In other words, had the maximum been two instead of three these 17 Members would have been able to put one less starred Question each per day, which in 17 days would have amounted to 289 out of a total of nearly 2,600 on the paper. The reduction would have been less than this, for in many cases the Members would have put the third Question down for answer on another day. In any case this was a period of exceptional activity at Question time. The reduction from three to two came at a time when the number of Members making full use of their rights was quite small, and the net effect was probably to reduce the potential number of starred Questions by only five hundred or so during the session. Even so were it still possible for a Member to have an unlimited number, or even eight starred Questions on the daily Order Paper the numbers asked each year would probably be several thousand higher.

(d) *Congestion of Question Time*

The fourth and final reason for the moderate increase in the number of starred Questions has been the increasing difficulty of securing an oral answer. This, however, is the subject of the next chapter.

4. UNSTARRED QUESTIONS

The daily average number of Questions for written answer has remained remarkably constant. On one-third of the sixty Sessions since starring was introduced the daily average has been either 17, 18 or 19. The annual average for the ten Sessions immediately after the introduction of the arrangement (including the remainder of the Session of 1902) was twenty, whereas for the ten Sessions ending with that of 1959–60 it was eighteen. There are fluctuations. Periods of low activity at Question time, e.g. in the early 1930s, are matched by a low

[1] Op. cit., p. 39.

number of Questions put down for written answer. During periods of high activity, however, a procedural factor gives an artificial stimulus to unstarred Questions. If a Member has more than the maximum number of starred Questions on the Paper on any day and does not arrange for the surplus to be deferred, the Table Office automatically remove the star from the surplus, strictly in the order in which notice of the Questions was received. This factor undoubtedly accounts for part of the big increase in the number of unstarred Questions in 1919 and 1920, for in addition to these being very active periods for Question time, they also saw the reduction of the daily maximum from eight to four and then to three. Nowadays two or three Questions a day are transferred from the starred to the unstarred category because of Members having more than two starred Questions down for answer that day.

The general factors which might have been expected to lead to a marked increase in the number of starred Questions might also have been expected to do the same for unstarred. Two of the factors which may account for this marked increase not having taken place do not apply in the same way to written answers, indeed they might have been expected to stimulate the use of this form. There has never been any daily limit to the number of unstarred Questions a Member may ask. The severity of the limit on starred Questions and the increasing difficulty of securing an oral answer might have led to a shift from starred to unstarred Questions. There is no indication of any such shift. There is indeed little or no evidence of any change in Members' attitudes to written answers during the past sixty years. Why is this?

Until recent years the reasons were clear. Starring his Questions had two advantages[1] and no disadvantage to the Member. First, if he was not satisfied with the Minister's reply he could ask a supplementary and second, he was thereby certain of getting the answer quickly and on a date fixed by himself. Probably the second factor was more significant in the majority of cases. The disadvantage is only real if the Member takes attendance in the

[1] In June 1902, immediately after the Balfour reforms, Mr. Joseph Chamberlain, then Colonial Secretary, minuted his staff, 'Please note that in order to encourage un-starred questions I desire that as full answers as possible should be given to them. They may be fuller than to ordinary questions to be answered orally.' Office Minutes, vol. 10, No. 124. There is little indication that Departments have answered the two forms of Question differently.

Chamber very seriously. Having put down the Question for oral answer he should be present in the Chamber on the day to ask it but if he forgets, or is prevented by another engagement he still gets a written answer.

When Mr. Balfour introduced the arrangement he said that one of the advantages of leaving a Question without an asterisk would be that Members would get an authoritative answer circulated with the Votes.[1] He did not, however, say when the answer would be circulated, but it may be inferred that Members expected replies to be available as quickly as replies to starred Questions. But whereas the Standing Order provided a minimum period of notice for starred Questions and by implication, if not in so many words, provided that the answer would be available when this minimum period had elapsed, no period of notice was required for an unstarred Question and therefore no implication could be drawn as to the date it was to be answered. There was no 'Question time' for written answers. A Member could put the Question down for answer on a stated day, but as Campion could say in 1929 'A department is not bound to supply the answer to an "unstarred" Question punctually on the day on which it is down.'[2]

The Clerk of the House agreed with the Chairman of the Select Committee on Procedure of 1931 that 'Ministers would really save themselves a lot of trouble if they would make it a rule in the Departments that all questions have equal value with regard to time . . .'. He said that instructions had been given by the Prime Minister to this effect but were not always carried out. Members were as much concerned with the uncertainty as with the delay; they did not know whether they would receive a reply on the day they had stated or a week or a fortnight later.[3] The Committee recommended that a new class of Question for written reply should be created, distinguished with a dagger. This would mark a Question not of general interest but for which a

---

[1] Unstarred Questions and their replies and starred Questions which received written replies were circulated with the daily *Votes and Proceedings* as well as printed in Hansard until September 1915. The practice was then discontinued on the understanding that a Department would send a copy of its reply to the Member as well as to Hansard. H.C. Deb. (1915), 74, c. 804–5.
[2] *An Introduction to the Procedure of the House of Commons*, 1st edition, 1929, p. 126.
[3] Special Report from the Select Committee on Procedure, 1931, qs. 4013–18 and 4313–16.

Member desired 'rapid information' and which should be answered as quickly as if starred.[1] Nothing came of the proposal. In 1937 Departments were instructed by the Prime Minister that if a written answer could not be provided within four days the Member should be informed that inquiries were being made.[2] The Select Committee of 1946, however, was of the opinion that 'Undoubtedly the volume of Questions put down for oral answer is to some extent attributable to the uncertainty of written answers. If Members could be assured that they would get a written answer within a reasonable time, they would be encouraged to make more use of the Question for written answer and so relieve the pressure of oral Questions.'[3] The Government accepted the Committee's recommendation that written answers should be provided within seven days of the Question appearing on the Notice Paper[3] and in February 1960 the period was reduced to three working days.

The difference in speed of answer secured by starring a Question is nowadays not very great. Unless a Member is very keen on questioning a Minister on the floor of the House he has more inducement now than ever before to omit the asterisk. Even so, the rules of procedure and other factors still favour the starred Question. Even if a Question is not reached at Question time a reply is certain to be available, except in those rare cases in which the Minister refuses to answer. By use of the expedited procedure, therefore, a Member can still secure an answer to a starred Question with barely two days' notice, as against at least three for the other form. And even the three days are not always certain to be honoured. Equally, perhaps even more important, answers to starred Questions not reached attract some of the glamour and publicity attaching to Question time, for it is Question time rather than Questions as such that continues to get attention.

These factors account for the reluctance of Members to leave their Questions unstarred, and to that extent they also account for the fact that the use of this form of Question has not increased. For whilst there are some kinds of Question that demand an oral answer, e.g. in a case when all the informal or

---

[1] Report (1932), para. 12 (ii).
[2] Second Report of Select Committee on Procedure, 1945–6, p. 2.
[3] op. cit., para. 12, and H.C. Deb. (1945–6), 420, c. 2161.

behind-the-scenes procedures have been exhausted, and some which obviously are more suitable for a written answer, e.g. those asking for long tables of statistics, the great majority of Questions do not fall into either category. If a hundred starred and a hundred unstarred Questions were taken at random and mixed up, even those experienced in handling Questions would have difficulty in sorting them into the two groups. The name of the Member and the political topicality of the subject matter would be the main guides, rather than the wording or apparent purpose of the Question. For example, on the 19 May 1960 the Colonial Secretary was asked whether he would make a statement about his discussions with Nigerian Ministers, and the Minister of State for Commonwealth Relations was asked how many full-time agricultural officers were now employed in the Bechuanaland Protectorate. The former was put down for a written and the latter for an oral answer. The fact is that if a Member is going to go to the trouble of asking a Question there is little or no inducement for him to omit the asterisk. If the answer involves a great mass of factual material he will usually decide against asking it in the House. If he is a Government supporter he will be more inclined to be considerate of the Minister. A few Members prefer written to oral answers. But to most Members the addition of the asterisk is fairly automatic. It provides a quicker and more certain answer; if it is reached it provides the Member with a rare opportunity to say a few words in the Chamber, and if it is not reached or if the Member cannot be present to ask it he suffers no harm.

CHAPTER 5

QUESTION TIME SINCE 1902

In the years immediately following 1902, it was unusual for all the starred Questions on the paper not to be reached. In the interwar years, excluding 1919–24, 1929–30 and 1938–9 the great bulk (possibly 90 per cent or more)[1] of starred Questions received an oral answer. Nowadays, only half to two thirds are answered during Question time.

We have seen that the number of starred Questions has not risen markedly during the period; indeed if certain years of high activity are excluded, the daily average in the 1950s is not appreciably different from that of many of the previous 30 years. Very little of the failure to give an oral answer to such a high proportion of starred Questions can, therefore, be attributed to this factor. The causes of the transformation must be sought in the marked decline, particularly in recent years, of the number of Questions dealt with during the time available.

The decline is striking. During the debates in 1902 Mr. Balfour suggested that the 40 minutes being made available would be sufficient to allow 60 or 70 starred Questions to be answered. This proved to be a reasonable estimate. In 1906, before the extension of Question time, Mr. Speaker Lowther thought that the House could get through about 60 Questions and 15 or 20 supplementaries each day.[2] On 14 March of that year, 66 starred and 29 supplementaries were answered. In 1914, after the extension of time, he could claim that the House often got through '80 questions, and perhaps 20 or 30 supplementaries besides',[3] but even at that time there were many occasions when the House only managed to get through about 60. In 1919 there were many days when 75 or more starred Questions were answered orally

[1] Professor McCulloch states: 'During the 1924–5 session, 1,600 starred Questions received written answer; 1,300 during 1926; 1,200 during 1927; 900 during 1928; and 1,300 during 1928–9.' *American Political Science Review*, 1933, p. 972. These figures account for about 15 per cent of the annual totals given at chapter 4, p. 88, but include starred Questions which Members were not present to ask.
[2] Select Committee on House of Commons (Procedure) 1906, qs. 36–7.
[3] Select Committee on House of Commons (Procedure) 1914, q. 2962.

but as the years went by the number declined. The daily average in 1938–9 and 1945–6 was about 60. By 1956–7, however, it was well below 50 and during November–December 1958 it was running just above 40. An average of 40–45 oral answers a day is now usual.[1] What are the reasons for the decline and what are the consequences?

It is well known that the most important reason is the increased use of the supplementary Question. But there are also important contributing factors, which can most simply be described as a general disinclination to try to get through more Questions. Fifty years ago there were fewer supplementaries than starred Questions; on average, one supplementary for every two to three main answers. Now there are roughly three supplementaries for every two main Questions. Question time has become supplementary time, the purpose of answering Questions of which notice has been given having declined in importance. Each supplementary is likely to take more time than each main Question for several reasons. The Member must give it in full, it is not already printed on the Paper; the Minister must consider how to reply, not just read a prepared answer; and both Member and Minister are likely to be less concise, thinking on their feet,[2] than drafting on paper. Thus an increase of ten in the number of supplementaries asked at each sitting will probably reduce the main Questions answered by a somewhat greater number. The total capacity of Question time as measured by answers given to Questions on the Paper falls as the proportion of supplementaries rises. Even so, in earlier years it was possible to get through both a larger number of supplementaries and a larger number of main Questions. Thus a sample analysis of 20 days in 1938–9 and 21 days in 1945–6 showed that on average more supplementaries were answered daily in those years than in 1958 and yet at the same time 50 per cent more starred Questions were answered.

We now propose to examine these matters in greater detail.

[1] On 26 November 1956 over 100 starred Questions were on the Paper but only 24 were answered orally. By way of contrast Mr. Speaker Fitz Roy in February 1930 could say that 'No. 82 is not very far down on the list'. H.C. Deb. (1929–30), 235, c. 2056.
[2] In some cases a Member may have prepared his supplementary in anticipation of the Minister's reply, and some Ministers have answers prepared ready for the more likely supplementaries.

INCREASED USE OF SUPPLEMENTARIES

During the last decade of the nineteenth century the main issue was between Questions which Ministers would answer, or could be expected to answer, without notice and those for which notice was required. Mr. Speaker Gully stated the position in 1901 quite clearly: 'Some hon. Members appear to think that when a question seems naturally to occur to the mind upon hearing an answer, it necessarily arises out of the answer.[1] Strictly speaking a supplementary question is only in order when it is asked in order to elucidate some ambiguity or to supply some omission in the original answer.'[2]

When Gully became Speaker in 1895 he did his best to curtail the use of the supplementary and with some success. Two years after his election Lucy could report that Mr. Speaker Gully had changed the Question hour which 'Under former Administrations . . . was one of illimitable possibility. . . . The rule remains unaltered. It is still permissible for a member who has a question on the paper or another interested in the subject to put a further question with the object of elucidating the point. The new manner of conducting proceedings has revealed the exceeding barrenness of the land on which such desires are assumed to grow. It is argument, not information, that in ninety-nine cases out of a hundred members using the phrase 'arising out of that answer' are after. Few of the ninety and nine succeed in getting to the end of their so-called question. Mr. Gully swoops down on them like a hawk on a sparrow, and before they know where they are the member whose name stands next on the list of printed questions is addressing it to the Minister.'[3]

After May 1902 a new factor emerged. If a Member merely wanted information he need not star his Question, whereas if he wanted to retain the right to ask a supplementary, he would add the asterisk.[4] It was perhaps inevitable, therefore, that an in-

[1] An Irish Member is reputed to have prefaced his supplementary with the phrase 'Arising out of the answer which the Minister has not given . . .'.
[2] Parl. Deb. (1901), 96, c. 264.
[3] *A Diary of the Unionist Parliament, 1895–1900*, pp. 133–4. Sir Henry Campbell-Bannerman speaking on 6 December 1900 also paid Mr. Speaker Gully the same tribute: '. . . in nothing has Mr. Speaker been more energetic and successful than in the preventing of unnecessary questions.' Parl. Deb. (1900), 134, c. 121.
[4] On 15 May 1902 the Speaker ruled that a supplementary could not be based on a written answer. Parl. Deb. (1902), 108, c. 372.

creasing proportion of those answered in the House should attract a supplementary. Even so, it is difficult to believe that Ministerial replies so deteriorated in clarity and fullness as to warrant a steadily increasing proportion needing supplementation. The House, and therefore Mr. Speaker, has gradually changed its attitude towards the purpose and use of the supplementary.

In July 1915,[1] Mr. Speaker Lowther was asked by a Member: 'Is there any fixed maximum number of supplementary questions permissible after the official reply of a Minister? Is there any definite limit to the number permissible to one particular Member during the whole Question Time of a single day, as is the case with notice questions? Is there any special method of giving precedence to different Members who may be anxious to interrogate a Minister in this way, and can any broad rule be laid down as to the scope and manner of such supplementary questions seeing that the gist of none of them can be known until it has been heard?'

The Speaker replied: 'The answer to all the hon. Member's questions is in the negative. I think I ought to remind him that all supplementary questions are out of order and irregular. I will read to him Standing Order No. 9. which deals with questions. It states:

"Notices of questions shall be given by Members in writing to the Clerk at the Table without reading them *viva voce* in the House, unless the consent of the Speaker to any particular question has been previously obtained."

The hon. Member will therefore see that all supplementary questions are irregular and are not provided for at all in any Standing Order. It is entirely a matter of grace. My predecessors have ruled somewhat differently as to supplementary questions. My immediate predecessor [Mr. Speaker Gully] was very strict in regard to them; he would hardly allow any supplementary questions at all. During my reign I have been rather more lax, and I must take the praise or the blame, as the case may be, for what has occurred. I may say generally that the object of supplementary questions is to elucidate any ambiguity in the reply of a Minister or to seek for some further information if he

[1] H.C. Deb. (1915), 73, c. 41-2

can give it; but supplementary questions should not be put, and ought not to be put, especially at such times as these, to embarrass a Minister or to lead him to give an answer in a hurry which at a subsequent time he might be sorry that he gave. I think I must ask the House to trust me. I will give as much freedom as I possibly can, but at the same time there must be some limits.'

Soon after he was elected to the Chair in 1928 Mr. Speaker Fitz Roy stated that there were far too many supplementaries and announced that he would take steps to control their number. On the whole, however, the general trend must have been to the liking of Members, for there was little complaint about the use of supplementaries in the evidence given to the Select Committee on Public Business during 1931. True, the Chief Government Whip (Mr. T. Kennedy) outdid the Mr. Balfour of 1902 by proposing, not only that a supplementary should be confined to the Member asking the original Question, but also that a Member should only be allowed one main Question at each sitting.[1] The general feeling, however, was against special restrictions being put on the use of supplementaries, for without them starred Questions would be much less effective.

Session	Percentage of Oral Answers followed by a Supplementary
1908	42
1918	51
1928	62
1938/9	70
1945/6	75
1948	85
1958/9	94

Source: Based on a sample count of Hansard.

The claim of the Member asking the original Question to ask a supplementary was by then fairly well recognized. If two or three Members rose as the Minister finished his answer the Speaker always called on the original questioner and, if he did not, the House would let him know.[2] The increase in the number of supplementaries came not from a large number being asked in respect of a few Questions and none in respect of others but from

[1] Select Committee on Public Business, 1931, qs. 605, 850–1.
[2] op. cit., qs. 311–12.

an ever increasing proportion of Questions attracting one supplementary. This is shown in the Table on page 118.

Thus it has become more and more unusual for the Minister's answer not to be followed by a supplementary. In the vast majority of cases the one who asks it is the Member who has asked the main Question. An analysis of 713 Questions reached in 1956–7, showed that 643 attracted supplementaries, the first of these being asked by the original questioners in 566 cases. There is now almost a feeling of anti-climax if, on hearing the Minister's reply, the Member asking the starred Question does not immediately ask a supplementary. Mr. Speaker automatically looks in the direction of the Member as soon as the Minister has read his answer, ready without doubt or hesitation to call the Member's name. This is now a ritual. Fifty years ago it was not so, and even twenty years ago neither Mr. Speaker nor Members presumed it to be an absolute right.

Immediately after the end of the Second World War Mr. Speaker Clifton Brown, spurred on by the large number of starred Questions on the Order Paper, made a special effort to maintain a high rate of answers. When in October 1945, for example, Miss Eleanor Rathbone followed up a Question about the importation of champagne by saying 'Is it not anomalous that a Socialist Government should facilitate the import of this costly luxury at a time when shipping is scarce...' Mr. Speaker intervened to say that she could not have a reply: 'She did not ask a proper Question; she only made an accusation. Questions should be asked to obtain information, and not to make accusations.'[1] When a few days later a Member started a supplementary: 'Does not my right hon. and learned Friend think that, until there is an agreed and economic settlement...' Mr. Speaker refused to allow him to proceed further, saying that the Member 'is asking for an opinion and not for facts. I am always suspicious of a question starting "Does not the hon. Member think...".'[2] On another occasion he rebuked a Member by saying: 'Silly, provocative Questions like that are out of place.'[3] On 24 June 1946 he startled the House by deliberately letting all supplementaries pass. As a result only 40 starred Questions were answered. Immediately after Prayers next day Sir Thomas Moore

[1] H.C. Deb. (1945–6), 415, c. 425.
[2] ibid., c. 882.   [3] ibid., 426, c. 33.

asked: 'On a point of Order. In view of what happened yesterday, may I ask, with deep respect, Mr. Speaker, whether it is your intention that this is to be a Question day, a supplementary day or a "free-for-all"?' Mr. Speaker Clifton Brown replied, 'Surely in vain the net is spread in the sight of any bird.'[1]

In vain indeed, for Members clearly liked supplementaries providing their use was not abused. Increasingly, when confronted at the end of Question time by irate Members whose Questions had not been reached, Mr. Speaker Clifton Brown would repeat that Members could either have 'lots of Questions and very few supplementaries or lots of supplementaries and very few Questions'. Increasingly, it has been accepted that the Member asking the main Question can claim to ask a supplementary. Even when a Minister gives a single answer to a series of starred Questions the claims of the Members who put them are recognized as far as possible. On 24 April 1958,[2] for example, the Financial Secretary to the Treasury gave a single answer to 19 Questions concerned with an imposition of a 5 per cent Purchase Tax on miners' protective clothing. Mr. Speaker allowed a number of supplementaries, but when he then proceeded to call the next Question Labour Members protested that only five of them had been allowed to ask a supplementary. The Speaker's reply did not satisfy the grumblers and Mr. Silverman said: 'The tradition by which the House allows a Minister to answer a number of Questions together has hitherto always been operated in such a way that the effect of answering them together is not to deprive any of the hon. Members who have put Questions on the Order Paper of their rights arising out of their having done so, and one of the customary rights . . . is to ask a supplementary question . . . it has become one of the most useful of the rights of private Members, on a particular issue, and to a particular Minister, for a number of hon. Members to put down Questions in order to have a review of the matter.'

Mr. Speaker Morrison replied: 'If there are perhaps half a dozen Questions, and the Minister answers them together, I always endeavour to call on any hon. Member whose Question has been answered, but when it comes to twenty Questions the matter becomes rather difficult, and the time of the House is

---

[1] H.C. Deb. (1945–6), 424, c. 689–90 and 1029.
[2] H.C. Deb. (1957–8), 586, c. 1142–52.

occupied with repetition. As I said, no hon. Member has a right to ask a supplementary question. It is, I think, Mr. Speaker's duty, if he can, to have due regard for the rights of other hon. Members who have Questions on the Order Paper.' He then refused to allow any further discussion, and went on to the next Question.

Any Member can, with the permission of Mr. Speaker, ask a supplementary, though it is usual to wait until the Member asking the original Question has had his chance. It is not a popular practice, indeed it has been said that asking a supplementary on another Member's Question is the lowest form of Parliamentary activity. Sometimes Members do it to present another point of view, sometimes in the hope of helping the Minister, and sometimes because opportunities of questioning Ministers are so limited.

The use of supplementaries by the Opposition Front Bench is not covered by that last remark. The practice has varied according to the Party in opposition and the political circumstances of the moment. Generally speaking, the more important Opposition front benchers do not put Questions on the Paper. They will, however, sometimes take advantage of a Question put by one of their supporters to pursue the Minister further. An analysis of the first 28 Question times of the Session of 1958/9 showed that Mr. Bevan asked only three starred Questions, but asked 29 supplementaries to Questions put by others, and Dr. Edith Summerskill asked 27 supplementaries and no starred Questions. Almost all Mr. Bevan's supplementaries concerned foreign affairs, and the bulk of Dr. Summerskill's concerned the health services. Altogether 8 per cent of the supplementaries during that period were asked by five members of the Labour Front Bench, who put only five starred Questions.[1]

The bulk of Questions attract only one supplementary. At times the original questioner will get in a second or another Member will add one. Occasionally some Question will arouse a barrage of supplementaries. It is clear, however, that if almost every answer now attracts one supplementary and yet on average there are less than two supplementaries per answer, not many answers can attract a multiplicity of supplementaries. When this

[1] See pp. 217–221 below for a fuller discussion of the use of Questions by the Opposition Front Bench.

does occur, the number of starred Questions dealt with during the time is likely to fall well below average.

INCREASING LENGTH AND COMPLEXITY

Whereas before 1946 the struggle had been to restrain the number of supplementaries, the emphasis in recent years has shifted to dealing with complaints about the length of both supplementaries and Ministerial answers. Complaints about the length of Ministerial answers are by no means new. In the 1870s and 1880s there was a good deal of criticism. Writing in 1882 a Member could say that Ministers 'who have few opportunities of distinction in debate, eagerly seize the opportunity afforded them [by answering Questions] of making brisk little speeches, full of sharp turns of phrase and bantering rebuffs, intended to excite laughter at the expense of their maladroit questioners, who have no right to reply'.[1] Mr. Speaker frowned on the practice, for quite apart from being time consuming, long answers made it more difficult for him to restrain questioners from entering into argument.

As the pressure on a fixed Question time increased there appears to have been an understanding that Questions and answers should be kept as short as possible. The following examples are taken from Hansard for 23 March 1911.[2]

IRISH FISHERIES (DEPREDATIONS OF TRAWLERS)

Mr. Boland asked the Chief Secretary whether, in view of the fact that the spring mackerel fishing will commence in about a week's time, and that the s.s. 'Helga' was unable to protect the whole coast of Ireland from the depredations of steam trawlers fishing outside legal limits, he would arrange to charter two fast-steaming trawlers on a time charter of three months, equipped with a crew of Irish sailors or of Irish Naval Reserve men, in order that the illegal operations of the steam trawlers may be put an end to during the coming season?

Mr. Birrell: The funds at present at the disposal of the Department of Agriculture in Ireland for fisheries would not permit of their carrying out the proposal. With the resources at their command they have succeeded in suppressing illegal trawling to a very great extent, especially since the passing of the Trawling in Prohibited Areas Act.

Mr. Boland. May I ask the right hon. Gentleman whether he is

[1] W. M. Torrens M.P., *Reform of Procedure in Parliament* (1881), p. 33.
[2] H.C. Deb. (1911), 23, c. 589–90 and 612–14.

aware of the steps which have been taken in Scotland to deal with the matter, and whether we in Ireland cannot have the same protection?

Mr. Birrell. I understand that the amount of protection given in Ireland is more satisfactory than that given in Scotland. I am not in a position to say that I can add to the resources of the Board of Agriculture.

Mr. Watt: Is the right hon. Gentleman aware that the protection in Scotland is not satisfactory?

Mr. Birrell: I have said that it is more satisfactory in Ireland than in Scotland.

Mr. Swift MacNeill: Is the right hon. Gentleman aware that we have only one cruiser in Ireland, whereas they have three cruisers in Scotland?

Mr. Birrell: I really do not think that the complaints in Ireland are very great. I quite admit that if the Board had more money at their disposal thay could make it more difficult for the trawlers to act illegally.

Mr. Malcolm: Would the right hon. Gentleman communicate with the Admiralty and see if he could arrange with them?

Mr. Birrell: We have been communicating with the Admiralty.

MINE INSPECTORS

Mr. Webb asked the Home Secretary whether it is necessary that candidates for mining inspectorships should be recommended by Members of Parliament in order to ensure their claims being considered; and, if this be not so, would he inform the House of the nature of the machinery that would be put into motion in the appointment of such inspectors?

Mr. Churchill: I am glad to have this opportunity of saying emphatically that it is not necessary that candidates for mines inspectorships or any Home Office inspectorships should be recommended by Members of Parliament; nor does it in any way advance a candidate's interests to be so recommended unless the recommendation is based on the same kind of personal knowledge of his qualifications for the post as that of a testimonial from any other person. As there is a widespread misapprehension on the point, I am inserting a warning against seeking political or social influence in the printed instructions which are issued to candidates by the Home Office. As regards the latter part of the question, candidates are required to fill in a form of application and forward it with testimonials based on personal knowledge of the candidate to the Private Secretary at the Home Office, from whom copies of the forms and all necessary information can be obtained.

Sir C. Kinloch-Cooke: Is it an open competitive examination?

Mr. Churchill: The conditions are well known.

Mr. Bridgeman: Is a nomination required to enter the examination, and, if so, who gives it?

Mr. Churchill: It has long been considered the proper practice not to judge entirely by examination, but to have some personal knowledge of the candidates. With those intentions the system of nomination has been in vogue for many years by the Secretary of State, but I cannot undertake myself personally the duty of discriminating between the candidates.

Mr. Bridgeman: How is the right hon. Gentleman certain the nominations are fairly and equally distributed?

Mr. Churchill: It is very difficult to know how you make certain of anything in this world, but I am quite certain the desire is to take the best and most suitable candidate, and if I thought there was any chance of any attempt to depart from that on grounds of favour, I should certainly exert my authority against that practice.

Mr. Stuart Wortley: Are we to understand that the nominations are nominations by himself and not by some outside authority?

Mr. Churchill: The nominations are by the Secretary of State, who is to be responsible to Parliament for them, but that does not mean that he necessarily sees every candidate.

Mr. MacNeill: Is the hereditary principle taken into consideration?

Sir C. Kinloch-Cooke: Will the right hon. Gentleman appoint a small committee to consider applications, similar to the Committee he appointed in the case of Factory Inspectorships?

Mr. Churchill: I do not think that that is a question that ought to be asked without notice.

On this day a new Member was sworn in, so that probably only about 45 minutes remained for Questions. Yet 65 starred Questions and 50 supplementaries were dealt with.

Examples of long-winded answers and supplementaries can be found throughout the history of Questions, but on the whole the examples taken from March 1911 give a fair indication of the practice prevailing until comparatively recent years. Nowadays, very few supplementaries are short. Many are barely in Question form. Many are complicated and argumentative and are indeed a series of questions. In some cases they appear to be a flow of words stimulated more by the subject than by the precise wording of the Minister's reply. Equally important, few Ministers now have the courage to ignore provocative supplementaries or to answer them shortly. They are inclined to read from their file, industriously and on occasion laboriously.

Where there are so many examples to choose from it is

invidious to pick on one Member, but an example or two is necessary. On the 27 November 1958, Mr. S. Swingler, having received a 78 word reply from the Under Secretary for Colonial Affairs about the alleged offer of a reward by the Mayor of Nicosia for the capture of the murderer of Mrs. Cutliffe, asked the following supplementary:

'Is not the Under-Secretary of State aware that when I asked him last week what offers of assistance in the discovery of the murderer of Mrs. Cutliffe had been made by Greek Cypriot authorities, he replied, "None"? Is not it clear that that answer was untrue? Cannot the Colonial Office read the *Cyprus Times*, in which the Mayor of Nicosia offered to raise a reward of £5,000, and appealed publicly to any Cypriot who knew anything about the murderer to come forward? Should not the Government have responded to this offer of assistance from a leading Greek Cypriot? Is not the hon. Member aware that the criticism made by Dr. Dervis was that when the Government had been given a description saying it was a fair-haired youth, they indiscriminately rounded up all the dark-haired youths? That is what is said. The fact is that the Mayor made an offer of assistance.'[1]

This contains 151 words. The Minister replied in 124 words. On this occasion the supplementary and the reply must have accounted for about 2 minutes of Question time. Several other supplementaries, each containing about 100 words, were asked at this same sitting. This is not a record nor is it an exceptional experience in recent years.[2]

In general, supplementaries tend to be longer than the original Question. It is most unlikely that any Speaker in the first forty-fifty years of the century would have allowed such lengthy supplementaries, or that Members would have tried to ask them.[3]

The asking and answering of supplementaries precisely are difficult arts possessed by only a minority of Members. The

[1] H.C. Deb. (1958–9), 596, c. 541–2.
[2] Mrs. McLaughlin's supplementary which Mr. Speaker thought to be 'rather on the long side' (supra, p. 4) contained 147 words.
[3] Commenting on the attitude of different Speakers, Earl Winterton has written: 'On more than one occasion Mr. Speaker Clifton Brown ... said that the remedy was in the hands of the House, and apparently the present Speaker [Mr. Speaker Morrison] takes the same view; but both Mr. Speaker Lowther and Mr. Speaker Fitz Roy believed that they had a duty to ensure that a reasonable number of questions were answered each day, and both of them were more strict in preventing lengthy or unnecessary supplementaries than either of their successors have been.' *Orders of the Day* (1953), p. 152.

supplementary has to a large extent been a victim of its popularity. Writers have painted vivid pictures of Ministers being unmasked and deflated and their answers shown to be misleading by the subtle supplementary asked by just the ordinary Member. This was never true of the mass of supplementaries. It was, however, more likely to be true when Members did not feel compelled to ask a supplementary as apparently they do these days. For not all Members are equally capable of the supplementary which goes to the heart of the Minister's answer. Indeed it would appear that most Members now regard the supplementary as an opportunity to say a few words in the House when it is reasonably full, an opportunity which otherwise seldom comes their way.

It is, however, possible to sympathize with the problems which supplementaries set for both Mr. Speaker and the mass of Members. Even though most supplementaries add little or nothing to the original Question and answer, and are only occasionally effective, it is still worth while to allow Members considerable freedom to ask them. When a Member rises to indicate that he wishes to say something it is difficult for the Speaker not to call on him. As Mr. Speaker Lowther said in his Memoirs 'until the question has been put the Speaker (not having the gift of divination) cannot tell whether [it] is a genuine desire for more light or only a cracker intended to cause diversion, disturbance, or dismay'.[1] Mr. Speaker Gully quite often did not allow a Member to say more than a word or so before ruling his attempted supplementary out of order. Once, however, a Speaker decides that he must listen to what the Member has to say before deciding whether or not he is in order most of the damage is done. A Member having been allowed to ask all or most of his supplementary, the Minister may want the chance to reply, otherwise the Question will stand unanswered in the day's record in Hansard. It may even be more time saving to allow the supplementary and the Minister's reply, rather than risk the Member raising a point of order upon his being refused.

[1] Viscount Ullswater, *A Speaker's Commentaries* (1925), vol. ii, p. 27. cf. also his statement to the Select Committee of 1906. 'When you suddenly get a Supplementary Question asked upon a subject with which you are not personally conversant, it is very difficult at a moment's notice to say how far that Question is relevant or not or is permissible or not; so much often turns upon a very small thing, it may be one word or one phrase in the original Question.' q. 26.

As Mr. Speaker Morrison once said: 'Very often if I interrupt a supplementary question because I think it is too long, there is a further expenditure of time.'[1]

In a sense, it is to no-one's direct advantage that there should be fewer and shorter supplementaries. There being only a limited amount of time, it benefits Ministers if Members 'misuse' what time is available. As for the individual Member, it is difficult enough for him to get a starred Question answered at all, and thus get the opportunity to ask a supplementary, so he feels he must take every advantage of the opportunity. If his supplementary is rather long and complex, or if he takes time to thank the Minister for his reply,[2] or to raise a point of order, or to give notice that in view of the unsatisfactory nature of the reply he will raise the matter on the adjournment, he is not being noticeably long winded. He may take up an extra half minute. He is forgetting that since the Balfour changes the output of Question time has depended on Members and Ministers exercising very considerable restraint. Quite a slight departure from that restraint has been sufficient to reduce the output. A few seconds 'lost' here and there is sufficient to reduce the output quite markedly. Indeed, the remarkable thing is not that the House now gets through only about 40–45 starred Questions in about 55 minutes, but that it was once capable of getting through 70–80 in the same time. In 1893 Mr. Gladstone could say that 'the humblest economies of time were not to be despised'. In recent years the House seems to have lost that sense of urgency. It has become reconciled to the fact that not all the starred Questions on the Paper will be reached.

[1] H.C. Deb. (1956–7), 564, c. 916.
[2] In February 1946 Mr. Thurtle called attention to the growing practice of Members thanking Ministers for their answers. He suggested it should be taken for granted that Members are grateful, 'for the good replies which they receive.' Mr. Speaker Clifton Brown's comment was 'anything that saves time is to be commended.' H.C. Deb. (1945–6), 419, c. 1554–5. A few Members still, however, continue the practice. In earlier years when top hats were worn in the House a Member would show his thanks by raising his hat at the end of a Ministerial reply.

CHAPTER 6

THE DEVELOPMENT OF THE ROTA SYSTEM

UP to 1902, Questions were taken in the order in which the Clerk had received the notices from Members. The only exception was Questions to the Prime Minister. Starting as a matter of courtesy to Mr. Gladstone in 1881 when he was aged seventy-two, Questions addressed to the First Lord of the Treasury, the title by which the Prime Minister was then usually addressed, were placed last on the day's list. If a Member was not in his place when his Question was called he had a second or even a third chance when the end of the list was reached. If a Minister was not present, the Questions addressed to him would be called either when he had entered the Chamber or at the end of the list or, in the unusual circumstance of his not being present at all, and nobody having been deputed to answer for him, would be carried over to the next Sitting.

The changes in procedure agreed by the House early in 1902 made it necessary for further thought to be given to the order in which Questions were taken. Precise limits having been fixed to the time during which Questions could be answered orally there was less excuse for the rather happy-go-lucky atmosphere that had prevailed under the old rules. Not only was there the possibility that on occasion the time available would prove insufficient. Now that the Sitting was to start earlier, there was also a danger that Ministers would have even less time to spend in their Departments.

In the words of Mr. Speaker Lowther, 'very often Questions were asked of a Minister who was not present, or who was just coming into the House when the Question happened to be asked, and it caused delay before the Minister could get up to the box. He then went back again, perhaps behind the Speaker's chair, and all that caused delay . . . if [the Minister] has one Question early and another Question halfway down the list, and another three parts of the way down, and another at the end of the list, his attention is taken away by other things. He has to yield his place at the box to other Ministers and it causes considerable loss of time.'[1]

On 2 May 1902, three days before the new Standing Orders were to come into operation, Mr. Balfour proposed to the House that the first fifty starred Questions should, as far as possible, 'be so arranged that those which are addressed to the same Minister shall be grouped together'. He frankly acknowledged that 'this would be convenient to Ministers of hard-worked Departments . . .' but he thought his proposal would be 'to the convenience . . . of Members asking Questions also'. Asked by Mr. Swift MacNeill what he proposed should be done with the questions subsequent to the first fifty, Mr. Balfour replied: 'At the doubtful margin of Questions there may be a little inconvenience to Ministers, but if so, I am afraid I cannot avoid that. It is clear that we must not interfere with the decision of the House.'[2] Mr. Dillon, Mr. James Bryce and Mr. Chaplin gave the proposal their blessing. Thus having rejected the idea that Questions should be arranged according to importance, the House accepted the idea that they should be arranged according to Ministers — but only the first fifty.

Quite shortly after this, though no announcement appears to have been made, the grouping was extended to all starred Questions on the daily list. No doubt this was unobjectionable when the number on the Paper was only a few more than fifty and it was quite clear that all could be answered. Questions to the Prime Minister were still usually grouped at the end of the list and, therefore, were more in danger of not being reached than those addressed to any other Minister.[3] On 7 March 1904, Mr. Swift MacNeill complained that Questions to the Prime Minister were being 'crushed out' and on 24 March, Mr. Speaker Gully said that, in order to comply with what he understood to be the wishes of the House, he had, with the assent of

---

[1] Select Committee on House of Commons (Procedure), 1906, qs. 5 and 28. 'In the old days we used to get through Questions at the rate of, I think, about one a minute; now we do about seven or eight Questions and often more, in five minutes.' q. 27.
[2] Parl Deb. (1902), 107, c. 572. The idea of grouping Questions had been suggested earlier: see, for example, Mr. Renshaw's Notice of Amendment to Mr. Balfour's proposal. Notices of Motions (1902), vol. i, p. 306.
[3] But occasionally they were put at around No. 45 or a little later, followed by one or more Questions to other Ministers.

the Prime Minister, directed that Questions addressed to the Prime Minister should begin not later than No. 51.[1] After further complaints Mr. Balfour made a statement on 27 June. He said that until recently he had thought that if his Questions came on at that number he would always be safe. But Members had become more inquisitive or Ministers' answers had become longer or more supplementaries had been put, and therefore he had been able to answer only half his starred Questions in the time. He would therefore ask the Clerks at the Table to put his Questions at No. 45 which he hoped would be safe.[2]

In the beginning there was no purposeful arrangement of the order in which Ministers were to answer Questions, other than the special position accorded to the Prime Minister. If, for example, the first Question put down by a Member for the Monday was addressed to the Postmaster General, that Minister would be placed first and any other Questions down to him on that day would precede those addressed to other Ministers. If the second Question submitted was addressed to the Chancellor of the Exchequer, his group of Questions would come second that day, and so on. This was an administrative device, obtaining results without anyone having to undertake the responsibility of deciding whose starred Questions should bear the risk of not being reached. There was no attempt to arrange the Departments in order of importance or current interest.

Whilst all starred Questions continued to be answered the order in which Departments appeared hardly mattered. But as the number of starred Questions rose the order became increasingly important. Quite apart from the possibility that there would not be time for the Minister to answer if he were placed late in the list, Members felt freer to ask him supplementaries if he appeared early. On 27 March 1905, on the Motion for the Adjournment, attention was drawn to the fact that at 2.55 several Questions addressed to the Secretaries of State for War and Colonies remained unanswered. One complaint was that sometimes Questions were put down and not reached which were of importance to a matter to be discussed later that day, e.g. the Army Estimates. But more generally the complaint was

---

[1] Parl. Deb. (1902), 131, c. 330 and 132, c. 642.
[2] Parl. Deb. (1902), 136, c. 1265-7.

that important Questions had been left unanswered whilst unimportant ones had been answered.[1] The Members who complained at this time placed great weight on Questions addressed to the War and Colonial Offices. As a result of these and other protests during 1905 a first attempt was made to see that Questions to certain Departmental Ministers came early enough in the list to be certain to be answered. In March 1906 the Speaker said that the Government had now directed that Questions to the Foreign Secretary should come first on Tuesdays and Thursdays, and that Irish Questions would come first on some days and last on others. Colonial Office Questions were put early from time to time.[2]

Notwithstanding the marked increase in the number of starred Questions on the paper during the period 1910–13 there were remarkably few complaints.[3] Indeed, for this and other reasons, it is most difficult to discover how the system operated. The arrangement of Questions is not mentioned in any edition of Erskine May. We have been unable to discover any lists or other official indication of the principles followed by the Clerks at the Table in arranging Questions. By 1914, however, it is quite clear that the order was no longer left to chance and had developed well beyond the first stage of securing prominence for a few important Departments. An analysis of the Order Papers for 1914 shows a high degree of regularity in the daily pattern in which Departments appeared. The Foreign Office appeared first on Monday, Tuesday and Thursday. Thursday was the main day for Irish Questions. The Chief Secretary to the Lord Lieutenant appeared immediately after the Foreign Secretary on that day but was either last or next to the last on the other three days. The War Office and the Chancellor of the Exchequer were very near the top on Tuesdays and Wednesdays, and the Colonial Office on Wednesdays and Thursdays. In contrast, the War Office and the Chancellor of the Exchequer were at the bottom

[1] One day, according to Mr. Swift MacNeill, two starred Questions had resulted in elaborate answers as to whether the public should be admitted between the hours of 3 and 4 p.m. to Hampton Court whilst on the same day the Secretary of State for War was prevented by time from answering some Questions. Parl. Deb. (1904), 143, c. 1309–12.

[2] Select Committee of 1906, qs. 23, 74–5.

[3] Mr. Speaker Lowther, who had been critical of the 1902 changes, said, in evidence to the Select Committee on House of Commons (Procedure), 1914, 'I think, on the whole, that rule works very well.' q. 2962. Mr. Balfour had not heard 'any great expressions of discontent'. q. 1238.

on Mondays and Thursdays, and the Colonial Office was low in the order on Mondays. Questions to the Prime Minister were put every day not later than No. 45.

Also by 1914 the machinery for deciding the order had been settled. In the years immediately after 1902 it would appear that the Clerks at the Table acted on the instructions of the Government. True, Mr. Speaker Gully in March 1904 said that the new arrangement about the order of Questions to the Prime Minister was made 'by my direction' though he added that the Prime Minister had given his assent.[1] But three months later he said 'They (Questions) are not arranged by me . . . I believe it is an arrangement made by Ministers, subject to requests from the other side', and later went on to add 'I can hardly take upon myself to dictate the order in which Questions shall appear on the Paper'.[2] In March 1906 Mr. Speaker Lowther when asked whether he would give an assurance that he was 'in absolute control of Questions' and that he would see that Questions were put down in such a way as to give a fair chance to everyone, replied that the Member 'has endeavoured to invest me with a great many powers which I am certainly not anxious to take upon myself'. He would do his best 'to prevent injustice from being done to any private Member or any member of the Government' and went on to add the significant sentence: 'If any arrangement is come to by the different sections of the House, of course, it is my duty to carry it out.'[3] Two days later when asked by a member of the Select Committee on Procedure whether any principle was adopted in the system of grouping Mr. Speaker Lowther replied: 'I believe the Clerks at the Table take their directions from the Members of the Government and those directions are altered from time to time.'[4] When the suggestion was put to him 'that the power of determining the order of the groups should remain with the guardian of our liberties, the occupant of the Chair' he replied: 'I am not very anxious to undertake it.'[5] In April 1914 Mr. Speaker Lowther said that the order of Questions 'is a matter which is generally arranged between the Whips of the two parties'. He added, however, that he would inquire whether the Questions to the War Office could be

---

[1] Parl. Deb. (1904), 132, c. 642.   [2] Parl. Deb. (1904), 136, c. 1266.
[3] Parl. Deb. (1906), 153, c. 1121.   [4] q. 23.
[5] Select Committee on House of Commons (Procedure), 1914, q. 32.

given a more advanced position.[1] Thus another function was added to those carried out through 'the usual channels'.

Mr. Speaker has tried to maintain that position. In 1920, in reply to a complaint from a Member about the change in the order of Departments, he said: 'The matter does not rest with me. It is a matter of arrangement between the hon. Member and the Patronage Secretary.' (i.e. the Government Chief Whip).[2] A little later in the same year he said apropos of a change in the order: 'I only call out the names. I do not settle the order in which the questions come.'[3] Nevertheless he could not stand aloof if there was a volume of complaint about a particular order or if the wishes of the House were clear. The grouping system was under considerable strain during the early 1920s and the Speaker, while continuing to insist that the determination of the order did not rest with him, was by this time prepared to take a direct interest in the matter.

Parliamentary conditions during the war of 1914–18 were exceptional and need not concern us. The new Parliament elected on 14 December 1918 showed a great increase in the number of starred Questions. The daily averages were 126 in 1919 and 110 in 1920. To make matters worse, there was an increase in the number of supplementaries. There were numerous complaints about Questions to a particular Minister not being reached, and from November 1919 until the end of the session of 1922 even the Prime Minister was put not later than No. 25 on Mondays and Thursdays to make certain he had the time to answer all the Questions addressed to him.

In the absence of measures[4] to bring the number of Questions, starred and supplementary, within the capacity of the time allowed, the only remaining possibility was to organize the order of Questions on the Paper in such a way that the greatest number of Members was satisfied. The principle of grouping of Questions was now well accepted and there was no suggestion of going back to the pre-1902 system of taking Questions strictly in the order that they were handed in by Members. The issue,

[1] H.C. Deb. (1914), 61, c. 1324. [2] H.C. Deb. (1920), 134, c. 1162.
[3] H.C. Deb. (1920), 134, c. 1367.
[4] From 25 October 1916 until the end of the Session (22 December 1916) Question time was extended by 15 minutes. During this period the number of starred Questions increased to a daily average of 146. Part of this increase was, however, due to the growing discontent with the Asquith Government, leading to Mr. Asquith's resignation on 5 December 1916.

therefore, was how best to arrange the order of Ministers. The arrangements which had existed for some years became formalized.

The first list we have been able to discover is dated 14 November 1924. This is a typewritten document which was available to Ministers, the Clerks at the Table, and the Whips, and was hung in the Lobby for Members to see.[1] The list was as follows:

ORDER OF QUESTIONS

Day	Beginning	Not later than No. 45	End
Monday	1. India Office 2. Colonial Office 3. Foreign Office 4. Overseas Trade 5. Ministry of Agriculture 6. Office of Works	1. Prime Minister	1. Board of Education 2. War Office 3. Home Office 4. Chancellor of the Exchequer 5. Secretary to Treasury 6. Ministry of Transport
Tuesday	1. Board of Trade 2. War Office 3. Scottish Office 4. Department of Mines 5. Ministry of Transport 6. Post Office 7. Ministry of Pensions 8. Ministry of Agriculture	1. Prime Minister 2. Chancellor of Exchequer 3. Secretary to the Treasury	1. Foreign Office 2. Ministry of Health 3. Ministry of Labour 4. Office of Works

---

[1] The Order of Questions was first printed in 1929 and copies of the list for 15 November 1929 were circulated to Members. H.C. Deb. (1929–30), 231, c. 2224–5.

See also H.C. Deb. (1929–30), 229, c. 1080, when a Member asked Mr. Speaker whether the Order of Questions 'which hangs in the Lobby, be made available to Members'.

Wednesday	1. Foreign Office 2. Admiralty 3. Ministry of Labour 4. Ministry of Health 5. Attorney General 6. Office of Works	1. Prime Minister	1. Home Office 2. Chancellor of Exchequer 3. Secretary to Treasury 4. Colonial Office
Thursday	1. Ministry of Pensions 2. Home Office 3. Board of Education 4. Air Ministry 5. Chancellor of Exchequer 6. Secretary to Treasury 7. Ministry of Agriculture	1. Prime Minister	1. War Office 2. India Office 3. Foreign Office 4. Admiralty

N.B. Questions to Ministers not mentioned in the Table follow those to the Ministers whose questions are to be placed at the beginning, subject to the condition that the questions to certain Ministers shall begin not later than No. 45.

14th November, 1924.

We call this the second stage, and it must have been reached some years before 1924. A fixed order at each of the four Question times had been agreed for most Departments. Questions were in effect divided each day into four groups: (i) those before the Prime Minister (six to eight 'Beginning' Departments); (ii) the Prime Minister himself (and on Tuesdays the Chancellor of the Exchequer and the Financial Secretary to the Treasury); (iii) the four to six Departments listed as coming at the end; and (iv) any other Department not listed for that day. The 'Beginning' Departments were put first on the Order Paper in the order listed, followed by Departments not on the day's list, i.e. group (iv). If there were less than 45 Questions addressed to the 'Beginning' Departments, the Questions to the fourth group would start before the Prime Minister's Questions. If there were more than forty-five Questions to the first group the

Prime Minister's Questions would be taken at No. 45 (and the Treasury on Tuesdays) and Questions to the 'Beginning' Departments would continue after his. Questions to the fourth group would then follow. At the very end of the Paper would be placed Questions addressed to Departments listed under the heading 'End'. As Questions to these Departments would be reached only after Questions to every other Department had been dealt with, to be listed as an End Department was a warning that such Questions would probably not be reached.

The average daily number of starred Questions fell quite markedly after 1924. In the 1924–5 Session the number was 91, falling to 71 in 1926, 74 in 1927, 67 in 1928 and 68 in 1928–9. Such an average was well within the capacity of the time available on most days, little pressure was put on the system, there were very few complaints and only minor changes needed to be made.[1] In 1929–30, however, the average number rose to ninety-three and there were again complaints in the House.

In June and July 1929, slight changes in the order were made but it was clear that something more radical was necessary. On 18 July[2] there was a long discussion in the House about the difficulties with regard to the Order of Questions. Mr. Neville Chamberlain began by complaining that not one of the forty-three Questions addressed to the Minister of Health had been reached. He asked whether it were not possible to reconsider the arrangements. The Prime Minister (Mr. Ramsay MacDonald) then put in the usual plea for fewer supplementary Questions, and several Members had their own suggestions as to how to ensure that all Questions had a reasonably fair chance of obtaining an answer in the House. Sir W. Brass asked if it would be possible for the first ten Questions, or possibly the first fifteen, to each of the Departments to appear first on the Paper, and for the rest to come after them[2] while Mr. Haycock asked whether it would be possible to arrange that priority should be given to those Members who did not ask three Questions every day. This was plainly an attack on the small number of persistent questioners. Major Colfox had a further suggestion: '... instead of taking a week of four Parliamentary days as the amount of time in this

[1] On 2 March 1925 a list was issued identical to the previous one except that the Air Ministry and the Ministry of Health changed places on Wednesdays and Thursdays. Lists issued on 5 July 1926 and in February 1928 were also identical.
[2] H.C. Deb. (1929–30), 230, c. 626–8.

THE DEVELOPMENT OF THE ROTA SYSTEM

matter we should take a fortnight of eight days and give a Minister priority on one day a fortnight instead of on one day in a week.'[1]

A great deal of discussion must have taken place, for in November 1929 a new list of the Order of Questions was issued with a most significant change. Scottish Members having felt themselves neglected for some years, it was appropriate that the news should be given in reply to a Private Notice Question by Mr. Macpherson. He asked the Government Chief Whip whether any arrangements had been made with regard to the position of Scottish Questions on the Order Paper, and received from Mr. Kennedy the following reply: 'Yes, Sir. It is proposed that on Tuesdays the Lord Privy Seal, the President of the Board of Trade, the Secretary of State for War and the Secretary of State for Scotland shall in turn take first, second, third and fourth places in order of answering questions. The new arrangement will take place from Tuesday next. . . . This arrangement will not affect the existing practice under which the group of Questions addressed to the Prime Minister, the Chancellor of the Exchequer and the Secretary of the Treasury commence at No. 45 on Tuesdays.'[2]

The new list printed and circulated to Members was as follows:

ORDER OF QUESTIONS

Day	Beginning	Not later than No. 45	End
Monday	1. India Office 2. Foreign Office 3. Ministry of Pensions 4. Overseas Trade 5. Ministry of Agriculture 6. Office of Works 7. Attorney General	1. Prime Minister	1. Board of Education 2. War Office 3. Home Office 4. Chancellor of the Exchequer 5. Secretary to Treasury 6. Ministry of Transport

---

[1] A similar suggestion was made to the Select Committee on House of Commons (Procedure), 1906, qs. 19–22.
[2] H.C. Deb. (1929–30), 231, c. 2224.

THE DEVELOPMENT OF THE ROTA SYSTEM

Tuesday to	1. Lord Privy Seal ⎫ Board of Trade ⎬ * War Office ⎭ 4. Scottish Office 5. Department of Mines 6. Post Office 7. Ministry of Pensions	1. Prime Minister 2. Chancellor of the Exchequer 3. Secretary to Treasury	1. Foreign Office 2. Ministry of Health 3. Colonial and Dominions Offices 4. Office of Works
Wednesday	1. Foreign Office 2. Admiralty 3. Colonial and Dominions Offices 4. Air Ministry 5. Ministry of Transport 6. Office of Works	1. Prime Minister	1. Home Office 2. Chancellor of the Exchequer 3. Secretary to Treasury 4. Ministry of Labour
Thursday	1. Ministry of Labour 2. Home Office 3. Board of Education 4. Ministry of Health 5. Chancellor of the Exchequer 6. Secretary to Treasury 7. Ministry of Agriculture	1. Prime Minister	1. War Office 2. India Office 3. Foreign Office 4. Admiralty

N.B. Questions to Ministers not mentioned in the Table follow those to the Ministers whose questions are to be placed at the beginning, subject to the condition that the questions to certain Ministers shall begin not later than No. 45.

---

* On Tuesdays the Lord Privy Seal, Board of Trade, the War Office, and the Scottish Office in turn take the first, second, third, and fourth places in answering questions. Thus on four successive Tuesdays (beginning on Tuesday 19 November) the order changes as follows:

THE DEVELOPMENT OF THE ROTA SYSTEM

1st Week	2nd Week	3rd Week	4th Week
1. Scottish Office	1. War Office	1. Board of Trade	1. Lord Privy Seal
2. Lord Privy Seal	2. Scottish Office	2. War Office	2. Board of Trade
3. Board of Trade	3. Lord Privy Seal	3. Scottish Office	3. War Office
4. War Office	4. Board of Trade	4. Lord Privy Seal	4. Scottish Office

15th November, 1929.

This was the third stage of development. It saw the beginning of the rotation of Departments, or the rota system, but it was rotation confined to a few Departments. At first, as can be seen from the list, the actual rotation was confined to four Departments on one day of the week, Tuesday. But once the principle was established there was little to stand in the way of its extension. One would have expected a certain amount of criticism, favourable or otherwise, of such a change, but in fact there is singularly little recorded comment in the House. From time to time small changes were made in the order of Departments. On 24 June 1930, the four-weekly rota of Departments on Tuesdays was altered, the Dominions Office being substituted for the Lord Privy Seal. On 25 November 1930,[1] the Chief Whip announced that the rota system on Tuesdays would be extended to five Departments by the addition of the Department of Mines, which until then had occupied a fixed position as fifth on that day.

In 1931 the Select Committee on Procedure heard evidence about Questions, including evidence from Mr. Kennedy who, as Government Chief Whip, had introduced the rota system in 1929. Nothing was said, however, either by him or by any members of the Committee, about the smooth working, or otherwise, of the new rota system. Perhaps they took it for granted, but the lack of criticism or proposals for a different system is significant. The big drop in the number of starred Questions after 1930 had greatly eased the situation.

For the next eight years there were very few changes in the Order of Questions and this again reflects the reduced activity at Question time.[2] The same five Departments continued to rotate

[1] H. C. Deb. (1930–1), 245, c. 1097–8.
[2] In 1936 the newly created Minister for the Co-ordination of Defence was put immediately after the Prime Minister on Wednesdays.

on Tuesdays. In 1938 a sharp rise in the number of starred Questions again caused some restiveness.[1] On 1 December 1938, the Leader of the Opposition (Mr. Attlee) asked the Prime Minister whether he could make any statement with regard to the Order of Questions on Wednesdays and Thursdays. Mr. Baldwin's reply, announcing a big extension of the rota system is worth quoting in full:

'The House will be aware that complaints have recently been made with regard to the difficulty of securing oral answers to questions addressed to the Air Ministry and the Ministry of Transport on Wednesdays, and to the Ministry of Health on Thursdays. The order of questions on both these days has been the subject of consultation through the usual channels and the following re-arrangement has been agreed to:

On Wednesdays, it is proposed that the Foreign Office questions should be taken first, as at present, and that the Air Ministry should be brought up to the second place. Then the Admiralty, the Colonial Office and the Ministry of Transport will be taken in rotation, so that each of these Departments occupies the third place once in three weeks.

On Thursdays, it is proposed that the Ministry of Labour should be taken first, as at present, and then the next four Departments, namely the Home Office, the Lord Privy Seal, the Board of Education and the Ministry of Health should be taken in rotation, so that each of these Departments occupies the second place once a month.

Mr. Speaker has been consulted with regard to this arrangement. A copy of this revised order of questions will be circulated to Members, and I would suggest that the new arrangements should take effect next week.

The House will be aware that the questions addressed to certain Departments on Tuesdays have been taken in rotation for some considerable time and this arrangement has, I think, worked satisfactorily. Any re-arrangement of the order of questions must be an experiment, but I hope that the proposal which I have announced will meet the convenience of hon. Members.'[2]

---

[1] One criticism, the difficulty of receiving answers to Foreign Office Questions while the Foreign Secretary, Lord Halifax, was in the House of Lords, was solved fairly easily from the point of view of the rota system by the Prime Minister answering the Questions, but in the position on the Paper usually occupied by the Foreign Secretary, thus keeping Foreign Office Questions and Questions to him as Prime Minister quite separate. This change accordingly had no effect on the order of Questions. A similar arrangement was made when Mr. Ramsay Macdonald was both Prime Minister and Foreign Secretary in 1924. This practice is now followed in other cases of this kind.

[2] H. C. Deb. (1938–9), 342, c. 608.

Thus the rota was extended to Wednesdays and Thursdays but not in quite the same form as already existed on Tuesdays.[1] Only on Mondays did the same Departments appear in the same order every week, probably because this was usually the day when least starred Questions were on the paper, many Members still not having returned from their constituencies. The inevitable next stage was to extend the system to Mondays and to more Departments. This occurred on Tuesday, 9 October 1945.[2]

ORDER OF QUESTIONS

MONDAY	TUESDAY	WEDNESDAY	THURSDAY
1. India Office	1. Fuel & Power	1. Air Ministry	1. National Insurance
2. Foreign Office	2. Labour	2. Civil Aviation	2. Home Office
3. War Transport	3. Scotland	3. Colonies	3. Pensions
4. Supply & Aircraft Production	4. War Office	4. Foreign Office	4. Health
5. Board of Trade	5. Town & Country Planning	5. Admiralty	5. Education
6. Overseas Trade	6. Works	6. Attorney General	6. Post Office
NOT LATER THAN NO. 45	NOT LATER THAN NO. 45	NOT LATER THAN NO. 45	NOT LATER THAN NO. 45
A. Prime Minister	A. Prime Minister	A. Prime Minister	A. Prime Minister
B. Agriculture	B. Treasury	B. Food	B. Labour
C. Dominions	C. Information	C. Board of Trade	C. Treasury

N.B. Questions to Ministers not mentioned in the Table follow those to the last of the Ministers so mentioned subject to the condition that the Questions to certain Ministers shall begin not later than No. 45.

The new arrangements were distinguished from the pre-war list in four ways. First, the rotation of Departments applied to each of the four Question times. Second, six Departments rotated each day over a six-weekly cycle and only the Prime

[1] The arrangements were now becoming so complex that the printed list started to give the order each day for some weeks in advance.
[2] The rota system continued to operate throughout the war years with increasing complexity there being only three sittings each week for most of the time and a number of new Departments had to be fitted in.

Minister and seven Departments had a fixed place. Third, the fixed place allocated to Departments which the House wanted to be sure of questioning was moved from the head of the list and the 'place of honour', as it was sometimes termed, became the one immediately after the Prime Minister's Questions, the place the Treasury had occupied on Tuesdays for many years. Fourth, for the first time the Foreign Office ceased to have a fixed top position; it was not included in the Departments that came immediately after the Prime Minister, even though the Board of Trade and the Ministry of Labour were given a position there as well as in the rota. It was, however, the only Department to appear on the rota list on two days a week.

This was the fourth main stage in the development of the order of Questions. Slight changes were made in the list from time to time, but the final stage, which brought in substantially the present system, did not come about until 21 April 1952. The number of starred Questions reached at each sitting fell markedly after 1950–1 and, therefore, Departments whose Questions followed No. 45, and so could only be reached when the Prime Minister had finished, had less and less chance of being reached. In April 1952, therefore, the distinction between Departments listed before and immediately after the Prime Minister's Questions was abolished. All Departments now took their place on one or other of the daily rota. There being seven Departments listed on Mondays and eight on the other three days, the order on Mondays rotated over a seven-week cycle and on the other three days over an eight-week cycle. Each day Questions were taken in strict order of precedence according to the Order stated. Not later than No. 45 any Questions to the Prime Minister were answered by him. In the time remaining after he had finished Departments were taken up again at the point they had reached before the Prime Minister came on.

The names of the Departments and the order in which they appeared for the first four days of the new system were as follows:

Monday 21st April	Tuesday 22nd April	Wednesday 23rd April	Thursday 24th April
Transport Supply	Housing & Local Government	Air Ministry Civil Aviation Foreign Office	Education Commonwealth Relations

Monday 21st April	Tuesday 22nd April	Wednesday 23rd April	Thursday 24th April
National Insurance	Works	Food	Board of Trade
Fuel & Power	Labour	Defence	Treasury
Attorney General	Scottish	Colonies	Agriculture
Foreign Office	Pensions	Admiralty	Home Office
Food	War Office	Post Office	Labour
	Board of Trade		Health
	Treasury		
Not later than No. 45	Not later than No. 45	Not later than No. 45	Not later than No. 45
Prime Minister	Prime Minister	Prime Minister	Prime Minister

Since that date various changes have taken place to take account of the abolition or creation of Departments and of changes in their topical importance judged by the number of starred Questions addressed to each. The Table Office keep statistics of the number of starred Questions addressed to each Minister each day during the Session. These and the extent of the Members' grumbling give the Government Chief Whip some indication of whether the rota is working reasonably well or whether adjustments are needed.[1] It is now appreciated, however, that no manipulation of the list can secure all Questions being reached and the only major point at issue is whether there is a fair chance of getting at each Minister in turn.

The only significant change has been in the position of the Prime Minister. As the capacity of Question time shrank No. 45 proved not sufficiently early on many occasions to give him time to answer all the Questions addressed to him and indeed sometimes he was not even reached.[2] In either case the Members concerned would usually transfer their unanswered Questions to a subsequent day thus adding to the difficulties on that occasion. The Select Committee on Procedure which reported in February 1959 recommended that 'the Prime Minister's questions be taken at 3.15 p.m. . . . but that . . . except by private notice (they) be limited to Tuesdays and Thursdays, as the 30 minutes

---

[1] In June 1957 Colonial Office Questions were given two days (Tuesday and Thursday) on the rota, the Ministry of Labour reverting to one day. In 1959, following a large number of Questions about unemployment, the Ministry of Labour was again made a 'double turn' Department.

[2] Should there be less than 44 starred Questions to Departments on the Order Paper then of course the Prime Minister's Questions start immediately after the last one. Thus, on 7 April 1959, the Prime Minister's Questions started at No. 36.

each week thus available for his questions will be an increase over the present practice'.[1]

On 8 February 1960, Mr. Butler, as Leader of the House, announced[2] that, instead of accepting the Committee's recommendation, the Government proposed that on Tuesdays and Thursdays Questions to the Prime Minister should begin not later than No. 40, remaining at No. 45 on the other two days. He thought that this would have much the same effect as the Committee's recommendation would be less of a break with the old tradition and could be fitted more easily into the existing procedures. It would also meet the criticisms of those who thought the effect of the Committee's recommendation would be to reduce the time available for questioning other Ministers. Mr. Mitchison who was handling the matter for the Opposition front bench thought this would be a satisfactory arrangement.[3] The new arrangement came into operation on 11 February 1960. The number of Departments on the list for Tuesday and Thursday was not altered.

On Tueday, 18 July 1961, following numerous complaints, the Government adopted the recommendation of the Select Committee. There were 87 starred Questions to other Ministers on the Order Paper for that day and these were listed first in the usual manner. Then, under a new heading '3.15p.m.: Questions to the Prime Minister', there appeared 16 starred Questions numbered Q1, Q2 ... and so on. This is now the practice on Tuesdays and Thursdays.

[1] Report, pp. xxii–xxiii.
[2] Previously (16 December 1959) he had said the Government preferred to make no change, in the hope that the proposed reduction in the maximum daily allowance of starred Questions from three to two would make any change unnecessary. See H.C. Deb. (1959–60), 615, c. 1456–66.
[3] H.C. Deb. (1960–1), 617, c. 144.

CHAPTER 7

THE EFFECT OF THE ROTA SYSTEM

At the beginning of the century it was possible for the same Minister to be questioned in the House day after day, four days a week during the Session. During the South African or Boer war, for example, there were few Question times at which the War Office Ministers[1] were not questioned on the floor of the House. The position in 1959–60 presents a stark contrast. The first Question time of that Session was on Monday, 2 November 1959.[2] The Secretary of State for War was sixth on the rota on Wednesday, 4 November, fifth on the following Wednesday, and fourth on the third Wednesday of the session. At none of these three sittings were his Questions reached even though there were several on the Paper. It was not until Wednesday, 25 November, when he was third on the rota, that Members received any oral answers from this Minister. He was again in action on the following two Wednesdays, but the next time after that was on the 17 February 1960, when he was fourth on the rota and answered one Question. Altogether he was reached on only twelve occasions during the Session.

This is a fair picture of the very limited opportunities offered at present to obtain oral answers from any Minister except the Prime Minister and the six Departments which appear on the rota list for two days each week viz: Foreign Office, Treasury, Colonial Office, Board of Trade, Ministry of Labour and Ministry of Agriculture, Fisheries and Food. Even providing a Department with a double turn each week does not greatly change the picture. For example, in that same Session starred Questions to the Foreign Secretary were first reached on Wednesday, 11 November, and again the following Wednesday, the Department being respectively second and first on the rota list on those two

[1] In addition to the Secretary and the Under Secretary for State, the Financial Secretary also answered Questions at this date.
[2] Previous to that, War Office Questions had been answered orally on 15 July 1959.

days. On Monday, 7 December, though not reached, the Minister answered Questions 83 and 84 after 3.30 p.m. Then came the Christmas recess and the next opportunity was on Wednesday, 27 January, but again he was not reached. On Monday, 1 February, the Minister was reached last and answered 3 Questions. He was not reached on the Wednesday nor on the following Monday. Then from Wednesday, 10 February, to Monday, 7 March, he was reached on six out of the eight occasions he appeared on the rota. This was followed, however, by a period of three weeks when he was reached only once. During the Session of 1959–60 the Foreign Secretary was reached on only nineteen occasions and on some of these he was reached too late for him to answer all his Questions on the Paper.

The startling contrast between Question time now and at the beginning of the century is not due to the introduction of a rota system but to the fact that the time available is no longer adequate. Nevertheless, the order in which Questions are answered orally has an important influence on the way Question time works. Thus if, as in 1901, all Questions were answered in the order in which notice had been given, a Member who particularly wished his Question to be reached would still be trying to get it within the first forty or so on the Order Paper. But he would not, as now, have to worry about whether the Minister concerned was at or near the top of the rota. Thus each of the methods used to achieve 'fairness' at Question time has its effects and characteristics. At the same time, each was designed to meet a particular set of circumstances, the dominant one being the number of Questions likely to remain unanswered at the end of each sitting.

The simplest index of the pressure on Question time is provided by the relationship between two daily averages — the number of starred Questions on the Paper and the number answered. These indicate that until 1910 the time available was usually sufficient. During the four Sessions 1910 to 1913 on average there was an apparent deficiency of say 10–15 a day. In the five Sessions 1919–1924 the average deficiency was about 30 to 40. Then come four Sessions with no apparent deficiency, followed by the Sessions of 1929–30 when it probably averaged 30 per sitting, and of 1930–1 with half that figure. In contrast, though the daily average in the 1950s was between 80 and 90, the marked decrease in the number of starred Questions answered at each sitting created an average daily deficiency of some 40 Questions.

These average figures conceal two changes in the habits of Members which have increased the pressure on Question time. First, the earlier statistics exaggerate the number of Questions actually asked at Question time. It was not unusual at one time for several Members to be absent when called to ask their Questions.[1] Many Members starred their Questions in order to make sure that the answer was forthcoming quickly and on a stated date, and, therefore, to them attendance in the Chamber though courteous, was not an essential part of the process. Thus, though only 60 or 70 Questions might be answered orally, the number on the Paper reached might be No. 100 or thereabouts. Even now, a day seldom passes without two or three Questions not being answered orally because of the absence of one or two Members, but the numbers are far fewer than in the period before 1939 or even immediately after 1945. If a Member wants a quick answer he need not bother about the rota system; he can put down a starred Question with the minimum notice, and, even though the Minister is not on that day's rota or is so low on it as not to be reached, he will receive a written reply. Only those who wish to have a good chance of receiving an oral answer need go to the trouble of putting their Question down for a day on which the Minister is at or near the top of the list. Thus the first 40–50 Questions are now more likely to be purposeful than the first 60–80 were in the period before 1914 and during most of the inter-war years. Members may still be prevented by circumstances beyond their control from attending to ask their Questions and may sometimes for political reasons decide at the last moment not to be present in the Chamber.[2] But now that each Member is limited to two starred Questions each day, even the

[1] Until it was amended in July 1948 the Standing Order governing Questions made provision for a Member to depute another Member to ask a Question for him in the event of his absence from the Chamber. The right was seldom exercised and in practice was only available on those days when time remained for Mr. Speaker to call a second round. When it became impossible to get through the Questions on the Paper the 'second round' fell into disuse and with it the right to ask another Member to deputize at Question time.

[2] Earl Winterton suggested to the Select Committee on Procedure in 1945 that, as a deterrent, a Member who failed to appear to ask his Questions should be required to put them down again but Mr. Speaker Clifton Brown thought it better 'to get him out of the way by letting him have his answer'. qs. 1543–5.

unavoidable absences will not have the same consequences as when the maximum was 3, or 8 as it was prior to 1919.

The second change concerns the spread of Questions during the Session. The high daily averages in certain pre-1914 Sessions conceal quite wide extremes — very large numbers well beyond the capacity of Question time on some days and numbers well within that capacity on other days. Questioning was usually heaviest in the early weeks of the Session and immediately after the recess and serious difficulties in reaching a particular Minister were largely confined to these periods. There is still quite a spread, but the purposeful search for an oral answer now means that Members try to avoid days which already look more than full, judging by the number of Questions of which notice has been given. More important, the capacity of Question time is now so low that on very few days are all the Questions reached. In the Session of 1938–9 up to the outbreak of war, for example, the number on the Paper, after making some allowance for the likely absence of Members, was within the expected or average capacity of Question time at some 20 per cent. of the sittings, whereas during the Session of 1959–60 this could not be anticipated at any sitting.

In the light of such factors as these it is worth looking for a moment at the different systems of ordering Questions tried since the early years of the Balfour reforms. The five main stages as explained in the previous chapter are:

(i) At first a few Departments were picked out for special treatment: in particular, the Foreign Office, Colonial Office, War Office, the Treasury and the Irish Secretary. This arrangement developed during 1906–1914.

(ii) Next, probably starting about 1912–13 but not perfected until later, there developed a fixed order of answering for most Departments for each of the four days.

(iii) From November 1929 until October 1945 there was a mixed system, some Departments rotating over a three to five-weekly cycle, others being taken in a fixed order as in the second period.

(iv) From October 1945 until April 1952 most Departments rotated, but a few were given a fixed favourable place on the daily list.

THE EFFECT OF THE ROTA SYSTEM

(v) Since April 1952 all Departments, great and small, have rotated. As a result the period of the cycle is longer now than at any time previously.

The arrangements in the first stage ensured that whatever the pressure Members could count upon reaching certain Ministers each week, but did not preclude these Ministers from being reached more frequently. The system provided a basic minimum, but for most of the period it was possible to reach most Ministers very frequently, if not day after day.

The second kind of arrangement made tolerably sure that certain Ministers could be reached when they were at the top of the list. It quite frankly recognized, however, that on some days certain Ministers were most unlikely to be reached i.e. those Ministers listed under 'the End'. In 1923, when the number of starred Questions was still quite high, 'Questions addressed to certain Departments which stood low in the order of proceedings were hardly ever reached.'[1] From 1924 to 1929 the daily number of starred Questions was usually well within the capacity of Question time and the order of Questions had therefore only occasional significance. This was still in the period when it was usual for only two or three starred Questions to be on the Paper for each Department. Only occasionally would a Department have to deal with double figures. On Tuesday, 28 April 1925 for example, fifteen Ministers, including the Prime Minister, answered 52 Questions; on the next day ten answered 32 Questions; and on the next, fifteen answered 72 Questions. In these circumstances the order of Questions was largely a reserve against emergencies, not a device to deal with a chronic state of congestion.

The partial transformation of a fixed order into a rotating order, in November 1929, was a recognition that a fixed order could not be relied upon to secure a fair chance of reaching the Departments listed fourth and fifth on Tuesdays. But the fact that the system was not extended until the end of 1938 shows that it was working reasonably well. The Session of 1929–30 was in any case rather exceptional. But in 1938–9 the number of starred Questions on the Paper was well above the capacity of Question time at nearly half the sittings and, in these circum-

[1] Select Committee on Procedure, 1931, Memorandum by the Clerk of the House, p. 443.

stances, it was clear that the House preferred the certainty of rotation rather than the hazards of a fixed order.

A fixed order is acceptable only if Members attach so much importance to questioning a few Ministers that they are prepared to forgo completely, if necessary, the chance of questioning other Ministers. Under the arrangement that obtained during the years after November 1929 the Foreign Secretary, for example, was first on Wednesdays and second on Mondays, and therefore was certain of being reached twice a week, whatever the pressure. Certain other Ministers were also certain to be reached at least once and in some cases twice each week. On the other hand, a Department such as the Ministry of Health, which did not appear among the 'Beginning' Departments on any day, would suffer if the number of Questions addressed to the Departments with a fixed opening place rose sharply.

The fourth stage was an attempt to get the best of both worlds. The system which operated between October 1945 and April 1952 was designed to enable a few Departments to be reached on a regular day (two days in the case of the Treasury) each week whilst the great bulk of the Departments rotated over a seven or eight weekly cycle. So long as about 60 starred Questions were answered each day the Departments with a fixed place were almost certain to be reached. When the capacity of Question time fell to 50, or even to 40 on occasions, then, even if the Prime Minister was reached, the two Departments which came immediately after him were not. In these circumstances it was preferable to have a place on the rota rather than a fixed place which was seldom reached, or, what was almost as bad from the point of view of Members, could not be relied upon to be reached. The situation could have been remedied for the Prime Minister and the two Departments which followed him by lowering his minimum starting point from No. 45 to say No. 35 or No. 30 but only at the expense of all the other Departments.

In the end, therefore, the House preferred to be able to reach every Minister, at however long an interval, to either (*a*) the certainty of reaching a few, reaching the rest being uncertain; or (*b*) the according of a special position to a few picked Departments, which even then did not always guarantee their being reached. The current system still retains a remnant of the special

THE EFFECT OF THE ROTA SYSTEM

position accorded to certain Departments, in that six of them rotate on two days a week, instead of on only one.

It is difficult to make any meaningful comparison between the different methods of ordering Questions. Each system can be judged only in relation to the pressure on or the congestion at Question time at that period. During the years 1902–39 there were many Sessions or parts of Sessions when the time available was sufficient for all the starred Questions to be answered and so the Order of Questions was not a significant factor. It decided the order in which Questions were placed on the Paper and answered, not whether they were answered orally. If these circumstances were to return even the current rota system would work quite differently. For though only seven or eight Departments are listed for each day, Members are not prohibited from putting down a starred Question to any Minister not listed for that day.

The rota is a priority list merely stating the order in which certain Ministers shall answer Questions each day. Should there still be time left after the Ministers listed have dealt with all their Questions, then any Questions remaining, to whichever Ministers they may be addressed, will be called in accordance with the order in which they appear on the Order Paper, which is the order in which notice has been given. It is still possible,[1] particularly on Mondays, to reach a Minister not on the day's rota list.

It is, however, when Question time is under pressure that the different systems come into their own and produce their different effects. It is clear, for example, that, whatever the pressure, the Foreign Secretary would be reached at least once a week during the period 1929–45; whereas under similar circumstances this is not provided for by the present rota system. The remainder of this chapter is devoted therefore to the present working of the arrangements for the order of Questions.

The working of the rota from 1945 onwards can be explained most simply in terms of the chance of a Department being reached. The Sessions of 1945–6 and 1946–7 were abnormal and therefore, we have chosen 1947–8, 1951–2 and 1958–9 as a basis of comparison in the following Table.

[1] So unusual is this, however, that, in the daily statistics kept in the Table Office, Questions to Ministers not appearing on that day's rota list are grouped under the heading 'Wrong Day'.

Session	1947–8	1951–2	1958–9
Number of Question times during the Session	133	118	125
Number of days on which:			
Only one Minister* reached:	0	6	11
2 or less Ministers* reached:	0	21	52
3 or less Ministers* reached:	6	46	77
Prime Minister's Questions not reached:	2	16	17

* Excluding the Prime Minister.

Thus, whereas as late as 1947–8 it was possible for four or more Ministers to be reached at all except 6 of the 133 sittings, this happened on only about a third of the days in 1958–9. There were in fact 11 days in 1958–9 when only one Minister was reached and 52 days when only two were reached.

These statistics understate the increasing difficulty of getting an oral answer from a particular Minister. For the fact that a Minister is reached does not ensure that he has time to answer all the Questions addressed to him. This is true of each of the three years but it affects the second and third years much more than the first. If the Table was confined strictly to Ministers who, when reached, answered all their Questions the general trend over the three years would be greatly emphasized. If further proof is needed of the very marked decline during this period in the number of Questions reached it can be seen in the increase in the number of days on which even the Questions to the Prime Minister were not reached.

The rota system has played a major part in this change. In so far as a Member puts an asterisk against his Question in order to obtain an oral answer he is likely to put his Question down for the day when he has most chance to reach the Minister. Increasingly in recent years finding the right day has become one of the arts of the questioner. If an answer is not urgently required the simplest thing for a Member to do is to put the Question down for answer on the day the particular Minister will next be at the top of the rota. The next best thing is to put it down for a day when the Minister is second or third and to arrange for the Question, should it not be reached, to be deferred to say the same day on the following week.

The regular questioner will know all the tricks of the rota and the rules governing its use. Finding on 31 October 1959 that the Secretary of State for War would not be third on the Wednesday rota until 25 November a Member might well decide to put his Question down for answer on 25 November and not to bother with the preceding Wednesdays. In making this choice he would be faced with a delicate matter of judgement. On Wednesday, 25 November, War Office Questions would be preceded by Questions to the Minister of Labour and to the First Lord of the Admiralty. Would there be so many Questions down for these two Ministers or would the progress be so slow as to make it unlikely that the Secretary of State for War would be reached or have time to answer all the Questions put to him? If there was no hurry for an answer the Member might judge it safer to put his Question down for answer on 2 December, or even, safest of all, for 9 December, when the Minister would be at the top of the list. To have Question No. 1[1] down for answer by the Minister at the top of the day's rota is to make as certain as is humanly possible of getting an oral answer.

Alternatively he could put his Question down for answer on the earliest Wednesday i.e. 4 November, but be on the alert to have it deferred to the following Wednesday as soon as it appeared the Question would be unlikely to be reached. This process he could repeat until the Question was reached. This alternative is troublesome to the Member though the extra time and vigilance may be rewarded by an earlier oral answer. But he runs the risk that even if the Minister is reached the Question may be too low on the Paper to be reached. For though deferred Questions are given precedence over other starred Questions handed in the same day as the Member gives notice of the deferment they rank behind Questions handed in earlier.

Both these devices are being increasingly used. To make certain of receiving an oral answer some Members put down Questions for answer many weeks in advance, thus, in the words of the Select Committee on Procedure of 1959 'pre-empting a favourable place on the order paper'.[2] The Report goes on to say: 'When this practice is carried to extremes, it will be found

[1] The very practised questioner prefers to have No. 3 or 4, when the House is more settled and attentive.
[2] Para. 40. On the 25 January 1960 Mr. Nabarro gave notice of starred Questions to the Chancellor of the Exchequer on 34 days, the last being put down for answer on 7 April 1960.

that the only questions to be reached for oral answer are those which have been down for some time; the more recent questions which are usually of greater topical concern receive written answers.' The Committee thought this practice to be open to abuse and recommended that no more than twenty-one days' notice should be given for any oral Question. The proposal was not accepted and therefore starred Questions can still be put down for answer many weeks ahead. The Select Committee did not comment upon the alternative practice of deferring Questions, which has grown considerably in recent years. A few deferments are for the convenience of Members unable to be present in the Chamber when their Question is called. The great bulk, however, are due to Question time having ended without these particular Questions having been reached.

Both practices have the same general effect. Both increase the number of Questions to each Minister at the top or near the top of the daily rota. This in turn emphasizes the long-term nature of the cycle. If, for example, 50 Questions were to be answered each day by Ministers in order of a stated priority it could well happen that the first five Ministers would each answer 10 Questions. But once Members start to doubt whether the Questions to the fourth and fifth Ministers on the list will be reached a bunching of Questions begins. Instead of 10 Questions each Tuesday to each of five Ministers the bunching might lead to each of the five having to answer 50 Questions one Tuesday in every five. This, in somewhat exaggerated form, is what has been happening to Question time in recent years.

The table on page 155 shows the number of starred Questions addressed to each Minister on the Tuesday rota list during the first seven weeks of the Session of 1958–9; the first Tuesday being 4 November 1958. A new cycle started on 20 January 1959.

The Departments are in the order in which they appeared on the list on 4 November. Each Department appeared at the top in the week corresponding to its order in the list e.g. the Board of Trade was fifth in the list when the cycle started and therefore is first on the fifth Tuesday. The step is drawn under the week each Department was at the top. The most popular day for six of the Departments was when they were at the top and one, the Scottish Office, had the greatest number addressed to it when second

THE EFFECT OF THE ROTA SYSTEM

on the list. If the occasions on which a Department was top are taken together with those when it was second it will be seen that these attracted the most Questions on 12 out of 13[1] occasions.

WEEK Department	1st	2nd	3rd	4th	5th	6th	7th
1 Colonial Office	44	6	4	4	3	13	31
2 Attorney General	—	4	1	1	—	1	6
3 Works	7	8	15	3	—	2	4
4 Scottish Office	9	14	33	26	10	14	15
5 Trade	4	3	5	14	44	4	6
6 Treasury	6	14	13	19	30	46	12
7 Housing & Local Government	3	3	17	20	23	27	46
Prime Minister	8	10	9	7	6	12	15
Other Ministers	11	2	5	4	3	7	5
Total starred Questions on Paper	92	64	102	98	119	126	140
Number answered orally	50	42	46	44	49	42	36

More important is the range of the fluctuation. The 44 starred Questions addressed to the Colonial Secretary when he was top on 4 November 1958 fell to 6, 4, 4 and 3 in the four following weeks and rose to 31 when he became second, on 16 December. Four of the seven Departments attracted over 40 Questions each on their top days with the result that only the top Department was certain of being reached. On 4 November, when 50 Questions were answered orally, the Colonial Secretary answered 40,[2] the Prime Minister 8 and the Minister of Works 2 out of 7. On the first of the other three days, when over 40 Questions were down to the top Minister, only 3 out of 30 Treasury Questions were reached; on the second, the Prime Minister had time to answer only 3 of his 12 Questions and the Department second on the list was not reached; and, on the third occasion, not even the Prime Minister's Questions were reached.

Thus a combination of the rota system and the decreasing

[1] Only 13 because the previous week for the Colonial Office is not included. The only exception, therefore, is the Attorney General, who attracts few Questions.
[2] Four starred Questions addressed to the Colonial Secretary were given written answers presumably because the two Members concerned could not be present to ask their Questions.

capacity of Question time has encouraged the concentration of Questions. The more anxious or uncertain Members have become that their Questions may not be reached, the more they have tried to ensure that they will be reached, and, the more they have taken such action, the more anxious they have had to become. Even if it is not so at present, it may eventually be considered absurd to put seven or eight Departments on each day's rota, just as it became absurd after 1952 to refer to Departments not on the daily list. A time may come when most Ministers will have 'their day' every seven weeks or so and therefore the rota would then need to show only two or three Departments of which the third and possibly even the second on the list would be there only in case by some chance the first Minister had not taken up the whole of the time.

The Select Committee of 1959 considered a proposal that the number of Questions for oral answer by any Minister on any one day should be limited to thirty. They did not recommend this even though they admitted it would result in Departments being reached more frequently. Their objection was that such a limitation would mean that 'answers would be given to the earlier, and therefore generally more stale, questions to the exclusion of the more recent and topical questions'.[1]

This brings us to a further problem created by present circumstances: the increasing difficulty of getting quick answers to topical Questions. There is a considerable element of chance in the speed of securing an oral answer, as can be seen from a comparison of two extreme cases. The War Office appeared at the top of the rota on Wednesday, 9 March 1960. For a Question to appear on the Order Paper for oral answer on that day notice must have been handed to the Table Office not later than 2.30 p.m. on Monday, 7 March. If, therefore, a Member's attention was drawn to some issue during the week-end visit to his constituency he could question the Minister about it three days later — very quickly indeed. If, however, the Member heard about the matter only on the Tuesday or Wednesday, or even on the Monday after 2.30 p.m., the earliest certain opportunity of questioning the Minister would be on Wednesday, 11 May, when he was again top of the rota. This period includes the eleven days of the Easter recess. This example gives a dramatic

[1] Report of Select Committee on Procedure, 1959, para. 41.

idea of the possible extremes of speed and delay. The speed of obtaining an oral answer is governed to a large extent by the chance relationship between the date on which the Member decides there is a need to ask a Question, the Minister's position on the rota at that date and the time needed to give notice. It is not affected by the relative importance or urgency of the Question.

An attempt is made, of course, to avoid such extremes in the case of 'important' Departments. The Foreign Office, Treasury, Colonial Office, Board of Trade, Ministry of Labour and Ministry of Agriculture, Fisheries and Food appear on two days a week and as they do not occupy the same place each day it is possible for a Department to be low down one day and high up on another day in the same week. The delay in receiving oral answers from the Ministers in charge of these Departments is, therefore, less than in the case of the Departments which appear on one day per week.[1] Even so it is not possible to arrange a simple daily cycle of eight Departments on four occasions a week so that six should be certain of being reached once every week. If on one day the Department is at the top and two days later it is at the bottom, the next week will see it at the bottom and next to the bottom, a fortnight later next to the bottom and third from the bottom and so on. For this reason even these 'important' Departments have periods when it is most unlikely they will be reached. Thus on Monday, 14 March 1960, the Foreign Office was at the bottom and on Wednesday, the 16th, it was fifth. As a result the Foreign Secretary answered starred Questions only once between Monday, 7 March, when he was at the top, and Wednesday, 30 March, when he was third.

Not all Questions addressed to these 'important' Departments are 'important', however judged. Some may be trivial in comparison to some of the Questions addressed to Ministers who are on only one daily cycle. Moreover even the general importance of a Department may vary from time to time. A marked rise in the figures of unemployment may suddenly increase the importance of the Ministry of Labour in the eyes of Members; a growth of public interest in road problems has done the same for

[1] According to the Colonial Secretary, the Foreign Secretary in 1956 was able to answer orally 486 of the 898 Questions addressed to him whereas he, who then appeared only once a week, was able to answer only 208 of his 958. H.C. Deb. (1956–7), 569, c. 758.

the Ministry of Transport.[1] The rota is adjusted from time to time to take account of these changes in demand. But it cannot be changed quickly or often. It is not a sensitive instrument for measuring or reflecting the changing moods of the House. It is a fairly blunt instrument which is adjusted only after sustained pressure and experience. The most that can be said is that it is less difficult to get a quick answer from a few Departments than it is from the rest.

The knowledge that a Minister answering Questions on the floor of the House may not again appear in that role for many weeks must account in some part for the rise in the number and the change in character of supplementaries. Mr. Speaker Lowther who in 1906 referred to a Minister having a *'mauvais quart d'heure'* would now talk of him having a *'mauvaise heure'*. It is, in effect, his day, so why should not Members take advantage of this rare opportunity? Equally important has been the effect on the strictness of interpretation given to the test of relevance as applied to supplementaries. At the beginning of the century, indeed even in the 1930s, if a Member's supplementary did not arise clearly and strictly out of the Minister's answer or the original Question, the Minister could ask the Member to put down a further Question, knowing that this probably would mean only a few days delay; or Mr. Speaker might disallow the supplementary with the same kind of timetable in mind. Most Ministers nowadays are in quite a different position. If they reply to a supplementary by saying that they 'want notice of that Question' or 'would the Member put the Question on the Paper' they know that several weeks may elapse before the Member will get his answer. The Speaker must also bear this in mind when considering whether to disallow a supplementary. It may be convenient, on occasion, for a Minister to ask for notice. But the Member concerned, and probably the House, appreciating the delay involved would dislike the Minister who used this answer frequently or without obvious reason.

There is another facet to this matter of relevance. The next best thing to asking the Question on the paper is to use it as the basis for one's supplementary. Let us go back to the example given earlier of the War Office for March 1960. Suppose a Mem-

[1] On 3 February 1960 the first 78 starred Questions were addressed to the Minister of Transport.

ber comes across an issue about which he wishes to ask a Question but is too late to get on the Notice Paper for answer on Wednesday, 9 March. He finds that he is unlikely to get another chance for about two months. He, therefore, if he is experienced, looks at the Questions already down for the Minister on Wednesday, the 9th, in the hope that one of them will be near enough to the matter worrying him to enable him to bring in his Question as a supplementary. The more urgent he regards his Question the less he will be worried about the exact degree of relevance. Indeed it may be to the liking of the Minister and of the House that the Minister should answer the supplementary however distantly it may be related to the original Question.

This desire to take every advantage of the rare occasions when a particular Minister performs at Question time emphasizes the 'bunching' effect. Many of today's supplementaries would, at an earlier period, have appeared as Questions on the Paper. Thus everything conspires to lengthen the time each Minister will have to spend answering Questions on his days, and by lengthening the time, lengthens the interval before his day will come again.

Even so, however much is squeezed out of each Minister's time, it is no help to Members wishing to obtain answers from a Minister low down the rota. Very occasionally, by the ingenuity of his supplementary or the tolerance or ignorance of the Minister replying, a Member may elicit an answer from a Minister on a topic which strictly speaking is the province of a different Department. But the rules do not allow a Member to ask a Minister to answer a supplementary arising out of an answer just given by another Minister.

One aspect of the strict rule of Ministerial responsibility is worth mentioning in this context. From time to time Members put down Questions to the wrong Minister, i.e. the Minister not responsible for dealing with that matter. These first appear on the Notice Paper addressed to that Minister, are then transferred by arrangement between the Departments concerned to the Minister responsible and appear on a subsequent Paper addressed to the proper Minister. Such transfers can be made without the permission of either the Member or the Table Office but it is now normal for the Department to notify the Member and not leave him to get the news by way of the Notice Paper. It is just an application of the general rule that a Question must be addressed to the Minister responsible. A transfer can cause considerable annoyance to a Member in either of two ways. On the one hand he may have put his Question to a particular Minister because he knew it was that Minister's turn to answer Questions. The Minister to whom the Question is transferred may not be high on the rota for several weeks. The choice may have been 'a try on' or a genuine mistake: the Member will still be annoyed. On the other hand, the transfer may cause his Question to miss the appearance at Question time of the appropriate Minister. For example, let us assume that on Monday morning, 7 March 1960, a Member put down a starred Question to the Colonial Secretary about, say Colonial troops, for answering on Thursday when he is top of the list. The Question reaches the Department on Tuesday's Notice Paper. The Colonial Office realizes that it should be addressed to the Secretary of State for War, arranges the transfer and notifies the Member. However quickly they do this it will be too late for the Member to switch the Question from Thursday, 10 March, to Wednesday, 9 March, (when the Secretary of State for War will be top of the list). The following Wednesday the Secretary of State will have dropped to the bottom of the list and will certainly not be reached; so all the Member can do if he particularly wants an oral answer is to defer the Question for about a month, by which time there would be some chance of it being reached. Yet if the Member had realized when he first put down the Question on Monday morning that he ought to address it to the Secretary of State for War he could have put it down for the Wednesday when that Department was top of the list. In such a case the Member is likely to feel annoyed and frustrated, and is unlikely to be soothed by being told that it was his own fault for putting the Question to the wrong Minister. Occasionally it may not be obvious that one Minister rather than another is responsible. There again, the annoyance is the greater nowadays in that the consequential delay in getting an oral answer may be so much the greater.

As we have already seen many matters can be dealt with more quickly and adequately by way of correspondence, interview or even by a written answer. If it is information that a Member requires or some explanation to give to a constituent any of these methods is suitable. If, however, he wishes to question the Minister in the House and regards the matter as being too urgent to wait until the Minister is high enough on the rota to be reached, four possibilities are open to him. None of these offers very much opportunity, but all are used from time to time.

The first possibility is to obtain Mr. Speaker's permission to ask a Question by Private Notice. One might expect that the number of such Questions would have risen steeply with the increase in the length of time it takes to receive an oral answer to a Question on the paper. This has not been so. During the Session of 1959–60 only forty Questions of this type were allowed.

Mr. Speaker takes a very strict view of the rules governing Private Notice Questions. The Question must satisfy the definition in the Standing Order by being 'of an urgent character and relate either to a matter of public importance or to the arrangement of business'. He does not regard the difference between oral and written answers as being significant for this purpose. Thus he will allow a Private Notice Question only if he thinks the matter urgent and important enough to warrant an answer more quickly than could be provided by putting the Question immediately on the paper, unstarred, in other words as requiring an answer more quickly than within three or four days. It is, of course, very difficult for a Member to prove that this is necessary.[1] Somewhat greater latitude is given to the Leader of the Opposition to proceed by way of a Private Notice Question but even he is bound by the Standing Order. The attitude of Mr. Speaker towards the use of Private Notice Questions has not been affected by the pressure on Question time, and there have been few complaints against his judgement.

The second possibility is that the Minister may agree voluntarily to answer the Question at the end of Question time. If so, Mr. Speaker having already been informed, the Minister will rise and say: 'With permission Sir, I will answer Question No. . . .' The phrase 'with permission' is purely a matter of form for no permission, neither of the Speaker nor of the House,

[1] Of the 40 Private Notice Questions allowed during the Session of 1959–60 more than half were asked by Labour front benchers and most of the others were asked by back benchers about 'disasters' affecting their constituencies. On 9 February 1960 Mr. Speaker allowed a Private Notice Question about a railway accident which had occurred in the Member's constituency the previous day. On 11 February 1960 he allowed two Private Notice Questions about a threatened railway strike but refused to accept an Urgency Adjournment on the same subject.

is required. The Question may be from the very end of the day's list or may be the next to be answered had not 3.30 p.m. intervened. Ministers very seldom excercise this right. If they were to do so frequently it would be in effect a regular extension of Question time. Sometimes, however, it is in the interest of the Minister as well as of the Member that a starred Question on the Paper should be answered quickly to kill a rumour, to refute an allegation or to remove a misunderstanding. Occasionally a Minister will answer at the end of Question time either because his answer is very long or is in the form of a statement or because he feels that Members should have rather more time to ask supplementaries than can be provided during Question time. During the Session 1959–60 only 43 out of 10,000 Questions were answered in this way and 15 of these concerned one issue, the report that German forces were to be trained in Spain.

There is the third possibility that the Prime Minister may be willing to answer the Question. Notwithstanding the introduction of a seven or eight week rota system for all Departments the Prime Minister has continued to appear on the list each day. At first glance, therefore, there exists a very big difference between the accessibility of the Prime Minister and of any other Minister, even that of the Foreign Secretary and the Chancellor of the Exchequer. It might be thought that the number of starred Questions addressed to the Prime Minister would have risen markedly in recent years because Members, finding it difficult to get quick oral answers from other Ministers, would increasingly have tried to get the Prime Minister to answer them. This has not been so. In the session of 1905, for example, some 426 Questions were addressed to the Prime Minister as against 476 in 1945–6. Since that Session the number of starred Questions addressed to the Prime Minister has fluctuated quite markedly from as low as about three per week in 1953–4 to about 15 per week during 1958–9. There are two reasons why the rota system has not resulted in more Questions to the Prime Minister.

On the one hand the Prime Minister is not head of an executive Department nor does he exercise much, if any, statutory power. Strictly speaking, therefore, only a very limited kind of Question can be addressed to him. For example, it is customary for him to handle questions concerned with the machinery of government, e.g. about the establishment of a new Department or the functions of a particular Minister; about the setting up of a Royal Commission or other general government enquiry and about any matter of importance which does not fall within the responsibilities of any one of the executive Departments. Anything beyond this is very much at the discretion of the Prime Minister. There are, however, two fields of activity about which most Prime Ministers will answer some Questions — foreign affairs and defence. Normally even in these fields he will not answer Questions which clearly fall within the duties of the Departmental Minister. But he is likely to answer where he has been personally involved, for example, in discussions with Commonwealth Countries, the President of the United States or the Heads of other Countries, or where a major issue of general Government policy is in question.

On the other hand, the decline in the capacity of Question time has affected the chance of reaching the Prime Minister more than it has any other Minister. At one time Prime Ministers were prepared to answer Questions on any of the four days, and before 1939 there are even examples of their answering orally on Fridays. In deference to Mr. Churchill after his illness in June 1953 the House accepted the arrangement that normally he would attend to answer Questions only on Tuesdays and Thursdays, an arrangement continued by Mr. Eden and Mr. Macmillan without the same reason. Questions can still be put down to the Prime Minister for answer on Mondays and Wednesdays but if they are reached are normally answered by the Leader of the House, who prefaces his answer by the phrase 'I have been asked to reply'. The separation of the functions of Prime Minister and of Leader of the House in recent years is one justification for this practice. Even when starred Questions to the Prime Minister came on not later than No. 40 on Tuesdays and Thursdays Members could never be certain that this number would be reached, or that if the Prime Minister were reached he would have time to answer all the Questions addressed to him. Since 18 July 1961 a quarter of an hour each Tuesday and Thursday has been available but this does not always prove sufficient.

The fourth and final possibility open to Members arises when a Ministerial statement is made at the end of Question time. (The term can also be applied to long Ministerial answers made during that time but as these add nothing to the time available they can be ignored.) Occasionally a statement is made in response to a Private Notice Question and is subject to the same strict rules. Each Thursday at the end of Question time the Leader of the House makes a statement about the Business of the House for the coming week and this provides back benchers with an opportunity to call attention to matters they think should be debated or to ask about the progress or prospects of particular items of legislation. Some of the starred Questions answered after 3.30 p.m. also take the form of statements, for the Minister, when the Question is reached, asks the Member to await the statement which he will be making at the end of Questions. There remains the Ministerial statement proper, i.e. an announcement about an important matter which a Minister voluntarily chooses to make at the end of Questions (or at 11.00 a.m. on Fridays). Examples are the reports the Prime Minister sometimes makes after a tour abroad and the annual announcement by the Minister of Agriculture, Fisheries and Food about the outcome of the review of farm prices and subsidies. During the Session of 1959–60 Ministers made forty-three voluntary statements of which more than half were concerned with Commonwealth or Foreign Affairs.

It will be seen that though three of the four possibilities, namely Private Notice Questions, answers to starred Questions after 3.30 p.m. and spontaneous Ministerial statements, add to the time available for questioning Ministers, they are very restricted in their use.[1] Moreover, they are more likely to be available for matters of concern to the House as a whole, not for the ordinary constituency Question or matters of similarly limited interest.[2]

The only other possibilities open to the private Member lie well outside Question time. There may be, for example, a convenient debate in which he may raise his point. There is also the

[1] Private Notice Questions are entirely under the control of Mr. Speaker. The other two devices are entirely at the Government's discretion and as they delay the start of Public Business they are co-ordinated and controlled through the Prime Minister's Office. Nevertheless on occasion the commencement of Public Business may be delayed by as much as half an hour.

[2] During the height of the Suez affair (November–December 1956), the bulk of the questioning of the Prime Minister and Foreign Secretary, some of it very spirited, took place on statements made by them at the end of Question time or on some occasion specially arranged. Other Ministers also used this device. The Foreign Secretary was reached on only 3 occasions during Question time, but answered several Questions at the end of Question time.

half-hour devoted to the Adjournment Motion at the end of each sitting. Usually a Member will attempt to raise a matter on the daily Adjournment only after he has failed to receive a satisfactory answer at Question time. But there is no need for him to wait for this. As, however, the right to raise a matter in this way is balloted for and arranged at fortnightly intervals and as there are usually twice as many Members wanting to exercise this right as there are days available, he is likely to have less chance of raising a matter in this way than by way of a starred Question.[1]

In comparing the working of Question time in the 1950s with most of the inter-war years two points are worth noticing. First, catching a Minister for an oral answer has now become a complicated operation requiring not merely a skilled knowledge of the rota system but also a real determination to succeed. On 16 December 1959, for example, Mr. Norman Dodds, an experienced questioner, put down three starred Questions for answer by the Secretary of State for War on 2 March 1960 concerned with the sale of surplus Army boots.[2] However, on 9 February he had to defer one of the Questions owing to the lowering of the daily maximum from 3 to 2. Because of this long notice his Questions were top of the War Office group on 2 March and, as the Department was second on the rota for that day, both were reached. The third appeared as Question No. 1 on 9 March and was answered. On 7 March he had followed up with a starred Question for answer on 16 March but as by then the War Office was at the bottom of the rota, it was not reached and Mr. Dodds, therefore, deferred his Question for a fortnight. On 29 March he deferred it for a further week when it appeared as No. 49, then deferring it for another week, only for it to become No. 56 owing to a barrage of Questions addressed to the Minister of Labour. Only 41 Questions were answered and Mr. Dodds was content with a written answer on this occasion. On 13 May 1960 he secured one of the places on the Adjournment before the Whitsuntide Recess when he made a good deal of use of the Ministerial answers. The merits of the particular issue do not affect the matter. The fact is that the Member had to book dates a long way ahead and alter them as soon as he found out that his Questions

---

[1] See chapter 10 for further explanation and discussion of Adjournment Motions.
[2] They were part of some 20 Questions asked over a longish period by Mr. Dodds, following criticisms of the War Office by the Public Accounts Committee.

were unlikely to be reached. As this Member had a number of matters being dealt with in this manner during this period it will be seen that considerable effort and planning were demanded of him. A Member not so attracted by the device of the starred Question, or less persistent, or not prepared to devote so much time to the matter would probably have been deterred from making the effort at all.

A second reflection on the present state of Question time is how much easier it now is for Ministers and for the Civil Service. A substantial number of Questions still receive an oral answer within a week of notice being given. But an increasing proportion remains on the Notice Paper much longer than this. Moreover there is very much less chance of a quick follow up. It can still happen, particularly in the case of Ministers who appear on the rota for two days each week, but quite often an unsatisfactory oral answer cannot be followed up by a further starred Question for six or seven weeks. Nowadays therefore, a Minister has much more time to deal with the matter and even settle it before the next Question is due to be answered. Question time is much more comfortable and much less exacting for Ministers and less spontaneous and exciting for Members.

CHAPTER 8

ANSWERABILITY, UBIQUITY AND PUBLICITY

THREE aspects or features of Questions must be borne in mind when discussing the significance of this form of Parliamentary procedure and the role it plays in the lives of Members, Ministers and the Civil Service. These are: the dependence of Questions on the concept and practice of the accountability and answerability of Ministers; the great range and volume of Questions compared with other forms of procedure; and the Press and other publicity which they attract.

MINISTERIAL ANSWERABILITY

The doctrine of individual Ministerial responsibility is one of the basic features of the British Constitution. In its widest and simplest form it means that some Minister must accept responsibility for every action of the Government. Usually this means the Minister who approved the action, or whose Department performed it or who had the power to perform it. In some cases the Prime Minister may himself have to accept responsibility. Ministerial responsibility is a standard test applied to all Questions before they are accepted for inclusion in the Notice Paper. According to Erskine May, Questions addressed to Ministers must relate 'to the public affairs with which they are officially connected, to proceedings pending in Parliament, or to any matter of administration for which they are responsible'.[1] Mr. Speaker Clifton Brown once said 'A Question is not in Order if it does not involve Ministerial responsibility'.[2]

Ministerial responsibility is not of course peculiar to Questions. It is also very much present in the Debates which occupy so large a part of the time of the House. Thus if the Government are being criticized for their inadequate road construction programme the Minister of Transport will handle the Debate and make the

[1] Sixteenth edition (1957), p. 356. [2] H.C. Deb. (1947–8), 446, c. 1816.

main statement on the Government side. Some of the rules governing speeches in the House are similar to those applied to Questions. In the case of Debates,[1] however, the main criterion governing admissibility is not Ministerial responsibility but whether the contents of a speech are relevant to the subject under debate. If the subject is the present state of the nationalized coal industry, Members may refer either directly or obliquely to matters which quite clearly are not within the jurisdiction of the Minister, e.g. to the appointment of a manager at a particular pit. The Member may not even be implying that the Minister is responsible, but merely be developing his general argument. Had he tried to deal with some of these matters by way of Questions they would probably not have been allowed on the Paper. Thus had he tried to address a Question to the Minister of Power as to why the appointment of a particular mine manager had been made he would have been told by the Table Office that this was the responsibility of the National Coal Board and not of the Minister.

In a sense, however, the strict application of the test of Ministerial responsibility makes things more, rather than less, difficult for the Minister. A Question places special obligations on the person to whom it is addressed. In the case of speeches made during a day's Debate, a large number of matters may be mentioned by Members with which the Minister who replies will usually make some show of trying to deal. But unless a senior Opposition leader has formally asked the Minister to deal with a specific point, or unless the same query has been raised by several speakers, the responder has a wide latitude in the manner in which he deals with criticisms and queries. He can use such time-honoured phrases as 'A large number of matters have been raised in this important Debate and though I will do my best to deal with as many as possible in the time remaining to me, I am sure that hon. Members will excuse me if I fail to deal with everything'. Or on a particular issue he may say some such words as 'My honourable Friend, the Member for X, raises a most interesting point which I only wish I had time to go into with the care and attention that it so obviously deserves'. Some of this is 'waffle' but a good deal is what a debating speech must

[1] Except in the case of Debates on the half-hour Adjournment, when the matter raised must be within the responsibility of the Minister asked to reply.

be. Members talk in roughly the same way — they develop an argument, they grumble, they praise, they criticize, they comment and they give the House information drawn from their experience or varied reading. They are not asking Ministers a series of precisely worded questions and they do not expect a series of precisely worded answers.

A Minister cannot handle a Question on the Paper in this way He and all other Members have had several days' notice of the Question. The more precisely it is worded the more difficult it is for a Minister to evade giving a precise answer, for it will be clear to all, much clearer certainly than in any Debate, that the Minister has not quite answered the Question. Ministers and their Civil Service advisers are quite clever in drafting answers in such a way as to appear to be answering the Question openly and fully, but without, however, giving everything away. Even so, the limits of clever drafting are quite narrow, if the Question is carefully framed. Moreover, in the case of an oral answer there is always the possibility of a supplementary to elicit the half-concealed information or to reveal the unsatisfactory nature of the reply.

Thus, whereas Ministers are guarded as far as possible against having Questions addressed to them about matters for which they are not responsible, once a Question has passed that test it is difficult for the Minister to avoid his responsibility. The rules governing Questions do not compel a Minister to reply and if he were to refuse the Speaker could not exercise any control over him.[1] But, unless the refusal was based on one or other of the well-accepted reasons, the House would not be at all happy about his attitude and would draw its own conclusions. Even a refusal based on the disclosure of the information being 'contrary to the national interest' has to be used most sparingly.

With the increasing powers of the central government and the current public attitude towards government activity, the range of Ministerial responsibility can be very wide indeed. At a minimum it includes every official act of the Minister, of his junior Ministers, and of all his civil servants. At this point, rather than get involved in any controversy about the exact meaning to be attached to the phrase 'responsible to Parliament', we prefer to use the word answerable. Any decision or act of a Department

[1] Many of the types of Questions at present refused by the Table are based on earlier refusals of Ministers to answer such types.

can be questioned and the Minister must answer, even if the decision or act was taken without his knowledge, and irrespective of whether it concerns some administrative detail, e.g. the rent charged by the Post Office for houses they own, or some major matter of policy, e.g. action taken by the British representative at the United Nations.

But Ministers are answerable for much more than decisions taken by or the actions of their Departments. In so far as they possess powers to do something, they can be asked why they have not exercised a particular power or whether they will exercise it in a particular way. A fuller explanation of the meaning given to Ministerial responsibility by Speakers' rulings and parliamentary usage is given in Appendix II. Here it is merely necessary to say that the experienced questioner can bring a very great deal under this heading, either by clever drafting or by the subsequent supplementaries.

VOLUME AND UBIQUITY

Each Session the House meets on some 160 days and spends about 1200 hours debating different issues. In contrast, it spends about 100–120 hours on Question time. At first glance therefore, it would appear that Questions play a much less significant part in the lives of Departments than does Public Business. In general this is not so, and for several reasons. The first is perhaps a statistical sleight of hand. Question time is not, of course, the limit of Questions. In addition to those which receive an oral answer there are the large number which, failing to be reached during Question time, are given a written answer. There are also the unstarred Questions. A rough indication of the relative volume of Questions and Debates can be obtained by comparing their relative bulk in the pages of Hansard. During the Session of 1957–8, for example, the Hansard for the House of Commons contained 28,459 columns of which 3,994 were taken up with oral Questions and answers and 2,583 with Questions which received a written answer. Altogether nearly a quarter of the space was devoted to Questions, a much higher proportion than might be expected in view of the limited time devoted to oral answers.[1]

The second reason is more significant. Most Departments

[1] The fact that starred Questions are printed in full, but not read out in the House, accounts for some of this.

have only intermittent direct concern with the activities of the House during Public Business. A high proportion of this Business is taken up with the discussion of legislation. During the Session of 1957–8, 83 of the 156 days were spent in this way. The Treasury was involved in a quarter to a third of these days and the Ministers concerned with local government, agriculture and coal had major measures to handle. But, apart from the Treasury, legislation is but an intermittent activity for most Departments. The Foreign Office, Post Office, Colonial Office, the Commonwealth Relations Office, and the three Service Departments seldom promote major legislation. Even on the rare occasions when a Department has a major Bill before the House only a limited side of the Department may be directly concerned, for the Bill is unlikely to bear on the whole range of its activities.

The other major element in Public Business is the discussion of Motions moved usually by the Government, but sometimes by the Opposition and in any case usually by agreement between the two Front Benches. On some occasions, e.g. during the six days devoted to the discussion of the Queen's Speech, any aspect of governmental activity may be raised. At other times, for example, on one of the 26 days devoted to the Committee of Supply, the activities of a particular Department may be discussed for six or seven hours, but not all Departments are discussed each Session on these occasions. For the rest there are the big set Debates on foreign, colonial or economic policy or some other major interest of the House. During times of strong political controversy, e.g. the Suez affair, the Department primarily concerned may be the subject of several major Debates within a short period. But on the whole, the affairs of most Departments are subject only to intermittent debate and their Ministers will be in action on only half a dozen or less occasions each Session. Moreover, as we have already seen, Debates are less precise than Questions and though they can wander over a great deal of ground, not every point raised in them need be dealt with by the Minister. Repetition, irrelevance or sheer verbosity reduce the effective volume of Debates more than they do that of Questions. On the other hand, it is possible to develop a sustained and telling argument in the course of a speech in a way made quite impossible by the asking of Questions, however clever the supplementaries. But this is more likely to concern the general policy of the Department or some single aspect of its work, and not touch on all its diverse activities.

In contrast to the Departments' intermittent concern with Public Business, Questions are there for answering every week for whether or not the Minister is reached, answers have to be prepared in the Department. Questions, starred or unstarred, come in a steady stream and in the major Departments there are very few days during the Parliamentary Session when |the answer to at least one Question is not being prepared.

In recent years some Departments have had to handle a thousand or more Questions, starred and unstarred, each year. The Colonial Office, Foreign Office, Treasury, and the Board of Trade have had to prepare answers for some 20 to 30 starred Questions a week during a Session lasting some 40 weeks. These are, however, Departments which also bulk large in Public Business. Agriculture, Housing and Local Government, Transport, Scottish Office, Labour and Health have not been far behind in the number of Questions, indeed in the 1958–9 Session the Ministry of Transport averaged some 30 Questions a week. Even the Post Office has had to answer about 400 Questions a year in recent years. This desire for information and answers bubbles up continuously and spontaneously. No Cabinet decision is needed, as it is with a Bill initiated by a Department; no getting together of the usual channels is needed, as it is with most of the Motions discussed in the House; all that is needed is a single Member to scribble his Question on any piece of paper, usually a sheet of House of Commons notepaper, and hand it in at the Table Office. Nothing which the Department does, nothing for which some responsibility can be attached to its Minister, can be certain of escaping attention. No other form of Parliamentary activity presents a Department with such a volume and variety of contacts with Members. If Members' correspondence with the Department is also included as part of the same phenomenon the volume and variety are increased manifold.

PUBLICITY

Even if Questions were given only the same proportion of space in the Press as they occupy in Hansard it would be quite a large amount. As it is they receive more.

Questions provide a continuous supply of news stories. The House may have spent six or seven hours debating some Bill, of interest only to those closely concerned with the subject matter. A few of the dailies which give a deal of space to Parliament will report these proceedings, but even these, with the possible exception of *The Times*, will give much less space to such a day than they would to a Debate on some major topical issue, e.g. relations with Russia. On that same day, some eighty starred Questions will have been answered, either orally or in writing. These will have covered a wide variety of subjects, and there will always be two or three concerned with topical issues. Every day there is something for all tastes.

Questions have several special advantages to the Press Gallery correspondents[1] in search of news and stories. First, the advance notice they receive is fairly precise, it does not just indicate a field of broad interest as do most Notices of Motions. The journalist, therefore, has time to do any necessary preliminary work. The Gallery correspondents are supplied with the Order and Notice Papers on which all Questions are listed. They can run their eye quickly through these lists and spot any which look interesting and likely to be news. In making their choice they will have clearly in mind the needs and policies of the newspapers they serve and the topicality of the matter. If they 'smell' a good story, they may get further information from the Member in whose name the Question stands on the Paper. They may even have a word with the Minister or one of his officials. Now and again the Editor may put a news reporter on to the matter to deal with aspects outside the sphere of his Gallery correspondent. In many cases all this can be done before the Question is answered and in preparation for it. Similar arrangements may be made for a Debate on a major subject, for the main business of the House is always announced on Thursday for the following week and the Monday afterwards. But this takes us back to the point made earlier: the subject of the Debate announced may or may not be of general news value to the mass of the press.

The advance notice of Questions may in itself provide a short newspaper paragraph. On occasions a paper will contain the news that such and such a Question has been put down for an-

---

[1] The nominal strength of the Parliamentary Press Gallery is 300 home and about 120 overseas correspondents.

swer two or three days hence. Sometimes it will mention the name of the Member, e.g. 'Mr. Fenner Brockway, the Labour Member for Eton and Slough is to ask the Colonial Secretary on Tuesday why . . .'; sometimes only the Minister will be named, e.g. 'On Wednesday the Foreign Secretary is to be asked about . . .'.

Second, Questions are answered at a very convenient time for the great mass of newspapers. The evening newspapers concentrate on Question time as their main source of Parliamentary 'copy'. The main edition of the evening papers in London and in other large towns is usually on sale by about 4 p.m., in good time to cope with the demands of the homeward-travelling public during the evening rush hour. Questions answered each day are therefore the only ones that can reach the newspapers in time. It is a tribute to the speed of the Press and a somewhat uncanny experience to come out of the Visitors' Gallery shortly after the end of Question time to buy a London evening paper and find already in print a Question and Answer, possibly even a newsworthy supplementary or exchange between Member and Minister, which one had listened to only an hour ago.

The deadline for the first edition of the morning newspapers is usually about 7.30–8 p.m. so far as Gallery correspondents are concerned. The first editions of the main dailies printed in London and Manchester are circulated in the areas remote from the newspaper's head office or source of distribution, e.g. in parts of Wales for a London newspaper. The earlier the correspondent can 'phone in his copy, consistent with not missing some important news, the better so far as the Editor is concerned. This means that the important Parliamentary news for the first edition is likely to come from Question time, Ministerial Statements (if any) and the opening Government and Opposition speeches in the Debate. These will be in time enough for even the main editions of most dailies. In passing, it is worth noticing that had Questions originally been placed much later in the daily sitting, it is very possible that they would not have developed to their present popularity. Mr. Balfour and his advisers knew what they were doing when they suggested transferring them to 7.15 p.m. or 9 p.m. or even later.

The third attraction of Questions and their replies is that they provide copy in a very convenient form. No newspaper has enough space to reproduce Members' speeches verbatim. Few if any readers would wish their favourite paper to read like a daily Hansard. All speeches, except a few leading ones on rare occasions, need to be summarized. Just how much depends on the newspaper. The amount of cutting will vary according to the importance of the speaker but nowadays most speeches obtain only a few lines of space. A Ministerial speech may last for forty or so minutes, a back bencher's for twenty or so. Sometimes the essence of the argument on some major point made in the speech can be conveyed in two or three sentences. But few speeches lend themselves readily to this treatment — they are either too closely knit or too woolly. In contrast, Question and Answer are succinct and ready-made for publication. Moreover, it is not necessary to publish the preceding argument in order to understand the answer. If the Chancellor of the Exchequer is asked whether he will introduce decimal coinage and answers, 'No Sir', he may be saying no more about this particular subject than he would have done during the course of a two-day Debate on, say, European economic integration. During such a Debate, however, this may be but one among twenty or thirty points embedded in a variety of speeches. It will have to be dug out and reconstructed by the Gallery correspondent from the proceedings of several hours Debate. When a Question is put down, none of this work needs to be done. The issue and the reply are clearly set out and both are usually quickly available.

In the room set aside for the use of the Press Gallery is a Question tray for each Department. A copy of every answer to Questions on the Order Paper, whether or not the Question was reached, is placed in the appropriate tray shortly after the end of Question time for any interested correspondent to look at but not to take away. A copy is also made available by government departments to each Agency: Reuters, Central News, Press Association, Exchange and *The Times*. When a very important Question is answered the Department concerned will usually send a batch of copies of it for the convenience of the Gallery. Copies of all Questions answered by Scottish Ministers go to all Scottish papers. Particular correspondents known to be interested in a certain subject or Department may receive copies of the replies on these matters for their individual use. The correspondent may have had to take his own notes of any supplementary exchanges, the rest is handed to him on the proverbial plate. Speeches have to be worked on, and save when a Minister reads a statement which is then made available to the press, the official record is not available until next day. Thus a Question may provide a correspondent and his newspaper with a news story in one highly concentrated minute of Parliamentary time and with very little trouble.

The evening and morning newspapers are but a fraction of the potential space available for reporting Questions. Almost every trade, profession and organized group has a special periodical devoted to its interests, with articles and news selected for a well-defined body of readers. Many will be weeklies, some monthlies and some may not even be on general sale. Debates of particular interest to this specialized group of readers will be reported. It would be unusual, however, for there to be continuous copy provided from this source and the amount of space available for such reporting is limited. In contrast, probably, hardly an issue will pass without the inclusion of some Question and Answer which the Editor knows will interest his readers. A journal devoted to local government, for example, will find plenty of material in the answers given by the Ministers of Housing and Local Government, of Transport and of Education. One or two pages in each issue will be devoted to reproducing Questions and Answers, usually for information and without comment.

It is also important to bear in mind the treatment of Questions of local interest. Few Questions will be judged to be of national interest, but many are likely to be of local concern. The big national papers with local editions will include in the appropriate edition Parliamentary news bearing on local issues, e.g. about the cotton industry in their editions circulating in Lancashire. In reporting what Members have said in the House, they will be more likely to report the local back benchers than those from other areas. The national dailies cannot, however, spare much space for news of highly local interest, such as the prospect for some road improvement in a particular town. A large number of medium-sized towns have an evening or morning daily and most rural areas have a weekly newspaper. So far as the reporting of Parliamentary proceedings are concerned, these local newspapers will pay special attention to local matters and the activities of some local Members. They will usually devote little or no space to general reports of Debates unless the matter is of major national or of local importance. A Question asked by a local Member about an issue concerning his constituency will almost certainly be reported and indeed given prominence.

Finally, there are the overseas newspapers. A Debate on some aspect of colonial affairs will be widely reported in the colony concerned and perhaps throughout Africa if it is an African colony. But such Debates occur infrequently. Questions are asked and answered continuously and many will be reported in the local newspapers. The same is true of many of the Questions answered by the Foreign Secretary. If they concern any major issue of foreign policy they are likely to be reported in the main newspapers of many countries. If they concern a particular area or country they are likely to be reported in the press of that area or country.

Thus Questions are a continuous source of publishable information and news stories for the national dailies, for the provincial press, for the thousands of specialized periodicals and for the newspapers of other countries.

Three glosses can be added to this account of the handling of Questions by the press. First, when reported in one of the dailies quite often the questioner's name is mentioned and it will certainly be mentioned in his local newspaper and usually also in any specialist periodical. Second, what is judged to be news may not correspond to the Department's judgment of the importance of the subject. When, in January 1958, Mr. Norman Dodds asked the Minister of Health whether he would give guidance to the public about the possible danger of food poisoning from the insertion of threepenny and sixpenny pieces in Christmas puddings[1] this may have been considered by the Department and by many Members as being among the lesser of their worries about the public health. But as it was asked shortly after Christmas and some public concern had been expressed the Question and Answer were very newsworthy. Third, so far as the evening papers and the dailies are concerned starred Questions have certain advantages over unstarred. A starred Question is an-

[1] The Minister replied: 'Tests have shown that the health risk from putting sixpences and threepenny pieces into Christmas puddings is very slight. A precaution would be to wrap the coins in greaseproof paper or to insert them into the pudding near the time of serving.' H.C. Deb. (1957–8), 580, c. *156–7*.

swered on the day it appears on the Order Paper and even if it is not reached during Question time the answer to it arrives in the room used by the Press Gallery shortly after the end of Question time along with the Questions which were reached. As a result a correspondent finds it fairly easy to keep track of starred Questions and their answers. In contrast, though an unstarred Question is put down for answer on a stated day he cannot be certain it will be answered on that day even though the position has very greatly improved since Mr. Butler's undertaking of February 1960. Unless an unstarred Question has some special interest for him, it is likely to suffer in competition with the greater convenience of the starred Question. The asking of a supplementary is also likely to add to the news value of Questions answered orally and attract his attention whilst he is sitting in the Press Gallery. The human interest of Question time is greater than the human interest of printed paper.

CHAPTER 9

THE QUESTIONS

A STATISTICAL analysis of Questions can be useful in throwing light on the use made of the device by different Members. But it may conceal quite significant characteristics for it assumes that one Question is so like another that they can be added and subtracted, and subjected to simple arithmetical processes and comparisons, whereas in fact Questions vary very widely in character. Compare, for example, Questions No. 45 and 54 asked on 4 November 1958. In the former Mr. Frank Allaun asked the Prime Minister 'if, in order to reach agreement with the two other nuclear Powers, and for other reasons, he will permanently stop all British test explosions of atom and hydrogen bombs forthwith'. In Question No. 54 Mr. Parker asked the Minister of Works 'whether he will thin the inside row of trees along Birdcage Walk during the winter'. One Question clearly concerned a matter of world interest and significance, the other concerned a very local matter (a road which runs alongside St. James's Park, near the House of Commons).

Again, compare No. 24 on that day with No. 106 on the following day. In the first Mr. Stonehouse asked the Secretary of State for the Colonies, 'how many prisoners are detained at Lokitaung Prison, Kenya; what is the number of warders at this prison; and what is the number of unofficial visitors the prisoners have received'. In the second the same Member asked the Postmaster General 'whether he will make provision for a letter box at The Square, New Invention, Willenhall, where there is much demand from local residents for this facility'. The former concerned an area far from the constituency of any Member, the latter concerned Mr. Stonehouse's constituency.

To appreciate the full range of Question time, its glory and triviality, its excitement, humour and dullness, the reader should sit through it for several days in the Visitors' Gallery of the House of Commons. The next best thing is to read the verbatim record in Hansard. Hansard, however, cannot convey that something which may be as important as the words — the atmosphere, the manner or the tone of voice in which the Ministerial answer was given and received. Even a selection of Questions and Answers, however carefully chosen as typical specimens, is unlikely to do full justice to the subject.

PURPOSE OF QUESTIONS

All Questions can be grouped into two main categories according to whether they ask for information or press for action.

Asking for Information

The information demanded may be purely statistical. Mr. Stonehouse's first Question quoted earlier is one example. Others are: a Question to the President of the Board of Trade asking him to state 'the number, size and value of new factory buildings erected in Wales during the period of twelve months up to the latest convenient date';[1] a Question to the Minister of Housing and Local Government asking 'how many alkali inspectors are employed by his Department in Manchester'; and one to the Chancellor of the Exchequer asking him 'the percentage increase in the amount of annual revenue provided from motor vehicle and petrol taxation in 1958 compared with 1938'.

The information required may be factual without being statistical. Thus the Colonial Secretary was asked 'what proposals have been made by the Government of Tanganyika during the last twelve months for providing funds for extra-mural work by Makerere College'; the Minister of Housing and Local Government was asked 'how many local authorities have provided schemes of training for the deaf; and whether he will give some indication of the nature of these schemes and of their results' and the Minister of Agriculture, Fisheries and Food was asked 'what research is being undertaken into the incidence of flukeworm and the means of combating it; and what steps are being taken by his Department to eradicate this pest'.

Many of the requests for factual information require a very precise answer. Thus on 4 December 1958 Mr. Swingler asked the Foreign Secretary 'on what date the United Kingdom Per-

[1] Unless otherwise stated all the examples in this chapter are taken from the period November–December, 1958. H.C. Deb. (1958–9), vols. 594–7.

manent Representative at the United Nations notified the Secretary-General that Her Majesty's Government had no objection to the release of the film "Blue Vanguard" '. To which the Minister replied 'On 11th September, 1958'. Others can be in more general terms, e.g. the Secretary of State for the Colonies was asked 'what progress has been made in introducing legislation in Hong Kong for the limitation of working hours in factories'.

Pressing for Action

Any official action taken by a Minister or by any member of the staff of his Department may be questioned and so may the absence of such action, if the Minister has the power to act. Thus the Minister of Agriculture, Fisheries and Food was asked 'why the subsidies offered for Grade I fat steers and heifers for the week commencing 10th November were 3/- per live cwt., nothing for the week commencing 17th November, and 6/- per live cwt. for the week commencing 24th November'.

A wide variety of Questions are put asking a Minister whether he will take a certain course of action. Thus the Chancellor of the Exchequer was asked 'when he proposes to reduce the rate of interest charged to local authorities by the Public Works Loans Board' and on the same day 'if he will review the provision for depreciation of ships'. A week later he was asked 'when he proposes to introduce a decimal coinage' and 'what steps he has in mind for increasing National Savings in the immediate future'. The Minister of Health was asked 'what he intends to do to relieve the shortage of hospital accommodation in East Kent'.

There is a fairly popular variation of the request for the Minister's intentions. The Member starts his Question by a statement of fact. As however the purpose of a Question is to ask for information, not to give it, the Member puts himself in order by prefacing his facts with the phrase 'whether he is aware that . . .' and ends by asking the Minister what he intends to do about them. Thus the Minister of Pensions and National Insurance was asked 'whether he is aware of the large number of old-age pensioners who are unable to purchase adequate supplies of clothing; and whether, in view of the recession of trade in clothing industries, he will consider the issue of an additional bonus to retirement pensioners in the form of clothing purchase vouchers'; the Minister of Defence was asked 'if he is aware of the official publication in the United States of information about a new North Atlantic Treaty Organization base for submarines to be placed on the coast of Ayrshire; what consultations have taken place on this matter; and if he will make a statement'; and the Minister of Health was asked 'whether he is aware that 69 per cent. of the outbreaks of food poisoning in 1957, in which a cause was found, were associated with processed and made-up meat dishes; what evidence there is that this danger is increasing; and what advice he is tendering to local authorities as to its prevention'.

In some instances the Member's Question implies or states the solution which he is advocating. Thus when Sir William Wakefield asked the Minister of Works 'the estimated cost of a lift up to the top of Big Ben; the estimated revenue likely to be obtained from visitors if the lift were constructed; and why proposals for the construction of such a lift have always been rejected by his Department' it was clear that he was an advocate of such a lift for such a use. A similar advocacy is to be found in a Question such as that in which the Secretary of State for Scotland was asked 'if he will now consider the introduction of legislation to enable awards of salary increases to teachers to be made retrospective'.

Sometimes a Member will ask a Minister to make a statement on this or that matter. Such Questions may take several forms. In many cases a Question has already been asked on a matter and in reply the Minister had said he was not yet in a position to reply (i.e. the matter was still not settled) or else had given what could be considered as an interim answer. The 'follow-up' Question is thus worded in some such form as 'whether he is yet in a position to make a statement about . . .' or 'whether he can yet make a statement about . . .' or 'whether he will make a further statement about . . .'. In these cases 'to make a statement' is used as a less exacting form of wording than 'to answer' or 'to make a further reply'.

A request for a statement is also used when a Member wishes to give a Minister greater freedom than he would have if the question were more precisely worded, or wishes to indicate that a more general, wider-ranging reply would be welcomed. This is often done with Questions about general matters of foreign policy. Thus on 15 December 1958 the Foreign Secretary was asked for four statements: 'whether he will make a statement regarding the course and conclusion of the Cyprus debate at the United Nations'; 'if he will make a further statement on his progress towards the resumption of diplomatic relations with the United Arab Republic'; 'whether he will make a further statement on the discussions which are taking place with regard to the future status of Berlin'; and 'whether he will make a statement on the progress made at the Geneva Conferences on the discontinuance of nuclear tests and safeguards against surprise attacks, respectively'.

In matters of this kind it is not always easy to frame a more precise Question. The Member is looking for a mixture of factual information, explanation of Government action or policy, and of Government intentions. He may also be looking for a peg on which to hang some rather wide-ranging supplementaries. Questions in this general form allow a Minister considerable discretion. He may take the opportunity to make a very full statement touching on all aspects of the subject or he may reply with some such phrase as 'Discussions are still proceeding' and give very much less information than if the Member had asked for precise factual information. Long general statements are usually made at the end of Question time.

A request for a statement is sometimes added at the end of a two- or three-decker Question. The Question asked of the Minister of Defence just quoted is a fair example. On the 16 December 1958, the Minister of Housing and Local Government was asked 'whether he has reached a decision on the question of restoring to agricultural use the land at Duggins Lane, Berkswell, in the County of Warwick, which was formerly the site of the Tile Hill Hostel, was derequisitioned on 20 September 1957, and is now derelict; and if he will make a statement'. In many Questions of this kind the phrase 'and if he will make a statement' is a general invitation to the Minister to say whatever he thinks necessary, or is added to make the Question as wide as possible. Here again the reply evoked may be a long paragraph or a mere sentence or that part of the Question may be ignored.

APPARENT AND TRUE PURPOSE

Too much significance must not be attached to the apparently different purposes implied in the wording of Questions. For providing the Question is reached, one form of starred Question can be turned into another by one or more supplementaries. A high proportion of the requests for statistics, for example, are really made to form the basis of a supplementary. Thus when the Home Secretary was asked 'how many prisoners are now housed three to a cell' and gave the answer of 5,925 men it would be no surprise either to him or to the House that the Member immediately arose and asked whether the Minister was not rather ashamed of the fact and called his attention to the remarks of a Judge in a recent case. Had the questioner merely wanted the statistics he could either have asked an unstarred Question or written to the Minister. It is indeed probable that he already knew the answer but preferred to put his Question in that form, partly to be more exact, partly for effect and partly as the best way of leading up to his primary purpose. Again, the Question quoted earlier asking the Chancellor of the Exchequer about increases in motor and petrol taxation was followed by a supplementary by the questioner (Captain Pilkington) which included the sentence, 'Does not he [the Minister] think that the motorist should pay rather less in taxation?'

If, however, a starred Question is not reached and receives a written answer its form is, of course, all important. If the Member asks for statistical or other quantitative information, he will receive that information if it is available. He will not, however, receive any comments by way of Ministerial intentions or explanations, except on the rare occasion when the Department may feel a purely factual answer to be misleading.

GENERAL AND PARTICULAR QUESTIONS

Questions can also be grouped according to whether they raise a particular case or whether they are concerned with a general issue. Thus the Postmaster-General may be asked when a particular person at a particular address may expect to have a telephone installed, or he may be asked how soon his Department expects to be able to deal with outstanding applications for new telephones in Oxford.

THE QUESTIONS

When a Question is asked about a named person, it is usually about someone in the Member's constituency. Thus on 25 November 1958 Sir David Robertson asked the Lord Advocate 'why the charge against Police Constables Gunn and Harper for assaulting and injuring John Waters, aged 15 years, was not proceeded with after the Procurator Fiscal, Wick, reported the case to him for instruction of Crown counsel; if he has yet considered the seventeen written statements made by witnesses and forwarded to him by the hon. Member for Caithness and Sutherland, together with the statement made by Dr. Fell who treated the boy on the night of the assault and two subsequent occasions; and if he will now give immediate instructions to have the case put down for trial?' Sir David Robertson is the Member for Caithness and Sutherland and the boy lived in his constituency.

It is not necessary to give the name of the individual. Thus, on 2 November 1959 Mr. Leslie Hale asked the Minister of Labour 'why the Chadderton man, whose name has been supplied to him and who is married with a son aged four years and whose wife is pregnant, has been ordered to report for military service on 5th November'.

Some Questions can be very detailed. On 17 December 1958 the Postmaster-General was asked 'why, as landlord of 34, Calthorpe Street, W.C. 1., his Department has increased the rent of four rooms there from £1.6.10 to £2.10.4 per week, especially having regard to the condition of the property and the lack of basic amenities'. On the same day two Questions were put to the Secretary of State for War as follows: 'if he will state the date on which the draught horse, Josephine, was selected for service at the Command Ordnance Depot, Didcot, the reason which prompted the commander to make a personal selection of this horse, the date on which it was taken on the Command Ordnance Depot, Didcot, strength, the number of occasions on which it has pulled the garbage cart since being taken on strength, and the last occasion on which it was so employed.' The second was: 'what was the date on which a privately-owned horse, Moira, was first stabled and fed at Government expense at the Command Ordnance Depot, Didcot; what was the date on which repayment to public funds was first made; and by whom the animal is owned.'

Most Members will not raise matters about individuals at

Question time until all other devices have been exhausted. Sir David Robertson, for example, had been pressing the case of John Waters for seven months. He had already asked a Question about the matter on 8 July but most of his work on the case had been done by correspondence and interviews.

Many Questions are asked about matters affecting named areas: for example, about hospital accommodation in East Kent; the commencement of a new road or the making of a road improvement in such and such a town; the extent of unemployment in Liverpool and particular measures for alleviating it; the closing of a Royal Ordnance Depot; or the erection of a nuclear power station. Again, Questions of this kind are usually asked by the Member for the constituency containing the hospital, the road, etc. About one fifth of the starred Questions refer to a matter within the questioner's constituency. In addition Questions not confined to a particular constituency may nevertheless be a constituency matter; for example, Questions from Lancashire Members about the cotton industry; from Scottish Members about some general Scottish grievance, and from Members for rural areas about agriculture. But by no means all Questions about particular cases are constituency matters. A high proportion of them nowadays concern the Colonies, ranging from Questions about individuals, e.g. the imprisonment of Dr. Hastings Banda, to Government policy in respect of a particular Colony. Mention must also be made of the many Questions concerned with the interests of particular groups or sections of the community: for example, the Question quoted earlier about the rate of interest charged on loans to local authorities and those asked about the deaf, old age pensioners, motorists or the unemployed. The great majority of these are concerned with general Government policy, e.g. whether old age pensions can be increased or the taxes on motorists reduced.

From time to time this distinction between local or constituency Questions and those concerning general issues of Government policy is used as a criterion of relative importance. This distinction has its uses and up to a point can validly be drawn. But it also has its dangers. It is dangerous, for example, to assume that all Questions addressed to the Foreign Secretary or grouped under some such broad heading as Foreign Affairs must be of greater importance than Questions addressed to the Postmaster-General or grouped under the heading of Local Government. The Foreign Secretary may be asked about the cost of rebuilding an Embassy or about the number of typists employed in it and even an enquiry about relations with another country may be rather pointless and of little current significance. On the other hand, the Postmaster-General may be questioned about such matters of public significance as the opening of letters or the tapping of telephone conversations for police purposes. Again a local case or a Question about a named person may involve a major issue of principle and arouse widespread interest. The one quoted earlier about the two policemen and John Waters led ultimately to the holding of a public enquiry and nationwide concern about the general issues involved.

QUESTIONS WHICH CANNOT BE ASKED

Notwithstanding the tremendous variety in the form, purpose and character of Questions, starred and unstarred, there are limits to the kind that can be asked. There is, however, nothing in the Standing Orders of the House that gives any indication of these limits. The whole of the procedure about wording and subject-matter, form and content, is contained in the innumerable rulings given during more than a century by Mr. Speaker and in the accepted conventions and practice of the House.

The latest edition (the sixteenth) of Erskine May's *Treatise on the Law, Privileges, Proceedings and Usage of Parliament* has this to say under the heading 'Rules of Order regarding form and contents of Questions': 'The purpose of a question is to obtain information or press for action, and it should not be in effect a short speech, or limited to giving information, or framed so as to suggest its own answer or convey a particular point of view; questions of excessive length have not been permitted. The facts on which a question is based may be set out briefly, provided the Member asking it makes himself responsible for their accuracy, but extracts from newspapers or books, quotations from speeches, etc., are not admissible. Where the facts are of sufficient moment the Speaker has required *prima facie* proof of their authenticity. A question which publishes the names of persons or statements not strictly necessary to render the question intelligible will be refused a place on the notice paper.'[1]

The official Manual of Procedure says that the purpose of Questions is 'to obtain information or press for action within the responsibility of the Member to whom it is addressed'. The current Manual, prepared in March 1959, contains 18 rules governing the form and content of Questions. It is clear from these definitions that a Question that only gives information and does not either ask for it or press for action arising out of the information provided is out of order. It is also clear that a Question will be out of order if the subject matter is not within the responsibility of any Minister. But these broad rules do not take us very far. For there are Questions which ask for information or press for action which are out of order on other grounds. And sometimes it may be a matter of opinion whether a matter falls within the responsibility of a Minister.

The starting point of procedure is that a Question must be a genuine question and not a statement or a speech couched in the interrogative. It follows also from the exceptional character of the proceedings, there being no Motion for discussion before the House, that a Question should not be couched in argumentative terms or even in a form likely to lead to an argumentative reply or to argument in the form of further Questions and Answers once that reply has been given. As a result, Questions seeking an expression of opinion, or containing arguments, expressions of opinion, inferences or imputations or containing epithets or rhetorical, controversial, ironical or offensive expressions, have been ruled as inadmissible. Under this heading of inadmissibility would also come Questions criticizing the decisions of the House or referring to debates in the current Session or asking for the solution of a hypothetical proposition or seeking, for purposes of argument, information on matters of past history.

Questions are also out of order if their form and content involve 'a breach of constitutional usage or parliamentary etiquette'[2] to use Campion's phrase. There has grown up over the centuries a whole series of conventions or usage concerned with the general behaviour of Members in the Chamber. The sixteenth

[1] p. 357.
[2] Introduction to the Procedure of the House of Commons (1950), p. 149.

THE QUESTIONS

edition of Erskine May devotes 14 pages to the rules governing the content of speeches. The rules are summarized as follows :
'A Member, while speaking to a question, [i.e. a Motion] may not introduce matter which is irrelevant to that question; allude to debates of the same session upon any question or bill not then under discussion; speak against or reflect upon any determination of the House, unless he intends to conclude with a motion for rescinding it; allude to debates of the same session in the other House; utter treasonable or seditious words, or use the Queen's name irreverently, or to influence the debate; speak offensive and insulting words against the character or proceedings of either House; refer to matters pending a judicial decision; reflect upon the conduct of the sovereign or of certain other persons in authority;[1] make personal allusions to members of Parliament; or obstruct the business of the House'.[2] To these rules should be added one not referred to directly in this list, viz. the rule prohibiting disorderly and unparliamentary expression, including the imputation of false or unavowed motives, charges of uttering a deliberate falsehood and the use of abusive and insulting language.

These rules have their counterpart in the rules governing the content of Questions to Ministers. It would indeed be a strange loophole in the procedure of the House if the Members could use language or behave very differently during Question time than they could under the rules governing their language and conduct during Debate.

Another group of inadmissible Questions is concerned with avoiding what has been thought to be an improper use of this form of procedure. Under this heading would come the following 'examples' from Erskine May :[3]

Suggesting amendments to bills, or asking for information which should be moved for as a Return.

Seeking an expression of opinion on a question of law, such as the interpretation of a statute, or of an international document, a Minister's own powers, etc.

---

[1] Including the heir to the throne or other members of the Royal Family, the Governor-General of a 'Dominion', the Speaker, judges of the superior courts but not, of course, Ministers.
[2] Sixteenth edition, p. 451.
[3] op. cit., pp. 359–61. This edition gives 29 numbered examples of types of Questions which have been ruled out of order.

Asking whether statements in the Press, or made by private individuals, or unofficial bodies are accurate.

Requiring information set forth in accessible documents (such as statutes, treaties etc.) or in ordinary works of reference (and not coming within the official knowledge or duties of the Minister).

Raising issues of policy too large to be dealt with in the limits of an answer to a Question.

Repeating in substance Questions already answered or to which an answer has been refused. A Question fully answered, whether orally or in print, cannot be renewed, nor can a Question which one Minister has refused to answer be addressed to another Minister.

Multiplied with slight variations on the same point.

Being trivial, vague, or meaningless.

Introducing the names of persons or bodies invidiously or for the purpose of advertisement.

Finally there are the Questions not accepted because their subject matter is not within the responsibility of a Minister. This rule was explained in the previous chapter and is dealt with more fully in Appendix II, pp. 292-313

INTERPRETATION OF THE RULES

It is clear that some of the rules and 'examples' of inadmissible Questions quoted are open to differences of interpretation. Mr. Speaker is the final arbiter[1] on these as on all matters of procedure of the House. Most of the discussion with Members on admissibility, is, however, conducted by the Clerks in the Table Office. Though the original form of the Question may offend against the rules, very often it can be converted fairly readily into a 'proper' Question by the deletion of a word or two or by some re-phrasing. Some, but by no means all, of the prohibitions can be avoided if ingenuity is exercised in drafting.

It should also be noted that though the rules also apply to supplementaries they are much more difficult to enforce. Thus, when the Minister of Agriculture, Fisheries and Food replied simply 'No, Sir' to Mrs. Mann's Question asking him if he was aware 'that shortage of petrol or increase in price of petrol will cause increases in prices of vegetables and other food; and, if he will take steps, by price control or otherwise, to avoid such

[1] See, however, pp. 311-13 below for his role in respect of the responsibility of Ministers.

increases for a period of at least six months', Mrs. Mann immediately asked: 'Am I to take it that the Minister is so blind that he cannot see what a blind man would feel with his stick . . .'[1] A phrase of this kind would not have been accepted had it been part of a Question submitted for inclusion in the Notice Paper.

[1] 6 December 1956. H.C. Deb. (1956-7), 561, c. 1425.

CHAPTER 10

THE QUESTIONERS

THE aim of this chapter is to show first, who asks Questions and second, what use they make of them.

WHO ASKS QUESTIONS?

Two general statements may be made. First, while most Members make little or no use of their right to put Questions on the Paper a few Members make a great deal of use of it. Second, Questions are by no means confined to Members of the Opposition, but are also extensively used by the Government's supporters. Each of these statements will now be developed.

Our starting point is a statistical analysis of Questions asked during two recent periods. The more recent is the first 38 days of the Session 1958–9. It began on 28 October but Questions could not be answered orally during the first three days.[1] Until the House adjourned for the recess on Thursday, 18 December, Question time occurred on 28 days. The general picture is shown by the Table on page 193.

During this period 332 of the 630 Members did not put a starred Question on the Paper. Including the Government Whips there were 68 Members who being Ministers or otherwise part of the Government did not ask Questions. Mr. Speaker, the Chairman and Deputy Chairman of Ways and Means do not ask Questions. The Leader of the Opposition does not put any on the Paper. This still leaves some 260 Members who might have asked a starred Question but did not. A further 67 Members put down only one starred Question.

At the other extreme 12 Members each asked 30 or more starred Questions. In all, these 12 Members put down 473 or one-fifth of the 2418 starred Questions. One of these (Mr. Stephen Swingler, Labour) put down 59. Next came Mr. G.

[1] Owing to the rule about minimum notice. Question time does not take place nowadays during the first three days of a new Session, but Private Notice Questions may be asked.

Questions Answered — October/December, 1958
Analysis by Party Membership

Number of Members who asked:

Party	Starred only	Starred & Un-starred	Unstar-red only	None	Total Members
Mr. Speaker, Chairman & Deputy Chairman of Ways & Means	—	—	—	3	3
Conservative					
In Government	—	—	—	68	68
Back Benchers	56	61	35	117	269
Labour	84	93	18	89	284
Liberals & Others	—	4	—	2	6
	140	158	53	279	630

(Based on a count of Hansard)

Nabarro (Conservative) with 47 followed by two other Labour Members (Mr. F. T. Willey and Mr. Fenner Brockway) with 46 and 43 respectively. These figures can be compared with the then possible maximum of three per day for 28 days, 84 altogether. Mr. Swingler asked three starred Questions on 13 and two on each of eight days, missing only one of the 28 days. Mr. Nabarro also went up to his maximum on 13 days but, because he was mainly hunting a particular Minister, missed putting Questions on 10 of the 28 days.

The second detailed analysis covered broadly the same period in 1948 and the same number of Question times. On this occasion, however, the Labour Party were in office and the Conservative opposition had 65 fewer Members than the Labour opposition in 1958. Otherwise the conditions were similar: it was the beginning of a new Session and the House had seen three years of its life. The general position is shown in the analysis on page 194.

During this period 341 of the 640 Members did not put a starred Question on the Paper, of whom only 74 are accounted for by the Government, Mr. Speaker, the Chairman and Deputy Chairman of Ways and Means, and the Leader of the Opposition. A further 61 asked only one starred Question. At the other extreme 10 Members each asked 30 or more starred Questions totalling 404 in all or one-sixth of the starred Questions put

Questions Answered — October/December, 1948
Analysis by Party Membership

Number of Members who asked:

Party	Starred only	Starred & Unstarred	Unstarred only	None	Total Members
Mr. Speaker, Chairman & Deputy Chairman of Ways & Means	—	—	—	3	3
Labour					
In Government	—	—	—	70	70
Back benchers	79	71	25	149	324
Conservative	71	63	11	73	218
Liberals & Others	6	9	—	10	25
	156	143	36	305	640

(Based on a count of Hansard)

down during the period. Of these, two Conservative Members, Mr. F. J. Erroll and Sir Waldron Smithers, respectively asked 61 and 54 starred Questions, followed by Mr. Platts-Mills (expelled from the Labour Party in April, 1948) with 49.

RANGE OF USE

The very wide range in the number of Questions asked by different Members is not a recent phenomenon. It goes back to the earliest days of Question time. In the Session of 1905, consisting of 114 days, about 200 Members did not ask any starred Questions and another 300 each asked less than 10 during the Session. Six Irish Nationalists, one Irish Conservative and one English Liberal each asked more than 100. Two-thirds of the 4120 starred Questions were asked by 35 of the 679 Members. Much the same pattern continued during the inter-war years. Professor McCulloch has estimated that during the period 1924–31, 50 Members asked 45,000 of the 80,000 Questions of all kinds, starred, unstarred and supplementary put to Ministers.[1]

The range is now less extreme. The reduction in the maximum number of Questions each Member can put down for oral answer has helped. Also the congestion of Question time has made Members less sympathetic towards those who try to make the maximum use of their rights. Earl Winterton has given a graphic

[1] *American Political Science Review*, December 1933, vol. 27, p. 974.

picture of the late Colonel Harry Day, the Labour Member for Southwark Central, a persistent questioner of the 1930s who 'endeavoured to break a parliamentary record by asking more questions than any member had done since the days of the Irish Nationalists. He had Questions "on the Paper" every day, usually going to the limit allowed. He frequently showed, in his original and supplementary questions alike some ignorance of the subject, which was not surprising, since the most erudite and painstaking member cannot have a personal knowledge of the affairs of every Government department, and Mr. Day interrogated every Minister in turn. The process became a parliamentary joke. Members using a well-known House of Commons formula in connection with the deferment of Business called out "Another Day" when he rose; the Speaker, who clearly disapproved of this excessive use of the Question Paper by an individual, because it meant a curtailment of other M.P.s' opportunities, used to rebuke him sternly, amid loud approving cheers, when, as often happened, he asked a supplementary question which did not have the slightest relevance to the original one. *Punch* chaffed him constantly, political commentators in the Press attacked him; but Mr. Day, grim-visaged and determined, ignored all this ridicule and resentment and continued without a smile, to ask his numerous questions until I, for one, began to admire his thick-skinned pertinacity.'[1] It is clear that nowadays Colonel Day would have aroused so much annoyance among his fellow Members that he would have required a very 'thick-skinned pertinacity' indeed to continue day after day with his questioning.

Again Members usually wish to receive an oral answer. For much of the period prior to 1939 Members could count on getting this far more often than they can nowadays. This combined with the reduction in the maximum number of starred Questions allowed means that questioners who confine themselves to a particular field, e.g. education or local government, are unlikely to have much oportunity to ask a large number of starred Questions during a Session.

Finally the number of Members who ask Questions has increased. Most back benchers now put at least one or two Questions on the Paper each Session. The analysis given earlier for 1948–9 and 1958–9 covered only a part of each Session — a

[1] Earl Winterton, *Orders of the Day* (1953), p. 222.

quarter and a third respectively. During the remaining period a big proportion of the private Members who had not already put a Question on the Paper would do so while the numbers asked by the regular questioners would continue to increase. During the Session of 1959–60 just under 60 Members (other than the Ministers and the conventional non-questioners) did not put a single Question on the Paper. A further 30 had put down only unstarred Questions. This is fewer than was usual in the pre-1914 period or even in the inter-war years. The change is due in part to the very big increase in the number of constituency cases which Members now have to handle; in part to the lessened opportunities to speak in the House; in part to the much higher proportion of 'full time' Members in the House.

THE PERSISTENT QUESTIONERS

The analysis for 1958 showed that eleven of the twelve regular questioners were Labour Members, while only Mr. Nabarro was a Government supporter. In contrast the analysis for 1948 showed that eight of the twelve regular questioners were Conservative, one (Mr. Piratin) was a Communist, and another Mr. Platts-Mills had recently been expelled from the Labour Party, leaving only two regular Government supporters. Whilst therefore those who ask most starred Questions are likely to be Opposition Members, the last seventy or so years show that certain Members who delight in putting Questions put them irrespective of whether or not their party is in power. True one will find more Labour and Liberal names among the persistent questioners of the inter-war years when the Conservatives, in one guise or another, were in power most of the time. But there have always been two or three Members in each Party who put down a large number of Questions not because they disliked the political complexion of the Government in power but because they had taken a strong liking to this particular device.

Between 1905 and 1942 an unofficial publication entitled 'The Parliamentary Gazette' usually gave a list twice a year of Members who asked the most Questions. Looking through these lists one is struck by the recurrence of certain names. For example, in the twenty years after 1920, the following names appear among the top dozen of such questioners for several

Sessions: Colonel J. C. (later Lord) Wedgwood; Lt. Commander J. M. Kenworthy (later Lord Strabolgi); Mr. Will Thorne; Mr. Wedgwood Benn (later Lord Stansgate); Sir Harry Brittain; Colonel Harry Day; Mr. Tom Williams (later Lord Williams of Barnburgh); Mr. (later Sir) Geoffrey Mander; Mr. (later Sir) Herbert Williams; Sir William Davidson and Mr. (later Sir) Rupert de la Bère.

We have now identified two groups of Members. At one extreme there are those who do not put Questions on the Paper: Mr. Speaker, the Chairman and the Deputy Chairman of Ways and Means, the senior and junior Ministers and other Members forming part of the Administration, and the Leader of the Opposition. At the other extreme are a very small group of questioners who account for a very high proportion of the Questions on the Paper. Together these cover less than 100 Members: there still remain some 530 or so Members. The Members in this large group vary considerably in the use they make of Questions. Some could almost be counted as persistent questioners, depending upon where the qualifying line is drawn. Others may go for months or even years without putting a Question on the Paper. There are indeed all the gradations from the Member who takes a delight in asking Questions and is, therefore, always on the look out for a suitable subject, through the Member who without going out of his way to look for Questions is quite ready to use the device, through to the Member who is only inclined to do so as a kind of last resort or in exceptional circumstances. More light will be thrown on this large group and in particular on the use made of Questions by the Opposition front bench, later in this chapter.

DISTRIBUTION BETWEEN THE PARTIES

The use of Questions by the Government's supporters as well as by its opponents can be illustrated from statistics of any period in the past 60 or 70 years. In the Session of 1905, for example, when Mr. Balfour's Conservative-Unionist Government was in power 211 Government supporters asked oral Questions against 232 Members of the Opposition, even though the latter included some 80 Irish Nationalists, most of whom were ardent questioners. Professor McCulloch's detailed analysis for the Session of 1929–30 showed that Labour Members asked 34 per cent of the starred Questions which, after allowing for the number of their Party in the Government, was almost equivalent to the share the Party had of non-governmental Members. The Conservatives asked 53 per cent. and the Liberals 13 per cent, both percentages being in line with the proportions the Parties had of the total Members (excluding the Government).[1]

The analyses already given for 1948 and 1958 ignore the numbers asked by each Member. When these adjustments are made for the 1958 period the following picture emerges:

	Proportion of Members*	Starred		Unstarred		Total Questions asked	
	%	Total	%	Total	%	Total	%
Conservatives (Govt. Party)	48	612	25	292	37	904	28
Labour (Opposition)	51	1756	74	481	61	2237	70
Liberals & Others	1	31	1	13	2	44	2
	100	2399	100	786	100	3185	100

* Excluding Mr. Speaker, the Chairman and Deputy Chairman of Ways and Means and the 68 Conservative Members who were part of the Administration.

It will now be seen that the Labour Members accounted for 74 per cent. of the starred and 61 per cent. of the unstarred, a very different picture from that disclosed by the earlier figures.

A similar analysis for 1948 shows the following position:

	Proportion of Members*	Starred		Unstarred		Total Questions Asked	
	%	Total	%	Total	%	Total	%
Labour (Govt. Party)	57	993	41	297	43	1290	42
Conservatives (Opposition)	38	1359	57	382	55	1741	56
Liberals & Others	5	49	2	19	2	68	2
	100	2401	100	698	100	3099	100

* Excluding Mr. Speaker, the Chairman and Deputy Chairman of Ways and Means and the 70 Labour Members who were part of the Administration.

[1] *American Political Science Review*, vol. 27, p. 974.

Again the Opposition Members asked the majority of the Questions. True they asked only 57 per cent. as against 74 per cent. of the starred Questions in 1958, but this is partly accounted for by the larger size of the Opposition in the latter year. If the average number of Questions asked per Member is calculated the comparison is as follows:

Average Number of Questions asked per Member

Period	Opposition			Government Supporters		
	Starred	Unstarred	Total	Starred	Unstarred	Total
1948	6.2	1.8	8.0	3.1	0.9	4.0
1958	6.2	1.7	7.9	2.2	1.0	3.2

It will now be seen that there is very little difference between the two periods. The Labour Members were slightly more active taking both kinds of Questions for the two periods: 11.9 as against 11.2. This is what one would have expected, for a higher proportion of Labour than of Conservative Members spend most, even all their time in the House, having no other occupation. It is also commonly held that they are more rebellious or more 'opposition minded' than the average Conservative Member. This probably accounts for the fact that the Conservatives when in power left a somewhat higher proportion of their Questions unstarred. Written answers are less embarrassing to the Minister and do not require the attendance of the Member at a particular time and day.

Analyses for other post-war periods might have produced slightly different results but the observable evidence and sample checks support the general picture presented by the contrast of 1948 and 1958. Questions are not purely an Opposition device. A high proportion of both starred and unstarred are asked by Government supporters. Having regard to the number of potential questioners the experience of these two periods shows that the Opposition are twice as prone to ask Questions.

THE USE OF QUESTIONS

Members of the House of Commons have two different kinds of obligations and as a result perform two different kinds of functions. On the one hand, each represents a constituency and in that capacity is concerned with the interests of the area and of his constituents. The activities of the Member in this, his individual capacity, include not only constituency interests but any other interests and public activities which do not directly arise out of his Party allegiance. On the other hand, he is a member of a political Party and as such must play a part in the struggle between the Government and its supporters and the Opposition leaders and their supporters. This is the Member in his Party capacity.

USE IN MEMBERS' INDIVIDUAL CAPACITY

Earlier chapters have shown that the use of most forms of Parliamentary procedure and in particular the arrangements for Public Business have been brought under control of the Government and the Opposition leaders acting through the Party Whips, otherwise known as 'the usual channels'. The significant difference between the use of Questions and participation in almost every other activity of the House is that Questions are not arranged by 'the usual channels' nor are their character and course dictated by the Party leaders. The Opposition leaders and Whips may stimulate their Members to harass the Government with Questions and the Ministers and Government Whips may advise their supporters to be less ardent in their Questioning. But Questions still remain much the most personal of all the activities of the House, reflecting much more closely than any other form of procedure the everyday activities of Members, the problems that concern them, their personal predilections and idiosyncrasies.

(i) *Information*

Why do Members want information? Why should Members not want information? If a Member is to be effective he ought to be more knowledgeable about public affairs and government activity and policy than other citizens. Much of this knowledge is obtained in the same way as others obtain it: from the press, books, conversation, Government publications (Blue Books, White Papers, etc.) and from Parliamentary Debates (in the last case he may listen or he may read). He can obtain some information more readily than the general public because he is constantly mixing formally and informally with other Members, whose interest and job it is to be well informed and to take part in and talk about public affairs. Even so, this is very far from saying that he has ready access to all the information he needs. In this connexion, it must be borne in mind that there are no Committees concerned with the administration and policies of a particular Department or of a sector of Government activity such as are found in many legislatures. There are, of course, the Committees on Public Accounts, on the Estimates, on Statutory Instruments, and, more recently established, on the Nationalized Industries. Membership of these Committees provides opportunities to examine witnesses and to obtain information from Departments. But only a small proportion of the House serves on these Committees, and, in any case, the subject they cover is limited. There are no Committees of the House concerned with, say Agriculture or Foreign Affairs, upon which the Members most interested in these subjects may serve and thus have fuller access to specialist information available in these Departments. Assuming that Members are likely to be more effective the better they are informed, any system of Parliamentary procedure must provide some formal opportunity for them to obtain information in the possession of the various Government Departments. In the British system this is provided by Questions to Ministers.

The rules governing Questions provide that the information for which Members ask should not be readily available in accessible documents, such as Statutes and Treaties, or in ordinary works of reference, including the statistical and other reports published by the Government. The rules are, however, liberally interpreted. A Member is assumed to be able to read but not necessarily to have the time to add, subtract or divide. Occasionally, therefore, he may use a Question to get a Department to make some calculations based on figures already published. More usually the information he wants is not readily accessible. Though Departments include a great deal of factual information in their Annual Reports or in one or other of the statistical returns there still remains a great deal unpublished. Sometimes only the national figures are published whereas the Member wants those for his constituency. In many cases the information demanded is not statistical but concerns Departmental practice or policy that would not be made available except in response to a Question. The Member may be specializing in a particular field and wish to keep abreast of affairs; he may want the information for a speech or an article or as ammunition with which to bombard the Department; or he may be asking for it on behalf of some group or activity with which he is connected.[1] Even University teachers have been known to invoke the aid of a friendly Member to obtain information in this way! The role of Questions purely as a device to obtain information is extremely significant and is often underrated.

(ii) *Pressing for Action*

The second purpose similarly springs from the everyday needs of Members. Whether or not his Party is in power a Member is concerned (*a*) to investigate and, if necessary, secure redress for the grievances and complaints brought to his attention, and (*b*) to exercise some influence on Government policy and action in favour of his constituency or some wider interest or even more generally.

(*a*) *Individual Complaints and Grievances*

Having regard to the large number of complaints, grievances and enquiries which come to the attention of Members, very few are raised by way of Questions. Normally they are raised in the first instance by a letter from the Member to the Minister concerned; there may indeed be a good deal of correspondence, there may be talks between the Member and the Minister, and the matter may go on for many months. Most of these cases will be settled by the Department making a concession, or altering its decision, or by the Member being satisfied, (even if the aggrieved person is not), that the Department has acted reasonably or that nothing further can be done. In a few cases the Member will remain dissatisfied, or at least will wish to press the matter further. He will then decide to raise the issue publicly in the form of a Question. The Department will very likely have

[1] A Department can refuse to provide information to an individual, a Trade Association or some interest group, but is reluctant to be put in the position of refusing such information to Parliament. Occasionally, an interest group will be advised by a Department to try to get a Question asked so that the Department may legitimately provide the information it requires. On this and the use of Questions by such groups see J. D. Stewart, *British Pressure Groups* (1958), pp. 79–83.

taken this possibility into account, indeed the Member may well have warned them that he would put down a Question failing a a satisfactory solution. It is unlikely, therefore, that they will be willing to change their decision merely because a Question has been asked, for had they intended to do this, they could have done so earlier and avoided a Question. Even so a starred Question causes a Department and, in particular, the Minister to think again. For the grievance now becomes public. One of the Gallery Correspondents seeking a good story may write it up; a national daily may even put several reporters on to filling in the background to the Question; the Member himself and the aggrieved person may be interviewed by the press. A story which was known to only a few people will now become general knowledge. It will become known also to the Minister's colleagues and to the mass of Members. All this publicity may not be unfavourable to the Minister, nor need it cause him to capitulate. It will mean, however, that he must take public opinion into account and re-examine the strength of his case. He will have to consider very carefully, not merely whether the Department's decision is right, but whether his explanation of it will sound right. This 'fuller consideration' will in some instances lead to the Minister giving a helpful reply, either by changing the decision or by saying that he will look into the matter further. The following exchanges recorded in Hansard[1] indicate the kind of thing that may happen.

Sir W. Smithers asked the Minister of Health if he is aware that Mr. E. Bowen, of Altham Cottage, Knockholt, who has had both legs amputated, is still awaiting information as to his future treatment and the supplying of a mechanical chair; and if he will take the necessary steps to see that Mr. Bowen's disabilities are attended to forthwith.

Mr. Bevan: No Sir. Mr. Bowen is perfectly satisfied with his treatment, which is almost completed, and knows that he will be provided with a mechanical tricycle as soon as possible.

Sir W. Smithers: Is the Minister aware that when this Question was put down he was not satisfied and that it is only because I threatened to put down a Question that Mr. Bowen got immediate treatment.

Mr. Bevan: That may reveal the efficacy of Questions in Parliament, and I have never under-estimated their importance. Why the hon. Member should reproach himself because on one occasion he has been useful, I do not know.

[1] H.C. Deb. (1948–9), 457, c. 1018.

Sir W. Smithers: On a point of Order. May I ask for your protection, Mr. Speaker? I object to being called 'vermin' in other words.

If the Member is not satisfied with the Minister's reply, he may be allowed to ask one, possibly two, supplementaries. If neither the original nor the subsequent Ministerial replies are to the Member's satisfaction, he may decide to pursue the matter further. He may resume discussions behind the scenes, and even follow up with a further Question some time later.

In many ways the following up of the original Question by further Questions on the Paper is more effective than the hurriedly prepared supplementary. For unless the supplementary catches the Minister completely off his guard, which is most unusual, little further information is gained by the Member. Moreover the Minister may not have adequate information with him and in any case he is likely to give an unforthcoming or defensive answer if pressed about a matter which he has not fully mastered. Having studied the Minister's answer to the original Question and perhaps checked it with his other sources of information, the Member can prepare a further Question. This will have to be considered carefully in the Department and as a result possibly a fresh approach may be made. A striking example of the persistent following up of a 'grievance' was the so-called Scarcroft affair. The issue was whether the newly established Yorkshire Electricity Board had contravened Defence Regulation 56A by spending more than they had been licensed to spend on the extension of the Board's headquarters at Scarcroft, near Leeds. Failing to get satisfactory answers from the Ministry of Fuel and Power Questions were put to the Minister of Works and the Attorney General in respect of their responsibilities. Ultimately the Board was successfully prosecuted. During the legal proceedings the Lord Chief Justice commented on the inaccurate reply given in the House to Mr. (now Sir) Donald Kaberry's Question on 4 December 1950. Later the Minister set on foot an enquiry to discover who was primarily responsible for the inaccuracy of the information supplied to the House.[1]

If a Member cannot get satisfaction by means of Questions the most suitable alternative form of parliamentary procedure is to raise the matter on the Adjournment. A Member will sometimes

[1] See H.C. Deb. (1951-2), 494, c. 866-8 and 2009-11 and numerous other references during the Sessions of 1950-1 and 1951-2.

THE QUESTIONERS

rise after the Minister's reply and say '... in view of the unsatisfactory nature of the reply, I beg to give notice I will raise the matter on the Adjournment'.[1]

There are three occasions when the motion 'That this House do now adjourn' can be used by a Member to initiate a discussion of some constituency case or similar administrative matter. First, whenever the House adjourns for one of its customary seasonal holidays the whole day is devoted to the discussion, on a motion for the adjournment, of topics selected either by the Opposition or by private Members. The day is divided into convenient periods and Mr. Speaker selects the Member and the matter for discussion during each period. There are four such days in the normal Session.

Second, there is the 'half-hour' available at the end of Public Business at each day's sitting. Standing Order No. 1. provides that on Mondays, Tuesdays, Wednesdays and Thursdays, Public Business shall be interrupted at 10.00 p.m., at which time the Adjournment is moved by one of the Government Whips and the Debate on this motion need not be brought to a close until half an hour has elapsed. The same rule applies to Fridays, but at 4.00 p.m.

Third, should all the business on the Order Paper be concluded before 10.00 p.m. (or 4.00 p.m. on Fridays), the Adjournment is immediately moved by one of the Government Whips, and the Member who was to speak on the Adjournment later that day may then initiate a discussion on the topic he has selected. Should this discussion go on until the hour fixed by the Standing Order for the interruption of business (10.00 p.m. or 4.00 p.m.) another Adjournment has then to be moved which results in a further half hour being available for the subject under discussion. This third category does not occur often, and when it does its effect, as a rule, is to extend the length of time available for the discussion of the point raised by a Member, although on occasion discussions on other matters have been initiated.

The main opportunity for a Member to raise a constituency or similar issue on his own initiative, without the need for support

[1] It is not necessary for a Member to give such notice, but having given it no further supplementaries are allowed. Nowadays, no further Questions can be put on the Paper concerning the subject, until the Adjournment motion has taken place, the prohibition ending if the Member fails to get a place on the next list of such Motions.

from either front bench, is thus during the daily 'half hour' Adjournment period. This is a comparatively recent development. In theory it existed before 1939 but it could not be relied upon, for the half hour was quite often taken up with 'exempted' business or largely eaten into by the voting on the Motion under discussion at the interruption of Business. It was made a more regular opportunity during the war of 1939-45 largely as recompense for the loss of other private Member's opportunities. Since 1947 the Standing Orders have guaranteed that there will be 30 minutes available for private Member's use after the evening Adjournment has been moved, it not being moved until any voting on the previous business has ended.[1]

The method whereby Members obtain the right to an Adjournment Motion has undergone many changes. At present, Members give notice by putting their name and the subject they wish to discuss in a book kept by the Secretary to Mr. Speaker. Once a fortnight, on a Thursday, there is a ballot and eight lucky Members obtain the right to raise their subject on the Adjournments taken on the Tuesday, Wednesday and Friday of the next week, and the Monday, Tuesday, Wednesday and Friday of the following week, and the Monday of the week after, a particular day being allocated to each. In addition, Mr. Speaker himself selects the subject and Member for Thursday Adjournments.

A Member must give written notice to the Speaker that he wishes to have an Adjournment Motion. Any statement to that effect that he may make during Question time does not count. He need not even have asked a Question about the subject. If he is successful one fortnight, he cannot submit a subject again until another fortnight has elapsed. If he is not successful, he will only be considered again if he formally renews his request, for it is not carried forward automatically as it used to be before February 1960. He cannot change the subject except on forty-eight hours notice, and not at all in respect of the Thursday Adjournment, for Mr. Speaker's choice is related to the subject, not to the Member.

Though the subjects discussed on the daily Adjournments are typical of the matters raised at Question time, probably less than

[1] Mr. Herbert (now Lord) Morrison has said of this development: 'it is becoming almost as distinctive, important and meritorious a part of our Parliamentary procedure as Question time itself.' Evidence to Select Committee on Procedure, Third Report, 1945-6, q. 3563.

half arise from Members' dissatisfaction at Ministerial replies. From the beginning of the Session of 1959–60 until the Easter recess there were 86 of these Adjournment debates. The kind of subjects raised can be seen from the list given at the end of the Weekly Notice Paper issued on Saturday, 27 February 1960:

> The case of Mr. S. K. Seisay (Colonial).
> New Technical and Grammar School, Blackburn (Education).
> Heavy traffic through narrow residential roads in Wembley (Transport).
> The death of Leading Aircraftman Thompson (Air).
> Treatment of migraine (Health).
> Delegation of health and welfare functions as it affects Worthing (Health).
> The operation of standard grants and improvement grants (Housing).
> High interest rates in building loans to local authorities compared to private firms (Treasury).
> Electricity supply — Fellbrigg Road, Sheffield (Power).
> The lack of adequate transport facilities in south Essex (Transport).
> Selection and appointment of general practitioners in the National Health Service (Health).

The Department concerned, i.e. the Department whose Minister has to reply to the Member raising the issue, is given in brackets at the end of each topic. Five Departments were involved in more than 50 of the 86 Debates — Transport (17); Housing and Local Government (10); Education (9); Home Office (9); and Health (7). In contrast, the Departments likely to be most involved in major current issues of national policy were seldom involved: Treasury (4); Colonial Office (2); and Foreign Office (1). In large part this reflects the constituency character of the majority of the issues raised. More than half of them concerned particular localities or persons, and most of the others were concerned with the administrative aspects of domestic affairs.

The value of the Adjournment Motion is that it enables a Member to speak at some length on an issue which is of great concern to him and for a Minister to reply at corresponding length. Usually, only these two will speak, and usually the Department's reply is made by the Parliamentary Secretary. On 10 February 1960, for example, Mr. T. W. Jones (Labour Member for Merioneth) raised the question of the shortage of hospital facilities in his area. He spoke for about 15 minutes, and the Parliamentary Secretary to the Ministry of Health replied in almost the same time.

Whilst the daily Adjournment is a useful adjunct to Question time, it is only a limited one. There are many more Members wishing to obtain one of these occasions than can be accommodated. A Member has, therefore, to be lucky or persistent in order to get a chance. Moreover, whilst the half hour is guaranteed, the time at which it occurs may be modified by the suspension of Standing Orders or for other reasons. Thus on 9 February 1960, the Adjournment Motion did not come on until 12.54 a.m., and it was 1.13 a.m. before the Assistant Postmaster-General rose to reply. The reason was that Mr. Speaker accepted an Urgency Motion under Standing Order No. 9, on Cyprus, which came on at 7.00 p.m., normal business not being resumed until 9.58 p.m. In any case coming as it does at the end of the day's proceedings, the Debate on the Adjournment almost always takes place in a very thinly attended House. On occasion only a Government Whip and possibly an Opposition Whip will be present in addition to the Member and the Junior Minister. Moreover, it is too late to catch the attention of most of the 'dailies'. It is, therefore, quite different from Question time.

Another possibility is open to the Member dissatisfied with a Ministerial reply. Under Standing Order No. 9, a Member may rise in his place immediately at the end of Question time and ask leave to move the Adjournment of the House for the purpose of discussing a matter of urgent public importance. The terms of the Motion must be given in writing to Mr. Speaker, who decides whether it satisfies the conditions of the Standing Order as interpreted by various rulings. If he decides it is in order, he reads it out and asks whether the Member has the leave of the House. If leave is given unanimously, or if, on objection being taken, Mr. Speaker asks those Members supporting to rise in their places, and forty or more Members rise,[1] the Motion comes up for discussion at 7.00 p.m. that same day.

For various reasons, an 'urgency Motion' is very difficult to obtain and is most unlikely to be accepted by Mr. Speaker if the primary purpose is to call attention to an unsatisfactory

---

[1] If 40 or more Members do not rise in support, but at least 10 have risen, the Member may demand a division and may receive leave to move the Motion by a majority vote.

Ministerial reply. Between 1945 and 1957, it was asked for on seventy-three, and allowed on only eight occasions. As a result of the recommendations of the Select Committee of 1959,[1] it is now a little easier to obtain the Speaker's permission to have such a Motion put to the House, but it is not intended to be a device for every day use.

(b) Relation to Parliamentary and Public Opinion

'But the question hour, touching on all subjects under the sun, is a microcosm of the Sitting. . . . If one wants to know what the House of Commons is thinking about at a particular period of a Session, he should study the list of questions.'[2] So wrote Lucy in July 1896. He was, of course, right about the great diversity of subject matter but he exaggerated the significance of Questions as an indication of Parliamentary opinion, probably because he wanted to chastise Mr. Balfour, then Leader of the House, for 'ostentatious indifference to the question hour'. Questions are not really a good indication of opinion and interest concerning the big issues; there are many better ones, including conversation in the lobbies and the Motions arranged through the usual channels. Any big issue of public policy creates a backwash in Question time but the number of Questions asked about it are unlikely to be a fair measure of the feelings of the House.

Questions are a much better guide to the smaller issues, for Members ask Questions about matters which interest or worry them. With more than 500 Members free to put Questions at any time during the Session any issue which excites them will lead to a sudden rash of Questions about the matter. It may be a comparatively small incident. Thus the announcement, in November 1955 that Sir Miles Thomas, then full-time chairman of British Overseas Airways Corporation, a Government body, had become Director of a private firm (Ferguson (Research) Ltd.) immediately provoked six starred Questions addressed to the Minister of Transport and Civil Aviation, all by Labour Members.[3] Sometimes in a case of this kind the Questions are so

[1] Report of Select Committee on Procedure, 1959, para. 34. The Committee quoted with approval Mr. Speaker Peel's remark of 1894 that the Motion was designed for 'the occurrence of some sudden emergency either in home or foreign affairs . . .'.
[2] Henry W. Lucy, A Diary of the Unionist Parliament, 1895–1900 (1901), p. 103.
[3] H.C. Deb. (1955–6), 546, c. 1454–8.

similar in wording or intention that the Minister can deal with them in one reply.

The subject matter of Questions reflects the changing interests of Members. In the early months of 1946, some 50 starred Questions a week were being addressed to the War Office, a clear indication of the great public interest in demobilization. This Department was by far the most questioned at that date. By the Session 1947-8 the War Office had fallen to seventh in the list of Departments arranged according to the number of starred Questions addressed to them. The Minister of Food was now the most questioned, averaging 38 starred Questions a week as against 18 for the War Office. Food was still at the top in 1950-1 but ceased to attract so much attention with the disappearance of rationing and a return to more normal conditions. In 1958-9 the Colonial Office was the most questioned Department (averaging 32 per week) followed by the Ministry of Transport (31), Foreign Office (28), Treasury (26), Board of Trade (23), Ministry of Health (21) and Ministry of Labour (20).

Most Departments are responsible for a variety of functions or subjects. The Ministry of Housing and Local Government has responsibilities for housing, town and country planning, water supply, local finance, local boundaries, and a variety of other matters. The Ministry of Power is concerned with steel, coal, electricity, petroleum and gas. Quite apart from any change in the volume of Questions addressed to a Department there will occur changes in emphasis within the total. Indeed marked changes from year to year in the number of Questions asked are more likely to occur in Departments with a single or limited range of functions, the former Ministry of Food and the War Office being good examples. For most Departments the total will not fluctuate markedly from year to year, an increase in interest in one aspect of the Department's work being probably offset by a decline of interest in another aspect. Thus, the Colonial Office has for many years now been among the top half-dozen Departments measured by number of starred Questions. But within the total there have been shifts in emphasis according to which of the Colonies was attracting most attention at the time.

A detailed study of Questions to the Post Office showed this changing interest. In 1906 when labour relations in the Department were not particularly good, 31 per cent. of the Questions concerned such matters, as against only 10 per cent. in 1946. In 1906 12 per cent. were concerned with alleged inefficiencies and inadequacies in the postal service as against 3 per cent. in 1936, and again 12 per cent. in 1946.[1] Some of the changes in the pattern of questioning reflected new responsibilities added to a Department. But whatever the reason, a rise in the number of Questions about a particular topic is usually not a precursor of rising public interest but an outward and visible sign that the topic has now reached the Parliamentary stage. The volume and changing content of correspondence which reaches a Department either direct from the public or by way of Members, will usually provide an earlier indication of popular feeling than the Order Paper. When in 1946 the War Office were handling 50 starred Questions a week, they also had to handle 1400 letters a week from Members and many more from the public direct. Neither Ministers nor Members need have attended Question time or even have glanced at the Order Paper during the period, to be made aware of the great public interest in demobilization — their correspondence, the press and their daily contacts were ample guides.

So far we have been proceeding on the assumption that what interests or worries Members will also interest or worry Ministers. Even the preparation of an answer to a single Question provides a Minister with an opportunity to reconsider not merely a particular case but also the general policy involved. If an issue or a particular aspect of the work of his Department suddenly attracts a large number of Questions he will be forced to give it special attention. Thus even though the major part of the 14,000 Questions asked each year are not organized but reflect the interests and worries of some 500 Members acting individually their impact on Government policy can be considerable.

From time to time, however, Questions are used as part of an organized campaign to secure a change in Government policy or to gain publicity for some cause. During the height of the campaign for equal pay a small group of Members (e.g. Dame Irene Ward, Mr. A. Lewis and Mr. Douglas Houghton) put

[1] Anne Phillips, 'Post Office Parliamentary Questions', *Public Administration* (1949) vol. 27, pp. 91–9. See also the Acton Society Trusts' study No. 5 in its series *Hospitals and the State*. (*The Central Control of the Service*) (1958) for a detailed analysis of the Questions asked about the Hospital Service during the six Sessions 1950–1 to 1955–6.

down a series of Questions. They asked about the pay of women in order to obtain particular information, to follow up a protest by the Equal Pay Campaign Committee against a particular case of discrimination, and primarily to keep the issue alive. On 9 March 1954 (Equal Pay Day), two petitions were presented and 25 Questions were put down for oral answer by Labour Members, Mr. Speaker refusing to accept any more.[1]

From time to time a Minister will attract a barrage of Questions on a particular issue. On the 4 April 1960 for example, over forty starred Questions were addressed to the Minister of Pensions and National Insurance, a number in very similar terms, and it is quite clear that most of them had been organized with a view to calling attention to the need to increase the level of the old age pension. On 23 May 1960 Questions Nos. 56 to 67 addressed to the Minister of Health were all concerned with the provision of tricycles to injured miners and certain other categories or the replacement of tricycles by two-seater vehicles. Many of the Questions were almost identical. For example four of twelve asked the Ministers how many injured miners in such and such a coalfield had been issued with [invalid] tricycles; and what would be the cost of replacing these tricycles by two-seater cars. The only significant variation in the wording was in the name of the coalfield; Lancashire, Durham, Yorkshire, Nottinghamshire, being substituted according to the constituency of the Member asking the Question. Somewhat similarly worded Questions were put down for sufferers from poliomyelitis. Other examples of a barrage of Questions on a particular topic are the successful campaign against the imposition of a 5 per cent. Purchase Tax on miner's protective clothing in April 1958 and the Questions organized by Scottish Members during 1960 to draw attention to the economic problems of Scotland. Occasionally a group of Opposition Members may concentrate on a particular Minister, for example, the large number of Questions addressed to Mr. Charles Masterman who as Chairman of the National Health Insurance Commission was answerable in the House for the National Health Scheme introduced in 1911 after bitter opposition.

Sometimes such tactics reflect a dislike of the Minister's

[1] Allen Potter, 'The Equal Pay Campaign Committee: A Case-Study of a Pressure Group', *Political Studies* (1957), vol. v. p. 57.

policy and actions and sometimes of his personality. An Opposition may resort to a greater use of Questions or of other Parliamentary devices to harass a Government with a small or uncertain majority and to encourage Ministers to give up Office.

The more organized the questioning the more likely it is to be a Party activity. Now and again two or three Members either from the same Party or from different Parties, out of their strong common interest in a particular subject, e.g. mental health or the development of atomic energy, will combine to ask a number of Questions. But the sudden appearance on the Paper of 10–20 starred Questions similarly worded usually indicates an Opposition device and is likely to have been organized by one of the Opposition Whips with the assistance of the permanent staff of the Parliamentary Party. This has certainly been the case in recent years with most of the barrages or campaigns conducted by groups of Labour Members.

Questions, however, enable a single Member to conduct a campaign in a way allowed by no other form of House of Commons' procedure. An earlier example is the campaign conducted by the late Mr. Fred Jowett to reduce anthrax. As Labour Member for Bradford West he knew at first hand the danger to workers in the woollen industry of the disease of anthrax contracted from certain diseased fleeces. Jowett entered the House of Commons at the election of 1906 and in the words of his biographer: 'Whenever a fatality from anthrax occurred he placed a question on the Order Paper, giving the name of the firm, the verdict, and any evidence of special significance.' His aim was to stimulate the government inspectors to a more careful inspection of the mills where wool sorting and combing were done, to encourage firms to be more careful about the wool they purchased and to exert constant pressure towards what he assumed to be the only proper solution — the entire exclusion of the dangerous fleece or its disinfection. 'For four years he maintained this deadly questioning almost every week, supplementing it by direct approach to the Home Office, [usually accompanied by representatives of the unions concerned]. At last, in 1910, he won. The Home Office ordered that dangerous wools must be disinfected at the Liverpool Wool Disinfecting Station before being sent to the mills.'[1]

[1] F. Brockway, *Sixty Years of Socialism* (1946), p. 85. Mr. Brockway very greatly exaggerates the number of Questions asked by Mr. Jowett.

Mr. Gerald Nabarro, the Conservative Member for Kidderminster, is an excellent example of a recent user of Questions to conduct a persistent campaign.[1] For several months prior to the Budget Day of 1958 (15 April) Mr. Nabarro put Question after Question to the Chancellor of the Exchequer about what he regarded as the 'anomalies' and 'absurdities' of the Purchase Tax. The Chancellor appears on the rota on Tuesdays and Thursdays and on almost every one of these days from Thursday, 23 January, to Tuesday, 1 April, Mr. Nabarro had three starred Questions on the paper about the Purchase Tax. The following is a fair sample day taken from the Order Paper for 13 February 1958:

*54. Mr. Nabarro: To ask the Chancellor of the Exchequer whether he is aware that a manufacturer of key holders was recently informed by the Customs and Excise authorities that a holder for the pocket, designed in such a way that the flap closing it would prevent the keys from falling out and damaging the pocket, would be subject to 60 per cent. Purchase Tax, but if the size of the flap could be reduced to $\frac{1}{2}$ inch in size, the holder would be free of Purchase Tax; and whether, in view of the fact that the holder with the $\frac{1}{2}$-inch flap would be ineffective from the point of view of protecting the user's pocket, he will instruct the officials to reconsider the matter.

*55. Mr. Nabarro: To ask the Chancellor of the Exchequer when the regulation was introduced laying down that doorknockers 5 inches or more in length shall be free of tax whereas doorknockers under that length carry 30 per cent. Purchase Tax; and what has been the revenue from Purchase Tax on doorknockers for each of the past five years for which figures are available.

*56. Mr. Nabarro: To ask the Chancellor of the Exchequer whether he is aware that, in view of the fact that a nutcracker is liable to Purchase Tax at 15 per cent. whereas a doorknocker over 5 inches in length is free of tax, there is an increasing practice of supplying nutcrackers with screw holes so that they could theoretically be used as doorknockers, with the result that with such modification these nutcrackers become free of tax; and what instructions have been issued to Customs and Excise staff with regard to this matter.

Questions like these persistently asked over a period, have three results. First, the accumulation of examples makes a more

[1] An interesting though less ambitious campaign was conducted by Mr. Arthur Lewis, Labour Member for West Ham North, who during February–March 1957 put some 30–40 Questions on the Paper all concerned with some aspect of the salaries of Members of Parliament, which he wished to see made more adequate.

considerable impact than any single Debate could have achieved. Whether or not Members agreed with Mr. Nabarro and whether or not they were Government supporters, they could not help chuckling at a Question which asked why 'corsets remain subject to Purchase Tax whereas corset laces are exempt' or why 'the fur of the Australasian red opposum, if undyed and in strips measuring not more than nine inches in length and one inch in width, is exempt from the 50 per cent. Purchase Tax charged on other furs'. Second, such a campaign attracts a good deal of attention in the press and Nabarro wrote articles and made public speeches about the matter. Under the title of one of these newspaper articles the editor had put, 'It is an open secret that the Chancellor is reviewing Purchase Tax. If he decides to make changes it will be largely due to the determined Conservative M.P. for Kidderminster.'[1] Third, as a result of the Questions it is very likely that the Chancellor of the Exchequer and his senior Treasury advisors learnt a very great deal more about the detailed working of the Purchase Tax than they would have done if left alone. We will, however, come to this aspect in a later chapter when we look at Questions from the viewpoint of Ministers. Here it is sufficient to say that in his speech in the House on 15 April 1958, introducing the Budget, the Chancellor of the Exchequer (Mr. Heathcoat Amory) said 'Although I am no lover of the Purchase Tax, and recognize its defects, I think that its shortcomings have been somewhat exaggerated in recent months. I know that there are anomalies . . . I have come to the conclusion that the most helpful thing that I can do is to simplify the tax and adjust it to a more sensible pattern.' He announced a number of reductions in Purchase Tax, including the tax on ties and the withdrawal of certain exemptions 'which have proved anomalous' the latter including 'the threads with which one does up stays' which Mr. Nabarro had cited as an anomaly.[2]

USE FOR PARTY PURPOSES

From the viewpoint of the party political battle Questions differ in three ways from most other forms of activity in the Chamber. First, they are not followed by the need to vote. The

[1] *Oxford Mail*, 12 March 1958.
[2] H.C. Deb. (1957–8), 586, c. 72–3. Mr. Nabarro conducted similar campaigns for several months before the Budgets of 1959, 1960 and 1961.

loyalty of the supporter of the Government is, therefore, not at issue. Emphasis on the monolithic character of the two major British political parties and the sternness of party discipline obscures the extent to which Ministers are at variance with their supporters in the House. The significant test applied in most cases is how the Member votes. A Member who votes against his Party leaders is a rebel indeed; a Member who openly or without good reason (e.g. sickness) abstains, is a significant figure if the issue is significant; but the Government supporter who, during the course of his speech, makes some remarks critical of or not wholly friendly toward the Minister and then votes with the Government is having the best of both worlds. Critical or awkward Questions do not involve the Member in voting.

Second, Questions are not part of a set piece staged by the Party leaders. The reasoned amendment to the Queen's Speech; Motions of no confidence; formal Motions for or against a particular Government policy are arranged through the usual channels for the purpose of securing a clash between Government and Opposition. The main speeches on both sides come from the front benches and the matters at issue usually reflect strong differences of political approach or, at least, reflect the desire of the Opposition to emphasize that it is thinking differently about them. There is much less political content in the majority of Questions. Many are asked purely for the sake of obtaining information and a good proportion of the remainder are about constituency matters or concern interests with which the Member is associated. Some will bring into play the political attitude of the Member; some he will be inclined to take up with more enthusiasm than others for reasons of personal rather than of Party interest; but a great many he will deal with just as any other Member would deal with them. It is true that Opposition Members ask more Questions than do Government supporters. The difference is not wholly due to the normal working of the Party struggle. Government supporters are likely to have closer personal contacts with Ministers than are Opposition Members. They find it easier, therefore, to use informal channels and need rely less on formal procedure. If the subject matter of their enquiry is likely to be awkward for the Minister to deal with at Question time their personal friendliness toward him quite apart from their political predilections, will incline them against dealing with the matter by way of a starred Question. Even the attitude of Members of the Opposition may be affected by their personal, and not wholly by their political, feelings about a particular Minister. Some Ministers are popular in the House, some are unpopular, even with their own supporters. If a Minister is popular, is thought to be doing a good administrative job and handles the 'behind the scenes' approach of Members in a helpful manner he is likely to attract fewer starred Questions than if he has not these attributes. Some of those that are asked will be couched in more friendly or less awkward terms and the supplementaries are likely to be less sharp and more easily handled.

Third, it is worth noticing that just as Questions are more personal in that they mostly reflect the wishes of the individual Member and are not organized through the usual channels, so they are more personal in the sense that they emphasize the role of individual Ministers rather than the responsibility of the Government as a whole.

ROLE OF THE OPPOSITION FRONT BENCH

The main Debates that take place in the House are dominated by the two Front Benches. For this and other reasons the Opposition leaders normally do not put many Questions on the Paper.[1] The Leader of the Opposition proceeds only by way of Private Notice Questions about matters which he thinks to be of urgent public importance. A similar attitude towards Questions is usually adopted by some of the other leading members of the Opposition Front Bench. In fact it is generally true to say that very few of the Opposition front benchers who ask a large number of Questions are from among the top half-dozen or so former senior Ministers or ultimately become one of the top half dozen or so when their Party achieves office.

There are, however, usually some Members on or aspiring to be on the Opposition Front Bench who use Questions as a party device to harass and criticize the Government. A detailed study[2] of the session of 1929–30 showed that 30 former Conservative

[1] cf. the remark of a Conservative Minister, Mr. Harry (later Lord) Crookshank, to the Select Committee on Nationalized Industries, 1952: ' by the convention to which at any rate our Party is subject ex-Ministers only ask ... very few Questions and ... they are always very straighforward ones.' q. 77.
[2] *American Political Science Review*, December 1933, vol. 27, p. 974.

Ministers asked 1,026 starred Questions (10.9 per cent. of the total) and 1,896 supplementaries (17 per cent. of the total). Professor McCulloch interprets this as an Opposition Front Bench campaign against the new Government. A good deal of the questioning, however, was done by Members who had just ceased to be quite junior Ministers, for example the former Assistant Postmaster-General.[1] Such leading former Ministers as Mr. Stanley Baldwin, Sir Austen Chamberlain, Mr. Winston Churchill, Mr. Leopold Amery, Sir William Joynson-Hicks and Sir Philip Cunliffe-Lister made little or no contribution. It is, moreover, generally the case that when a Government is in a weak position, as was the Labour Government in 1929–30 and again in 1950–1, that the Opposition will make greater use of every Parliamentary device to harry Ministers and so induce the Government to resign. An increased number of Questions will then be part of a general campaign entered into with vigour by the more energetic and politically enthusiastic Members.

For a good many years now the leading front bench Members of whichever party is in Opposition have been referred to popularly as the 'Shadow Cabinet'.[2] A Conservative Leader in Opposition is assisted by a Consultative Committee appointed by him and also by a larger Business Committee consisting of the principal officers of all the main functional committees of the Parliamentary Party.

The Labour Party has a Parliamentary Committee, composed of the Leader and Deputy Leader and a number of others mainly elected by the Parliamentary Party. In 1955, however, the then Leader (Mr. C. R. Attlee) decided that, in addition to having this Committee, he would allocate responsibility for watching the work of each major Department to one or more Members of the Party in the House. This practice was continued and developed by Mr. Gaitskell when he became Leader shortly afterwards. During the Session of 1959–60, for example, Mr. Harold Wilson, Mr. Douglas Jay and Mr. Roy Jenkins had special responsibility for the Treasury and the Board of Trade;

---

[1] Sir Kingsley Wood, who had been Parliamentary Secretary to the Minister of Health, who became Chancellor of the Exchequer in 1940 was, however, one of the prolific questioners during 1929–30.

[2] See R. T. McKenzie, *British Political Parties* (1954), pp. 55–57 and 411–26 and Herbert Morrison, *Government and Parliament*, second edition, 1959, pp. 121–46 and 348–51.

Mr. F. T. Willey for Agriculture; and Mr. J. Callaghan and Mr. G. M. Thomson for Colonial and Commonwealth Affairs. Altogether, excluding Mr. Gaitskell himself, Mr. Aneurin Bevan who was not able to attend owing to ill-health, and Mr. J. Griffiths who acted as Deputy Leader of the Opposition, 29 Members had 'shadow' Departmental responsibilities. These responsibilities include speaking in the appropriate Debates and taking a particular interest in the formulation of the Party's attitude to current problems and to Government action and policy. They also involve taking an interest in Question time. During the Session of 1959–60 these 29 Members gave notice of some 1,300 Questions, rather over 10 per cent. of the total number of starred and unstarred Questions asked during the period. Not all of these were in respect of the Members' departmental responsibilities, only some 700 being for this purpose, and 200 of these were put down by three of the group: Mr. G. de Freitas, Mr. D. Healey, and Mr. Willey. The fact that even these Members asked nearly as many Questions about constituency and other matters outside their special Party responsibility and that the specialized organization of the Labour Front Bench produced only about 6 per cent. of all the Questions asked during 1959–60, shows what a predominantly back bench device Questions still remain.

Three other points must, however, be made about the use of Questions by the Opposition for attacking the Party leaders in power. First, the leaders of the Opposition are more active in asking supplementaries than putting Questions on the Paper. After the Member asking the main Question has had his chance of a supplementary the Labour Member charged with a special responsibility for watching that particular Minister and his Department may come in either in support of the original questioner or to try to gain some advantage from the exchange. This usually happens only when the Member or the party leaders feel that it will be of advantage to subject the Minister to more thorough cross-questioning. It is more likely to happen in the field of foreign and colonial affairs or in respect of Questions which raise topical issues of public controversy. But even a constituency case which appears to show the Minister in an unfavourable light may occasionally be hunted in this way by a front bench Member. Sometimes, however, the more experienced front bencher is merely coming to the rescue of one of his friends who looks to be having the worst of the exchange with a Minister.

Second, there usually exist at any one time several issues on which Party feeling runs high. During the time a subject is in serious political dispute much of what has just been said about the political attitudes of back benchers needs to be modified. For any mention of the subject in the House, even by way of the most harmless looking Question, is likely to arouse Opposition Members and possibly provide them with an opportunity not only to embarrass a Minister but also gain a good deal of publicity in the process. When a subject becomes politically 'live' Opposition Members are likely to put down most of the Questions. They are likely to look for Questions or at least not have the same hesitation about raising, for example, personal cases by way of a starred Question.

The establishment of the Unemployment Assistance Board by the Government in 1935 and the transfer to the Board of responsibility for financial assistance to a large number of unemployed, aroused considerable anger and bitter criticism in the Labour Party. Over 800 Questions were asked about various aspects of the Board's activities in the first four years of its life. The Opposition's Questions, many of them quoting individual cases, were directed to showing the higher costs of the new form of administration or the bad effect of the new scales of assistance. When more favourable scales were introduced the Government's supporters put down Questions to reveal the numbers receiving more generous assistance. On 18 February 1937 when the Minister concerned was twitted about the number of his supporters who were putting down Questions which he could answer favourably, he replied, 'The hon. Member and his friends [i.e. the Opposition] are constantly asking for information about decreases, and there is no reason why my hon. Friend should not ask about the increases.'[1] Government supporters continued to ask Questions of this kind. During the winter of 1937–8 they asked some thirty Questions about the number receiving increased assistance due to the season and the higher cost of living, in order to demonstrate how the unemployed were benefiting from these concessions.[2] But in the political circumstances of the time few, if any,

[1] H.C. Deb. (1936–7), 320, c. 1333.
[2] John D. Millet, *Unemployment Assistance Board* (1940), pp. 162–71.

THE QUESTIONERS

Government supporters would put down Questions critical of the Board.

Third, from time to time the Party in Opposition will organize a campaign on a particular issue or against a particular Minister and use Questions by back benchers as part of it. Some of the small campaigns by Labour Members during 1959–60, referred to earlier, were of this kind. A particularly amusing form of campaign occurred on Thursday, 18 February 1960. With the normal rate of progress on that day Questions to the Prime Minister would not have been reached until about 3.15, possibly even later. But the Labour Members who had 28 of the first 39 Questions on the Paper asked only 12 of them and very few supplementaries, with the result that No. 40 was reached at 2.48. As a result, the Prime Minister, to whom 23 Questions had been addressed by Labour Members was subjected to some forty minutes of questioning, mainly about African problems.[1]

INSPIRED QUESTIONS

It is convenient at this point to mention briefly the so called 'inspired' Question. Strictly speaking this is a Question put down by a Member at the request of a Minister, and excludes Questions put on the paper because the Member thinks it will be helpful or pleasing to a Minister to answer. Inspired Questions are used for a variety of purposes: to announce the name of the Chairman and Members of a Royal Commission, or some governmental committee, or important changes in the membership of such bodies; to give publicity to some change of Government policy or some action taken by a Department; to correct or to answer a statement reported in the press; and to get in an explanation or statement in advance of some anticipated criticism.

---

[1] One Question asked about the possibility of appointing a Select Committee 'to consider the televising of parts of the proceedings of the House of Commons' and also whether the Prime Minister would consider 'arranging for experiments to be made by the taking of a film at Question Time, so that it can be used by the television service at their peak period'. This led to a supplementary by that great humourist of Question time, Mr. Emrys Hughes. He asked: 'Is the Prime Minister aware that there is a growing custom now to televising religious services? Will he consider having discussions now about whether Prayers in the House of Commons should be televised in order to attract the Government Front Bench?' Mr. Macmillan replied. 'It might also attract today's absent questioners.' H.C. Deb. (1959–60), 617, c. 1421–2.

In part, the use of this device stems from the long-established doctrine that governmental announcements should first be made in the House, a doctrine perhaps more honoured by some of the older Departments than others. In part it reflects the news and publicity value of Questions in the eyes of the press. Quite often, however, such Questions are not starred, and therefore do not attract the greater publicity associated with Question time. If, however, a Department particularly wishes an answer to receive publicity, duplicated copies of the Question and Answer are used by the Department's Public Relations Officer as press 'handouts'. In any case, the information has been made available to Members and this, in many cases, is the primary concern of the excercise.

An inspired Question is put down in the name of a back bencher. It is regarded as improper for even junior members of the Government, e.g. Parliamentary Secretaries or the junior Whips, to be used for this purpose. Very occasionally, however, a Parliamentary Private Secretary may be used but not to put an inspired Question to his own Minister. It is not, however, difficult for the Minister concerned to find one of his party willing to be used for this purpose.

PERSONAL PUBLICITY

It is often said, not of the occasional questioner but of those who make a habit of asking Questions, that they do so primarily for the publicity they obtain. Undoubtedly a Question is likely to receive far more publicity than any equivalent amount of Parliamentary effort. The front benchers on both sides of the House hit the headlines either for their speeches on major occasions or because they are involved in important or interesting political events and manoeuvres. But they constitute only a small part of the total membership. It is not easy for the general run of back benchers to catch more than the very occasional headline in the national press. They may work hard for their constituents' interests dealing with individual cases etc; they may serve on important committees, either of their Party or of the House; they may be unfailing in their attendances and their voting; they may be among the first to arrive each day and among the last to leave; all these and many more things they can do without getting the briefest mention in any newspaper report of Parliamentary proceedings. In contrast, a Question has a much greater chance of being mentioned if not in one of the national dailies, at least in a paper or journal, either circulating in the Member's area or concerned with the subject matter. Moreover the opportunity to ask Questions occurs almost every day and both frequency and subject matter are very largely under the control of the Member. A starred Question, if reached, also provides a back bencher with Parliamentary publicity. His few chances of speaking in a major debate are likely to occur at a time when the House is not well attended. Attendance at Question time is comparatively high, being excelled only by those occasions when a Minister or Opposition leader is speaking on some issue of general interest.

It cannot be denied, therefore, that Questions provide plenty of opportunity for personal publicity, and that some Members may be tempted to use them largely for this purpose. But all who wish to succeed in politics like to be well known and are not averse to seeing their names and political activities featured in the press. If personal publicity is acceptable in the case of the Party leaders why is it less so in the case of back benchers? Why should an allegation of using Questions to secure press publicity carry an implied criticism?

There are many different types among the 630 Members who constitute the House of Commons. Upon being first elected each Member is faced with the issue of what he should try to make of his new position. Some will be ambitious to become a Minister, even to become Prime Minister; some will already be quite clear that they do not wish to strive for Ministerial office. To some Members, attendance at the House will be a full-time occupation; to others very much a part-time one. Some will wish to mould their party's policy, others will be content to give their leaders unquestioning support. Some will have solid majorities unlikely to be lost except for some unforeseeable catastrophe, others will be in marginal, unsafe constituencies. Some will be good speakers and aim at contributing to major debates; others will be much happier in taking part in other forms of parliamentary activity. Some will be lethargic: others very energetic.

Asking Questions corresponds neither to the unpublicized but important work of the back bencher nor to the highly publicized and important work of the front bencher. A Question may attract press publicity quite out of relation to its importance in the eyes of the House and a persistent questioner may get more publicity and appear to be a harder working Member than those who ask only the occasional Question. The significant thing about the publicity which the persistent questioner attracts — in and out of the House — is that it seldom if ever leads to the top political posts. The typical persistent questioner comes not from that group of Members whose Parliamentary efforts are concerned with attaining high political office but from that less ambitious, but still very important group, who do not particularly want to be a Minister, or have no particular hopes of achieving this even if they wished. The young newly elected Member asking advice from experienced Parliamentarians as to the surest way to the top in politics would generally be told to make a name for himself in Debate: none would tell him that he could do it by asking more starred Questions than any other Member.

There are several reasons for this. Obviously Members of the party in power do not endear themselves to the Cabinet by harassing their Ministers with a heavy dose of Questions. This may have sufficient nuisance value to secure the Member an offer of a minor Ministerial post to keep him quiet, but usually the persistent questioner prefers his freedom and independence to being muzzled by minor office. When the Member's party is in opposition the vigorous use of Question time will give him a chance to impress his front bench with his qualities, but there are dangers, and any good impression may easily be more than offset by certain other features. The issue turns on the subject matter of the Questions.

Questions can be concerned with matters which achieve national importance and publicity or with purely local affairs and other matters of limited interest. The subject matter of the former will vary from time to time, but will usually include topics of current controversy in defence, foreign and colonial affairs. A good example of a Question of limited political interest is that by Mr. Henniker Heaton in 1896 asking why the Post Office charged father-in-law as three words on a telegram whereas mother-in-law was treated as one word.[1]

The back bencher who wishes to use Question time to its

---

[1] He succeeded in getting father-in-law treated as one word in May 1898. See Henry W. Lucy, *A Diary of the Unionist Parliament* 1895–1900, p. 78 and p. 214.

maximum is in considerable difficulty about dealing with matters of major current importance. For, even if the matter were not important until it caught the public's attention, once it has done so it is likely to become a matter for the Front Bench. Very likely the leaders of his party will wish to challenge the Government to a Debate. The Leader of the Opposition may wish to ask a Private Notice Question about it, and other Opposition front benchers may join in the supplementaries. If the matter is important enough, the Opposition will try to have an agreed policy, and may possibly work out a Parliamentary campaign. In any case, the matter is unlikely to be left to the free enterprise of a solitary back bencher.

The subject matter of the Questions of persistent questioners is therefore unlikely to be concerned with issues of current major controversy between the Government and the Opposition. This means that, in order to ask a large number of Questions, a Member must find either (a) a theme or series of themes which he can pursue over a period but not important enough to be taken over by his Front Bench, or on which the Front Bench has not an agreed policy, or (b) collect a miscellany of points, whose only link is that they provide a subject for a Question.[1] This is the difference between the campaigner and the random questioner.

Mr. Gerald Nabarro's campaign against the Purchase Tax is an excellent example of the use of a continuous series of starred Questions in an effort to change Government policy — a 'drip by drip' campaign. Some Members will concentrate their attention on a particular field of Government activity and policy, and draw all their Questions from it. But it takes a great deal of effort and ingenuity to find and frame suitable Questions day after day, however intensive the campaign or, however, broad the theme. Moreover, a campaign or theme usually involves only one, or possibly two, Ministers, and the chance of these being available nowadays for frequent questioning is not very great. Mr. Nabarro's main attack was against the Chancellor of the Exchequer, who appears on the rota on two days a week. Colonial and foreign affairs are other possible themes for which

---

[1] Commander Kenworthy (later Lord Strabolgi) 'employed no fewer than four private secretaries, whose sole and constant task it was to ferret out suitable subjects for questions'. A. Baker, *The House is Sitting* (1958), p. 239.

Ministers concerned are available more frequently for questioning on the floor of the House than are most other Ministers. These two are major fields of political interest, and are, therefore, likely to be dominated by the Opposition leaders.

For these and other reasons, the Questions put down by a persistent questioner are likely to cover a wide variety of matters. A Member who wants to make a regular practice of asking Questions will find material for them in every field in which he is interested, or in his constituency, or from any source. He is likely to be approached by people outside his constituency, even occasionally by other Members to ask a Question on their behalf. Thus Mr. J. S. Weir, who was Liberal Member for Ross and Cromarty during the period 1892–1911 and who was a major reason for the first limit imposed on the daily number of Questions, quite often had ten or more Questions on the Paper. Lucy[1] describes four of his Questions. 'Mr. Weir wanted to know whether all the Lee-Metford rifles are fitted with this particular bolt-head? Curiosity was contagious, and an hon. member on the opposite benches timidly asked what a Penn-Deeley patent bolt-head might be? This indicated a degree of ignorance that evidently pained Mr. Weir. Fortunately he was prepared for it. Amongst other ammunition packed about his person, there chanced to be a Penn-Deeley patent bolt-head. This he produced out of his waistcoat pocket, and holding it daintily between finger and thumb, he in his deepest chest notes, with just a touch of commiseration in their tone, called the hon. member's attention to it. Another Question detects the continuance in office, contrary to the Order in Council, of two district auditors in the employment of the Local Government Board who have attained the respective ages of seventy-one and sixty-five. No. 3, addressed to the President of the Local Government Board, inquires if he is aware of the existence of an excessive up-flow of sewer air in Hampstead. No. 4. also deals with sewage, which at the present moment divides Mr. Weir's attention with patent bolt-heads and district auditors who linger superfluous on the stage. It appears that the sewer drain going through the Nonikiln Burying Ground, and a sewer drain of

---

[1] *A Diary of the Home Rule Parliament 1892–5* (1896), pp. 139–40. Lucy's stories, as in this case, seldom tally exactly with the record in Hansard but this does not detract from the vivid pictures he paints of Members and of the proceedings of the House.

Nonikiln Steading and House, run into the water which supplies the town of Invergordon. Does Sir George Trevelyan, in his capacity of Secretary for Scotland, know of these things?'

Obviously Mr. Weir was treated as a 'character' by other Members except when they were annoyed about the amount of time he took for his Questions. In recent years, there has been no one quite like either him or Colonel Harry Day among the persistent questioners. But experience shows that no Member can ask several hundred Questions each Session without asking a number that most Members regard either as trivial or as more appropriately dealt with by methods which do not take up the time of the House. This has become increasingly the attitude since Question time became quite inadequate to deal with the number of starred Questions. Such a Member is unlikely to be popular with his colleagues, or to make the kind of Parliamentary reputation that will take him to the very top. They may say that he is just a publicity seeker; what they really mean is that they do not think Question time is for that kind of use, at least they themselves do not intend to use it that way. For this reason, Members have acquiesced in the lowering of the maximum daily number of starred Questions that a Member may put, knowing that it will affect the persistent and not the ordinary questioner. As the most persistent questioners are strong individualists, they are probably not much concerned with what other Members think.

CHAPTER 11

MINISTERS AND THEIR ANSWERS

THE PROCESSES OF NOTICE AND ANSWER

FOUR sets of people are directly concerned with the process whereby a Question is asked and answered: Members; the Speaker and Clerk of the House, with their assistants; the Civil Service; and Ministers. The use made of Questions by Members has already been described. The primary purpose of this chapter is to deal with the part played by the last two groups. It is, however, convenient to explain at this point the method whereby Departments receive notice of Questions and this involves saying something briefly about the handling of Questions in the office of the Clerk of the House of Commons.

The process starts by a Member wishing to ask a Question. He has to decide on the form of the Question, whether he wishes an oral or a written answer and, if the former, the day on which he would like an answer. The Member experienced in the rules and arrangements governing Questions will usually have no difficulty about these matters. But the infrequent questioner, and these are the majority of Members, will want advice which he may get from a more experienced Member or quite likely from the Table Office.

The Question may be typed or written, sent by post or handed in at the Table Office, the only proviso being that unless it is handed in by a Member in person, it must be signed by a Member though not necessarily by the one asking the Question. Special forms are not provided. If the Member wants an oral answer he must place an asterisk by the side of the Question. If he omits the asterisk, either consciously or unconsciously, the Question will be treated as requiring a written answer. In the case of a starred Question, if the Member does not indicate the date when he requires an answer, the Clerks will usually put the Question down for the first day the Minister concerned appears on the rota. The Clerks will also assign a date to any undated unstarred Question, allowing three days' clear notice.

Nowadays, except during a recess, the great majority of Questions are handed in at the Table Office. This Office is a recent development. Until 1939 it was usual for the Second Clerk Assistant to deal with Members about Questions but the Clerk of the House and Clerk Assistant were also directly concerned a great deal. Though the work was heavy, involving as it did the constant search for references, precedents and so on, it was thought that Questions did not warrant a separate section with its staff to assist the Clerk. Instead help continued to be obtained from such other sections as the Public Bill Office and the Journal Office. This arrangement seriously upset the work of these sections, particularly at times when Questions were very numerous. In 1939 a separate office was started to help the Clerks at the Table with Questions and certain other matters. It was started with one Clerk and increased to two in 1943. After the report of the Pethick-Lawrence Committee in 1945 the new arrangement was confirmed and so the Table Office came fully into being.[1]

There are now four Clerks in the Table Office. They handle Questions and also act as general assistants to the three Clerks at the Table. Subject to the Clerk of the House and ultimately, of course, to Mr. Speaker, the Table Office Clerks are responsible for advising Members on Questions, ensuring that Questions conform to the rules and conventions of the House before they appear on the Notice Paper, dealing with any points of procedure raised by Departments, and arranging for Questions to appear in the Order Paper on the right day, in the right order and form.

Except during a recess or when a major debate is taking place in the Chamber there is a steady stream of Members to the Office. Some will merely hand in their Question but a good many will wait while one of the Clerks makes certain that it conforms with the rules. The Clerks are empowered either to edit Questions so as to bring them into line with Parliamentary usage or to refuse them if they conflict with the rules. Before the Table Office will place a Question on the Paper they have to satisfy themselves that it satisfies the general rules of Order; has not

[1] For the development of the Table Office see the evidence of Mr. D. J. Gordon to the Select Committee on Nationalized Industries, (1951–2), qs. 369–74. For the Report of the Pethick-Lawrence Committee see Appendix J to the Report of Select Committee on House of Commons Accommodation, 1954, H. of C. Paper 184.

already been answered in the Session; and comes within the sphere of responsibility, if not of the Minister to whom it is addressed, at any rate of some Minister.

If a Question is 'edited' without the knowledge of the Member, the Table Office may send him a printed letter in the following form.

Dear Sir,

Your Question to .... has required slight amendment to bring it into order. In order to save delay it has been sent to the printer in its amended form and will appear in the next issue of the NOTICE PAPER.

If the amended Question does not meet with your approval would you kindly call on this office as soon as convenient.

Yours very truly,

....
Second Clerk Assistant.

This is usually sufficient for extensive verbal alterations and slight changes of substance; for slight verbal alterations no warning need usually be given, though some Members are more touchy than others about them. If, however, a substantial change needs to be made to bring the Question within the rules or if the Question is likely to be unacceptable in any form, the following printed card is sent to the Member concerned.

Dear Sir,

Would you kindly see me at the Table or call at the Table Office, when convenient to you, with reference to your Question.

Yours very truly,

....
Second Clerk Assistant.

The Member can then discuss the matter with the Table Office or if the House is sitting, the Clerk at the Table. In most cases the issue will be settled at that level either by rewording or by the Member accepting the ruling that such a Question cannot be put. In some cases, however, the Member will not be convinced; and if on reconsideration, and perhaps after discussion with his other colleagues at the Table, the Second Clerk Assistant still considers the Question to be out of order it is referred to the Speaker. During the Session the Speaker is consulted probably a couple of times a month about the proper form or acceptability of Questions which have not yet reached the Notice Paper.

MINISTERS AND THEIR ANSWERS

When checked and accepted the Question is ready for printing. Before the development of an extensive rota system and when shorter notice was required most Questions would be printed straight away on the Order Paper of the day on which the answer was required. Nowadays, however, there is frequently quite a gap in time between the first and the final stage — the handing in and the appearance among the business for the day.

The first stage of printing is a mere listing in the Blue Notice Paper under the heading 'Notices given on. . . . [the date of the previous day.]'. This comes out daily during the Session but on Saturdays a consolidated edition appears and is known as the Blue Order Book. The Blue Paper is printed primarily for the benefit of the Departments. A copy is sent to each Department and is usually the first notice they receive of the Questions addressed to their Minister. Each Minister also receives a copy of the Blue Notice Paper and the Blue Order Book.

The day before they are to be asked Questions are grouped according to Departments in the White Order Book which comes out at about 2 p.m. This and the weekly editions are mainly used by the Clerks of the Table Office for their own convenience. The White Order Book is not circulated to Departments but Members may obtain copies on request at the Vote Office.

Finally, the Question appears on the Order Paper for the day. Each day's business so far as Questions are concerned is built up from the White Order Books. The Order Paper for the following day's business is completed each evening at the rising of the House, starred Questions having been arranged in accordance with the order of the Ministerial rota. Should it happen that any Member has more than two starred Questions on the day's Paper, any excess is transferred to the list of those requiring a written answer.[1]

To understand the process it must be appreciated that a considerable number of Questions are now sent in to the Table Office at least a week before the day on which the Member wants an answer. In many cases the notice given will be much longer. On occasions a Member may give notice of a series of Questions to a particular Minister stretching over a number of weeks. At

---

[1] Before the Order Paper is finally printed a Member can choose which two starred Questions he wishes to ask and whether he wishes to transfer the surplus to some other day.

the other extreme a number of Questions are put down for answering at the earliest possible moment allowed by the rules.

The rules about notice are that a starred Question must appear on the Blue Notice Paper circulated two days (excluding any Sunday) before that on which an answer is desired. However, Questions handed in before 2.30 p.m. on Mondays and Tuesdays and before 11 a.m. on Fridays may, if the Member wishes, be put down for answer on the following Wednesday, Thursday or Monday respectively; these are known as Expedited Questions. Thus some starred Questions may be listed on the Blue Notice Paper only the day before they appear on the Order Paper for answering, whilst others may have been reprinted in one or more editions of the weekly Blue Order Book. Unstarred Questions are put down for answer on a stated date in the same way as starred Questions. But they can be put down for answer on the following day, thus never appearing on the Notice Paper. Departments are, however, not bound to provide the answer on the day specified. At any time while it is going through the process a Member may withdraw his Question, or defer the date.

The result of all this is that on each morning when Questions are due to be answered in the House there appears on the Order Paper a list of Questions for oral answer that day. If, for example, it is a Wednesday some of the Questions will have been handed in at the Table Office one or more weeks before, some will have been handed in as late as 2.30 p.m. on Monday. They will conform to the rules of the House. They will be grouped according to the Ministers to whom they are addressed and will be in the order of the day's Ministerial rota. Within each Ministerial group they will be in the order in which they have been handed in.

The arrival of the daily Blue Notice Paper in a Department is usually the starting point of the process by which the Minister's answer is prepared. Most Departments, however, send across to the Table Office for typewritten copies in the late afternoon on days when Expedited Questions can be handed in, particularly on Monday and Tuesday and particularly when their Minister is high in the rota on Wednesday and Thursday. By doing this, instead of waiting for the arrival of the Blue Paper next morning, they gain a valuable few more hours in which to prepare the answer.

Different Departments organize the preparation of answers in different ways. A good deal depends on the number with which a Department has to deal. The organization is also affected by the nature of the Department's work, e.g. whether information will have to be provided from overseas or from distant parts of the country, whether the answers are likely to need much technical or specialized knowledge and so on.

In all Departments Questions have a special urgency and importance. Provision of an answer cannot therefore be left solely to the normal working of the Department's machine, there must be someone in the Department whose special responsibility it is to start and watch over the process of preparation and to see that the time table, which may be very tight, is kept.

There appear to be two basic differences in Departmental methods of handling Questions. First, in most Departments the official responsible is primarily an organizer and chaser but in at least one he is also responsible for preparing the final draft for the Minister. Second, the official responsible may be in the office of the Minister, or in a Parliamentary or other special section of the Department.

In the case of Questions addressed to the Chancellor of the Exchequer one of the Chancellor's Private Secretaries is responsible for 'organizing' the answers. These are, however, prepared in the branch of the Treasury concerned with the subject matter, the Private Secretary acting very largely as router, chaser and go-between with the Minister. He is responsible for searching the Blue Paper for Questions addressed to the Chancellor and for collecting Expedited Questions. He arranges for each Question to be cut out of the Blue Paper and affixed to the front sheet inside the file, red in this case. He must see that the files containing the draft answers and notes are ready in time for the Minister to consider. If the Chancellor has any queries he may deal direct with the senior civil servant responsible for the subject matter of the Question, or he may ask his Private Secretary to deal with the point. In contrast to this decentralized system the War Office use a centralized system. A Principal in the Secretariat of the Army Council does not merely do what is done by the Private Secretary in the case of the Treasury, he also drafts most answers, the branches providing the information. The present War Office system is suited to a Department which is not wholly composed of branches staffed by the regular Civil Service grades with long experience. A high proportion of answers to Questions involve information provided by Army Commands and units throughout the world and collected by branches with military staffs, serving for comparatively short periods in the War Office, who are specialists in particular fields of Army administration. A Principal at headquarters acquires the knack of drafting suitable replies and also is well placed to appreciate what other information the Minister is likely to need. For the draft answer is only part of the departmental process; equally important is information on any points which might possibly arise in the form of supplementaries or which the Minister may need in order to decide the proper form of his answer.

Nowadays, in many Departments Questions are too great a burden for the Minister's Private Office. It requires some person or branch who can give their undivided attention to the process. In many Departments there is a Parliamentary branch which, along with other duties, acts as organizer and chaser. The actual preparation of answers and the provision of other material for the file is, however, usually part of the work of the division of the Ministry concerned with the subject matter of the Question. In fact, apart from the special provision of the processer and chaser, Questions are handled by the great majority of Departments in very much the same way as any other business but, of course, much more quickly.

From time to time Questions are addressed to the wrong Minister, i.e., the subject matter is the responsibility of some other Minister. The Department to whose Minister the Question is addressed is responsible for transferring it to the correct Minister, having first obtained the agreement of that Department. The transfer is then made by the Table Office at the request of the Department. Sometimes a Department will claim that neither their Minister nor any other Minister has any responsibility for the subject matter of a Question or that for some other reason their Minister does not wish or intend to reply. Once a Question has appeared in the Blue Paper, however, it can be withdrawn[1] only with the consent of the Member concerned or, very rarely indeed, at the express direction of Mr. Speaker. In any dealings the Department may have with the

---

[1] Notice of Questions withdrawn is given on the Notice Paper.

MINISTERS AND THEIR ANSWERS

Table Office on problems of this kind it is clearly understood that, within the limit of the rules of the House and the Speaker's authority, the Table Office's loyalty is to the Member, not to the Department.

Usually a first draft answer and supporting information are provided by a Principal in the Division. The P.Q.[1] files in any Department always have a distinctive colour. They have a high priority and must be circulated specially and quickly. The Principal passes the file to the Assistant Secretary concerned, who may or may not be satisfied, and who, if he feels that some important issue or new point of departmental policy is at issue will consult his superior, and so on up the hierarchy. Questions vary considerably in importance. Some can be answered by a Principal without involving anyone higher in the hierarchy. Others may raise major issues of governmental policy and involve the Permanent Secretary, the Minister and possibly other Ministers. Whether of minor or major importance the answer has to be provided quickly. The processer and chaser, whether Private Secretary or Parliamentary branch, must therefore have a good eye for this kind of point. Even though primary responsibility rests on, say, a Parliamentary branch, the Blue Notice Paper will be carefully read by others in the Department including, very likely, the Minister and his Parliamentary Private Secretary, his Private Secretary and the Permanent Secretary or someone in his private office. A number of copies are circulated in each Department. Little is likely to escape attention.

Thus as the time nears for the Minister to answer the Questions the number of green, pink, red or other distinctive coloured files in his office will grow until all are ready for his attention. Each file will contain the Question from the Notice Paper, a draft answer and also supporting information. Some Ministers like to have possible supplementaries and draft answers on the file; others prefer to answer them 'off the cuff' with the aid of the information on the file. But however much preparatory work there may have been done in the Department, the answer in the House, whether to the main Question or to any supplementary, is that of the Minister, personally and in full hearing of a well-attended Chamber. It is his responsibility, therefore, to decide

[1] Civil Servants talk about P.Q.s but the abbreviation is not used in the House or by the Clerks

the final form of the answer, after consulting such of his civil servants, or even other Ministers, as he thinks necessary or desirable. It is his responsibility to see that he has all the information with which to face the House. Thus armed, he takes his place on the Treasury Bench ready to rise when his group of Questions on the day's Order Paper is reached. He is then on his own, subject to the rules of the House and any protection from any irrelevant supplementaries which the Speaker may afford him. One by one the Questions with their supplementaries are answered in their order on the Paper until either none remains or the time allowed is exhausted.

During this time the Minister's Private Secretary will be sitting in the official box at the side of the Chamber making a note of any last minute changes the Minister may have made to his answers, of the supplementaries and of any points for further Ministerial action.

The Department sends a copy of the Minister's answer to the Member asking the Question — this is available to him shortly after Question time is over. Supplementaries and their answers are, of course, not available in this way though a Member can obtain them from the Hansard Reporter.[1] The Department also sends copies of the Minister's answer to the room set aside for the use of Gallery Correspondents. Finally, if the Minister's answer involves a promise to provide further information, or to deal with a particular case in a stated way, or for some other reason involves the Department taking action, it is the responsibility of the appropriate section of the Department to take note of this and see that the promise, etc. is fulfilled.

So the four parties directly concerned have played their part — two in public, two behind the scenes. A Question has been asked and answered.

MINISTERS

However much thought and labour the Civil Service may put into the preparation of the answers they cannot take over or in any way reduce a Minister's personal responsibility. If he is answering them on the floor of the House his responsibility is

[1] The Editor of Hansard is responsible for seeing that the Questions and answers, including all supplementaries and their answers, are recorded. They will appear in the next day's issue of Hansard.

clear and direct. But he is equally responsible in both theory and practice, for the written answers: these are not the Department's replies but the Minister's and in form they do not differ from the form of oral replies. In Hansard they appear as 'Mr. X asked the Secretary of State for the Home Department . . .' and the reply as 'Mr. R. A. Butler' (or whoever is the Minister) followed by the wording of his reply. It will be obvious therefore that the Minister's relations with the House of Commons will affect the way he handles Questions and also dominate the Civil Service attitude towards the drafts and information they prepare.

Almost all Ministers are ambitious. The junior Minister, usually a politician *de carrière*, wishes to get senior office: the senior Minister may still have hope of becoming Prime Minister. Even if not particularly ambitious they are at least anxious to make a good show in their office. A Minister's reputation depends largely on the opinion of the House of Commons. 'For this reason (no doubt there are others) Ministers are extraordinarily careful about Parliamentary business, and in all dealings with their fellow-members; they often take what appears to a civil servant a disproportionate amount of time and trouble over a speech on some unimportant topic, or over the exact terms of a reply to some foolish question or letter.'[1]

We have already seen that Questions have certain important characteristics from the viewpoint of Ministers. Hardly any aspect of the Department's powers and activities can be shielded from Questions, their range is very wide indeed and any Member however new or politically insignificant can ask them. They and their answers may attract a good deal of publicity, at least it is safer to work on this assumption. They reflect not only public opinion but opinion which has achieved expression in the proceedings of the House. The Minister has to consider not only the Member who has put the Question but also the many other Members who may be listening to his reply or who will read it in Hansard or hear of it in some other way. A Minister cannot make a great Parliamentary reputation by the manner in which he answers Questions, but if he cannot handle them effectively in the House he is unlikely to go far or even last long as a Minister. The handling of Questions gives a new or junior Minister a

---

[1] H.E. Dale, *The Higher Civil Service*, (1941), p. 114. Parliamentary Secretaries, he says, are more anxious than their chiefs about what the House will think.

chance to show his paces, to show whether he is at home in the House and has that sixth sense for the mood of Members without which a politician however clever cannot hope to climb far up the greasy pole.

Question and answer are a personal activity: one Member *vis à vis* another Member. There is no vote at the end but neither is there a three-line Whip. There is no chance of being defeated but neither can a Minister rely on his Party's majority to get him out of a difficulty. Over a wide range of Questions Party passions seldom run high. True, if Opposition Members are harrying a Minister the Government's supporters will usually avoid doing so on that subject, or occasionally may even try to come to his aid with a helpful supplementary. True the political content of Questions to the Prime Minister and to one or two other Ministers is likely to be quite high. But in the majority of cases it is a matter of a back bencher asking a Question about a subject in which he is interested being answered by another Member who is for the time being the political head of the Government Department concerned with that subject.

The answers to many Questions are straightforward and present Ministers with few if any problems. Unstarred Questions are easiest in so far as there is no need to prepare for the supplementaries but even they may present difficulties and cannot be treated in an offhand way. It is, however, the starred Questions which need most thought and preparation. A request for factual information readily available in the Department can be easily answered, indeed the answer may be exactly the same whether the Question is starred or for written answer, but if it is starred the Minister will have to consider what supplementaries are likely to be asked and how he should handle these.

There are many ways of answering Questions. A former Permanent Secretary has written: 'The wording of replies to Parliamentary Questions requires special care and knowledge of the psychology of the House of Commons, in order to secure that the reply will convey clearly the information desired, will, if possible, give satisfaction, and will not cause embarrassment to the Minister or to the Government as a whole.'[1] Mr. H. E. Dale in his classic analysis of the Higher Civil Service had this to say: 'as regards truthfulness and candour — to his superiors in his

[1] Sir Francis Floud, *The Ministry of Agriculture and Fisheries* (1927), p. 41.

own Department and to his own Minister the obligation of an official is of course absolute: he must speak not only the truth but the whole truth as he knows it. . . . But it is a different affair when we come to statements which are intended or likely to become public. These are of course always made on the responsibility of the Minister, and usually with his personal approval; all the most important will in fact be made by him, whenever possible, in Parliamentary debate or in replies to questions. The rule here is simple. Nothing may be said which is not true: but it is as unnecessary as it is sometimes undesirable, even in the public interest, to say everything relevant which is true; and the facts given may be arranged in any convenient order. It is wonderful what can be done within these limits by a skilful draftsman. It might be said, cynically, but with some measure of truth, that the perfect reply to an embarrassing question in the House of Commons is one that is brief, appears to answer the question completely, if challenged can be proved to be accurate in every word, gives no opening for awkward 'supplementaries', and discloses really nothing.'[1] Earlier in the same book Mr. Dale had written of a Permanent Secretary being satisfied with a draft reply which was: 'brief, completely accurate, courteous, exhibits the Minister as modestly surprised to find his own attitude so clearly right, and gives no opening for awkward "supplementaries".'[2]

These are the views of civil servants who have spent many years preparing drafts of replies for Ministers. Ministers themselves seldom write about their craft, usually being more interested in the major political issues in which they have been involved, but they would be unlikely to dissent from these views. They would however want to add a great deal about the kinds of answers to deal with different situations.

Generally speaking the questioner rather than the Question is the more important element in the situation. Among the factors which the Minister will want to take into account are:

(i) is the Member a Government supporter or in the Opposition;
(ii) does he carry weight in the House, or is he regarded as rather a joker, a bore or a lightweight;

[1] H. E. Dale, *The Higher Civil Service of Great Britain* (1941), pp. 104–5.
[2] op. cit., p. 37. Quoted with approval by T. A. Critchley (a serving civil servant) in his *The Civil Service Today* (1951), p. 76.

(iii) is he quick witted and likely to be able to frame a very awkward supplementary on the spur of the moment;

(iv) is he completely free lance or is he connected to movements or interests which the Minister must take into account, e.g. he may be a leading member of a specialist Party Committee or known to be raising the point on behalf of some major national organization;

(v) is he a specialist or expert on this matter and therefore likely to have a well-prepared supplementary or be a good judge of the adequacy of the Minister's reply or has he taken up the issue casually;

(vi) is he likely to accept a negative or unforthcoming answer or may he pursue the matter further, e.g. on an Adjournment Motion.

To mention these personal factors is not to ignore the content of the Question. Obviously some Questions are more tricky, more awkward to answer than others, whoever is the questioner. And in general the Minister will try to give an answer which will satisfy or not unduly annoy the Member. It pays a Minister in the House of Commons to be helpful and forthcoming whenever he can, irrespective of the Member. If the Question does not involve anything which is politically controversial, for example, if it is purely a constituency matter, the Minister will try to be as helpful as possible in his reply. He appreciates that the Member is but doing his job and though the Question may appear trivial and tiresome it will not benefit the Minister, either with the Member or the House, if he is offhand or rebuffs the Member without good reason. He may get away with this attitude on a few occasions, but not if he adopts it as a general rule. This attitude of being, or giving the appearance of being, helpful and forthcoming will not differ greatly whether the Member concerned is a Government supporter or an Opposition back bencher, unless the questioner is trying to score off him. Of course, the Minister will wish to please his Party's supporters, his political future depending to a large extent on their appraisal of him.

It is in handling the awkward Questions that the Minister will have to pay particular attention to the character and capabilities of the questioner. In this assessment the Minister will also be aware of his own position. He may be popular in the House, full of political confidence, have a mastery of the subject and of the work of his Department, and be quick witted in seeing the point of a supplementary and framing his reply. Or he may be a new or junior Minister still having to find his feet and get the feel of the House, or his political star may be on the wane, temporarily he hopes, or he may be not too confident about his capacity to handle supplementaries.

A Minister who is uncertain of himself *vis à vis* a Member who has the ear of the House and is quick witted can adopt either of two methods of handling the awkward Question. He may be so forthcoming and helpful in his answer as to leave little or no room to be attacked or he may read a carefully prepared answer and refuse to stray very far from it in answering critical or awkward supplementaries, e.g. by saying the same thing in the same or slightly different words,[1] by saying he has nothing to add, or even by remaining seated and not answering. The popular and confident Minister *vis à vis* the bore or unpopular Member may take many liberties, even to the point of giving but a cursory answer and ignoring the supplementary.

On the whole courtesy, straightforward answers, an apparent desire to be helpful and the occasional witty remark or joke are the well-tried ingredients of Ministerial answers and attitudes at Question time. A Minister does not need to be clever or witty if it is clear that he is trying to answer the Question as fully and as helpfully as he can and that he understands what he is talking about. If he can score off an opponent, particularly off a leading Opposition Member who may have intervened, or if he can get the better of a sharp exchange on a currently active political issue he will gain marks with his supporters.

Mr. Asquith when Prime Minister frequently left a bad impression with his answers and was accused of snubbing Members. The reason was that he seldom took the trouble to be conciliatory and his replies were skilful rather than informative. His answers sounded curt even though they were never discourteous. Some of his familiar phrases at Question time became part of the stock in trade of Ministerial answers, or might still be so if they had not been so overworked: 'there will be no

---

[1] When one Under Secretary of State for Foreign Affairs (Sir James Fergusson) was asked, Am I to understand that the rt. hon. Gentleman means so and so Lucy says he replied, 'The hon. Member is not to understand me to mean anything more than I have said.' *A Diary of the Salisbury Parliament 1886–1892*, p. 394.

unavoidable delay,' 'every avenue is being explored,' 'all relevant matters will be taken into consideration.'[1]

Sir Winston Churchill was most careful in the preparation of his answers to Questions but as might be expected they quite often embodied some of his wit and humour. As Prime Minister he was once asked by Mr. Norman Dodds whether in view of the present international situation, he would reconsider taking the initiative in an effort to arrange a meeting at top level, representing the United States, the Soviet Union and the United Kingdom. Churchill replied: 'Perhaps on this somewhat delicate topic I may be permitted by the House to take refuge in metaphor. Many anxieties have been expressed recently at the severe character of the course of the Grand National steeplechase, but I am sure it would not be improved by asking the horses to try to jump two fences at the same time.'[2] Quoting this and other answers a former chief of the Parliamentary Staff of *The Times* has written, 'I am convinced that Churchill thought out his answers to questions very carefully, down to the last detail, and he was prepared for all eventualities. That he made frequent last-minute alterations to his prepared replies is well known. In some of the official typed answers that used to come up to *The Times*' room I have seen small changes made in his own handwriting — just a word here and there, and the whole balance of a sentence, or even the emphasis of the answer, would be changed. His hand was firmly stamped on all the answers he gave.'[3] On the same day in 1954 that he gave the answer just quoted, he was asked whether he would reconsider his refusal to separate the Ministry of Agriculture from the Ministry of Fisheries in view of the national importance of the fishing industry. Churchill replied, 'It would not, I feel, be a good arrangement to have a separate Department for every industry of national importance' and went on, 'These two industries have been long associated departmentally and, after all, there are many ancient links between fish and chips.'[4]

Not all answers are so entertaining and not by any means even all of Sir Winston Churchill's. Most are brief, formal and

---

[1] Alexander Mackintosh, *From Gladstone to Lloyd George* (1921), p. 275, and *Echoes of Big Ben, A Journalist's Parliamentary Diary, 1881–1940* (1941), p. 55.
[2] H.C. Deb. (1953–4), 528, c. 2275.
[3] Arthur Baker, *The House is Sitting* (1958), p. 118.
[4] H.C. Deb. (1953–4), 528, c. 2274.

courteous. Readers may have wondered what kind of answer was given to some of the Questions quoted in Chapter 9. The reply of Mr. Molson (Minister of Works) to Mr. Parker's concern about the trees in Birdcage Walk was, 'I am considering what treatment should be adopted for these trees, and I hope to come to a decision shortly.' The reply of Mr. Profumo (Under Secretary of State for the Colonies) to Mr. Stonehouse's query about the number of prisoners detained in Lokitaung Prison was, 'There are five convicts serving prison sentences and one detainee at Lokitaung. The prison staff consists of one sergeant, one lance corporal and six warders. Four unofficial visitors have visited the prisoners.' Mr. Stonehouse then asked: 'Why is it considered essential to keep these six men in such an isolated place, to all intents and purposes without contact with the outside world.' Mr. Profumo replied: 'That is a very much wider question. Perhaps the hon. Gentleman would put it down.' The Question about 'the subsidies offered for Grade I fat steers and heifers' having received an answer from Mr. Godber (Joint Parliamentary Secretary to the Ministry) was followed by a supplementary, 'Does the hon. Gentleman mean to say that between the weeks commencing 17th October and 24th October there was an average difference of 6s. per live cwt. for fatstock entering markets or slaughter houses? Does not this state of affairs mean that a farmer who sends his cattle one week gets a bigger subsidy although there is not a comparable variation in the market price?' Mr. Godber replied: 'The figures accurately reflect the operation of the formula which we use, but I must point out that this occurred at a time when seasonal standard prices at the latter part of the period the hon. Gentleman mentioned were rising sharply, thus accentuating the difference.'

As this book is about Parliament readers may like to have the answer and the subsequent exchange on the Question asked by Sir W. Wakefield about a possible lift to the top of Big Ben. The Parliamentary Secretary to the Ministry of Works replied:

'There would be considerable practical difficulties in installing a lift. It is estimated that if these difficulties could be overcome the cost might be in the neighbourhood of £20,000. I do not feel able to estimate the likely revenue but, owing to limitations of space, the number of visitors at any one time would be severely restricted. In rejecting previous proposals my Department has had in mind the heavy capital cost, and the doubt whether the project would be economic. There is also, of course, the question of whether it would be acceptable to the authorities of the Palace of Westminster and to hon. Members themselves.'

The Member's supplementary and the Minister's reply were :

'Is my hon. Friend aware that his reply will cause great disappointment not only to the people of this country but to the many visitors from overseas ? Further, is he aware that towers like the Eiffel Tower in Paris, the Campanile in Venice, and others provide great pleasure for people visiting those places, as this would do for those who visit London? Can he tell us what are the economic difficulties which prevent the placing of a lift in Big Ben for the enjoyment of the public?'

'I can assure my hon. Friend that there is no question of our being spoil-sports in our attitude to this matter. It is hardly fair to compare Big Ben with the Eiffel Tower and the others mentioned by him. The practical difficulty here is that the Clock Tower would take a lift with a maximum capacity only of about ten people, and with the number of hours during which it could be opened it is extremely doubtful whether in charging, say, 1s. for adults and 6d. for children, we could get the capital expenditure returned.'

Finally, two other examples, the Waters case and Mr. Nabarro's campaign against the Purchase Tax. The Lord Advocate did not reply himself to Sir David Robertson's Question quoted at page 185 but left it to the Solicitor-General for Scotland, who read the following answer:

'As my right hon. and learned Friend stated in reply to a Question by my hon. Friend on 8th July, Crown Counsel did not order proceedings in this case because in their view the evidence did not justify proceedings being taken. On receiving the statements referred to, my right hon. and learned Friend carefully considered them and caused further investigation to be made. Having done so he decided that on the evidence before him he would not be justified in instituting criminal proceedings against the constables concerned, and he so informed my hon. Friend by letter dated 28th July. My right hon. and learned Friend is still of the same opinion.'

The Member then asked :

'Does not my right hon. and learned Friend know that, during the whole of the seven months I have been pressing the case, none of the statements contained in this Question has been challenged? Does he also know that many of the people of Caithness know that this assault took place and they will be gravely and grievously disappointed at the reply given today denying a trial? Why should there be all this covering up and lack of informing this House why a trial has not taken place?'

To which the Minister replied:

'The mere fact that there is local feeling that something has happened is no ground for taking proceedings in a case where the evidence does not justify it.'

The Member then said:

'In view of the unsatisfactory nature of the answer, Sir, I beg to give notice that I will raise this matter again at the first opportunity.'

His opportunity came when he spoke on a half-hour Adjournment Motion on 3 February 1959,[1] the Lord Advocate replying. Still being unsatisfied and by now having been assured of public interest and support the Member put a Motion on the Paper asking the House to set up a Select Committee to enquire into the case. This led the Prime Minister to announce on 16 February 1959 the Government's decision to establish a Tribunal of Inquiry and this was done and the names announced on 17 and 19 February.

Mr. Nabarro's long series of Questions resulted in a kind of running battle between him and the Treasury Ministers. The Hansard record[2] of the three Questions quoted on page 214, their answers and resulting supplementaries is as follows:

54. Mr. Nabarro asked the Chancellor of the Exchequer whether he is aware that a manufacturer of key holders was recently informed by the Customs and Excise authorities that a holder for the pocket, designed in such a way that the flap closing it would prevent the keys from falling out and damaging the pocket, would be subject to 60 per cent. Purchase Tax, but if the size of the flap could be reduced to $\frac{1}{2}$ inch in size, the holder would be free of Purchase Tax; and whether, in view of the fact that the holder with the $\frac{1}{2}$-inch flap would be ineffective from the point of view of protecting the user's pocket, he will instruct the officials to reconsider the matter.

The Financial Secretary to the Treasury (Mr. J. E. S. Simon): Yes, Sir. The matter has been reconsidered and, as my hon. Friend is aware, the anomaly has been rectified.

Mr. Nabarro: I think it will be agreed that good progress is now being made in this field. Will my hon. and learned Friend now deal with the matter sensibly and objectively and give instructions to the

[1] H.C. Deb. (1958–9), 599, c. 349–58. [2] H.C. Deb. (1957–8), 582, c. 572–4.

Customs and Excise authorities to endeavour conscientiously to abolish all these quite ridiculous anomalies that are wasting so much of the nation's trade and time?

Mr. Simon: I cannot accept the implications of that supplementary question, but we should be grateful to my hon. Friend for drawing attention to the anomalies which unquestionably exist.

55. Mr. Nabarro asked the Chancellor of the Exchequer when the regulation was introduced laying down that doorknockers 5 inches or more in length shall be free of tax whereas doorknockers under that length carry 30 per cent. Purchase Tax; and what has been the revenue from Purchase Tax on doorknockers for each of the past five years for which figures are available.

Mr. Simon: Following consultation with the trade, doorknockers over $4\tfrac{3}{4}$ inches long have been treated as free of tax under a relief for builders' hardware introduced in 1948. On the second part of the Question, I would refer my hon. Friend to the reply which my right hon. Friend the Member for Monmouth (Mr. P. Thorneycroft) gave him on 17th December.

Mr. Nabarro: Why is there this invidious distinction between doorknocking nutcrackers and nutcracking doorknockers —

Mr. Speaker: Order.

Mr. Nabarro: This is an invidious distinction, Mr. Speaker.

Mr. Speaker: It may be an invidious distinction, as the hon. Member says, but I rather think he is now anticipating Question No. 56. Is not that about nutcrackers?

Mr. Nabarro: I understood the Financial Secretary to say that he was answering the Questions together. It is a quite understandable mistake, because that is how the Chancellor of the Exchequer generally rides off these difficulties. Will my hon. and learned Friend put this matter into good order?

Mr. Speaker: The hon. Member should ask Question No. 56 if he wants to get on to the subject of nutcrackers.

56. Mr. Nabarro asked the Chancellor of the Exchequer whether he is aware that, in view of the fact that a nutcracker is liable to Purchase Tax at 15 per cent. whereas a doorknocker over 5 inches in length is free of tax, there is an increasing practice of supplying nutcrackers with screw holes so that they could theoretically be used as doorknockers, with the result that with such modification these nutcrackers become free of tax; and what instructions have been issued to Customs and Excise staff with regard to this matter.

Mr. Simon: No, Sir; I do not think Customs staff need instructions to help them distinguish a nutcracker from a doorknocker.

Mr. Nabarro: Now will my hon. and learned Friend apply himself to the Question that I have put to him? Why is there this invidious distinction between doorknocking nutcrackers and nutcracking doorknockers? Is he aware that this is a perfectly well known device, practised by manufacturers? I have evidence of it in my hand. Is he aware that this ridiculous position, which was mentioned in a leading article in *The Times* on 11th February, is bringing the whole of the Purchase Tax Schedules into disrepute? Is it not time that the matter was drastically overhauled by abolition of the Purchase Tax and substitution of a sales turnover tax at a very small and uniform rate over the whole field?

Mr. Simon: My hon. Friend tempts me to reply in the words of the conductor Richter to the second flute at Covent Garden — 'Your damned nonsense can I stand twice or once, but sometimes always, by God, never.'

Mr. Shurmer: Is the hon and learned Gentleman aware that while this may be a jocular matter for some people, in Birmingham a number of firms which manufacture brass goods are continually coming into conflict with the Customs and Excise about exactly what Purchase Tax must be paid due to the anomalies referred to by the hon. Member for Kidderminster (Mr. Nabarro)? Is he further aware that when the present Leader of the House was Chancellor of the Exchequer, and I brought up the question of the corkscrew on the dog's tail the right hon. Gentleman admitted that Purchase Tax had got into such a mess that it ought to be completely reorganized?

The stream of Questions from Mr. Nabarro resulted in a duel between him and the Treasury Ministers each trying to score off the other, sometimes good-humouredly and at other times with ill-concealed annoyance. Not all the replies were as witty as the Financial Secretary's reference to Richter. Some of the 'repartee' was distinctly knockabout.

Most experienced Ministers do not fear Question time; they do not find it difficult or alarming and feel reasonably well at home answering and parrying supplementaries. Some positively enjoy the occasion and are skilled and experienced in combining a generally helpful attitude with a capacity to score heavily with a witty remark against any Member trying to be clever at their expense. Others are not very quick at thinking on their feet or adapting themselves to the variety of situations. They may be tongue-tied or long-winded; they may cling to such clichés as 'I have nothing further to add to my answer'; they may be firm when a more forthcoming attitude would be better in keeping with the atmosphere in the Chamber or be unnecessarily forthcoming when they could have got away with a witty, noncommittal or evasive reply. All Ministers have their difficult moments and the least expert may never feel at home at Question time.

In assessing the difficulties with which supplementaries may confront Ministers it is worth bearing in mind three factors which help them. First, they have at hand a well-prepared file from which they can draw information and even prepared answers. True the Speaker may nowadays allow supplementaries rather wide of the Question and answer and which, therefore, cannot always be anticipated. Also in some cases the Minister may have had very little time to study the file. But unless he is below normal wits for a politician, in which case he is unlikely to last long as Minister, he can, if he keeps his head make good use of the file prepared for him by his civil servants.[1]

Second, it is easy to exaggerate the penetrative effect of supplementaries. It is obvious in a good many cases what the supplementary is likely to be and what the Member is after and the Minister can be prepared with a ready answer. More important, supplementaries seldom become a cross examination. Notwithstanding the growth in their number it is unusual for a Member to be allowed to ask more than one, two at the outside. A Member is never in the position of the Barrister who can continue examining the defendant until he is satisfied that the point has been completely cleared up. Even on the rare occasions when ten or a dozen supplementaries are allowed much of the effect is lost by their being dissipated among half a dozen or more Members pursuing possibly different hares.

Finally, there is the protection afforded by Mr. Speaker. He is expected to maintain a fair balance between the Government and other Members and not to favour any side. All supplementaries are, however, allowable only at the Speaker's discretion and there are constant complaints about too many being asked. If a Minister can be made to look foolish in the course of one or possibly two supplementaries then Mr. Speaker is unlikely to be involved for this number is now fairly normal. But should a series of supplementaries be needed, in other words should it

---

[1] It is not unknown for a Minister to lose his place in the file and either answer the wrong Question or read out a note meant for him personally and quite inappropriate or embarrassing in the House.

appear that by pursuing the Minister he could be got into trouble, Mr. Speaker is faced with a very difficult decision. If he allows the supplementaries to continue he is penalizing the Members whose starred Questions have still to be reached. If, however, he stops further supplementaries he may be felt to be favouring the Minister. Usually he will be guided by his sense of feeling of the House. If it is quite clear that there is widespread interest in this particular Question he will allow more supplemantaries than usual. Otherwise he will call the next Question, much to the relief of the Minister on many occasions.

Nevertheless, it is not always possible to anticipate the supplementary or to handle it effectively when it comes. This is particularly the case when a perfectly straightforward and innocuous Question has been put down either to conceal the nature of the intended supplementary or to get round the rules of the House governing the form and content of Questions. A particularly nasty supplementary was put to Mr. Lloyd George in April 1913[1] when, as Chancellor of the Exchequer, he had been accused of taking advantage of his official knowledge to make a profit out of Marconi shares. Mr. Kebty-Fletcher's simple starred Question was: 'To ask the Chancellor of the Exchequer if there are any emoluments or allowances attached to his office other than his salary.' Lloyd George replied, 'The answer is in the negative' (nowadays the more usual form would be 'No, Sir'). Kebty-Fletcher then rose and asked, 'Should not the right hon. Gentleman's salary of £5000 per annum be sufficient to prevent him from wrongfully and improperly gambling?' This supplementary greatly angered Mr. Lloyd George and his supporters but was received with enthusiasm by most of the Opposition, Mr. Speaker Lowther having some difficulty in restoring order.

Mr. Emrys Hughes makes a practice of putting Questions to the Prime Minister. The subsequent supplementary can be barbed and raise a laugh at the Government's expense. His exchanges with Mr. Churchill at Question time were a popular diversion, each good-humouredly trying to score off the other. The Question Mr. Hughes puts on the Paper is usually simple and innocuous. Thus on 26 January 1960,[2] he asked the Prime Minister 'what study of prison conditions he made during his tour of Africa'. Mr. R. A. Butler, replying for Mr. Macmillan

[1] H.C. Deb. (1913), 51, c. 195.   [2] H.C. Deb. (1959–60), 616, c. 29–30.

who was visiting Africa, answered, 'None, Sir.' Whereupon Mr. Hughes asked: 'Would not the Home Secretary agree that the Prime Minister is missing a unique opportunity for completing his political education? Could not he arrange to be taken into protective custody, where he might meet Dr. Banda and have the experience which a good many Prime Ministers who will attend the Commonwealth Conference already have had?' Mr. Butler treated Mr. Hughes and such a supplementary in the only way possible by entering into the joke and paying tribute to Mr. Hughes's reputation at Question time. He said: 'I have already promised my right hon. Friend that on the resumption of Parliament the first supplementary question put by the hon. Member would be immediately telegraphed to him for his delectation and amusement, and I shall certainly do that.'

On occasion, even the best-prepared Minister at the head of a well-organized and powerful Department may find himself without an adequate answer to a supplementary. On 14 April 1959[1] for example, Mr. J. Callaghan asked the Chancellor of the Exchequer 'what steps are taken to preserve the confidential nature of Income Tax returns when they are disposed of'. Mr. Callaghan had been an official in the Inland Revenue Department before he became a Labour Member and probably the Treasury thought the Question arose from this earlier interest. The Chancellor replied:

'Income Tax returns are normally disposed of with other Government waste paper of a confidential nature by pulping in paper mills, the pulping arrangements being subject to inspection by officials of the Stationery Office or the Post Office. The sacks containing the waste are sewn up securely and sealed before leaving the Tax Office.

In any area where satisfactory arrangements for pulping cannot be made, the returns are disposed of by burning or other means.'

The opening words of Mr. Callaghan's supplementary gave no indication of the bombshell that was to follow. 'I am sure', he said, 'everybody will be delighted to have that reassurance, but,' and here he held up a variety of letters, accounts and returns, 'can the Chancellor tell me how I came to pick up on the docks at Cardiff last week these Income Tax returns? I agree that they are old, but they relate to pottery firms in the Midlands and give

[1] H.C. Deb. (1958–9), 603, c. 807–8.

full details of their income and correspondence between inspectors about all their affairs. Is the Chancellor aware that these returns, in company with others, are regularly shipped to the Continent for disposal without any regulation? When a bale breaks open, as they often do, these things are left lying about on the docks for anyone to pick up and examine people's private affairs.' Mr. Callaghan had been visiting his constituency and being familiar with income tax administration had seen the significance of the papers lying on the docks. The Chancellor, taken aback, replied:

'No; I admit I am rather concerned by what the hon. Gentleman has said. All I can say is that if he will give me the most complete information he can give, I shall look into it as a serious matter if what in fact he alleges is capable of taking place.'

On 7 May 1959[1] Mr. Callaghan asked about the result of the enquiries and the Financial Secretary replied:

'The arrangements for disposal of confidential waste paper, including Income Tax returns, are designed to ensure that it is pulped at a British mill under conditions which preserve its confidentiality. In the case of the Income Tax returns found by the hon. Gentleman on Cardiff dock, it is clear that the stipulated rules were not complied with, and investigations are proceeding. But the incident has shown that the present system can be improved, and my right hon. Friend has therefore set in train a review of the arrangements in the Departments concerned. My right hon. Friend is grateful to the hon. Gentleman for calling his attention to this matter.'

Thus a Minister can never be absolutely certain just what awkward turn the questioning may take or what may develop from even an innocuous-looking Question.

ADMINISTRATIVE ASPECTS AND IMPLICATIONS

There is a good deal of ambivalence towards Questions in the Civil Service. In the words of a former Permanent Secretary to the Treasury:

'I often hear my colleagues in the Civil Service complaining about Questions. It is annoying when you are busy to have to break off to prepare an answer to a tricky question. And the fact that Government departments have to be ready to answer questions at very short notice

[1] H.C. Deb. (1958–9), 605, c. 536–7.

means that they have to keep elaborate records, which are expensive. Question time is not, therefore, an unmixed blessing to the Civil Service, but there is no doubt that it is a very good thing. It is a great safety valve and a safeguard against abuses, and it makes sure that Government departments cannot get very far out of line with public opinion without being pulled up short.'[1]

We will start by looking at the value of Questions to Ministers and their Departments.

Administrative Advantages

It would be easy to fall into the error of thinking of Questions primarily in terms of a Minister having to stand up in the House and answer all and sundry — a kind of public ordeal. It is this aspect which impresses all foreign observers; they are interested in Question time rather than in Questions. Administratively, however, Questions affect many more people in a Department than the Minister and their effects are more pervasive than any possible discomfort suffered by the Minister while answering them in the House.

In the modern large Department a good deal of administrative discretion is delegated. Decisions are taken at different levels in the hierarchy. The lower down the administrative hierarchy the less the degree of discretion permitted and the more the official is required to apply the departmental rules or policy to particular cases. Those at the top of the hierarchy nearest the Minister are most likely to be concerned with the formulation of new policy and the settlement of unusual cases in the light of existing policy. As such, though politically neutral, these senior civil servants must, if they are to be effective advisers, develop some sensitivity to the way the winds of political and popular opinion are blowing. To that extent they are not unlike the Minister. Moreover, though they are likely to know much more than he does about the activities of the Department, they are likely to be equally in the dark about many of the day to day decisions. In considering the impact of Questions on a Department it is, therefore, more helpful to consider the Minister, his Parliamentary Secretary, his Permanent Secretary and a small number of his senior civil servants as one, even though the picture so presented has to be adjusted from time to time.

[1] Extract from a talk by Sir Edward (now Lord) Bridges to a Youth Conference of the Hansard Society. *Whitley Bulletin*, December 1949, p. 206.

Questions serve three purposes for this group:
  (i) They call attention to what are possibly wrong decisions or failings on the part of the Department.
  (ii) They are some guide to what the public are thinking about this or that aspect of the Department's functions and work.
  (iii) They provide an opportunity for the Department to deal with criticisms or misunderstandings and as such can constitute an important element in a Department's 'public relations'.

The first of these mainly concerns the application of the Department's policy to particular cases, to a person, a firm, or a local authority. The general policy may not be at issue but the Member is implying that the rule has been applied harshly or unjustly in this case, or that the decision might have been different if the Department had had fuller knowledge of the facts, or even that the Department slipped up and applied the wrong rule or applied the right rule wrongly. In most Departments a large number of decisions in respect of individual cases are made each week which never get anywhere near the Minister or his senior advisers. They are made by members of the Executive and Clerical Classes, possibly in the outstations or local offices of the Department, or even overseas. In so far as the Administrative Class is involved it may be only at the Assistant Principal or Principal level. The Minister and his senior advisers, and indeed all the Civil Service must work on the assumption that these thousands of decisions are being made correctly, or at least in an acceptable way, in so far as they do not arouse criticism and protests. Equally the assumption is that any case brought to the attention of the Department as being harsh, unjust or wrong will be carefully reconsidered. This is true whether the issue is raised by way of a letter from the Member or by way of a Question. By either way it is likely to secure the attention of those at the top of the Department for the first time. They may be horrified to find that such a decision could have been made and order its revision immediately, or further enquiry may show that the Member is not in possession of all the facts or that the Department did not have all the facts at the time. The Question may throw doubt on the rule, even though correctly applied in this instance and lead not only to a change in the decision but to a change in general policy. Contrariwise the fullest enquiry may confirm the Minister in the wisdom of the decision, in which case, he will presumably decide to abide by it.

It will be noticed that the absence of such 'individual grievances' is just as valuable to the Minister and his senior advisers. If Questions were prohibited (and Members' letters also) the Ministries would be saved a good deal of trouble but they would be like actors used to appearing in public condemned to act only in radio plays without even a studio audience. They would be acting in the dark (to change the metaphor) and have much less confidence in the correctness of the actions of their Departments.

Moreover it is reassuring for a Department to know that there exists a means whereby such grievances can be voiced in public. Thoughtful Ministers and civil servants appreciate that they are involved in making decisions affecting the lives of large numbers of people. They make these decisions to the best of their ability but they are not infallible. Few of the grievances raised by Questions are justiciable i.e. involve the alleged infringement of legal rights which could be tested in the Courts. In most cases they arise from the exercise of administrative discretion. If Questions were abolished some other method would have to be found for dealing with such cases for as Lord Bridges implied there must be a 'safety valve and a safeguard against abuses'.

This is also true of the general policies and activities of the Department. No Department expects to escape public criticism entirely but in providing services for which there can usually be no economic calculus, no profit and loss account, the volume and kind of criticism is not without its merits as a test of whether a Department is doing its job well, or at least in the way the public want it done. Ministers and their Civil Service advisers operate in a world of public opinion about the activities of their Departments.[1] Some opinion must be given instant attention, some must

---

[1] 'There is little doubt that the weekly flow of questions in Parliament provides, by and large, the best means of keeping government policy broadly in step with popular sentiment, and at any rate of warning members of the government if they are in danger of separating themselves widely from opinion in the country. The vigilance of Parliament sets up a state of tension at all levels in the administration, among Ministers and officials alike, which is relaxed as soon as Parliament goes into recess.' Lord Strang (a former Permanent Under Secretary of State for Foreign Affairs) in his 'The Formation and Control of Foreign Policy', *Durham University Journal*, June 1957, p. 105.

be mollified, some may be safely discounted — but none can be left entirely out of account.

Public opinion takes many forms. There is the press — the dailies and the periodicals — some with large national circulations, some with small local circulations. There is radio and television with talks, discussions and news stories. There are books and reports some of which have an instant and profound effect on public opinion. There are the many representative bodies or interest groups — the T.U.C., the British Legion, the National Union of Farmers, the Association of Municipal Corporations; the Council for the Preservation of Rural England and so on. There are the people who write letters — to the papers, to their Associations, to the Departments, and to Members of Parliament. Finally there is the House of Commons with its variety of ways of attracting and mirroring current opinion.

Questions are therefore not by any means the only contact Ministers and Departments have with the outside world, are not the only touchstone of whether the Department is doing the right thing. In a great many cases it does not require a Question to warn a Department that this particular matter is currently attracting a good deal of attention or is agitating all or a significant section of the public. A large air liner crashes on some houses; a scientist makes a statement about the amount of Strontium 90 in the atmosphere; there is a shortage of butter after the summer drought and prices rise; there are riots in one of the Colonies; there are criticisms of a newly constructed major road: all these items will appear prominently in one or more daily papers; all will be the subject of current conversation, whether in the Club, in the pub or during the course of a chatty afternoon's bridge; all are likely to become the subject of a Question to a Minister.

It is one thing, however, to read about such a happening and, as a private citizen pass the time of the day discussing it and distributing praise and blame. It is quite a different thing if one is a Minister. If the matter remains only in the press or in private discussion he is not compelled to make a public statement about it. If, however, it becomes the subject of a Question, he is brought in personally, he has to give an answer, an answer which may receive a fair amount of publicity and which may affect his standing in his Party and in the House generally.

Questions therefore reflect public opinion at a point at which Ministers are very sensitive. This does not mean that all Questions are equally valuable as indicators of opinion. Many, of course, imply no criticism of the Department either for its actions or for not taking action or if they do the criticism reflects the division of opinion between the Government and the Opposition. Occasionally there is an element of 'crankiness' in a Member's Question which allows the Department to ignore the criticism. There is also the differing attitudes of Members to be taken into account, some being ready to raise what are apparently trivial matters, others reserving Questions for cases on which they feel strongly. A substantial proportion of Questions therefore have little influence on the policies and actions of Departments; but there still remain a good number that may.

In some cases they do so merely because the very act of preparing an answer causes the Minister to think afresh or to reach a decision. A Department may have been pursuing a particular policy for some time out of inertia rather than recent conviction. A Question, whether critical or friendly, may cause the Department to ask itself the reasons for the policy; it provides an opportunity for fresh consideration. It may be that the Minister is brought to give his full attention to the matter for the first time or a new Permanent Secretary may bring a fresh viewpoint. In other instances the Department may have been putting off making a decision either because of the inherent difficulty of the problem or pressure of other work or sheer inertia. Even a Question may not result in the Minister making the decision but quite often it will. This is why when a Member cannot get a satisfactory decision by correspondence he threatens to ask a Question.[1] Occasionally these decisions may be of major importance. Thus, the declaration by the Prime Minister (Mr. Neville

[1] The late Sir Herbert Williams, who made great use of Questions, records the following: 'I remember, on one occasion, corresponding with a busy Minister on a matter where it seemed clear to me that his Department was making a muddle of a certain matter. I received from the Minister a letter which indicated to me that he had not really been into the matter himself, but had just signed the letter which had been prepared and put before him by one of his subordinates. I wrote back and said I did not think this letter was quite up to his standard, and perhaps the time had come to ask a Question; so I tabled one and sent him a copy. Within twenty-four hours he had telephoned me to say that he thought the matter required further investigation, and would I oblige by taking the Question off the Order Paper; and the result I desired was effected two or three days later.' *Papers on Parliament A Symposium* (1949), pp. 37–8.

Chamberlain) in the House of Commons on 31 March 1939 guaranteeing British aid to Poland in the event of a threat to her independence, made in reply to a Question suggesting that a German attack on Poland was imminent and enquiring what action the British Government would take in such a case, had been improvised only the previous day.[1]

Finally Questions give a Department the chance to explain and to defend its policies and actions. As regards explanation Mr. Kenneth Younger has this to say:[2] 'It is by the continuous stream of replies from the Prime Minister and Foreign Secretary far more than by the occasional full-length speech, that awareness of government policies is gradually built up in the public mind. At each stage the policy is open to attack, and Ministers are subjected to every kind of comment and criticism. From the Minister's point of view, ill-informed or even stupid questions may be quite as informative as those of the experts, and the murmurs of approval or protest evoked from different sections of opinion in the House can be as significant as anything that is said. Although these exchanges do not all percolate to the public through the press, much more goes out over the B.B.C. and the keenest political groups get a good idea of it from their M.P.'s.' Quoting this with approval Lord Strang added: 'The point to note here is that the process is two-fold. It helps to build up knowledge of the issues of foreign affairs among the public, to the extent that the public pay attention to what happens in Parliament; and it helps the government in a regular way to sense the feeling of the public, in so far as this can be reflected by members of Parliament.'[3] Both these writers, a former Member of Parliament and a former permanent head of the Foreign Office, are experienced in the handling of foreign affairs. Others could testify to the explanatory value of answers to Questions in domestic affairs. Indeed the fact that inspired Questions are regularly used by Departments shows their public value.

Even though Ministers may be very sensitive to Parliamentary opinion and generally try to be helpful and forthcoming at Question time this does not mean that they must give way to the

---

[1] Lord Strang, *Home and Abroad* (1956), p. 161.
[2] 'Public Opinion and Foreign Policy', *The British Journal of Sociology*, June 1955, vol. vi, pp. 172–3.
[3] 'Formation and Control of Foreign Policy', *Durham University Journal*, June 1957, p. 105.

questioner's demands or accept his criticisms. Indeed it is said, possibly with some justification, that Ministers are more ready to climb down in private e.g. when a grievance is handled by way of correspondence, than in public. Asked by Mr. Noel-Baker 'Which has the more explosive effect in the Department — a Parliamentary Question or a letter?' an experienced Post Office official replied:

'Well, if you had said which has the more constructive effect I should have said the letter on the whole. When a letter comes in you feel this is an endeavour to co-operate with the Department in getting something put right which is apparently wrong, and feeling like that everyone approaches it with a desire to do the very best he can. A Question in the House, on the other hand, I think is always received in rather a defensive way. You cannot answer it in full; you answer it as clearly and concisely as you can, but you cannot really get down to it in the way you can with a letter. You are therefore left in a rather defensive position. You try to answer the Question and to give the Minister such information as will enable him to handle any Supplementary Questions which may come along.'[1]

No Minister would like, as a regular thing, to have to admit in public that he and his Department were in the wrong. If he clearly is in the wrong he will admit it, though being human he may try to disguise the extent of his admission. But in many cases it will be a choice between the Member's opinion and his. Providing he does not misjudge the extent of the Member's knowledge of the matter or the extent of the interest of the House in it the Minister is usually in a strong position. The Departmental position if examined in detail and impartially might be shown to contain flaws but it is not being examined in this way, probably one or two not very well-designed supplementaries is all the examination it will receive.

A public body without a Minister to answer for it in the House of Commons lacks these advantages. This was quickly discovered after the nationalization of the coal and other major industries. Members of Parliament had grievances and criticisms brought to their attention and many of these were voiced in the press and in public speeches. But because no Minister was responsible for the day to day activities of the Boards managing

[1] Select Committee on Nationalized Industries, 1952, q. 638. See also Sir Herbert Williams, 'A Question in Parliament', in *Papers on Parliament*, A Symposium (1949), p. 35.

these industries these grievances and criticisms could not be raised at Question time. This was not without advantage to the Boards but it had one major disadvantage — it was difficult to make an explanation or defence which would have the same strength and get the same publicity as the answer to a Question. This last aspect of Questions is not always realized and appreciated by critics in the Civil Service.

Administrative Problems

Questions are said to create four problems for the administration and organization of a Department and in particular for the methods whereby the Department operates and for the attitudes of its Civil Service staff.

The first problem is the very high priority that must be given to the preparation of answers. Parliamentary business of any kind normally takes precedence over everything else in the work of a Department. It is not merely that the Minister must be more concerned with proceedings in Parliament than with anything happening elswhere. It is also that 'the Department itself, as an entity distinct from the Minister for the time being, suffers some temporary loss of influence if its chief makes a bad speech on an important occasion or is severely battered at question-time'.[1]

In the case of starred Questions there may be very little time to prepare the answer, not more than two days in many instances though one effect of the rota has been to increase the period of notice normally given. In contrast the time allowed to Departments for answering unstarred Questions has recently been greatly curtailed.

Some answers will be readily available and easy to draft, others will present considerable difficulties: they may involve communication with a colonial territory[2] or with some distant army base; a Town Clerk may have to be consulted; other Departments may need to be brought in; fresh data collected and analysed; scientific advice sought, and so on. Moreover, in so far as the Member is not just asking for information but is questioning the Ministry's action in some particular case, the affair may have to be considered afresh. The Minister may not have looked

[1] H. E. Dale, 'Parliament in relation to the Civil Service' in *Parliament. A Survey*, by Lord Campion and others (1952), p. 125.
[2] Some 70–80 per cent of the Questions addressed to the Colonial Secretary have to be referred to one or other Colonial Governor before they can be answered. H.C. Deb. (1956–7), 569, c. 760.

at it more closely before, indeed it may have been brought to his attention for the first time. He may therefore want to read the file and consult the civil servants directly concerned. He may even find it desirable to ask the advice of one or more of his Cabinet colleagues, even of the Cabinet itself. Drafting the answer may be straighforward or it may call for considerable care, skill and forethought, having regard to the political and even international implications.

These kinds of problems arise in all aspects of a Department's work but in the case of a starred Question the time allowed for doing all these things is so short and so definite. As a result, the preparation of answers to Questions are always carefully and highly organized. They receive priority over other work. Moreover, unlike much of the work arising out of the Department's Parliamentary activities, which concerns only the Minister's Private Office or the Department's Parliamentary branch, the preparation will need the help of staff concerned with the day to day activities of the Department. An Assistant Secretary in the Ministry of Housing and Local Government may have to suspend his preparation of the Ministry's views on an important town planning appeal and concentrate immediately on preparing the answer to a Question. Moreover, not only has an answer to be drafted but also a good deal of background material, indeed possibly the whole story of the case has to be put on the file. This can be a time-consuming occupation. If the issue involved is significant neither the Minister nor the staff concerned is likely to begrudge the time and effort involved. But it is easy to see how exasperated they may be if it should appear that the Question is mere idle curiosity or publicity seeking on the part of the Member.

The direct costs of preparing answers to Questions are probably less significant than the indirect costs. In addition to taking several hours of the time of highly paid staff each Question diverts the branch of the Department concerned from dealing with other matters. In the words of one civil servant: 'there is no doubt that the system tends at times to clog the higher administrative machinery. Questions are generally asked about subjects that are "in the news", and it (is) reasonable to suppose that it is just these subjects that are already placing a strain on the division concerned. The strain is merely increased if the attention of the assistant secretary or under secretary is constantly being diverted from his proper task of administration by the need to explain himself and his work — an example of what happens when priority must always be given to Parliaments' current business.'[1]

This is not a fair general picture of the impact of Questions on a Department. The number asked is not large in relation to the present-day size of most Departments. An average of 10–15 — or even 20 starred Questions a week during a Session, some of which are perfectly straightforward and readily answerable and no Questions for some 20 weeks of the year can hardly be said to overwhelm or clog the administrative machine. True the 'bunching' of starred Questions on the weeks when the Minister is at or next to the top of the list must be a specially heavy period but it is counterbalanced by fewer Questions during the other weeks of the cycle. Undoubtedly, however, Questions must impinge particularly severely on a Department or a section of a Department engaged on a matter which is attracting a great deal of Parliamentary attention. When one thinks of the worries of the Colonial Secretary in recent years in dealing with the rapidly changing, sometimes explosive situation in various Colonies, one cannot but wonder at the added strain of having to prepare careful answers to more than 1,000 Questions a year, knowing that each answer will receive publicity and be examined carefully, not only by the Member but by thousands of people in this country and abroad.[2]

This brings us to the core of the charge that can be justly

---

[1] T. A. Critchley, *The Civil Service To-day* (1951), p. 76.
[2] The strain could be very much greater when a Minister could be reached day after day. In 1912, for example, when C. F. G. Masterman was both Financial Secretary to the Treasury and Chairman of the National Health Insurance Commission, he was subjected to a barrage of Questions from Opposition Members violently critical of the National Health Insurance Act passed in 1911, part of 'a deliberate move . . . to break the Minister and wreck the Bill'. On 19 February Masterman answered 39, on the 20th he answered 24, on the 21st, 28, on the 26th, 45 and on the 27th 11. These were the number of starred Questions: if written answers were included the numbers would rise to 40 on the 19th, 30 on the 21st, 49 on the 26th and 34 on the 28th. The daily encounter continued, the volume of Hansard for 20 February–7 March showing 30 columns of index on National Health Insurance alone. Worthington-Evans in January 1913 said, 'We bombarded him (Masterman) with questions and he has more questions to answer off his own bat than all the rest of the Ministers put together on many and many a day, and the skill he has developed in answering questions is perfectly prodigious. . . . He has earned his reputation of "Masterman Ready".' Lucy Masterman, *C. F. G. Masterman* (1939), pp. 230–51.

levied against Questions — the priority of treatment is decided by the Member without his knowing what is involved. In part this is due to the great unwillingness of Ministers either to ask for further time in which to answer or to refuse answers on grounds of the cost and trouble involved. Indeed there is a convention that unless there are overwhelming reasons to the contrary an answer will be provided on the date demanded. As a result there must be occasions when important and urgent current business has to be put aside by the Minister or by a civil servant to deal with a Question, which, and this is the point, the Member would not have wished to see put aside had he known what was involved. The same can be said of the cost and trouble involved in the preparation of certain factual answers. This is not true of the great bulk of Questions but when it does occur it must not only cause annoyance and exasperation in the Department, but also reduce efficiency.

The second problem concerns the keeping of records. Mr. H. E. Dale put the point quite well when he wrote: 'the high official must have at his command full records, always quickly available — which means "paper work" in quantity, for his subordinates if not for him. Unlike his compeer in private business, he has to fight on two points at once, so to speak; he has to do the work or see that it is done, and he has to provide for its public defence, in detail and at short notice, against questions and attacks from a numerous, acute and well-organized body of professional critics.'[1] Critchley puts the point more strongly: 'the Civil Service must anticipate every conceivable Question likely to be raised in Parliament about any one of its myriad activities. It must be prepared, at a few days' notice, to supply any information about anything it has done and most things it has failed to do, for Ministers are understandably reluctant to have to declare that 'the information is not available.' Elaborate statistics must be maintained, and detailed records kept showing what everybody thinks and says and does, and what they might have thought and said and done in slightly different circumstances. Files grow and papers multiply, but they must all be kept and faithfully recorded in case the inevitable Question turns up.'[2]

[1] 'Parliament in relation to the Civil Service' in *Parliament. A Survey* by Lord Campion and others (1952), p. 126.
[2] *The Civil Service To-day*, p. 61.

It is difficult to assess how much weight to give to these charges. Undoubtedly Government Departments do use an elaborate system of minuting and filing but it does not follow that this is due to Question time. Even before Questions became a major Parliamentary device Government files and records were elaborate. Paper work is indeed a major characteristic of central administration in all countries, even where no system of Questions to Ministers exists. Private firms of a similar size also have to keep considerable records. Opening a file for each new subject, keeping all the relevant papers on it and having a system of minuting are obvious administrative devices and it is not easy to see how they could be eliminated for the kind of work Government Departments have to handle. There are what Sir Josiah (later Lord) Stamp once called 'deep rooted differences in the very nature of the task' between the administration of Business and Public affairs. He said: 'The usual reply of the Civil Service to criticism or explanation of the difference between business and Civil Service methods generally ends up by a reference to the Minister in the House, who has the responsibility for the doings of his subordinates. It is undoubtedly an important feature, but there is something even more fundamental than that and of which answers to Parliamentary questions are a mere consequence ... something which permeates the whole theory and task of government.'[1] The two major deep-rooted differences according to Stamp are that Government Departments are administering Acts of Parliament which they have to apply consistently to all cases and they operate on a scale seldom found in private enterprise. To these characteristics can be traced most of the administrative features of the Civil Service.

The third and fourth problems can be taken together — Questions are said to lead to over-centralization and to delay and timidity on the part of Departments. As long ago as 1902 Austen Chamberlain, when Postmaster-General, could complain, 'In a great administration like this there must be decentralization, and how difficult it is to decentralize, either in the Post Office or in the Army, when working under constant examination and answer in this House, no hon. Member who has not had experience

[1] 'The Contrast between the Administration of Business and Public Affairs', *Public Administration*, (1923), vol. i, p. 158.

of official life can easily realise....'[1] He went on to add that at a low estimate a third of the time of the highest officials in the Post Office were occupied in answering queries. In 1932 Mr. (now Earl) Attlee wrote that because the action of any postal servant may be challenged on the floor of the House of Commons, 'the minutiæ of administration come right up to the highest officials, diverting their minds from broad matters of policy. The effect is also', he said, 'felt throughout the service in a cramping of initiative and a tendency to stick too closely to the letter of regulations which prevent the evolution of a proper public relations attitude.'[2] And later he wrote, '... it was this fear of the effect on administration of detailed day-to-day Parliamentary supervision that was a factor in setting up public boards in nationalized industries instead of following the Post Office precedent.'[3]

The point was put by Dale in this way:[4] 'business must sometimes go more slowly than it would if the House of Commons did not exist; for the official is cautious about deciding without reference to the Minister some things in themselves trivial, if they are likely to provoke discussion in the House. It is not that he doubts the wisdom of his own views or is afraid to act on them; it is the feeling of fair play. This may mean trouble in the House, and my chief will have to face it, not I; it is not fair to run him in for it without giving him a chance of objecting.'

The only Parliamentary examination of criticisms of this kind was undertaken by the Bridgeman Committee in respect of the Post Office. Lord Wolmer, who had been Assistant Postmaster-General, made a scathing attack on the inefficiency of the Post Office and was supported in his demand for an enquiry by the majority of Conservative Members. He was extremely critical of Parliamentary control and wished the service to be operated on business lines by an independent Board. He had this to say about Questions: 'Question-time resembles a game which schoolboys play called "French cricket", wherein one individual has to defend his legs with a cricket bat, without shifting his ground, against

[1] Parl. Deb. (1902), 106, c. 733–4.
[2] The Bridgeman Committee Report, *Public Administration* (1932), vol. x, p. 355. See also Lord Wolmer, *Post Office Reform*, pp. 227–31.
[3] *The Civil Service in Great Britain and France*, edited by W. A. Robson (1956), p. 20.
[4] op. cit., pp. 125–6.

the balls of a dozen friends in front of and behind him. If he makes a slip he has to cede his place to his successful rival. And similarly with Parliamentary debates. The questions directed to the Postmaster General from the Opposition benches aim largely at showing his administration in as unfavourable a light as possible; and the arguments which he will have to answer in debate will be equally tendentious. Theoretically this steady flow of hostile criticism might make for good administration, and provide an essential safeguard against slackness or corruption, but, in practice, what the critics are looking for is not administrative improvement conceived on long-sighted and well-informed grounds, but a party score. A Minister must offer as small a target as possible to the snipers of other parties, and he therefore tends to only adopt a forward policy on the rare occasions when the risks of doing nothing are judged to be greater than the risks of doing something. Post Office policy exemplifies the operation of this rule. I have known important decisions held up for months because of the awkward questions they might provoke in Parliament. Political exigency weights the scales permanently in favour of hesitation and delay.'

'Further, this Parliamentary sharpshooting is one of the principal causes of the over centralization of the Department. The idea that the Postmaster General may any day be hauled over the coals for the error of some provincial postman exercises a cramping effect on the Department out of all proportion to the non-political importance of such questions and results in a centralization of authority which is at once expensive and dilatory. The Secretary will not delegate to the provinces matters which any ordinary business undertaking would delegate, for fear that his chief may be questioned about them, although, when his chief *is* questioned, the Secretary knows very well how to frame a suitable answer which leaves the questioner much where he was.'[1]

The Government appointed a Committee under the chairmanship of Lord Bridgeman which found some things wrong with the Post Office and its organization but did not agree with Lord Wolmer's diagnosis. 'It cannot be denied' they said in their Report 'that Parliamentary intervention in the minor details of daily administration may be harassing and sometimes vexatious;

[1] Lord Wolmer, *Post Office Reform*, pp. 227–8.

it indubitably involves in many instances an expenditure of time and effort quite disproportionate to the importance of the matter in question. At the same time, we are inclined to think that this insistence on the supposed results of Parliamentary intervention in matters of detail is somewhat unduly stressed and that in the long run, the advantages of the power of Parliamentary intervention outweigh its disadvantages. It seems to us that where complaints are expressed against a business so closely in contact with the everyday lives of the public as the Post Office, some means of ventilation is necessary, and on the whole we believe that the House of Commons provides the best machinery for this purpose. In effect, we do not consider the relationship in which the Post Office stands to Parliament is a factor which essentially and inevitably makes the efficient performance of its duties impossible, or that the position of the Post Office in this respect differs substantially from other Government Departments subject to Parliamentary control.'

'We do, however, consider that the main causes of such defects as may exist, are the two described in paragraph 46, viz., the relationship between the Post Office and the Exchequer, and the internal organization of the Department, and we believe that the faults to which attention has been drawn, can be eradicated by certain modifications of financial status and by changes in organization at least as effectively as by the revolutionary step of removing the Post Office Communications Services from direct Government control.'[1] This view was later borne out by Sir Thomas Gardiner, Director General of the Post Office during the period 1936–46. Asked whether Questions made it difficult to run the Department conveniently he replied that if it was just a matter of abolishing Questions and leaving the rest of the Parliamentary control as it was the Department would merely be relieved of some irksome work 'but generally I do not think it would go beyond that'.[2]

The fact that a Minister is answerable to the House of Commons for all the actions of the Department must obviously result in a different attitude on the part of administrators than if no such responsibility were involved. It is difficult, however, to see

---
[1] Report of Committee of Enquiry into the Post Office (1932), Cmd. 4149, paras. 55–6.
[2] Select Committee on Nationalized Industries 1952, q. 623.

any alternative. The Civil Service is exercising powers not possessed by any private body. If a citizen is not satisfied with the treatment he has received at the hands of the Home Office he cannot take his custom elswhere, except by leaving the country. Failing a system of administrative tribunals covering every activity of government there must be some method whereby grievances and criticisms can be voiced. As one former civil servant put it 'A wholesome fear of Parliament is the best safeguard against harsh or hasty decisions . . . and against the careless application of rules which may be based on good grounds but which fail to take account of exceptional circumstances.'[1] There must also be a great many occasions when a Question or criticism in the House stimulates a Department into taking action. Moreover a Minister who is popular in the House and experienced in handling Members can be a very powerful defender of his Department and so disarm its critics or enable it to pursue a settled course of action irrespective of sectional criticism.

This book is concerned only with Questions. One thing is clear: the abolition of Question time and Questions would not remove the four problems. As Lord Stamp said, these problems arise mainly from certain deep rooted differences between public and private administration. Moreover, Questions are part of the general relationship between the Departments and the House of Commons. If Questions were abolished Members would have to find some other method of handling this aspect of their functions, possibly by Committees concerned with the administration of each Department or sector of government activity. Finally, as we saw earlier, Questions are now overshadowed in volume by correspondence between Members and Ministers. Apart from the fact that the answer is not given in the House and published in Hansard Members' letters raise most of the problems attributed to Questions. It is noticeable that neither Dale nor Critchley paid much attention to them.

This prompts one last reflection. The Civil Service have few if any direct contacts with the House of Commons. The Permanent Secretary and one or two of his senior officials may appear each year before the Public Accounts Committee and, occasionally,

[1] F. Elliott, 'Questions in Parliament', *The Fortnightly Review*, March 1934, p. 342.

civil servants may be called upon to give evidence to other Committees, in particular the Select Committee on Estimates. Questions are, in a sense, the nearest that most civil servants get to Members.

CHAPTER 12

CONCLUSIONS

THE number of testimonials, British and foreign, to the value of Question time is legion. President Lowell of Harvard could say, 'the system provides a method of dragging before the House any acts or omissions by the departments of state, and of turning a searchlight upon every corner of the public service . . . it helps very much to keep the administration of the country up to the mark, and it is a great safeguard against neglect or arbitary conduct, or the growth of bureaucratic arrogance which is quite unknown in England.'[1] Sir Ivor Jennings refers to the 'practice of asking questions . . . now of the utmost constitutional importance'.[2] Mr. J. R. Clynes wrote: 'The freedom of the House is never better illustrated than during the daily question hour. Important Ministers may be questioned by the humblest Members; and if the Members master the rules and procedure, they can often render substantial service to their constituents.'[3] In 1906 Mr. Speaker Lowther declared: 'If I had the decision of it, I would not limit the right of asking Questions at all. I think it is a very valuable right.'[4] In 1946 another Speaker, (Mr. Speaker Clifton Brown) giving evidence to a Select Committee expressed the clear opinion: 'I regard the Question hour as a vital part of our proceedings'[5] and a little later said, 'I think the Question Hour is the most important Private Members' hour, so to speak. I think it is a frightfully important hour.'[6] Lord Campion, one of the most able and prominent Clerks of the House of Commons, wrote that Questions 'are the one procedural invention of the democratic period'.[7] Before the Select Committee on Procedure in 1931 Stanley Baldwin said: 'There is no more unalienable

[1] A. L. Lowell, the *Government of England*, 1919 edition, vol. i, p. 332.
[2] *Parliament*, second edition (1957), p. 99.
[3] *Memoirs* 1924–1937, p. 270.
[4] Select Committee on House of Commons (Procedure), 1906, q. 18.
[5] Select Committee on Procedure, 1945–6, Minutes of Evidence, Second Report q. 1506.
[6] q. 1535.
[7] Lord Campion and others, *Parliament. A Survey*, p. 165.

right ... than that right of putting questions to the Ministers' (q. 306); Lloyd George said that he regarded Question time as 'Very valuable, and supplementaries are very valuable' (q. 1012); Sir Archibald Sinclair, the Liberal leader, said he attached great importance to Questions and particularly to supplementary Questions (q. 1271-2); an experienced Chief Government Whip, Sir Bolton Eyres Monsell, said that Questions and supplementaries were 'the one effective way of criticizing the Government at the present moment' (q. 1469). And so we could go on. Few elements in the procedure of the House of Commons, indeed in the British constitution itself, have attracted so much attention or been so universally praised as the system of allowing Members to question Ministers.

It is, however, Question time rather than Questions that has attracted attention and praise. Nobody has waxed lyrical about Questions which receive a written answer though their usefulness has been admitted. Question time, however, is little or nothing without the right to ask supplementaries. A growth of the late nineteenth century, frowned on by Balfour and a great many others in the earlier years of the present century, the supplementary has become the most significant part of the process of questioning. Picturesque phrases such as 'the right to wring the last drop out of the orange'[1] or, 'It is the man's own "hare", he finds it, so let him hunt it'[2] have been used about the asking of supplementaries. Commander Kenworthy (later Lord Strabolgi), a very insistent and practised questioner, once said: 'without the supplementary a question is of very little value. Unless you can put supplementary questions ... you will not get the truth in many cases. ...'[3]

If an institution or device is praised and generally regarded as 'a good thing' one would expect it to flourish and its use to expand. In this particular case two other factors would add to that expectation. On the one hand there has been the great growth in the powers and activities of Government Departments, a big increase in the number of voters and a changed public attitude towards state intervention. Inevitably these have led to an increase in the number of 'individual grievances', and have

---

[1] Stanley Baldwin, Select Committee on Procedure, 1931, q. 312.
[2] Mr. Speaker Morrison, Select Committee on Procedure, 1959, p. 152.
[3] Select Committee on Procedure, 1931, q. 3154.

provided Members with many more matters about which they need to take action or, at least, to ask for information. On the other hand the opportunities for the back bencher to play an active, public and independent role in the proceedings of the House of Commons are not as great as they were in the early years of the century. In so far as Question time remains primarily a back bencher activity and in so far as 'individual grievances' are largely constituency matters which in turn are the bread and butter of the back bencher's life it might be expected that an increasing use of this procedure would have led to more time being made available for it. Instead, the number of minutes available are the same now as they were in April 1906 and though the number of supplementaries has increased in the last fifty years this has been at the expense of a more than corresponding decline in the number of Questions receiving oral answer. This in turn has inhibited growth of the number of Questions on the Paper.

Since 1906, when the time available was increased to its present 45–55 minutes, the House has tried to deal with the problems raised by the increasing pressure on Question time in four ways:

(1) By reducing the maximum number of starred Questions any Member may ask on any one day. The maximum is now two as against eight until 1919 and three from 1920 to 1960;

(2) By developing the rota system so that the chance to question Ministers on the floor of the House comes round according to a regular and predetermined cycle;

(3) By appealing to Members not to ask so many and such long supplementaries, the Speaker being asked to make such appeals and also to be tougher in not allowing supplementaries; and

(4) By trying to get Members to use such other methods as correspondence and unstarred Questions.

Each of these ways of treating the problem has involved limiting the use of Question time.[1] There has been no serious move to increase the amount of time available. The Select Committees on Procedure which reported in 1932, 1946 and 1959 not merely did not recommend any extension of time, they did not

[1] The increase in the amount of notice required is a further limitation.

even discuss it in order to reject it. They discussed many other aspects of Questions (period of notice, restriction on numbers etc.) but not increasing the time available.

When the Government's proposals arising out of the recommendations of the Select Committee of 1959 were put before the House on 8 February 1960 an amendment was moved by Mr. Tom Driberg which, if accepted, would have made the so-called Question hour really an hour. Question time, he said, never lasted an hour for there was always Prayers to be taken out of the period between 2.30 p.m. and 3.30 p.m. and, on occasions, Private Business, Petitions and other items of Business which altogether could take up a quarter of an hour. He had found little disagreement with 'this modest proposal'; it was thought not to be very important but there was no harm in it. Mr. R. A. Butler, replying for the Government, rejected the amendment on the grounds that the matter had not been examined by the Select Committee and was not one of its findings, that various devices were to be introduced to improve what he continued to call the 'Question hour' by speedier written answers and 'Mr. Speaker has undertaken to check as far as he can the length and number of supplementary Questions'. The amendment was not pressed to a division, Mr. Driberg saying, 'Since it is so generally agreed that this is a reasonable suggestion, I have great pleasure in asking the leave of the House to withdraw the Amendment.'[1] Though it is a small point it is interesting psychologically to notice how Members will talk about Question hour knowing full well that it is not an hour and refusing to make it an hour. To continue the words of Mr. Speaker Clifton Brown quoted earlier: 'I regard the Question Hour as a vital part of our proceedings. I would not extend it.'[2]

A similar fate has met the more drastic suggestion that there should be a Question time on Fridays. Replying to such a suggestion in 1956 the Prime Minister (Sir Anthony Eden) said: 'To have Oral Questions on Fridays would be contrary to the practice of the House and it would not, I think, be convenient to adopt the hon. Gentleman's suggestion.' In answering a supplementary he was able to point out that his answer coincided

---

[1] The proposed amendment was: 'When 1 hour has elapsed after Mr. Speaker has called the Member whose question is No. 1. on the Order Paper, no further questions shall be taken.' H.C. Deb. (1959–60), 617, c. 175–7.
[2] Second Report of Select Committee on Procedure, 1946, p. 36.

closely with an answer given by Mr. Herbert Morrison when he was Leader of the House, and added, 'I have had no representations . . . in favour of this practice. . . .'[1] Yet for a long time after 1902 it was possible for Members to put down Questions for oral answers on Fridays and sometimes a Minister would, by voluntary arrangement, attend to answer. Even as late as the 1930s Questions were quite often answered orally on the Friday the House adjourned for the Whitsuntide, the Summer or the Christmas Recess.

Finally, mention must be made of the proposal of Sir Edward Fellowes as Clerk of the House, to the Select Committee of 1959.[2] In order to get more Questions answered orally he proposed that three Grand Committees should be established. Each Committee would have several Departments allotted to it by Mr. Speaker, and would meet for one hour every Monday and Wednesday during the Session for what in effect would be the present Question time. On Tuesdays and Thursdays Questions could be answered in the House (i.e. not in the Grand Committee) but Sir Edward suggested that on these days Questions should be limited to the Prime Minister, Foreign Secretary, Chancellor of the Exchequer, Minister of Defence and Leader of the House, with Mr. Speaker having power to add to this list. The net result would be that instead of four periods each week there would be eight, six in the Grand Committees and two in the Chamber. Apparently this proposal had no sympathizers much less supporters in the Select Committee, for Members did not take the opportunity to discuss it with the Clerk when he gave evidence nor was it even mentioned in the Committee's Report. Probably the major objection was that Questions would cease to be an activity of the House as a whole, except on two days a week. Even so the Committee did not feel it necessary to discuss the proposal.

There are three main explanations why the House has been content to attempt to remedy the problems of Question time by restrictive rather than by expansive measures. The first probably lies in the fact that the proceedings of the House of Commons are dominated by the two Front Benches and, in particular,

[1] H.C. Deb. (1955–6), 551, c. 1611–12. For Mr. Morrison's reply see H.C. Deb. (1945–6), 418, c. 1713.
[2] Select Committee on Procedure, 1959, pp. 9–10.

by the Treasury Bench. The introduction of a limited Question time altered the attitude of all subsequent Governments. Before May 1902 any exuberance, excess of zeal or dilatoriness on the part of questioners affected the time at the disposal of the Government. After that date it was merely a matter of one Member getting more of the time at the expense of another. Since that date, therefore, there has been no inducement for Governments to concern themselves with the reform of Question time, their only concern being to avoid more time being made available. If as a result of more and longer supplementaries fewer starred Questions are answered orally this is to the advantage of Ministers. If a Minister is reached only once in five or six weeks this is generally more palatable and more convenient to him than being available every day. Ministers are, therefore, unlikely to take the initiative in extending the time available for questioning them. Moreover it is not for a Minister, but for Mr. Speaker reflecting the general wishes of the House, to admonish a Member who asks lengthy supplementaries and raises unnecessary points of order, so preventing two or three more starred Questions being reached. The time is available for private Members and if they choose to use it this way rather than the way they used it in say the 1930s that is their affair.[1]

The Opposition Leaders are not so differently placed as to feel compelled to take an opposite viewpoint. For one thing they anticipate being Ministers themselves one day. For another, Questions are not a major Front Bench activity. The leading Opposition Members make their main contribution during the major debates and get sufficient opportunity to do this. They are unlikely, therefore, to wish to expand Question time at the expense of the time available for debates.

Though neither Front Bench has any inducement to bring forward spontaneously proposals for the extension of Question time both are responsive to strong currents of opinion on the part of

[1] Mr. Stanley Baldwin put the issue very clearly to the Select Committee of 1931 (q. 305). 'If private Members who put these questions and supplementaries feel that the thing is getting a bit of a bore, and that enough people cannot ask their questions, it is open to them at any time to make their suggestions to Mr. Speaker, who, of course, would consider them. I do not think you could lay down any hard and fast rules. I would leave the House during that hour to enjoy the perfect freedom it enjoys now, either to put supplementary questions or not, as they think fit. I have never had any objection to questions which have been put to me, and if they choose to waste time it is their business. It is their hour, and I would not interfere with it.'

their supporters. The conclusion cannot be avoided therefore that there has been no expressed desire on the part of the majority of Members to have more time made available. Indeed the 'restrictive' measures have been due to pressure from private Members and the initiative has not been taken by the Government.[1] This brings us to the second explanation.

Most Members ask very few Questions: some because they take very little public part in any form of Parliamentary activity, others because they hold the view that a starred Question is a device to be used sparingly, usually when other methods have failed and the issue at stake is important. Some of the latter group are politically ambitious and feel that speaking in major debates or taking part in general party activity are more likely to get them to the top than asking Questions. Whatever may be their reason the majority of Members have broadly the same attitude towards the small group of Members who make continuous use of this device.

In general most Members quite like to see Ministers questioned. A great variety of matters is touched upon, it is interesting to see how different Ministers handle their Departmental problems and there is always a chance of a laugh, a scene or some other titbit. Question time is the hors d'oeuvre to what may be a very plain bill of fare. Even so, they are not enthusiastic about seeing the time extended. They appreciate that probably all or most of the extra time would be taken up very quickly by the comparatively few Members who already take up a high proportion of the available time. For this reason they agree to a reduction in the maximum daily number of starred Questions that any Member can ask. This restriction does not harm or even restrict the great majority of Members, but merely limits the persistent users and thus makes more time available for the occasional questioner.

In fairness it must be pointed out that the problem of guaranteeing an oral answer for all starred Questions has long since passed the stage when a small extension of time would be sufficient. To enable all the starred Questions asked during the Session of 1959–60 to be answered orally another 40 to 50 minutes each day would have been necessary. But had this extra time

[1] Select Committees on Procedure are mainly composed of back benchers and never contain Ministers.

been available the number of starred Questions on the Paper would have been very much higher, for the difficulty of reaching a Minister regularly is now a major deterrent. Moreover it would have been less easy for Mr. Speaker to restrain supplementaries. Thus even if the present period were doubled many starred Questions would probably still remain unanswered. To ensure that a full hour is available would make little impact on the present problem.

The indifference of front benchers and the unwillingness of back benchers to press for more time to be made available in case it is mostly taken up by the persistent questioners may explain but can hardly be said to justify a state of affairs in which the amount of time available for questioning Ministers remains the same as it was half a century ago and is less than it was at the beginning of the century. The House of Commons has conferred vast new powers on Government Departments, yet appears unable or unwilling to provide even an extra half hour on four days a week for questioning Ministers. It can hardly be a defence to say that the time available has been made inadequate by the growth of supplementaries. For, if supplementaries were to be the exception rather than the rule, there would be no particular merit in a Minister answering orally rather than in writing. True, many supplementaries are long-winded and a very blunt instrument indeed but there are occasions when a Member could with profit be allowed to ask more than one or two supplementaries.

This brings us to the third reason. At present the House normally meets for eight hours a day on four days a week and for $5\frac{1}{2}$ hours on Fridays. This, however, by no means indicates the extent of the claims on Members' time. Some Committees meet in the morning; Ministers have their Departments to administer; and Members have their correspondence to answer and their constituencies to visit, other public activities to perform and also probably a substantial part of their living to earn by some other occupation. The hours the House meets could be extended only on the assumption that Members need attend only a smaller part of the time.

It is argued, therefore, that any extension of Question time would have to be at the expense of the time at present devoted to Debates. At present normally $6\frac{1}{2}$ hours are devoted to the discussion of legislation, Supply, Motions, etc. (about 5 hours on Fridays) and half an hour to a private Member's Adjournment Debate. Already the House devotes three-quarters of an hour less on Mondays to Thursdays to Public Business than it did in 1947. This time has to suffice for the Government's legislative programme, the Budget and other financial legislation, the discussion of major issues of public policy and a certain amount of private Members' business. It is difficult enough as it is for private Members to take part regularly in such Debates, and their chances would be even less if part of the time were diverted to Question time. In so far as Members face up to the problem of Question time they see it as a choice between Questions and Debates. The Government's preference is clear, so on the whole is that of the Opposition leaders, and the great majority of the back benchers are ready to accept this view. Not many Members give much thought to Parliamentary procedure and fewer are very knowledgeable about it. But even the thinking ones, though not happy about the present state of Question time, are not inclined to attempt a remedy that would reduce the time available for Debates.

The House is faced with the same problem that has faced it since the 1830s — how to secure a fair balance between the business which only one or two Members wish to discuss and the business which is of interest to the majority of Members. The point was forcefully put in the following exchange between Sir Stafford Northcote and Sir Thomas E. May as Chairman and Witness respectively, before the Select Committee of 1878.

'542. Which do you think is the more important, that every individual should have an opportunity of airing a crotchet, or of bringing before the House that which he may imagine to be a grievance, but which the great majority would not consider to be such, or that greater facility should be given for the important business of the country being carried on with due expedition and certainty? — The first object, of course, is to carry on the important business of the country, which is at present very much hindered.

543. And in order to obtain that due expedition and that certainty you think it would not be hard to restrict, in some measure, the privileges of individual Members? — That is my opinion.'

This, however, was in 1878 when the private Member still could dominate the daily timetable of the House if he so wished.

Northcote's questions could be put today and get the same answers but equally well his opening question could be worded quite differently: 'Having regard to the greatly increased powers of Government Departments and the corresponding increase in the responsibilities of Members for the welfare of their constituents, which do you think is more important, that a Member should be able to question a Minister whenever he feels that a grievance needs airing in the House or that his chance to do this should be limited in order that he should have more chance to take part in Debates organized through the usual channels?' The answer would probably be that the right of individual Members to question Ministers in the Chamber is more than ever needed as a constitutional safeguard but that, as sufficient time must be available for the discussion of important legislation and issues of general public policy, there still remains the problem of whether every Member can be trusted in his judgement of what issues were important enough to take up the time of some 600 other Members.

Members are little nearer solving the problem of the kinds of Questions which should or should not be put down for oral answer than they were when the issue was discussed in 1902. They are aware that many Questions are starred which in the opinion of the mass of the Members are not important enough to warrant the use of the very limited time of the House. They are also aware that pure chance may decide that a trivial Question may receive an oral answer whereas a Question of greater interest and importance may not be reached. They also know that the regular questioner, familiar with the complexities of the rota system, is more likely to get his Questions answered orally than the occasional questioner and is more willing to take the trouble to do so.

Mr. Balfour's proposed solution was to empower either Mr. Speaker or a Committee of Members to make a choice so that Questions least likely to be reached were of the least general importance. The point was touched upon in the evidence before the Select Committee of 1906 when Mr. Speaker Lowther said if he were given the task of arranging for Questions involving answers in great detail or of purely local interest to be put down unstarred he could do it, but he was afraid that his decisions would give rise to considerable dissatisfaction.[1] Before the Select Com-

[1] Select Committee on House of Commons (Procedure), 1906, q. 54.

CONCLUSIONS

mittee of 1931 Sir Austen Chamberlain rather hesitantly suggested that the Speaker should be empowered to transfer a Question from the starred to the unstarred list 'if in his opinion it was a question of no general interest'.[1] He added that 'In the general interests of those who are putting questions of public interest, I should like to clear the House of a certain proportion of questions which a more reasonable man would have put either in a private letter to the Minister or in unstarred form'.[2] But he did not attach much importance to the suggestion. The problem was again touched upon during the evidence to the Select Committees on Procedure of 1946 and 1959. On each occasion Mr. Clement Davies asked Sir Edward Fellowes about the possibility of keeping certain types of Questions from being starred. On the second occasion Sir Edward replied: 'your suggestion is a power which no Clerk can possibly be asked to exercise ... it would destroy the (I hope) friendly relations between the Table and Members which do exist about Questions at the moment. If we had powers of that sort, I am quite sure that we should be in conflict with Members.'[3]

Mr. Asquith, when Prime Minister, put the difficulty very strongly to the Select Committee of 1914. True he was expressing a view on the possibility of an arrangement whereby the discussion of petty matters on the Estimates could be taken in a Committee, reserving the 'broader issues and great questions in which the House would be interested' to the House as a whole, but his remarks are equally applicable to Questions. He said:

'Yes; theoretically, of course, that is perfectly true, but I do not know that in practice you could frame any boundary line between that which is in your sense petty and that which is not petty. This is one of the great safeguards for the real control of the House of Commons of administration. Take, for instance, a War Office question, dismissing an officer, in itself a matter of very limited interest, but every Minister acts with the knowledge that his action may be called in question upon the floor of the House when his Estimates come on, and that he may have to vindicate it, and that knowledge is, I believe, a very important and useful safeguard, not only for the control of the House of Commons over the administration, but for honest and efficient administration itself, and I

[1] Select Committee on Procedure, 1931, q. 2500.   [2] q. 2524.
[3] Select Committee on Procedure, 1959, q. 86. See also Select Committee on Procedure, 1946, qs. 1284–95.

should rather deprecate any attempt to draw what I might call a scale of dimensions as to the relative importance of particular topics or particular items in any given Department of Administration. I do not believe you would find in practice that it would work out. A thing which seemed small on paper might turn out very big indeed, and the thing which seemed big might turn out to be non-controversial and capable of being disposed of in a few minutes. I doubt the practicability of it.'[1]

It is thus not merely a problem of finding the right machinery to carry out the sifting process. Any form of control, even if excercised by a Committee chosen entirely by back benchers, would gradually, but inevitably, establish a system of rules and precedents that would increasingly limit the choice of Members to what the majority thought significant. One of the great merits of Question time is that it has remained a private Members' device, that any Member can within very wide limits ask any Question without having to secure the approval of or consult either the Government, the Opposition front bench or 'the usual channels'. Nevertheless the ease with which Questions can be put on the Paper presents a problem about which the Select Committee of 1946 had this to say:

'Before dealing with specific points Your Committee desire to make certain observations of a general nature. They regard the right to put Questions to Ministers as one of the most important possessed by Members. The exercise of this right is perhaps the readiest and most effective method of parliamentary control over the action of the executive. They would therefore deprecate anything which tended to diminish the effectiveness of this right. On the other hand the very powerfulness of the right imposes upon Members a proportionate responsibility in its use. The Departments very properly accord a high degree of priority to the answering of parliamentary Questions. It is important therefore that Questions, especially oral Questions, should only be put down when other and less formal methods have failed to produce a satisfactory result, or when some information or action is urgently desired. Similarly, in deciding the date for which a Question is put down, regard should be had to the time which may be needed for the preparation of the answer and to the real urgency of the case. In fine, the smooth working of this form of parliamentary procedure (as indeed of all parliamentary procedure) depends to a great extent upon the individual Member.'[2]

[1] Select Committee on House of Commons (Procedure), 1914, q. 2204.
[2] Second Report of Select Committee on Procedure, 1945-6, para. 3.

CONCLUSIONS

On the whole Members follow this advice. The vast mass of individual cases as well as many other matters are now handled by correspondence. True, more Questions could be put down for written instead of oral answer but so far as the Department is concerned there is not a great deal to choose between the two. A careful and precise answer has to be prepared quickly to each kind. In any case the large proportion of starred Questions which fail to receive an oral answer is not due to a marked increase in the number of such Questions but to more and longer supplementaries and the replies they bring forth.

So far we have been assuming that the inability of Question time to provide for oral answers to all, or at least the great bulk of, starred Questions is a serious defect which needs remedying. It will indeed come as a surprise and a shock to many whose knowledge of the working of Question time dates from an earlier period to learn that the opportunity to question the Foreign Secretary in the House occurred on only 19 occasions during the Session of 1959–60 and that the possibility of questioning most other Ministers was even less. It is, however, worth considering whether there may not be quite another way of looking at the change for may not the present working of Question time reflect more faithfully the current needs of Members than would a return to an earlier usage?

It is, of course, true that the House has got itself into its present position by chance and not by a clearly expressed wish. It was inevitable that the Members asking starred Questions would more and more take advantage of the 'right' to ask a supplementary. As the number of supplementaries increased, the number of starred Questions reached decreased, leading to the development of the rota system. In order to make sure that their Questions were reached Members were bound to use the rota system intelligently, thus leading to a bunching of Questions for Departments at or next to the top of the list. As it became more difficult to get a Question answered orally and more difficult to reach a particular Minister, Members inevitably wanted to make the most of the occasions when he was reached. The more they did this the more difficult it became to get a Question answered orally or to reach a Minister. Thus step by inevitable step there may come a time when only one Minister will be reached at most sittings. Question time will have become 'the Foreign

Secretary's day' or 'the Minister of Transport's day' and so on, rather like Supply days.

There is little or no reason to believe that the recent trend will, or could be, reversed. Question time has on many occasions been referred to as a safety valve in the procedures of the House. The present use of the supplementary is a kind of safety valve for Question time is one of the rare occasions when back benchers can create an opportunity both to address the House and to deal with a specific matter that interests them. The supplementary developed and was allowed to develop in the late nineteenth century because other forms of expression were being curtailed. The way it is now used and the inability of Mr. Speaker to restrain this use reflect in part an unsatisfied need on the part of back benchers. The device of Question and Answer, strictly interpreted is sometimes unsatisfactory, for both parties would like a little more elbow room — the questioner to explain the background of his question or complaint, the answerer to give more information and a fuller explanation. Two post-war developments illustrate this desire for something fuller and yet still reasonably specific. First, there is the greatly increased use of the daily Motion for the Adjournment for the purpose of a very short debate on a specific issue, during which usually only the opener and a Minister take part. Second, there is the use of Ministerial statements followed by questions. Procedurally this is bad and Mr. Speaker quite often has to stop such occasions degenerating into 'irregular debate'. But the general idea of there being an occasion for a short airing of a particular issue appears to be attractive to Members.

The desire to ask supplementaries is in some ways a manifestation of this general need. If supplementaries were not allowed there would be little point in Question time. Why, however, should a Member be confined to one supplementary and why should his supplementary and the Minister's reply be kept short, except on the ground of lack of time? Once Questions ceased to be merely a method of obtaining information and were accepted, though reluctantly at first, as a form of cross-examining Ministers why should the examination be confined to one supplementary or even two? In all this the House has shown itself somewhat illogical, even if eminently practical.

Lord Eustace Percy was responsible for the most critical

estimate of Question time before the Select Committee of 1931 and to some extent his criticism turned on this point. He said the House spent nearly one-eighth of its whole time, and about one-sixth of its best publicity time, 'in putting and discussing a farrago of miscellaneous questions; and the growing habit of asking supplementary questions is only a futile attempt to concentrate a little attention on some question which the Member concerned thinks of special importance.' It had always seemed to him, and it had been his small experience as a Minister, 'that Ministers are no more afraid of questions than a public speaker is afraid of hecklers. . . . If you really wish to make a Minister uncomfortable, or to drive him to justify points on which he may be really weak, you would do much better to have short debates.' He therefore proposed that oral Questions be abolished and the time thus released be used for short debates which would serve 'to drive home points arising out of answers to written questions on points of policy'. Speeches might be limited to ten minutes for the mover and the official reply and five minutes for other speakers.[1]

This proposal received no support from the Select Committee nor would it receive much if any support if it were put forward today. It is mentioned here as an extreme example of the idea of using the limited time available to examine a few points thoroughly rather than a larger number of points cursorily. Clearly a number of Members would like to spend a little more time on delving rather further into the subject matter of their Questions than is possible by way of one or even two supplementaries. That is why, on occasion, they try to cram several Questions into their supplementary. The Minister also usually wishes to deal with the Questions fully and not to appear to be unforthcoming or withholding information. Occasionally so clear are the wishes of the House that the Speaker allows six or eight supplementaries, there being a kind of miniature free-for-all.

Unless Members are firmly restrained the long-term trend, therefore, may be for fewer and fewer starred Questions but for many more supplementaries. This would not turn Question time into a series of short debates but it would allow for greater cross-examination of Ministers. At the moment the House does not quite know what it wants. Most Members seem to be agreed

[1] qs. 1886–95.

that many Questions now put down for oral answer could without loss be put down for a written answer (indeed a third to half of the starred Questions fail to get an oral answer). If this is so it surely follows that Question time is primarily an occasion for supplementaries. There is nothing significant in hearing the Minister read the answer to the Question on the paper, his voice adds little if anything to what can be read in print.[1] What then is the logic of insisting that Mr. Speaker should try to limit Members to one supplementary in almost all cases? It can hardly be argued that one supplementary, however lengthy, is sufficient in every case to produce an adequate explanation.

The present and future use of Question time must also be reviewed in relation to the great increase in the number of matters, particularly personal cases and constituency issues, dealt with by correspondence. The volume of such dealings is likely to go on increasing.[2]

A procedure has been perfected and accepted for dealing with the great mass of personal and local matters. In a sense it is an extra-Parliamentary device and possibly because of this has received too little attention from writers on the Constitution. In most Departments Members' correspondence is of much greater consequence than Questions as a means of calling attention to matters needing reconsideration and as an indicator of the reactions of public opinion to the activities of the Department.

In the long run, the greater use of correspondence should have the effect of emphasizing the significance of starred Questions or, at least, of changing their character. Such Questions are likely increasingly to become a device of last resort, other 'behind the scenes' methods having failed; or be concerned with major issues which must be ventilated in public and cannot be dealt with adequately except on the floor of the House; or be from Members who wish to embarrass or score over the Minister. There will, of course, remain the attraction of the publicity which Questions receive, though so far as the local press is concerned a

---

[1] There is even something to be said for the Minister's reply to be printed on the Order Paper so leaving the whole of Question time for supplementaries.

[2] From the point of view of Parliamentary procedure it would be most unfortunate if the decision of the House not to treat Members' letters to Ministers as part of the proceedings of Parliament and therefore as privileged should make Members reluctant to show constituents' letters to Ministers for fear of libel action or drive them to bring themselves within the rules of privilege by putting down a covering Question in each case.

CONCLUSIONS

Member's correspondence with a Minister is available to receive just as much publicity if the Member passes a copy to the local editor.

It is thus possible to regard the increasing proportion of Question time devoted to supplementaries not as a deterioration but as an adaptation to the changing needs of the House. Correspondence and unstarred Questions provide ample opportunity for the gathering of information and the raising of individual cases and constituency matters for the consideration of Ministers. The House has had to choose between oral answers and supplementaries and has compromised, trying to get a good many starred Questions reached but still allowing more and longer supplementaries. A rota system has been evolved which makes certain that each Minister will be available for answering on days stated well in advance. Matters about which Members feel particularly strongly are accumulated until the particular Minister becomes available and then he has to undergo 30 to 50 minutes of questioning. Having regard to the many other claims on the time of the House it can be argued that this is a reasonable use of Question time. But it could equally be argued that the House is getting the worst of both worlds, for present procedure ensures neither that Ministers are frequently and regularly available for questioning, say once a week, nor that, once available, there is time to cross-examine them thoroughly. It can hardly be denied that the trend of events has favoured Ministers and that once again the procedures of the House have failed to keep pace with the increasing powers of the Executive.

Nevertheless it is still significant that Question time has remained important in the lives of most Members during a period when more and more of the proceedings of the House have become dominated by the two Front Benches. It still remains one of the few elements in the Parliamentary timetable in which the newest or the humblest or the most disliked Member has the same rights as any other. In this respect, comparatively speaking, Question time is more important and more unique a feature of procedure than it was at the beginning of the century. Moreover, its ultimate value as a sanction and control depends not so much on the precise number of starred Questions reached and supplementaries asked, but on the ever present possibility that they may be asked. This also applies to Questions for written answer.

True, nowadays only 5,000 starred Questions may be answered on the floor of the House each Session as against say 8,000 in the same period before 1939, or even before 1950, but this is still a significant number. Yet if pressure on the time available has caused Members to be more thoughtful and selective about the kind of issues they raise at Question time these 5,000 may be more significant than were the 8,000. When considering their policies and decisions Ministers and civil servants still have to take into account that the Minister may have to answer a Question about the matter in the House or at least have his answer circulated for all to see.

It is also possible that the significance of Question time was over dramatized in the past. It is, of course, a colourful period with the House fairly full, a wide variety of matters dealt with in a short time and always the possibility of an angry scene or roars of laughter. It is seldom, however, an occasion that attracts the most thoughtful and most ambitious among the back benchers. As for Ministers it is seldom the ordeal that most writers on the subject appear to think it is. It can be a great nuisance when a Minister is engaged on an urgent and important problem to have to give time to framing thoughtful answers about something else, but much of this drafting can be done by the Civil Service. A Minister who is not by training a politician may find it difficult on occasions to deal with the House but the majority of supplementaries present little if any terror for the experienced politician. There are some who would have lasted longer as Ministers or risen higher in Government circles had they been able to answer Questions better. But it is likely that their inability to handle Questions was but a reflection of their general inadequacy as Parliamentarians.

Most writers on Questions quote some spectacular example in which a major change of Government policy was brought about or a great wrong redressed because of Questions asked in the House. As there have been some half a million starred Questions answered on the floor of the House since 1902 it would indeed be remarkable if a few examples of spectacular results could not be found. Moreover Questions are by no means a unique method of achieving such results; probably as many are achieved by Members privately without resort to any Parliamentary action.

CONCLUSIONS

The significance of Questions and Question time is to be found in three other directions. First and foremost it is pre-eminently a device for emphasizing the individual responsibility of Ministers. In the House of Lords Questions are addressed to the Government, there being so few Ministers available. When it was proposed to introduce Question time into the American Congress it was made clear that Questions would have to be addressed to the President.[1] In the House of Commons Questions are addressed to and answerable by the Minister responsible. No other Minister can regularly answer for him. His personal responsibility for his actions and for those of all the civil servants in his Department is pinpointed. In the ever increasing scale of governmental activity and the great strength of the leaders of monolithic Parties this stress on personal responsibility stands out as being of the utmost significance.

Second, Questions enable a large number of miscellaneous issues to be dealt with quickly within the framework of Parliamentary procedure. Opinions may differ as to the extent that Question time is 'abused' but few would deny that if this occasion were abolished some other opportunity would have to be found for handling such matters and that this would probably be more consuming of Members' time. It may be a matter of regret that fewer starred Questions are now dealt with at each sitting but nevertheless 40 to 50 items dealt with in less than an hour on each of four days a week is a pretty high rate of productivity. The rest of the time of the House is at best no more productive.

Third, there can be little doubt that some Questions are not worth the upset to the work in a Department and the general trouble involved in preparing the answer. Some Questions are still put down for oral answer when a written answer would give the Member most of what he requires. Many supplementaries are clumsily worded, irrelevant and merely time-consuming. Some Members waste the valuable minutes of Question time on points of order of no immediate significance. These things cause annoyance and do not add to the efficiency of the Departments. But these criticisms are not peculiar to Questions. A good deal of debating time goes in speeches that might with advantage have been shorter and more to the point. It would be demanding a standard of excellence and thoughtfulness not found

[1] G. B. Galloway, *The Legislative Process in Congress* (1955), pp. 445–51.

in any large group of men and women that everything each did should be well considered.

There are some 550 Members who are not part of the Administration or leaders of the Opposition or involved in running the business of the House. Nowadays some 12,000 to 15,000 starred and unstarred Questions are put on the Paper each Session, an average of 20 to 25 per Member. This can hardly be said to be a large number. After all, each of these Members represents a constituency of some 50,000 voters and each has to concern himself with the mass of decisions and activities of over twenty Government Departments and the great power for good or ill which now resides in them. Moreover the House has large responsibilities for the welfare of Colonial territories. Any annoyance and reduced effectiveness caused by inconsiderate Members seem but a small price to pay for a method of bringing to public notice, with the minimum use of Parliamentary time, the grievances of individual citizens and of groups and the matters about which Members feel strongly. Notwithstanding the changes brought about in recent years Question time and Questions still continue to perform this function effectively. Whether they secure results must always depend on the willingness of Ministers and civil servants to reconsider their decisions and policies and to take account of criticism. There is no reason to believe that they are less willing to do this now than they were 30, 40 or more years ago. There is even less reason to believe that they would be more willing to do so if Questions did not exist.

APPENDICES

I: STANDING ORDERS OF THE HOUSE OF COMMONS REFERRING TO QUESTIONS

THE first Standing Order specifically concerned with Questions was passed on 7 March 1888, when the Resolution of 12 March 1886, was converted into Standing Order No. 20. It read:

'Notices of Questions shall be given by Members in writing to the Clerk at the Table, without reading them *viva voce* in the House, unless the consent of the Speaker to any particular Question has been previously obtained.'

It was converted into Standing Order No. 9, passed on 29 April 1902. S.O. No. 9 read as follows:

(1) Notices of questions shall be given by members in writing to the Clerk at the Table, without reading them *viva voce* in the House, unless the consent of the Speaker to any particular question has been previously obtained.

(2) On days when there are two Sittings of the House, questions shall be taken at a quarter past two of the clock.

(3) No questions shall be taken after five minutes before three of the clock except questions which have not been answered in consequence of the absence of the Minister to whom they are addressed, and questions which have not appeared on the paper, but which are of an urgent character, and relate either to matters of public importance or to the arrangement of business.

(4) Any Member who desires an oral answer to his question may distinguish it by an asterisk, but notice of any such question must appear at latest on the notice paper circulated on the day before that on which an answer is desired.

(5) If any Member does not distinguish his question by an asterisk, or if he or any other Member deputed by him is not present to ask it, or if it is not reached by five minutes before three of the clock, the Minister to whom it is addressed shall cause an answer to be printed and circulated with the votes, unless the Member has signified his desire to postpone the question.

This was modified on 3 April 1906, by deleting paragraph (2), and substituting:

(2) Questions shall be taken on Monday, Tuesday, Wednesday and Thursday, after private business has been disposed of, and not later than three of the clock.

Also 'a quarter before four' was substituted for 'five minutes before three' in the opening line of paragraph 3 and in paragraph 5.

On 28 September 1915, paragraph (5) was amended by leaving out the words 'and circulated with the votes' and by inserting 'in the Official Report of the Parliamentary Debates'.

On 14 November 1933 it became Standing Order No. 7, and the words 'before questions are disposed of' were inserted before 'signified his desire' in the last part of paragraph 5.

On 4 November 1947 the Standing Order was amended to require longer notice to be given of starred Questions.

Paragraph (4) was amended to read as follows:

(4) Any member who desires an oral answer to his question may distinguish it by an asterisk, but notice of any such question must appear at latest on the notice paper circulated two days (excluding Sunday) before that on which an answer is desired.

Provided that questions received at the Table Office on Monday and Tuesday before half-past two of the clock and on Friday before eleven of the clock, may, if so desired by the Member, be put down for oral answer on the following Wednesday, Thursday and Monday, respectively.

A further clause was added:

(6) Whenever the House is adjourned for more than one day, notices of questions received at the Table Office at any time not later than half-past four of the clock on either of the two last days on which the House is not sitting (excluding any Saturday or Sunday) shall be treated as if either day were a day on which the House were sitting at half-past four of the clock and the notice had been received after half-past two of the clock, and notices of questions received at the Table Office at any time not later than half-past four of the clock on a day before the penultimate day shall be treated as if they had been so received on the penultimate day.

Certain amendments in the times were made consequential upon changes in the daily timetable of the House.

In (2) the time was changed to 'quarter-to-three of the clock'.

In (3) the time was changed to 'half-past three of the clock'.

In (5) the time was changed to 'half-past three of the clock'.

On 28 July 1948 Standing Order No. 7 became No. 8. It has not been altered since, and the present Standing Order No. 8 reads as follows:

(1) Notices of questions shall be given by members in writing to a clerk at the table and shall not be read *viva voce* in the House.

(2) Questions shall be taken on Monday, Tuesday, Wednesday and Thursday, after private business has been disposed of, and not later than a quarter to three of the clock.

(3) No questions shall be taken after half-past three of the clock, except questions which have not been answered in consequence of the absence of the minister to whom they are addressed, and questions which have not appeared on the paper, but which are in Mr. Speaker's opinion of an urgent character, and relate either to matters of public importance or to the arrangement of business.

(4) A member who desires an oral answer to his question shall distinguish it by an asterisk, but notice of any such question must appear at latest on the notice paper circulated two days (excluding Sunday) before that on which an answer is desired: Provided that questions received at the Table Office on Monday and Tuesday before half-past two of the clock and on Friday before eleven of the clock, may, if so desired by the member, be put down for oral answer on the following Wednesday, Thursday and Monday, respectively.

(5) If any member does not distinguish his question by an asterisk, or if he is not present to ask it, or if it is not reached by half-past three of the clock, the minister to whom it is addressed shall cause an answer to be printed in the Official Report of the Parliamentary Debates, unless the member has before half-past three of the clock signified his desire to postpone the question.

(6) Whenever the House is adjourned for more than one day, notices of questions received at the Table Office at any time during the adjournment shall be treated —
  (a) if received not later than half-past four of the clock on the last day but one, as if they had been received after half-past two of the clock during a sitting of the House on that day;
  (b) if received after half-past four of the clock on the last day but one and not later than half-past four of the clock on the last day, as if they had been received after half-past two of the clock during a sitting of the House on that day; and
  (c) if received after half-past four of the clock on the last day, as if they had been received before half-past two of the clock on the day the House meets :
Provided that if the last day of the adjournment be a Sunday, the Friday and Thursday immediately preceding shall for the purposes of this paragraph be deemed to be respectively the last day and the last day but one of the adjournment; and that if the last day be a Monday the preceding Friday shall for the purposes aforesaid be deemed to be the last day but one of the adjournment.

II: MINISTERIAL RESPONSIBILITY AND ANSWERABILITY

There is nothing in Standing Order No. 8 which confines Questions to Ministers, indeed only the word Member is used in the title and rubric and Ministers are not even mentioned. But nowadays Questions to Members other than Ministers are unlikely to be allowed unless there is some very special circumstance, e.g. to the Chairman of the Kitchen Committee, and unless there is no other more appropriate proceeding.

According to the sixteenth edition of Erskine May 'Questions addressed to Ministers should relate to the public affairs with which they are officially connected, to proceedings pending in Parliament, or to matters of administration for which they are responsible.'[1] This definition has remained virtually unchanged since it first appeared in the tenth edition in 1893. The pur-

[1] ibid. p. 356.

pose of this Appendix is to explain in greater detail than was possible in the body of the book the meaning given to this definition in practice. In order, however, to avoid argument about the precise meaning of 'responsible' we have preferred to use the word 'answerable' i.e. matters about which Ministers can be asked Questions and be expected to answer.

THE EXTENT OF ANSWERABILITY

The simplest and clearest form of Ministerial answerability arises from the official actions of Ministers and their Departments. A Minister can be questioned about his decisions or actions, which also means the official decisions or actions of any of the staff of his Department. The Member has not to show that the Minister or his officials were acting under such and such a power, it is sufficient that they have acted, though, of course, it is in order to ask the Minister what authority they had for taking the action. A Minister can also be asked why he has not exercised a power he is known to possess. The case of non-action, however, is different in that it may not be certain that the Minister has the power to act. Some Departmental powers are well known being clearly expressed in a statute, either as permissive or compulsory. Thus the Education Act, 1944, requires the Minister to establish a Consultative Committee and to have regard to certain rules in its composition. The non-appointment of such a Committee could be questioned, as well as the reasons why particular persons had been appointed by the Minister of Education. Again the Minister of Housing and Local Government can be asked why he has not used the power given him by Section 15 of the Town and Country Planning Act, 1947, to require a particular Local Authority to submit a decision for his approval and whether he would now do so. The great bulk of Departmental powers are set out in Acts of Parliament and in case of differences of opinion responsibility can be fairly clearly ascertained.

Some of the powers under which Ministers act are, however, not granted and defined by Statute but derive from the 'prerogative' or ancient powers of the monarch, now the Cabinet, to undertake the basic and long-established functions of the State — defence, conduct of external affairs, securing law and order.

These prerogative powers mainly concern the Foreign Office, Colonial Office, Defence Departments and the Home Office. Any event which affects the peace, order or well-being of the country may be said to be the concern of the Government in so far as it may be held that these are objects for which government exists.

To these ancient functions of the State there has been added in recent years a new range of general responsibilities, sometimes by Act of Parliament but more often by the attitude of successive Governments and the expectations of successive Parliaments. Thus it is now accepted that a Government has general responsibility for securing a high level of employment, for increasing the standard of living and for many other aims of financial and economic policy. The Minister of Health has a general responsibility for matters concerning the general health of the nation, the Minister of Education for education and by implication if not by Statute the Minister of Labour for all matters concerning the labour side of industry in general. Thus it is possible to ask a Minister about the decline of a particular industry or about a general increase in unemployment or about some new medical discovery or about a dispute between two trade unions which is affecting output and productivity in a particular industry. Indeed it can even be said that if there is sufficient concern about any matter either among Members or in the country generally there is a correspondingly less need to show that a Minister has specific responsibility for the matter. It is an ancient function of the House to be concerned with general grievances whether these arise out of the actions of Ministers or the failure of Ministers to act under powers which they admittedly possess or for reasons which have nothing to do with Ministers and their powers. Even so there are important practical limitations to this wide view of responsibility.

First, there is a very big difference between questioning a Minister about his action, or his non-action in respect of a matter for which he is statutorily responsible, and questioning the same Minister about some general grievance or complaint in respect of which it is agreed that he has no specific powers to act. In the former the questioner can ask about a particular case, even the case of some individual, and it will be difficult for the Minister not to give a precise answer which shows that he fully appreciates his responsibility. In the latter, however, the wording of the Question must inevitably be in general terms and the answer correspondingly general. It can seldom be in terms of asking why the Minister did (or did not) do such and such a thing but usually has to be worded: 'Will the Minister consider doing such and such a thing' or 'Is the Minister aware that such and such a thing has happened and what, if anything, does he propose to do about it?' In other words Questions concerned with the general grievances and well-being of the nation are more likely to have to be concerned with the future intentions of Ministers than with responsibility for past acts or for any failure or unwillingness to exercise certain powers. It is a different level of answerability, there is less opportunity to use it and even when used the results are likely to be less definite than Questions directed at the exercise of the specific and established powers of Ministers.

Second, there are clearly a number of matters about which Ministers and even the House itself are powerless to do anything, for example, the internal affairs of foreign countries. Thus, while it is admissible to ask the Foreign Secretary whether a *coup d'état* in a particular country has had any bad effects on current negotiations between the two countries, it is not admissible to ask for his views on the merits of the change or indeed for any information about the events and actions of political leaders in that country except in so far as those events or actions can be clearly related to the direct interests of the U.K. and the Commonwealth. It is obvious that Ministers cannot be expected to accept responsibility for the internal affairs of other countries and therefore these matters can hardly be held to be the business of Parliament. On the whole the House proceeds on the assumption that it is not much use devoting time to matters about which the House is powerless either to legislate or take any effective action. Moreover just as the House would not like the internal affairs of the U.K. to be the subject of discussion in foreign Parliaments so it is prepared to adopt the same attitude to the internal affairs of other countries.

A similar situation arises when a Colony becomes an independent member of the Commonwealth. Most of the Colonies are governed under powers exercised under the prerogative and therefore Government action and policy in the use of those powers are properly a subject of Questions. Once a Colony becomes independent, however, it becomes in effect, a foreign country for the purpose of Questions even if it remains within the Commonwealth and broadly the same prohibitions apply. Questions about the relations between the U.K. and the independent members of the Commonwealth are, however, a matter for the Secretary of State for Commonwealth Relations, not the Foreign Secretary. The same thing occurred when a separate Parliament was established for Northern Ireland: the matters which were made the responsibility of that new Parliament ceased to be the responsibility of Whitehall

There are also certain other matters which though apparently within the control of the House have been accepted as being matters about which Questions cannot be put to Ministers. Thus a Minister cannot be asked to interpret the wording of a Statute or a Treaty or even his own statutory powers or the meaning of the law on a particular matter. Nor can he be questioned about the internal proceedings of a Royal Commission.

A somewhat similar limitation though nothing like so extreme in its application arises when Parliament has vested the power to administer a public service not in a Minister but in a Local Authority, Board or other statutory Authority. Thus in Oxford and other large towns the only governmental body which has powers to provide and maintain a library service for the public is the City Council; no Minister has any such power. Again whilst the Minister of Power has statutory obligations to appoint a National Coal Board it is the Board, once established, and not the Minister, who alone has the power to appoint and dismiss staff and other employees. It is not the practice for specific administrative responsibilities to be shared between a Minister and another public body so that both might be held responsible. The Statutes usually distinguish quite clearly between those administrative acts which lie within the province of the Minister and those which lie within the province of the Local Authority or Statutory Board. It follows in these cases that the Minister cannot be questioned about matters which Parliament has made the statutory responsibility of some body other than a Minister. Thus whereas a Question about the hours of opening and closing of a particular post office could be put to the Postmaster-General, a Question about the hours of opening and closing of a Municipal library or of a showroom of one of the Electricity Boards would not be accepted for they concern a matter which is specifically within the statutory power of another body and not of a Minister.

It is in this area, however, that most of the disputes about answerability arise and for three main reasons. First, it cannot be denied that the services provided by Local Councils and Public Corporations are part of the total public services of the country. In the minds of a Member's constituents and even of Members themselves the distinction between the different forms of public administration and their respective powers are not always very clear. Quite often therefore a constituent will approach a Member about a matter which is the statutory concern of say the Borough Council, e.g. about his difficulty in getting a Municipal house in the area. Strictly speaking the Member should refer this complaint to the Council but in many cases he will treat it like other complaints and pass it to the appropriate Minister for comment. The Ministry may refer the matter to the Borough Council and provide the Member with an answer. But it is unlikely that the matter could be raised by way of a Question.

Second, however autonomous the statutory body may be in general, Parliament will usually have endowed a Minister with some powers in respect of the service and possibly some responsibilities for its general efficiency and development.[1] Thus though the power and responsibility for establishing and maintaining local police forces have been vested by Parliament in local Police Authorities the Home Secretary also has certain important powers in respect of police in England and Wales. He pays a grant of 50 per cent. of the approved expenditure on these County and Municipal police forces and may withhold payment of the grant in certain instances, e.g. if he is not satisfied that a particular force is efficient. In other local services a Minister may have both a general and certain specific statutory powers. The Acts which nationalized certain industries gave a Minister a number of powers, e.g. to appoint the Members of the Board; to approve schemes of capital expenditure and to issue Directions of a general character to the Board.

In these circumstances it is difficult for a Minister to deny all responsibility for a service administered by another statutory

---

[1] To this extent the wording in the sixteenth edition of Erskine May (p. 356) 'raising matters under the control of bodies or persons not responsible to the Government' is ambiguous.

body and therefore a very great deal will turn on the form the Question takes, and in the long run on the attitude of successive Ministers and of the House to Questions concerning these services. Thus the Home Secretary cannot be questioned as to why a particular policeman had not been promoted in a particular County Police Force but he could be asked about any regulation he had prescribed dealing with the procedure for promotion. The Minister of Power cannot be asked about the installation of a new piece of machinery at a pit but he can about the general progress of the National Coal Board in mechanizing production. Everything depends on the statutory wording of the powers given to the Minister. The Minister of Power can for example be asked about the welfare of pit ponies employed underground and about colliery accidents because he has powers in respect of both these matters, not under the nationalization Act, but by virtue of other Acts.

Third, the appropriate Minister usually has the statutory power to require Local Authorities and Public Boards to provide him with statistics and other information about the services they perform. Prima facie, therefore, a Member is in order in asking a Minister to supply him with such information. Where the data are collected by the Ministry for general use such Questions will be accepted. But a Minister will usually refuse to answer Questions asking for information not collected in the course of his Department's responsibilities for to do so might lead directly or by implication to the Minister being held responsible for the state of affairs revealed by the facts given in his answer. Thus if the Minister of Transport is asked 'how many motorists were awaiting their driving tests in Birmingham at the end of 1958 and 1959?' the figures supplied may give rise either to praise or blame. If, for example, the Question is starred and the oral answer shows a marked increase in those awaiting a test the Member will almost certainly ask whether the staff of examiners in the area is sufficient or when will the number be reduced. This is in order, for the administration of driving tests is the statutory responsibility of that Minister and the supplementary can be said to arise out of the answer.

Questions asking for the numbers on the waiting list for houses of a particular Borough Council at different dates or for the output of coal and the numbers employed at a particular

APPENDICES

colliery would carry the same implications and [...] down for oral answer, lead to the same kind of s[...] In these cases, however, the statutory administrat[...] vested in another body. The Minister could, of cou[...] statistics and refuse to answer supplementaries ab[...] ministrative policies or practices associated with th[...] refusals if frequent, however, would be unsatisfactor[...] Minister, to the Member and to all concerned. The M[...] would be in danger of being given and accepting an im[...] responsibility for the actions of another body. He is not likel[...] be in a good position to defend or to criticize the Council [...] Board on such a point of detail unless, as in the case of a Question arising out of an act of his own Department, he gets fully briefed. Wishing to be helpful to the Member he may if he is not careful, be led by a persistent Member into saying that he will take some action about the matter, if only by way of drawing the attention of the Council or Board to the point made by the questioner. The Member may feel frustrated in the performance of what he regards as his public duties or that the Minister is not being as helpful as he might be or that the Authority or Board are not under adequate control. Even if no supplementary were to be asked or only a written answer were to be required the Borough Council or the Board might feel that some explanation of the state of affairs revealed by the statistics ought to have been given to the Member at the same time.

Whereas, therefore, in theory the criterion of Ministerial responsibility is clear, in practice there is a substantial area of governmental activity in which the application of the rule raises delicate problems. A very great deal depends on the precise wording of the Question and perhaps even more on the case law that has been built up over the years based on the attitudes Ministers have adopted to answering Questions about matters for which their responsibility is not beyond doubt.

QUESTIONS WHICH MINISTERS MAY REFUSE TO ANSWER

Right from the earliest days of Questions the Speaker has always made it clear that he has no power to insist on a Minister answering a Question admitted to the Order Paper or even to in his place to answer such Questions. Had the Speaker ruled otherwise he would have had to devise some form of disciplinary action suitable for extracting an answer out of a stubborn Minister.[1] But, of course, there was never any need for any Speaker to take a different attitude for as we saw in chapter 2 Questions developed in such a way that Ministers were always ready to answer the great bulk of them without complaint and the House would now need a very good excuse indeed from any Minister who tried to make a habit of refusing. From the earliest days a Minister has been able to refuse to answer a Question only if he can give some good reason, good in the sense that it would be acceptable to the general feeling of the House, even if not to that of the questioner.

The two main reasons acceptable are (*a*) that to give the information required by the Question would be contrary to the public interest, and (*b*) that the matter is not his responsibility. There is also a miscellaneous category of reasons that warrant a refusal. A Minister will not normally divulge information about the prices paid by departments for different kinds of supplies, particularly military supplies or of the prices tendered by competing firms. Occasionally a Minister may reply that the information required by the Member is either not available or would be so difficult and costly to collect as to make it not worth while.

Surprisingly few Questions are refused an answer on the ground of public interest. Members appreciate that it is undesirable to ask Questions about such matters as the details of national defence or of some delicate negotiations which the Government may be engaged upon. Also Ministers are usually adept at answering such Questions without giving away any worthwhile secrets and stonewalling or ignoring any supplementaries. But from time to time a Minister will refuse to answer a Question and give 'grounds of national interest' as his reason. The House usually accepts the refusal but occasionally the Opposition may remonstrate and imply that the Government are trying to hide some scandal. A dispute of this kind is a matter

[1] 'The Minister is always entitled on public grounds to refuse an answer. That is perfectly clear. If he refuses to give an answer, that is the Minister's responsibility, and it has nothing to do with me. Therefore I cannot authorize the Table to go behind the Minister and insert a Question a second time. The ... remedy is to put down a Motion of Censure on the Minister ... for refusing to reply.' Mr. Speaker Clifton Brown, H.C. Deb. (1947–8), 445, c. 565–71.

for the general relations between the two major Parties in which the majority usually gains the day.

The Table Office may occasionally allow a Member to put a Question on the Paper only to find the Minister refusing to answer on the grounds of having no responsibility, but if there were many such occasions both Ministers and Members would grow annoyed and some new understanding and possibly a ruling by Mr. Speaker would be indicated.

Such a situation arose in the early life of the Boards established by the Labour Government in 1946–50 to administer certain major industries — coal, gas, electricity, railways, canals and certain other forms of transport, and the Bank of England. The relations between the Board and Ministers and between Parliament, Ministers and the Boards are highly complex and depend partly on the wording of various Acts of Parliament, partly on the distinction to be drawn between matters of general policy and of day-to-day administration and partly on the precise status which Ministers and the House wish to give the Boards. It is too complicated a story to be fully told here[1] but part of it is worth telling for the light it throws on the answerability of Ministers. Sufficient to say that the nationalizing Acts vested these industries in particular Boards and gave the Ministers certain powers of control and that the Board form was chosen instead of the normal Ministerial Department in order that these industries should not be answerable to Parliament in the detail that for example, the Post Office is.

In the early days of the Boards the Table admitted to the Order Paper a number of Questions which the Ministers to whom they were addressed were not prepared to answer, the reason for refusal being that the Questions were concerned with the day-to-day administration of the industries for which a Board and not the Minister was responsible. Subsequently when Members attempted to put similar Questions on the paper they were ruled out of order being inadmissible as 'repeating in substance questions already answered, or to which an answer has been refused'.[2] The late Mr. D. J. Gordon then the Second

[1] For a fuller analysis of this issue see A. H. Hanson, *Parliament and Public Ownership* (1961) and W. A. Robson, *Nationalized Industry and Public Ownership* (1960).
[2] This wording was first used in the 14th edition of Erskine May and has been repeated in the 15th and 16th editions.

Clerk Assistant in the House, with a major responsibility for dealing with Questions explained that 'in substance' was interpreted to exclude not only individual Questions but also whole classes of Questions concerned with the subject matter of the Question and answer used as the precedent. If, for example, the Minister had refused to answer a Question about a breakdown in the supply of electricity in a particular area then not only all Questions about this particular breakdown but also all Questions about such breakdowns were treated as inadmissible.[1]

Feeling came to a head in May 1948 when the Speaker following precedent, refused to allow Questions about a particular severe and widespread breakdown in electricity supply on the grounds that there had already been questions about power failures that Session. It was clear that Members were no longer prepared to accept such a severe interpretation and on 7 June 1948, Mr. Speaker announced a new ruling. After giving the rule about Ministerial responsibility in Erskine May, he went on as follows:[2]

'The rule requiring Ministerial responsibility has had the effect of excluding a certain number of Questions about nationalized industries, but not very many since the responsibilities of Ministers under the relevant statutes are very wide, so far as obtaining information is concerned.

It is the rule against the repetition of Questions already answered, or to which an answer has been refused that has had the largest share in excluding Questions. The Government, in their desire not to interfere in the day to day activities of the Boards of nationalized industries, have by what might be termed a 'self-denying ordinance' refused to answer many Questions on subjects which by a strict interpretation of the statutes, might be held to fall within their responsibility. They are fully entitled to do so — that is a matter for their discretion. But such a refusal ... prevents the admission to the Question Paper of all future Questions dealing with the class of matters dealt with by the Question to which an answer is refused.

I have come to the conclusion that in the case of an entirely novel branch of administration, such as that relating to the nationalized industries, the strict application of this Rule might operate more harshly than either Ministers or Members generally would wish. I am, therefore prepared to make a suggestion which I hope will recommend

---

[1] On the manner in which the Table Office applies the test of Ministerial responsibility see D. J. Gordon's evidence to the Select Committee on Nationalized Industries (1952), qs. 124–254.
[2] H.C. Deb. (1947–8), 451, c. 1635–43.

itself to the House, for the power of dispensing with its recognized rules belongs to the House alone and not to me.

I propose to leave the Rule which excludes Questions on matters outside Ministerial responsibility unchanged. But I am prepared, if it is generally approved, to exercise my discretion to direct the acceptance of Questions asking for a statement to be made on matters about which information has been previously refused, provided that, in my opinion, the matters are of sufficient public importance to justify this concession. "Public importance" is one of the tests for Motions for the Adjournment of the House under Standing Order No. 8 and in my experience it is not an unduly difficult test to apply.

One other condition, I think, is essential if this experiment is to succeed. The allowance or disallowance of Questions after the application of this test must be left to my discretion. I will not refuse to hear representations privately if good grounds are alleged. But I cannot allow my decision, once it is given to a Member, to be questioned or argued in the House.

I should like to add that, of course, it by no means follows that Ministers will be bound to answer any Question which I have allowed as being of "public importance"; that is their affair. In their case, considerations may arise of which I can have no knowledge.'

When Mr. W. S. Morrison was elected Speaker in October 1951 he announced that he would follow his predecessor's ruling:

'The practice in the last Parliament was one whereby my predecessor exercised a certain discretion to allow certain Questions which otherwise would not have been allowed. For my part I am prepared to continue to try to exercise that discretion, but on the same terms as my predecessor, namely, that my discretion shall not be questioned nor argued about in the House.'[1]

The new Government established a Select Committee on Nationalized Industries whose first report dealing wholly with Questions was published on 29 October 1952. The conclusions most relevant to the aspect at present being analysed and discussed were:

'17. The basic feature of the Parliamentary Question is that it is answered by the Minister ultimately responsible for the decision about which he is questioned. Under their existing constitution, the Nationalized Industries are not subject to any direct control by Ministers in individual matters of detail. Your Committee, therefore, feel that without altering the terms of the statutes under which the public corpora-

[1] H.C. Deb. (1951-2), 493, c. 648.

tions are constituted, which they are not empowered to recommend, Questions on matters of detail in the Nationalized Industries are inappropriate.

18. On the other hand, Your Committee are convinced that the present method of placing the onus of determining in the first place whether a Question which is not obviously ruled out under paragraph 17 above should be placed upon the Order Paper should not rest upon the Clerks at the Table. Where the identical Question, or the same Question in slightly different terms, has been previously asked, the Clerks at the Table are clearly obliged to refuse it. But in the case of questions which are not obviously matters of repetition or matters of detailed administration the questions should be allowed to appear on the Order Paper and the Minister would have to answer or refuse to answer on the floor of the House.'

The Committee's proposal was accepted. If a Member now wishes to put a Question on the Paper about the administration of a Nationalized Industry and the Table is uncertain whether it should be excluded as being repetitive or concerning a matter of detailed administration the Question is allowed to appear and the Minister is left to answer or to plead absence of responsibility. This and the excercise of Mr. Speaker's discretion in respect of Questions which would be out of order but for their being judged to concern a matter of public importance thus give a certain amount of flexibility whilst maintaining intact the general rules governing admissibility.

The matter has been raised at various times subsequently and on 25 February 1960 Mr. R. A. Butler made the following statement on behalf of the Government:

'With your permission, Sir, may I say that we must adhere to the view that Ministers can answer Questions only on matters for which they have a recognized responsibility. Otherwise, they would inevitably find themselves encroaching upon the managerial functions entrusted to the nationalized boards.

Ministers would, of course, answer for the matters which the industries are required by Statute to lay before them, and for appointments, finance and matters on which they themselves have statutory powers or duties. In addition, they may from time to time be concerned with other questions of broad policy affecting the industries.

There is no hard and fast formula by which these matters could be identified and opened to Questions in the House, but provided Questions on the Paper relate to Ministers' responsibilities for matters of general policy, they will consider sympathetically the extent to which they can properly reply.'[1]

Though these rulings have special application to the problem of the division of responsibility between Ministers and the Boards for the affairs of the nationalized industries, they are of general application and indeed one would have thought that they have been part of the spirit if not the letter of Questions from the earliest days. Whether a major industry is in private or public ownership its general misfortunes are usually of sufficient weight to justify use of the time of the House to discuss them. There was, for example, a good deal of discussion of the affairs of the Coal Industry in the House in the inter-war years, long before it was nationalized and many Questions were allowed about it. The distinction lies, of course, in the character of responsibility attributed to the Minister. He cannot be asked why he has allowed something to happen or why he has not done something about a matter if he has no power to act. But his attention can be called to the happening and he can be asked whether he can do or intends to try to do anything about it. The more important the matter the more admissible is a Question. This must be even more true of an industry over which a Minister has important powers of supervision and also some general responsibility for its success or failure.

Similarly it must surely always be and always has been the duty of the staff of the House of Commons to give the benefit of the doubt to the private Member. For the Minister always has the right to refuse an answer whereas the Member's only right is to raise the matter of inadmissibility as a point of order with the Speaker. Had the nationalized industries not been so politically controversial and Members so excited about them no doubt the precise way of handling Questions about them might have been worked out over a longish period without any special rulings.

WHO IS THE MINISTER ANSWERABLE?

The manner in which Parliament confers powers on particular Ministers and the usage concerning the prerogative and other non-statutory powers and duties of the Government usually make it quite clear who is the Minister answerable for a par-

[1] H.C. Deb. (1959–60), 618, c. 577–82.

ticular action or lack of action. Statutory powers are never conferred on the Cabinet in general but always on specific Ministers. In strict constitutional theory the powers of one Secretary of State may be exercised by any other Secretary of State, i.e. the Colonial Secretary could legally exercise the powers of the Home Secretary, but Parliamentary and constitutional usage are against this. Where a Department is apparently in charge of a board e.g. the Board of Inland Revenue or the Board of Admiralty, it has been made clear in practice which Minister is answerable to Parliament for the actions and policy of the Department. It is indeed one of the merits of the Parliamentary Question that it pinpoints responsibility for policy and administration by translating responsibility into answerability.

From time to time, however, it may not be immediately clear which Minister is responsible for answering a particular Question. Thus the Minister of Housing and Local Government has a general statutory responsibility for the finances of local government, the Chancellor of the Exchequer has a responsibility for public finance in general which in its widest interpretation must include the finance of local government; and the Minister of Education has responsibilities for education, and therefore for the finance of education. Just which of these three Ministers would have to answer a Question about the financial relations between central and local government including grants to aid local education would depend on the precise wording and purpose of the Question. It might well require consultation between the three Departments as to who was the most appropriate Minister to answer it. Similarly a Question concerned with some aspect of wages and conditions in agriculture though probably answerable by the Minister of Agriculture, Fisheries and Food might, because of its wording or purpose, be answerable by the Minister of Labour. Only one Minister, however, will answer any one Question and therefore if the wording submitted is such as to involve two or more Ministers either the Member will be asked to divide it into Questions related to the responsibility of the different Ministers or the Minister to whom it is addressed will deal only with his part and ask the Member to put down another Question so that he can get an answer to the remainder from another Minister or Ministers. The necessity to decide upon the precise division of responsibility of different Ministers is an important factor nor merely in relating the work of Ministers to their answerability in the House but also for securing a clear and detailed division of functions between the several Departments of government.

Any constitutional changes or Ministerial arrangements which blur the lines of responsibility so that the House is left uncertain as to who is answerable are greatly disliked by Members and never last for long. Thus the occasional attempt to give a Minister some general but undefined responsibilities in respect of a field of activity in which one or more other Ministers have clear and defined responsibilities has always failed. This does not apply to Ministers who are Chairmen of Cabinet Committees, even for specific fields, e.g. social services, for just as the fact that the Prime Minister is Chairman of the Cabinet does not make him responsible for the actions and policies of all Ministers who are members of the Cabinet, similarly the position of Chairman of a Cabinet Committee does not involve a transfer of responsibility from individual Ministers to that Chairman. Even so, Governments are seldom willing to reveal the current structure of Cabinet Committees in case this leads to confusion either as to the over-riding collective responsibility of the Cabinet or, more important from the viewpoint of Questions, as to the responsibility and answerability of the various Ministers.

It was failure to recognize the very different position of the Chairman of a Cabinet Committee from that of a Minister who had been announced as having special responsibilities for a particular segment of Governmental policy that led first to the confusion and annoyance and soon to the abandonment of Mr. Churchill's so-called Overlords in 1951–2. Under this arrangement Lord Woolton, for example, was appointed Lord President of the Council to supervise and co-ordinate the policies of the Ministers of Food and of Agriculture and Fisheries. The situation was less difficult than it might have been by reason of that fact that the three Ministers named as having these special responsibilities were all in the House of Lords and, therefore, someone else had to answer for them in the Commons, this someone usually being the appropriate Minister who was being co-ordinated by the absent 'Overlord.' This fact, however, exacerbated the feelings of the Opposition for though they could question a Minister they were left uncertain as to whether he was acting as a mouthpiece for a superior Minister or whether he was answering entirely on his own responsibility.[1]

The problem has not arisen to anything like the same extent with the Minister of Defence for when this department was created in December, 1946 the Government issued a White Paper setting forth the matters for which the new Minister would be responsible and for which therefore the individual ministerial heads of the three Service departments (Air, Army and Navy) were no longer responsible.[2] Nevertheless the existence of several Ministers one with general and the three others with specific powers in the same broad field of activity has led to argument and occasional confusion. There has been, for example, controversy as to whether the Minister of Defence or the Secretary of State for Air should answer Questions about rocket bases and inter-continental missiles.

Ministerial responsibility as interpreted for House of Commons procedure generally and for Questions in particular thus means not that the Government must answer and that they have a choice as to who should answer but that a particular Minister decided automatically by the subject-matter of the Question must answer and answer in person if the Question be starred. There are a few apparent exceptions to the rule about the Minister answering in person.

First, there is the occasional difficulty as to the range of responsibility of the Prime Minister. On the whole the rules are fairly clear and their application should therefore be straightforward. On the one hand the Prime Minister will not normally answer Questions about matters which are clearly the responsibility of a particular department Minister. On the other hand he will answer Questions about matters of which he has been personally and publicly concerned, e.g. Mr. Macmillan about his visit to Moscow and his talks with Mr. Kruschev. He will also answer Questions about such matters as the general arrangements of the Government and its administration e.g. about the

[1] See Herbert Morrison, *Government and Parliament*, Second edition (1959), pp. 45–56.
[2] This division was helped by most of the defence powers being prerogative and not statutory. Had the powers been statutory they would have required a formal Order in Council made under the Ministers of the Crown (Transfer of Functions) Act, 1946.

functions of the Minister of Defence, and usually about matters that affect several Departments or Government policy in general. In the field of international relations most Prime Ministers work closely with their Secretary of State for Foreign Affairs and while a Prime Minister would not normally answer a Question on a particular matter which fell within the responsibilities of the Foreign Secretary he would be likely to answer if the issue involved was a matter of grave importance or affected the policy of the Government as a whole, particularly if the Question were put down by the Leader of the Opposition. For the rest it is a matter for the discretion and temperament of each Prime Minister. Some are very willing, others strongly insist on their Ministers dealing with as many matters as possible; some take a particular interest in some general field which may transcend the normal department arrangements, e.g. atomic energy; others prefer to keep themselves aloof from all except their obvious Prime Ministerial duties. If any issue becomes big enough and controversial enough the Prime Minister may be brought in but usually only as a very last resort if the matter is clearly the responsibility of a departmental Minister; after all if it is as serious as this a Motion and not a Question is the most appropriate proceeding. A Question put by Private Notice by the Leader of the Opposition to the Prime Minister will always be answered by him for it is in effect a challenge by the leader of one major party to the leader of the other; but such a device has to be used very sparingly.

Second, the Minister responsible may not be available. If he has just died or resigned his successor must be appointed very quickly but if the interregnum is likely to be long the Prime Minister will usually announce which other Minister will act and take responsibility in the interim. If a Minister is seriously ill or out of the country and unlikely to be able to attend the House for some time, again the Prime Minister is likely to announce the arrangements for securing answerability during that absence. In the case of the absence of a Minister for only a few days it is usual for the Parliamentary Secretary to answer Questions there being no need to announce this automatic and normal arrangement or, in the case of the Foreign Office, the Prime Minister or one of the Ministers of State may answer. The Parliamentary Secretary usually answers should the Ministerial head of the department be in the House of Lords. Such Ministers cannot attend the Commons to answer Questions and as all the normal Ministerial departments have at least one Parliamentary Secretary he is the person to whom Questions are addressed in the Commons.

Third, the Ministerial head of the Department may ask his Parliamentary Secretary to answer for him. In recent years the increase in the burden on Ministers and the growth in the size and scope of some Departments has led to a feeling in some quarters that Parliamentary Secretaries should be given more responsibility and therefore a higher Parliamentary status. In part this is reflected in the appointment of a new category of junior Minister, Ministers of State, for though these are subordinate to the Minister and do not take away any of his ultimate responsibilities they are intended to have a higher status than a Parliamentary Secretary and indeed are paid a higher salary. It is now more usual for Ministers to allow their Parliamentary Secretary, or their Minister of State if they have one, to answer some Questions. It may even be made known that Questions about a particular side of the Department's work will normally be answered by the Parliamentary Secretary and not by the Minister. But Questions must always be put on the Paper addressed to the Minister and not to the Parliamentary Secretary (except when the Minister is in the Lords).

Since Mr. Macmillan's appeal on 5 November 1957[1] asking Members to help to relieve the burden on Ministers by accepting Ministers of State or Parliamentery Secretaries as Departmental spokesmen the House has been more tolerant of the practice. But it is still apt to be resentful if a Minister leaves too many Questions to his juniors, or if Questions the House considers important are left to them. The Minister usually carries more weight with the House and the public than does his Parliamentary Secretary, who is likely to be a younger, less well-known and less experienced politician. Moreover for a Minister not to answer personally a Question about a matter in which there is a great deal of Parliamentary and public interest is likely to give the impression that he does not share that interest and concern or is contemptuous of it.

[1] H.C. Deb. (1957–8), 577, c. 27–8.

APPENDICES

WHO DECIDES ON MATTERS OF MINISTERIAL RESPONSIBILITY?

The sixteenth edition of Erskine May states that 'The Speaker's responsibility in regard to questions is limited to their compliance with the rules of the House. Responsibility in other respects rests with the Member who proposes to ask the question.'[1] This dates from a ruling given in 1880. Thus it is the responsibility of the Member, not of the Speaker, to make certain that any facts stated in his Question are accurate, though, of course, the Table Office may enquire of a Member whether he has checked his facts.

Mr. Speaker has, however, always refused to arbitrate in any dispute as to whether the subject-matter of a Question is one for which any Minister is responsible and if so, which Minister. A clear statement of the position was made by Mr. Speaker Clifton Brown in 1948. On 4 February[2] Mr. Churchill as Leader of the Opposition asked a Private Notice Question about Questions that the Table was refusing to accept about various aspects of the administration of the nationalized industries. In the course of his reply Mr. Speaker gave an account of the procedure: 'I am responsible,' he said 'first of all for seeing that the Question is in Order. A Question is not in Order if it does not involve Ministerial responsibility. That is the first proposition. Very well: a Question comes to the Table; the Table thinks that it does not involve Ministerial responsibility; then possibly, the matter is put to me — but more usually, I think, I am by-passed to save trouble. Anyhow, it does sometimes happen that a Question comes to me and I have to give a ruling. The Question, we will say, is about the transport industry or another of the nationalized industries. It comes to me, and the question I have to answer, is whether this is a matter of internal administration within the industry, or whether there is Ministerial responsibility. I am not prepared to answer questions about railways, about civil aviation, about telegraphs, about everything else that is nationalized. The only thing I can do is to go to the Minister, or telephone him, and ask him what his opinion is, and whether this is a matter for which he has responsibility. That is the only possible course. Can I know all about these industries, and say whether

[1] Sixteenth edition, p. 355.   [2] H.C. Deb. (1947–8), 446, c. 1816–17.

every Question about them is in Order or not — that it is a matter affecting a Minister's responsibility or not? I am bound by the rules of the House to see that only Questions that are in Order are put down on the Order Paper. Therefore, if a Minister says that it is not his responsibility, then the Table does not allow the Question. I hope that makes the situation plain.'

The Speaker and the Table take a similar view about the extent of their jurisdiction to interfere in any dispute as to which Minister should accept and answer a Question. From their vast experience in handling thousands of Questions each year the staff of the House are often in the position to advise a Member as to which Minister a particular Question should be addressed and Members will usually take such advice. But if they do not or, if it is not clear which Minister should be asked, the Table will let the Question go forward placing the onus of rejection on the Department addressed. If the Member has guessed wrongly the Department will arrange with the Table Office for the Question to be transferred and this will be shown on the next Notice or Order Paper.

From time to time Members complain to the Speaker of these transfers either by approaching him informally or by raising a point of order in the House at the end of Question Time. Mr. Speaker's reply is always similar to the reply quoted earlier in respect of Ministerial responsibility for the nationalized industries. As recently as 9 December 1958, for example, the Speaker in reply to a request from Miss Elaine Burton said, 'I have no authority whatever over the transfer of Questions from one Department to another.'[1]

This attitude of Mr. Speaker and therefore of the Table is inevitable. He cannot be an expert on the law governing all the vast powers of contemporary government. Moreover any attempt to act as an arbiter on such matters would open the possibility of his appearing to support a Minister against another Member or vice versa. He may have to do this when presiding over the proceedings of the House but he is then dealing with the rules and practice of the House of which he is a master. It would be quite different if he were to be involved in a dispute which turned on a point of law for which Ministers with their Civil Service advisers have all the resources to handle and Mr.

[1] H.C. Deb. (1958–9), 597, c. 209–10.

Speaker has little or none. At the same time this attitude is only possible because of the operation of certain other factors.

It assumes that Ministers and departments will not knowingly wrongfully plead lack of responsibility as a reason for not answering a Question and will not use it as an excuse for avoiding awkward Questions. It also assumes that the Clerk and his staff are quite independent of Ministers and Departments and can, without fear or anxiety as to their tenure or prospects, admit Questions to the Paper which Departments would prefer to avoid being given publicity or having to answer. This staff are also quite free to help any Member so to word his Question that it is in order. The Table Office staff who handle Questions not only accumulate a great experience but can draw upon their collection of precedents. If it is not certain that the Question is out of order on the ground of lack of any Ministerial responsibility for the subject-matter the Table Office may still allow the Question to appear on the Notice Paper for there is one further factor: the right of any Minister to refuse to answer.

III: QUESTIONS IN THE HOUSE OF LORDS[1]

At first sight the arrangements for Questions in the House of Lords bear a strong resemblance to those in the House of Commons. There are Questions put on the Order Paper for oral answer; Questions which may be asked for answer in the Official Report; and Private Notice Questions which may be asked about matters of urgent importance or about the arrangements for the future course of business. But there the resemblance ends. There are three major differences between the two Houses.

First, in the Lords a Question may be asked to enable a Member to make a speech and initiate a debate. When a Question is starred it means that it is asked for information only. Starred Questions are answered orally at 'Question time' and supplementaries may be asked, provided they are confined to the subject of the original Question, but a debate may not take place. If only a written answer is required the questioner signifies to the Table that the Question is 'for written answer'.

[1] On this and the House of Lords generally see P. A. Bromhead, *The House of Lords and Contemporary Politics* (1958).

If, however, a Question is put on the Paper without an asterisk it signifies that the questioner wishes to initiate a general debate on the subject. If he wishes to reserve to himself the right to reply to the debate he adds at the end of his Question the words 'and to move for papers'. This form of Question has no exact equivalent in the House of Commons where debate at Question time is out of order. The nearest equivalent is the half-hourly Adjournment Motion which though formally a debate on the motion 'That this House do now adjourn' is in effect a method of allowing a Member to raise and speak to a limited issue and a Minister to reply. In the Lords an unstarred Question is in effect a notice of motion and is therefore not a Question in the sense used throughout this book.

Second, very few Questions are asked. Until 1954 starred Questions for oral answer could be asked only on Tuesdays and Wednesdays and not more than three such Questions were allowed on any one day. Now oral answers are given on any day the House meets, usually Tuesdays, Wednesdays and Thursdays, but on occasion additional sittings are held on Mondays and Fridays. There is still, however, a daily maximum, now four. Each year only about 200 Questions are put down for oral answer.

It follows that there is no real equivalent to Question time. There is little or no pressure on time and business proceeds at a more leisurely pace. Ministers' replies are usually longer and more supplementaries are asked. The person presiding over the proceedings, unlike the Speaker in the House of Commons, has no power to bring the interchange of supplementaries and answers to an end and no time limit is fixed for the proceedings.

Third, Questions are not normally addressed to a particular Minister, as they must be in the Commons, but to Her Majesty's Government. This practice is almost inevitable, for most of the Departments are not directly represented in the Lords and a Minister in the Commons cannot speak in the Lords.

IV: STATISTICS

There are two basic sources of statistics about Questions: the Order Papers and Hansard. The figures quoted in official publications are usually based on a count of the Order Paper.

Since 1896 the number of Questions on each day's Order Paper has been entered in a book now kept in the Votes and Proceedings Office. They are totalled at the end of each Session. This annual series goes back to 1873. Before that, official figures are available for only five isolated years: 1847, 1848, 1850, 1860 and 1870.

The figures for 1873–87 were published in House of Commons Paper 131 of Session 1887 and for 1888–1901 in the Parliamentary Debates for 1901 (vol. 100, p. xcii). For 1902–4 they are in H. of C. Paper 194 of 1905, but the division between starred and unstarred Questions is wrong for 1902, all Questions in that Session before 5 May being treated as unstarred, instead of starred. No general returns either by way of a separate Paper or in *Hansard* have been published since 1905.

Another source sometimes quoted as though it were a published book is 'Statistics relating to the Sitting of the House' by A. A. Taylor, printed in 1911. Mr. Taylor was in the Votes Office and must have had a passion for compiling statistics and records of every aspect of the work of the House. He must have originated the present daily count of Questions in the so-called Black Book (because of its covers) which dates from 1896. Several copies of the book are available in the House of Commons — and one copy is kept up to date.

Statistics based entirely on a count of the Paper minimise the number of Questions actually asked before 1886 and exaggerate the number after that year. The first Question appeared on the Paper in February 1835 but the practice of giving formal notice in this way developed slowly and for some years after 1835 many more Questions were asked than appeared on the Paper. It is difficult to estimate the difference with any accuracy for not all Questions and Answers were reported in Hansard. There is, therefore, nothing with which to compare the numbers on the Paper. A count for 1850 showed 232 reported in Hansard as against 212 on the Paper. A count for 1870 showed an even narrower gap; 1216 in Hansard as against 1203 in the Paper. A study of the reports of Parliamentary proceedings in *The Times* for about this period indicates that though *The Times* was fuller there was not much difference between it and Hansard in the number of Questions reported.

After Question time became a limited period in May 1902 the

number of starred Questions on the Paper may be greater than the numbers actually asked because of the practice of deferring Questions.

Since May 1902, when the distinction between written and oral answers was first made, the Order Paper may differ from the Hansard record in another way. The numbers of starred and unstarred Questions on the Paper do not correspond with the numbers of oral and written answers recorded in Hansard. On 28 April 1960, the day chosen to illustrate the working of Question time in Chapter 1, the count based on the Order Paper would show 75 starred and 8 unstarred Questions. The count based on Hansard would, however, show 40 oral and 31 written answers. The difference between 75 and 40 is due to 20 starred Questions not being reached and being given a written answer, another 13 being deferred and the remaining two being given written answers because the Member was not present

House of Commons
QUESTIONS TO MINISTERS
1847–1900

Session	Number of Questions on the Paper	Session	Number of Questions on the Paper
1847	129	1886 (Session II)	827
1848	222	1887	5,030
1850	212	1888	5,549
1860	699	1889	4,049
1870	1,203	1890	4,407
1873	1,002	1890–1	3,770
1874	851	1892 (Session I)	2,889
1875	1,171	(Session II)	55
1876	1,346	1893–4	6,534
1877	1,332	1894	3,567
1878	1,283	1895 (Session I)	3,304
1878–9	1,628	(Session II)	569
1880 (Session I)	377	1896	4,464
(Session II)	1,169	1897	4,824
1881	3,243	1898	5,155
1882	3,663	1899 (Session I)	4,290
1883	3,185	(Session II)	231
1884	3,555	1900 (Session I)	4,792
1885	3,354	(Session II)	314
1886 (Session I)	1,994		

when his name was called. The difference between 8 and 31 is accounted for by the 22 starred Questions which received written answers plus 3 unstarred Questions answered but not down for that day less 2 unstarred Questions on the Paper but not answered.

V: SOURCES AND SELECT BIBLIOGRAPHY

There are disappointingly few manuscript or unprinted sources. The only papers of Sir Thomas Erskine May are two diaries in the House of Commons Library. They cover the period 1857–82, but only intermittently, and add very little to the printed material. Apart from those in current use, there are no files or records of the Officers of the House such as are available for the historical study of government departments. A great deal of the business of these Officers is conducted verbally, and even where paper work is involved, e.g. the Questions put in by Members, the vast bulk of it is recorded in the Notice Papers and for this and other reasons is soon destroyed. There are, of course, references to Questions among the papers of former Ministers and politicians and in the old files of government departments, but we cannot pretend to have done more than to have looked at those records which seemed most likely to throw light on some major change in procedure.

The main printed sources are:

1. *Parliamentary Debates and Proceedings*

A very useful guide to Parliamentary Debates is given in House of Commons Library Document No. 2 'A Bibliography of Parliamentary Debates of Great Britain' (1956). What₁ is usually referred to as 'Hansard' started in 1803. It was not until 1909 that 'Hansard' became a strictly verbatim report. Before that, the fullness and accuracy of the reports varied from time to time, being particularly inadequate for the period before 1830–40.

There have been five series as follows:

1st Series,	1803–20	41 vols.
2nd Series,	1820–30	25 vols.
3rd Series,	1830–91	356 vols.
4th Series,	1892–1908	199 vols.
5th Series,	1909–	

Until 1909 the reports of the House of Lords and the House of Commons were contained in the same volume, but since that Session they have been bound separately. Our references are, therefore, shown as Parl. Deb. up to and including 1908, and after that year as H.C. Deb. or H.L. Deb. We give the Session, the number of the volume and the number of the column. Thus 'Parl. Deb. (1902), 132, c. 642' refers to column 642 of volume 132, the figure in brackets being the Session.

The Hansard reports can be supplemented for the period 1828–41 by the 60 volumes of *The Mirror of Parliament*, edited by J. Barrow. This is fuller than Hansard for the period 1828–1833.

The Journals of the Lords and Commons, published annually, are an essential source for decisions of the House about procedure. They are, however, not particularly useful as a guide to the development of Question time, except in so far as the procedure was affected by Standing or Sessional Orders or by the occasional Resolution. Speakers rulings are not recorded and neither is Question time. The same can be said of the Votes and Proceedings of the House.

More useful are the Notice and Order Papers bound under the title of 'Notices of Motions'. These provide a continuous record of all the Questions put on the Paper.

2. *Reports and Evidence of Select Committees*

After Hansard the most important official source of information about the development of Questions and of procedure generally is the reports and evidence of the following House of Commons Select Committees:

Select Committee on the Public and Private Business of the House, 1837, Paper 517.

Select Committee on the Public and Private Business of the House, 1848, Paper 644.

Select Committee on the Public and Private Business of the House, 1854, Paper 212.

Select Committee on the Business of the House, 1861, Paper 173.

Select Committee on Business of the House, 1871, Paper 137.

Select Committee on Public Business, 1878, Paper 268.

APPENDICES 319

Select Committee on Parliamentary Procedure, 1886, Paper 186.

Select Committee on House of Commons (Procedure), 1906, First and Second Reports and Evidence 1906, Papers 89 and 181.

Select Committee on House of Commons (Procedure) 1913–14. Report with Evidence, Papers 246 (1913) and 378 (1914).

Select Committee on Procedure on Public Business, 1931–2: Special Report with Evidence. Papers 161 of 1930–1 and 129 of 1931–2.

Select Committee on Procedure, 1945–46:
First Report with Evidence, Paper 9
Second Report with Evidence, Paper 58
Third Report with Evidence, Paper 189.
(The Second Report is devoted to Questions.)
Select Committee on Procedure: 1959. Paper 92.

There is also some discussion of Questions in the reports of the following Select Committees:

Select Committee on the Official Secrets Acts:
First Report, 1938, Paper 173 of 1937–8.
Second Report, 1939, Paper 101 of 1938–9.
Fifth Report from the Committee of Privileges, 1956–7, Paper 305.
Select Committee on Nationalized Industries, 1952, Paper 332 — I (1951–2).

3. *Guides to Procedure*

There are four main guides to the Procedure of the House of Commons:

(*a*) The most important is Sir Thomas Erskine May's *Treatise on the Law, Privileges, Proceedings and Usage of Parliament*. This is popularly referred to as 'Erskine May' and sometimes by the shorter title, *Parliamentary Practice*. The first edition was prepared by Mr. Thomas Erskine May, then an Assistant Librarian in the House, and published in 1844. He was knighted in 1866 and became Clerk in 1871, though he had in effect been undertaking the work for some ten or so years before that. His treatise superseded the four volumes of *Precedents of*

Proceedings in the House of Commons by John Hatsell (1781) (4th edition in 1818). Altogether, Erskine May edited 8 further editions: in 1851 (2nd), 1855 (3rd), 1859 (4th), 1863 (5th), 1868 (6th), 1873 (7th), 1879 (8th), and 1883 (9th). The 10th edition, published in 1893, was edited by Sir Reginald Palgrave and Mr. A. Bonham Carter; the 11th in 1906 by T. Lonsdale Webster and W. E. Grey; the 12th in 1917 and the 13th in 1924 also by Webster; the 14th and 15th in 1946 and 1950 by Sir Gilbert Campion (later Lord Campion) and the 16th in 1957 by Sir Edward Fellowes and Mr. T. G. B. Cocks.

(b) *The Manual of Procedure in Public Business*, first published in 1854 and revised at intervals since.

(c) *The Standing Orders of the House of Commons for Public Business*, published at intervals since 1919. Nowadays a new edition is published each Session.

Both the *Manual* and the *Standing Orders* are published with the authority of the House of Commons and are now made available free to Members. Erskine May's *Parliamentary Practice* is, however, commercially published by Butterworth & Co. Ltd., London.

Mention must also be made of *An Introduction to the Procedure of the House of Commons* by Sir Gilbert Campion, later Lord Campion, first published in 1929, with a 2nd Edition in 1947 and a 3rd Edition in 1958.

Erskine May is the fullest and most authoritative guide to procedure and is constantly used by the Speaker and Members. The *Manual* is based on it but is nothing like as exhaustive. Should there be any conflict between them on major points, which is most unlikely, the view expressed in Erskine May will be accepted, if only for its abundance of references to precedents and Speaker's rulings and for its fuller treatment of all branches of procedure. The *Manual* is not adopted by the House and differs, therefore, from the *Standing Orders*, but it is an attempt to give Members what they need to know about procedure, whether derived from practice, Speaker's rulings or Standing Orders. Campion's book is important only because Campion had a long experience of the procedure of the House and was in some ways the twentieth century equivalent of Sir Thomas Erskine May. None of these publications, however, gives the Member a full account of the procedure governing Questions.

The Table, Journal of the Society of Clerks-at-the-Table in Commonwealth Parliaments provides a very useful survey of procedural developments. It is published annually.

4. *The Diaries of H. W. (Sir Henry) Lucy*

Mr. H. W. Lucy, who became Sir Henry Lucy in 1909, wrote the 'Essence of Parliament' for *Punch* under the nom de plume of Toby, M.P., from 1881 until 1916. He also wrote on Parliament for the *Daily News* and the *Observer*. Altogether he published 19 books, a good many of which were compiled from his daily or weekly eye-witness reports of happenings in the House. The most significant are:

A Diary of Two Parliaments:
   The Disraeli Parliament, 1874–80, (1885)
   The Gladstone Parliament, 1880–5, (1886)
A Diary of the Salisbury Parliament, 1886–1892, (1892)
A Diary of the Home-Rule Parliament, 1892–1895, (1896)
A Diary of the Unionist Parliament, 1895–1900, (1901)
A Diary of the Balfourian Parliament, 1900–1905, (1906)
Memories of 8 Parliaments, (1908).

5. *Memoirs and Recollections of Speakers, Members and Parliamentary Journalists*

Charles Abbot, Lord Colchester, *Diary and Correspondence* (1861). 3 vols. (Abbot was Speaker from 1802 to 1817)

J. E. Denison, *Notes from my Journal when Speaker of the House of Commons* (1899). (Denison was Speaker from 1857 to 1872)

Viscount Ullswater, *A Speaker's Commentaries*, 2 vols. (1925) (Lowther was Speaker from 1905 to 1921)

D. Anderson,	*'Scenes' in the House of Commons,* (1884)
A. Baker,	*The House is Sitting,* (1958)
H. Graham,	*The Mother of Parliaments,* (1910)
M. MacDonagh,	*The Book of Parliament,* (1897)
(Sir) Alexander Mackintosh,	*From Gladstone to Lloyd George 1876–1921,* (1921)
	Echoes of Big Ben, 1881–1940, (1945)

Sir Richard Temple,	*Life in Parliament 1886–1892*, (1893)
Lord Wedgwood,	*Testament to Democracy*, (1942)
William White,	*The Inner Life of the House of Commons*, 2 vols. (1897)
Earl Winterton,	*Orders of the Day*, (1953)

6. *General Publications*

HISTORY

C. Bradlaugh,	*The Rules, Customs and Procedure of the House of Commons*, (1889)
Patrick Howarth,	*Questions in the House*, (1956)
Sir Courteney Ilbert,	*Parliament, its History, Constitution and Practice*, 3rd edition (1948), revised by Sir Cecil Carr
W. Law,	*Our Hansard*, (1950)
A. L. Lowell,	*The Government of England*, 2 vols. New edition (1919)
H. W. Lucy,	*A Popular Handbook of Parliamentary Procedure*, (1880)
R. W. McCulloch,	*Parliamentary Control. Question Hour in the House of Commons*, Revised version (1947) of Doctoral Dissertation. Unpublished, University of Michigan Library
K. Mackenzie,	*The English Parliament*, (1950)
J. Redlich,	*The Procedure of the House of Commons*: a Study of its History and Present Form, (translated from the German by A. E. Steinthal, with an Introduction and Supplementary Chapter by Sir Courteney Ilbert), 3 vols. (1908)
E. and A. G. Porritt,	*The Unreformed House of Commons*, 2 vols. (1903)
Alpheus Todd,	*Parliamentary Government in England: its origin, development and practical operation*, 1st edition, 2 vols. (1867–9)

APPENDICES

W. M. Torrens, — *Reform of Procedure in Parliament*, 2nd edition (1881)
W. C. Townsend, — *History of the House of Commons from 1688 to 1832.* 2 vols. (1843–4)

PARLIAMENT

L. A. Abraham and S. C. Hawtrey, — *A Parliamentary Dictionary*, (1956)
P. A. Bromhead, — *The House of Lords and Contemporary Politics*, (1958)
Lord Campion and others, — *Parliament: A Survey*, (1952)
Sir Ivor Jennings, — *Parliament*, 2nd edition (1957)
H. J. Laski, — *Reflections on the Constitution*, (1951)
Parliamentary Government in England, (1938)
H. Morrison, — *Government and Parliament*, 2nd edition (1959)
Hansard Society, — *Papers on Parliament*, (1949)
P. G. Richards, — *Honourable Members*, (1959)
E. Taylor, — *The House of Commons at Work*, (1951)

GOVERNMENT AND CIVIL SERVICE

Acton Society Trust, — *Nationalized Industry: No. 1. Accountability to Parliament*, (1950)
Lord Campion and Others, — *Parliament. A Survey* (1952)
T. A. Critchley, — *The Civil Service Today*, (1951)
H. E. Dale, — *The Higher Civil Service*, (1941)
A. H. Hanson, — *Parliament and Public Ownership*, (1961)
J. D. Millett, — *The Unemployment Assistance Board* (1940)
J. D. Stewart, — *British Pressure Groups* (1958)
W. A. Robson, — *Nationalized Industry and Public Ownership* (1960)
Lord Strang, — *Home and Abroad*, (1956)

ARTICLES

H. A. Bone,	'The Presidential Press Conference' (A comparison with Question Time), *Parliamentary Affairs*, Spring 1958, pp. 142–54
K. Bradshaw,	'Parliamentary Questions', *Parliamentary Affairs*, vol. vii, 1954, pp. 317–326
K. E. Couzens,	'A Minister's Correspondence', *Public Administration*, Autumn 1956, vol. 34, pp. 237–44
F. Elliott,	'Questions in Parliament', *The Fortnightly Review*, March 1934, pp. 341–8
A. H. Hanson,	'Parliamentary Questions on the Nationalized Industries', *Public Administration*, Spring 1951, vol. 29, pp. 51–66
E. Hughes,	'Sir Erskine May's Views on Parliamentary Procedure in 1882', *Public Administration*, Winter 1956, vol. 34, pp. 419–24
N. Johnson,	Parliamentary Questions and the Conduct of Administration. *Public Administration*, vol. 39, 1961, pp. 131–148
Colin Leys,	'Petitioning in the Nineteenth and Twentieth Centuries', *Political Studies* vol. III, 1955, pp. 45–64
R. W. McCulloch,	'Question Time in the British House of Commons', *American Political Science Review*, December 1933, vol. 27, pp. 971–5
Anne Phillips,	'Post Office Parliamentary Questions', *Public Administration*, Summer 1949, vol. 27, pp. 91–9

Lord Strang,	'The Formation and Control of Foreign Policy', *Durham University Journal*, June 1957, pp. 98–108
D. Thompson,	'Letters to Ministers and Parliamentary Privilege', *Public Law*, Spring 1959, pp. 10–22
Sir Herbert Williams,	'A Question in Parliament', *Papers on Parliament*, Hansard Society (1949)
K. Younger,	'Public Opinion and Foreign Policy', *British Journal of Sociology*, vol. vi, 1955, pp. 169–75

INDEX

A

Abbot, Mr. Speaker (later Lord Colchester), 14, 15
accountability, *see* answerability, ministerial
adjournment of the House, *see* Parliamentary procedure
administration and Questions: Advantages, 251–9
  Problems, 259–68
  see also departments and Civil Service
Admiralty, 104 n, 107 n, 153, 306
Agriculture, Fisheries and Food, Ministry of, 2, 102, 107 n, 145, 157, 164, 172, 180–1, 190, 306–7
Air Ministry, 104 n, 107 n, 308
Allaun, Frank, 179
Amery, Leopold S., 218
Amory, Heathcoat, 215
answerability, ministerial, 28, 92, 94–96, 159, 167–70, 188, 190, 230, 236–7, 266, 287, 292–314
  extent of, 293–9
  Ministers answerable, 305–11
Asquith, H. H., 133 n, 241, 279
Attlee, C. R., 140, 218, 264
Attorney-General, 155

B

Baker, A., 225 n
Baldwin, Stanley, 140, 218, 269
Balfour, A. J., 32, 50 n, 52, 55–84, 111, 114, 118, 129, 130, 174, 197, 209, 270, 278
Balfour reforms 1902:
  effects of a limited Question Time, 80–84
  need for certainty, 62–63
  origin of, 51–61
  period of notice, 77–80
  proposals to the House, 61–67
  proposals debated, 67–75
  time for Questions, 54–57, 64–65, 70–77

views on Questions, 56–59, 65
  See also Questions, Parliamentary and Parliamentary procedure
Barber, Anthony, 10
Bellenger, Frederick, 2
Benn, W. Wedgwood (later 1st Lord Stansgate), 197
Bentinck, Lord George, 17
Bevan, Aneurin, 121, 203, 219
Birrell, Augustine, 122, 123
Board of Trade, 1–3, 107 n, 145, 154, 157, 172, 180, 210, 218
Boland, J. P., 122
Borthwick, P., 14 n
Bowles, Gibson, 67, 75
Brand, Mr. Speaker (later Viscount Hampden) 19, 26, 40, 45 n
Brass, Sir William, 136
Bridgeman, W. C., 124
Bridgeman Committee, 264–5
Bridges, Sir Edward (later Lord Bridges), 252 n
Brittain, Sir Harry, 197
Brockway, Fenner, 8, 174, 193, 213 n
Brodrick, St. John, 73 n, 78
Brown, Mr. Speaker Clifton, (later Lord Ruffside), 119, 120, 125 n, 127, 147 n, 167, 269, 272, 311
Bryce, J., 82, 129
Butler, Mrs. Joyce, 3
Butler, R. A., 10, 106, 144, 249, 250, 272, 304
Burton, Miss Elaine, 312
Buxton, Foxwell, 17

C

Cabinet, the, 51, 293, 307
Callaghan, J., 9, 219, 250–1
Campbell-Bannerman, Sir Henry, 67, 85, 116 n
campaigns, use of Questions in, 211–15
Campion, Sir Gilbert, (later Lord Campion), 111, 188, 269, 320

INDEX

Canning, George, 15
Castle, Mrs. Barbara, 6
Chamberlain, Austen, 218, 263, 279
  Joseph, 51, 66 n, 105, 110 n
  Neville, 136, 256–7
Chancellor of the Exchequer, 2, 10, 131, 162, 180–1, 184, 214, 225, 233, 273, 306
Chaplin, H., 70, 82, 129
Churchill, Lord Randolph, 59, 60
Churchill, Sir Winston, 60 n, 123, 124, 163, 218, 242, 249, 307, 311
Civil Service, 92, 166, 167, 169, 228, 236, 251–4, 259, 263, 267–8, 286, 288
  See also departments, Government
Clerk at the Table, 18, 20, 21, 47, 48, 72, 73, 82, 128, 130, 132, 134, 304, 313
Clerk of the House, 24, 42, 111, 228, 229, 273
Clerk, Assistant, Second, 302
Clynes, J. R., 296
Colfox, Major W. P., 136
Colonial Office, 66 n, 104, 107 n, 131, 132, 145, 157, 171, 172, 207, 210, 294
Colonies, 288, 295
  Sec. of State for, 2, 113, 125, 155, 179, 180, 181, 261, 306
Commonwealth, 164, 295, 296
Commonwealth Relations Office, 2, 113, 171, 296
Conservative Members, 102–3, 193–4, 196, 198–9
constituents, grievances and letters, 96–99
  questions, 185–6, 278, 297
Cornwall, Mr. Speaker, 14 n, 15
correspondence with Ministers, 94, 96–108, 160, 184, 202, 211, 254–8, 267, 271, 279, 281, 284–5
  number of letters, 96, 103–5
Couzens, K. E., 103 n
Cowen, Joseph, 19, 43, 44 n, 60
Cowper, Earl, 12
Craig-Sellar, A., 60
Crichel Down case, 102–3
Critchley, T. A., 262, 267

Crookshank, Sir Harry, 217 n
Crouch, Robert, 102
Cunliffe-Lister, Sir Philip, 218

D

Dale, H. E., 237 n, 238, 239 n, 262, 264, 267
Davidson, Sir William, 197
Davies, Clement, 279
Day, Colonel Harry, 195, 197, 227
debate
  rules of, 13–15
  contrasted with Questions, 167–177
Defence, Minister of, 182, 183, 273, 308
  Depts., 294
De Freitas, Geoffrey, 219
De la Bère, Sir Rupert, 197
Denison, Mr. Speaker, 37, 39, 40, 41 n
departments, Government
  and Questions, 80, 106, 170–2, 210, 232–6, 253, 256, 257, 287–8
  See also administration, Civil Service, correspondence and rota system
Dilke, Sir Charles, 18 n, 20, 44 n
Dillon, J., 70, 76, 81, 129
Dillwyn, L. L., 19
Dodds, Norman, 164–6, 177, 242
Driberg, Tom, 6, 7, 272
Dyke, Sir William Hart, 70

E

Eden, Sir Anthony, 163, 272
Education, Ministry of, 2, 104, 176, 207, 293–4, 306
equal pay campaign, 211–12
Erroll, F. J., 194
Erskine May. *See* 'Treatise on the Law, Privileges, Proceedings and Usage of Parliament' *and* May, Sir Thomas Erskine

F

Fellowes, Sir Edward, 107, 273, 279
  his proposals for Question Time, 273
First Lord of the Treasury, 128
Fitzroy, Mr. Speaker, 115 n, 118, 125 n

INDEX

Flynn, J. C., 83
Food, Ministry of, 210 (*see also* Agriculture, Fisheries and Food)
Foreign Office, 66 n, 107 n, 131, 145, 157, 171, 172, 207, 210, 294, 295, 309
  Secretary, 59, 81 n, 146, 150, 151, 162, 164 n, 177, 180, 183, 186, 187, 257, 273, 281, 296, 309
fourth Party, 22, 33
Fowler, Sir Henry, 51
front benches, 171, 222, 225, 273, 276, 285
  See also Treasury bench *and* Opposition front bench
Fuel and Power, Ministry of, 107 n

G

gallery correspondents, 173–8, 203, 236
Galloway, G. B., 287 n
Gaitskell, Hugh, 218, 219
Gardiner, Sir Thomas, 266
Gibbs, Vicary, 104
Gladstone, W. E., 18, 19 n, 20, 25, 58, 60, 62, 127, 128
Godber, J. B., 243
Gordon, Alexander, 58
Gordon, D. J., 229 n, 301
Gorst, Sir John, 46
Gourlay, H. P. H., 5
Government and Question time, 274
Government departments, see departments, Government
Graham, Sir James, 40
Grey, Sir Edward, 82
Grey, C. F., 4, 6
Gresham Cooke, R., 8
Griffiths, James, 219
Gully, Mr. Speaker (later Viscount Selby), 24, 78 n, 116, 117, 126, 129, 132

H

Hale, Leslie, 185
Hansard, 6, 9–11, 23, 66, 111 n, 126, 175, 179–80, 236, 267, 316, 317–18
Harcourt, Sir William, 21, 29, 30 n, 60

Hartington, Lord, 47
Hatsell, John, 22
Haycock, A. W., 136
Healey, Denis, 219
Health, Ministry of, 107 n, 136, 150, 172, 177, 181, 182, 207–208, 210, 212, 294
Heaton, Sir John Henniker, 224
Hoare, Sir Samuel, 70 n
Hobhouse, Charles, 79, 81
Home Office, 2, 3, 10, 107 n, 184, 207, 267, 294, 297, 298, 306
Houghton, Douglas, 211
House of Commons,
  committees of, 34, 39, 53, 67, 68. *See also* Supply and Ways and Means
  composition of, 53
  debates. *See* debates
  door of honour, 54
  Journals, 23–25 n
  Leader of, 6, 59, 81 n, 144, 163, 164, 273
  order of daily business, 22–25, 49–50, 54–56
  sessions, *see* sessions, Parliamentary
  sittings of the House, 1, 25, 35, 49, 53, 67–68, 71, 74
  time of meeting, 1, 25, 49, 53–55, 68, 85
  Votes and Proceedings, 23 n, 60, 66, 81, 111
  See also Parliamentary procedure and Questions
House of Lords, 12, 69, 85, 140 n, 287, 309–10
  Questions in, 69, 313–14
Housing and Local Government, Ministry of, 104, 172, 176, 180, 183, 207, 210, 260, 293, 306
Howarth, Patrick, 12, 15
Hughes, Emrys, 3, 10, 221 n, 249, 250
Hughes, Hector, 1, 4, 11

I

Inland Revenue, Board of, 306
Irish Members, 30, 33, 46, 51, 56, 58, 79, 81 n, 83, 105, 116 n
Irish Nationalists, 76–77, 194–5, 197

INDEX

Irish Questions, 30, 58, 61, 91, 92, 131

J

Jay, Douglas, 218
Jenkins, Roy, 218
Jennings, Sir Ivor, 269
Jones, T. W., 207
Jordon, R. Donaldson, 66 n
Journals of the House, 23 n, 318
Jowett, Fred, 213
Joynson-Hicks, Sir William, 218

K

Kaberry, Sir Donald, 204
Kebty-Fletcher, J. R., 249
Kenealy, Dr., 26–27
Kennedy, T., 118, 137, 139
Kenworthy, Lt. Commander J. M. (later Lord Strabolgi), 197, 225, 270
King-Harman, Colonel, 58
Kinlock-Cooke, Sir Clement, 123, 124
Kirby, B. V., 107
Kitchen Committee, Chairman of, 292

L

Labour Governments, 94, 218, 301
Labour, Ministry of, 94, 104 n, 107 n, 145, 153, 157, 172, 210, 294, 306
Labour Party, Parliamentary, 218–219
  front bench, 121, 218–19. *See also* front bench; Opposition front bench
  use of Questions, 2, 89, 120, 192–9, 209, 212–13, 220–1
Lawson, Grant, 80
Lawson, G. M., 4
Leader of the House, 6, 59, 81 n, 144, 163–4, 273
letters to Ministers, *see* correspondence
Lewis, A. W., 211, 214
Liberal administration 1906–16, 90, 92
Liberal members, 194, 196, 198
Lipton, Marcus, 2
Lloyd George, David, 89, 249, 270
Local Authorities, 94, 97, 296, 298

Lord Advocate, 244, 245
Lord President of the Council, 307
Lowell, A. L., 269
Lowther, Mr. Speaker (later Viscount Ullswater), 19 n, 114, 117, 126, 128, 131 n, 132, 158, 249, 269, 278
Lucy, Henry, 31, 46, 58, 59 n, 116, 209, 224 n, 226, 321

M

McCulloch, Prof. R. W., 22, 114 n, 194, 197, 218
MacDonald, Ramsay, 136, 140 n
McLaughlin, Mrs. Patricia, 2, 4, 125 n
Mackenzie, R. T., 218 n
Macmillan, Harold, 7–9, 163, 221 n, 249, 308, 310
MacNeill, Swift, 86, 123, 124, 129, 131 n
MacPherson, J. I., 137
Malcolm, I., 123
Mander, Sir Geoffrey, 197
Mann, Mrs. Jean, 190, 191
Manners, Lord John, 45
Manual of Procedure, 25, 188, 320
Marples, Ernest, 11
Marquand, Hilary, 7, 8, 9
Massey, W. N. 40
Masterman, Charles, 212
Maudling, Reginald, 3–5
May, Sir Thomas Erskine, 12, 19 n, 20, 24, 25, 36 n, 37, 40, 42, 43, 46, 187, 277, 317
  See also 'Treatise on the Law, Privileges, Proceedings and Usage of Parliament'
Members of Parliament
  claims on time, 53, 55, 276
  correspondence, 96–108
  and Press, 176–7
  Ministers' appraisal of, 239–40
  obligation and functions, 199–200
  personal publicity, 222–7
  Questions to private Members, 16, 28
  salaries, campaign about, 214
  use of Questions, 192–217
  status of private Members, 31
Millan, B., 4
Millett, J. D., 94, 220 n

INDEX

Ministers: answerable, 305–11
  answers to Questions, 4, 45, 80, 99, 117, 122–7, 166, 169, 179–180, 183, 236–51, 256–7, 258
  correspondence with Members, 96–108
  in House of Lords, 309–10
  junior Ministers, 59, 169, 310
  relation with House of Commons, 237–41
  right to refuse to answer, 21–22, 28, 169, 299–305, 313
Ministerial responsibility, *see* answerability, Ministerial
Mirror of Parliament, 22–23, 318
Mitchison, G. R., 144
Molson, Hugh, 243
Monsell, Commander Sir Bolton Eyres, 270
Moore, Sir Thomas, 5, 119
Morrison, Mr. Herbert, 218 n, 206 n, 273
Morrison, Mr Speaker, 120, 125 n, 127, 303
motions, *see* Parliamentary procedure
motions, notices of. *See* Parliamentary procedure.

N

Nabarro, Gerald, 153 n, 192–3, 196, 214–15, 225, 244, 245–247
National Coal Board, 168, 296, 298
nationalized industries, 95, 258–9, 264, 301–5, 311–12
Noel-Baker, Philip, 258
Northcote, Sir Stafford, 277, 278
Northern Ireland, Government of, 91, 296
notice paper process, 1, 231–5
  first Questions on, 17–18, 23
  See also order paper
Nugent, G. R. H., 102

O

Opposition, 50–5, 89, 199, 213, 225, 265, 300
  front bench, 3, 57, 81, 121, 144, 217–21, 280
  Members, 55, 196, 199, 216–17, 220, 238, 274

  Leader of, 6, 140, 168, 192, 193, 197, 217, 225, 274, 277, 309, 311
  Whips, 208, 213
order book, 231–2
orders of the day, *see* Parliamentary procedure
order paper, 1, 11, 66, 173, 231–4, 316
  See also notice paper
order of Questions, *see* rota system
Osborne, Bernal, 17
Owen, W. J., 1, 3, 4

P

Palmerston, Viscount, 17, 28 n, 45
Parker, J., 179
Parliament, *see* House of Commons, House of Lords *and* Parliamentary procedure
Parliamentary Debates, *see* Hansard
Parliamentary opinion and Questions, 209–17
Parliamentary Practice, *see* 'Treatise on the Law, Privileges, Proceedings and Usage of Parliament'
Parliamentary privilege, 99 n
Parliamentary procedure
  adjournment motion (urgency), 34–41, 43, 45–46, 49–50, 54, 69, 72, 74, 130, 208–9, 303
  adjournment debate, 165, 168 n, 204–8, 240, 245, 314
  Balfour's proposals 1902, *see* Balfour reforms
  changes in 1906, 84–86, 271
  divisions, 50, 52–3, 74 n, 75
  notices of motions, *see* public business
  order of business, 22–25, 49–50, 54–56
  orders of the day, *see* public business
  private bills, 22–25, 38–39, 41, 49–50, 54, 56, 68, 70, 75, 272
  private business, *see* private bills
  public business, 25, 27, 33–42, 47, 49–50, 54–57, 61–64, 70, 72, 74, 76, 84, 164 n, 170–2, 200, 205
  resolutions, 25, 29, 47–48, 60
  rule of progress, 37

standing orders
  about Questions, 6, 21, 24, 26, 47, 74, 82, 106, 161, 187, 289–92
  about other matters, 36, 38, 40–41, 50, 52, 62, 67–68, 71, 85, 129
  Struggle between public and other business, 38–41, 276–7 for Parliamentary time, 31–33
Parliamentary Questions, *see* Questions
Parliamentary Secretaries, 59, 101–102, 207–8, 309–10
Parnell, Charles, 30 n
Patronage Secretary, 133
Peel, Mr. Speaker (later Viscount Peel), 46, 48, 209 n
Pensions and National Insurance, Ministry of, 98 n, 107 n, 181, 212
Percy, Lord Eustace, 282
Pethick-Lawrence Committee 1945, 229
petitions, 22–25, 38–39, 49, 75, 212, 272
Phillips, Anne, 211 n
Pilkington, R. A., 184
Piratin, P., 196
Platts-Mills, J. F. F., 194, 196
Post Office, 91, 103, 171–2, 184–5, 187, 208, 210–11, 224, 263–266, 296, 301
Potter, Allen, 212
Power, Ministry of, 104, 210, 296, 298
prerogative, 293–4, 295, 305
press and Questions, 167, 172–8, 203, 223–4, 284
press gallery, 173–5, 178,
Prime Minister, Questions to, 2–3, 6–9, 82, 128, 129–30, 132, 133, 135, 137–44, 145, 150, 155, 162–3, 164 n, 167, 179, 221, 257, 273, 307–9
private business *see* Parliamentary procedure
private Members, *see* Members of Parliament
private office, 100, 234, 260
Privileges, Committee of, 1957, 99 n
Profumo, J. D., 243
Publicity, 172–8, 203, 223–4

public business *see* Parliamentary procedure
public opinion, 209–17, 255–6, 284
Pulteney, Sir William, 15
purchase tax, campaign against, 214–15

Q

Question, avoiding devices, 92–96
Question 'hour', 86, 116, 209, 269, 272
Questions, administrative aspects and implications, 251–68
  answers, 44–47, 54, 122–7, 156–157, 236–51
    by Ministers after Question time, 161–2
  business, 6, 11–16, 28, 47, 57, 64
  changing attitude to, 41–43
  committee for *see* Questions local and imperial
  costs of, 260–1
  days on which answered, 1, 24–25, 64, 78–79, 88, 272–3
  deferred, 10 n, 90–91, 153–4, 165, 316
  developments, 1832–1900, 16–28
  editing of, 20, 229–30
  expedited, 112, 232–3
  Friday, 64, 78–79, 88, 272–3
  general and particular, 184–7
  House of Lords, 69, 313–14
  inspired, 221–2
  local and imperial, 58–61, 65, 70, 72–73, 82, 184–7, 278–80
  maximum limit, 108–10, 117
  notice, 17–22, 44, 47–48, 77–80, 106, 154, 228–36
  numbers (1847–1900), 316, (1901–60), 87–88; 29, 50, 87–92, 105, 114–15, 133, 136, 146–7, 261, 286, 288
  number answered per day, 114–115, 124, 127, 146–7, 271
  oral or starred, 1, 64–65, 72, 80–81, 103, 106–7, 160
  order of, *see* rota system
  origins, 12–16
  place in daily timetable, 22–26, 68, 75–77
  Prime Minister, *see* Prime Minister

INDEX

printing of, 58, 60, 66, 70, 83
private notice, 47, 72, 105–6, 108 n, 137, 161, 164, 192 n, 217, 225, 309, 311
procedural significance of, 12–16
purpose of, 180–4, 187–8
reading of, 18–19
safety-valve, 43, 73, 77, 252, 282
scope and content, 26–29, 170–2, 179–91
second round of, 82–83, 128, 147 n
significance of, 286–8
standing orders, 6, 21, 24, 26, 47, 74, 82, 106, 161, 187, 289–292
starred *see* Questions oral
statistics, 87–88, 118, 152, 155, 193–4, 198–9, 314–16
supplementary or 'subsidiary', 3–4, 29, 43–48, 56, 59, 61, 65–66, 115–27, 158, 178, 183, 190, 204, 219, 248, 270, 271, 276, 281–3, 285, 299
time of, 1, 6, 23, 54–57, 64–66, 69–73, 75–77, 80, 83, 85, 161
transferred, 160, 234, 312
urgent, 47, 72, 80, 83, 161–6 (*see also* Questions private notice)
which cannot be asked or answered, 187–91, 299–305
written or unstarred, 9, 11, 60–61, 65–66, 74, 80, 89, 106, 109–13, 160, 165, 170, 184, 199, 271, 279, 281, 284–5
See also procedure, rota system, Select Committees on procedure, Speaker and Speakers' rulings
questioners, 192–227
distribution between parties, 193–9
Members who do not ask Questions, 192
personal publicity, 222–7
persistent, 196–7
range of use, 192–6
Question time, 1–11, 22–25, 50, 61, 74, 112, 115, 146, 165–6, 170, 178, 179–80, 192 n, 252, 281
capacity of, 114–15, 127, 146–50, 156, 163
conjestion of, 109, 194

future of, 284–8
length of, 76, 86, 271–4
significance of time of, 56–57, 84, 174–5
testimonials to, 269–70, 285

R

Randall, H. E., 4
Randles, J. S., 57
Rathbone, Miss Eleanor, 119
Redlich, J., 16, 22, 51 n
Redmond, John, 48, 67, 85, 86
Renshaw, C. B., 129 n
responsibility, Ministerial, *see* answerability, Ministerial
Richards, Peter G., 96 n
Robertson, Sir David, 185, 186, 244–5
Ropner, Sir L., 11
rota system, 90, 231–2, 271, 278, 281, 285
development of, 128–44
effect of, 144–66, 231, 261, 281
grouping of Questions, 72, 81–82, 129–33
order of Questions, 1924, 134–5
1929, 137–9
1945, 141
1952, 142–3

S

Salisbury, Lord, 59
Salt, T., 43
Scotland, Secretary of State for, 182
Solicitor-General for, 244
Scottish Members, 137, 212
newspapers, 175
Office, 104, 154, 172
Questions, 4–5, 137, 175, 212
Select Committees; estimates, 201, 268
nationalized industries 1952, 201, 217 n, 229 n, 303–4
procedure 1848, 35, 42 n, 318–9
1854, 42 n
1861, 16, 27, 37, 39–40
1871, 18, 19 n, 36 n, 37–38, 40, 42, 44
1878, 20, 42, 43, 45 n, 277
1886 (Hartington committee), 20, 47

1906, 85, 86, 114 n, 129 n, 137 n, 278
1914, 114 n, 131 n, 132, 279–280
1931–2, 111, 118, 139, 149 n, 271, 283
1945–6, 106, 107 n, 109, 112, 147 n, 206, 271, 279, 280
1959, 143–4, 153–4, 156, 209, 271, 272, 273, 279
public accounts, 165, 201, 267,
statutory instruments, 201
Selwin-Ibbetson, Sir Henry, 20, 29, 44 n
service departments, 171, 308
sessions, parliamentary, length of, 32, 170
1800, 62
1901, 50, 52, 62
Sexton, T., 46, 48
shadow Cabinet, 218–19. *See also* Opposition front bench
Shaw-Lefevre, Mr. Speaker (later Viscount Eversley), 35–41
Shinwell, E., 1, 4
Shurmer, P. L. E., 247
Silverman, Sydney, 120
Simon, Sir Jocelyn, 245, 246, 247
Sinclair, Sir Archibald, 270
Smith, W. H., 61 n
Smithers, Sir Waldron, 194, 203–204
Soames, A. C. J., 11
South African War, 51, 71, 145
Speaker, 1, 26, 46, 190, 192, 197, 278, 311–13
and private notice Questions, 161, 164 n
and Questions, 20, 47, 230, 234, 299–300
and rota, 129–33, 140
and supplementaries, 45–47, 117–21, 125–7, 158, 248–9, 276, 282
Speakers' rulings, 12, 14, 15–16, 20, 26–29, 170, 187, 190–1, 301, 302–3, 311–12
interpretation of rulings 190–1
See also under names of Speakers
Stamp, Sir Josiah (later Lord), 263, 267
Standing Orders of the House of Commons refering to Questions, 6, 21, 24, 26, 47, 74, 82, 106, 117, 161, 187, 289–92
statements, Ministerial, 163–4, 174, 182–3, 282
statistics, 314–17. *See also under* Questions
Stewart, J. D., 202 n
Stonehouse, J. T., 179, 180, 243
Strang, Lord, 257
Strauss case, 99, 284 n
Suez, 104, 164 n, 171
Summerskill, Dr. Edith, 121
Sunderland, Earl of, 12
supplementary Questions, *see* Questions, Supplementary
Supply, Committee of, 33–34, 36–38, 43, 46, 171
Swingler, Stephen, 125, 180, 192, 193

T

Table, 169 n, 279, 301, 311, 312
Table, Office, 98, 99, 110, 143, 151 n, 156, 159, 168, 172, 190, 228–32, 235, 301, 311–313
development of, 229
Taylor, A. A., 32 n, 35 n, 315
Thomson, G. M., 219
Thorne, Will, 197
Thorneycroft, Peter, 246
Thurtle, Ernest, 127 n
Tierney, G., 14, 15
Times, The, 66, 73, 173, 175
Todd, Alpheus, 44
Torrens, W. H., 122 n
Trade, Board of, 1–3, 107 n, 145, 154, 157, 172, 180, 210, 218
Transport, Ministry of, 158, 167, 172, 176, 207, 209–10, 298
Treasury, 107, 145, 150, 157, 171, 172, 207, 210, 218, 233 *and see* Chancellor of the Exchequer
bench, 3, 81, 236, 274
Financial Secretary to, 103, 120, 251
First Lord of, 73, 128
'*Treatise on the Law, Privileges, Proceedings and Usage of Parliament*', 319–20
1st Ed (1844), 12, 13, 24, 26

INDEX

2nd Ed (1851), 24
4th Ed (1859), 36 n
5th Ed (1863), 36 n
6th Ed (1868), 18
7th Ed (1873), 44
10th Ed (1893), 26
16th Ed (1957), 167, 187, 189–190, 292, 302, 311

U

Unionist party, 51, 53
United States, President of, 287
'usual channels', 132–3, 140, 200, 209, 278, 280

V

Vincent, Sir Edgar, 61
visitors' gallery, 1, 179
Votes and Proceedings of the House, 23 n, 60, 66, 81, 111, 318
Vote Office, 231
Votes and Proceedings Office, 315

W

Wakefield, Sir William, 182, 243–244
Walton, Joseph, 71
Walrond, Sir William, 50 n, 52, 55, 64
Warbey, W. N., 10
Ward, Dame Irene, 211
Waring, Colonel T., 20
War Office, 104, 107 n, 131, 132, 145–6, 153, 156, 158, 165, 185, 210–11, 233–4
  correspondence, 211
Waters case, 185–6, 187, 244
Watt, H. A., 123
Ways and Means, Committee of, 33–34, 36–38
  Chairman and Deputy Chairman of, 193–4, 197–8,
Webb, H., 123
Wedgwood, Colonel J. C., (later Lord Wedgwood), 197
Weir, J. S., 19 n, 226–7
Whips, *See* usual channels
Whips, views on Question and procedure, 51–55, 64, 77, 139
Whitley, J. H., 77
Wigg, George, 3
Williams, Sir Herbert, 197
Williams, Tom, 197
Willey, F. T., 193, 219
Wilson, Harold, 6, 218
Winterton, Earl, 125 n, 147 n, 194, 195 n
Wolmer, Lord, 264, 265
Woolton, Lord, 307
Wood, Sir Kingsley, 218 n
Wortley, C. B. Stuart, 124
Works, Ministry of, 107 n, 155, 179, 182, 243

Y

Younger, Kenneth, 257